Thos Spencer

The portrait & autograph are perfect Thos Raffles.

"A Burning and a Shining Light;"

BEING THE

LIFE AND DISCOURSES

OF

REV. THOMAS SPENCER,

OF LIVERPOOL.

BY REV. THOMAS RAFFLES, D.D. L.L.D.

HIS SUCCESSOR IN THE PASTORAL OFFICE.

WITH AN INTRODUCTION.

NEW YORK:

SHELDON, LAMPORT AND BLAKEMAN,

115 Nassau Street.

1855.

JOHN J. REED,
Stereotyper and Printer,
16 Spruce street.

CONTENTS.

CHAPTER IV,

CHAPTER V.

CHAPTER VI.

SPENCER'S SERMONS.

SERMON XI.

SERMON XII.

SERMON XIII.

SERMON XIV.

SERMON XV.

SERMON XVI

SERMON XVII.

SERMON XVIII.

SERMON XIX.

SERMON XX.

SERMON XXI.

SERMON XXII.

ADDRESS,

PREFACE.

THE volume now presented to the public, owes its origin to one of those mysterious events in Providence, which seem commissioned, at distant intervals, to alarm and admonish the church of God. A loss so sudden, so awful, so universally deplored as that of Mr. Spencer, demanded improvement. Many impressive discourses were delivered on the sad occasion, several of which have issued from the press. But his *life* was not less instructive than his *death*; and the more it was contemplated by his friends, the more deeply they felt the importance of rescuing from oblivion those traits of his character, and circumstances of his history, by which their own private circles had been interested. Upon my acceptance of the solemn office from which he was so unexpectedly removed, his bereaved people anxious to see some authorized memoirs of their beloved pastor embodied and preserved, committed the mournful duty to my hands. My respect for the honored dead, and attachment to the living, induced me to accept the charge; how I have executed the important trust reposed in me, I must now leave it with a candid public to decide.

Various causes have contributed to create the delay which has attended the publication of the book. It was with considerable difficulty that I collected the materials necessary for my purpose. I had imagined, from the general impression which prevailed, at least among Mr. Spencer's friends, of the propriety of such a publication, that information would have been spontaneously offered from every quarter whence it might be furnished. But in this I was disappointed; and it was some considerable time from the annunciation of my design, before I was sufficiently supplied to commence, with any degree of prudence, the composition of the volume.

In addition to this, the laborious duties of a new and most extensive charge, conspired often to suspend the prosecution of the work, for the appearance of which I knew many to be anxious, but none more so than myself.

Had I at first anticipated the extent of these Memoirs, I should most probably have shrunk from the undertaking. But the volume has grown almost imperceptibly beneath my hand. What I have recorded of the dear departed is strictly true, so far as the veracity of the most excellent men can warrant the assertion; and whatever opportunity the narrative has afforded of administering instruction I have gladly seized, and conscientiously improved, leaving the issue to a higher agent.

I have at length completed the work; and now, with the deepest humility and diffidence, I resign it to the blessing of God—the consideration of friendship—and the candor of the public. If to those who knew and loved him, it shall sometimes recall, with grateful emotions, the image and the excellences of their departed friend; if it shall induce any to emulate the bright example of his manly virtues, and his Christian graces; or if but one, anticipating or commencing the laborious duties of the Christian ministry, shall derive from the contemplation of Spencer's character, instruction, caution, or encouragement —I am amply recompensed—I have not labored in vain!

THOMAS RAFFLES.

INTRODUCTION.

"How many fall as sudden, not as safe."—YOUNG.

THE first half of the Nineteenth Century was adorned with some of the rarest illustrations of youthful genius. Among these might be named many whose gifts have shone with resplendent lustre in some of the most elevated pursuits of life; but, among them all, none are more conspicuous than those whose noble and rich endowments have been consecrated to the great work of preaching Christ. The memories of such men as PEARCE, and McCHEYNE, and SUMMERFIELD, and SPENCER, are familiar and dear to the people of God every where, and the influence of their deep piety, and the honor awarded to their distinguished talents may be justly claimed as a precious heritage by the entire church.

True, their earthly career was exceedingly brief; but the history of their labors and the measure of their usefulness are not to be estimated by years. Their work was accomplished with prodigious speed. They witnessed as much impression and effect in the labors of a few months as many would rejoice to observe after the toil of long years, and the moral power of their lives will be felt down to the end of time. One of the strongest circumstances, perhaps, tending to the support of this view, is the fact that every day witnesses an increasing demand for their biographies and works.

Nor is it a little remarkable, that, while some years have elapsed since the death of one of these, the sensation excited by his extraordinary labors, and the circumstances attending his sudden removal have not subsided nor abated much of their force. We are led, therefore, to conclude, that, "The unequalled admiration he excited while living, and the deep and universal concern expressed at his death, demonstrate him to have been no ordinary character; but one of those rare specimens of human nature, which the great Author of it produces at distant intervals, and exhibits for a moment, while He is hastening to *make them up amongst his jewels.*

The Rev. Thomas Spencer was in every respect a wonderful youth, and the deep interest felt in his history, and the general astonishment awakened by his distinguished abilities, are fully justified by the most judicious estimates that can be formed of his character as a christian, and his gifts as a preacher.

Before noticing these, however, it may not be amiss just to allude to a few of the points which mark the progress of his brief career. He was born, we are informed, at Hertford, January 21, 1791. In his twelfth year he considered himself to have become the subject of serious impressions, and "to have felt something experimentally of the power of religion." In his fifteenth year he was placed under the care of the Rev. Wm. Hordle, of Harwich, to enter on his preparatory studies. In January, 1807, he was admitted into Hoxton College. During the vacation in the following midsummer, he preached his first sermon in public, at Collier's End, a small village near Hertford.

Three years subsequent to this, he spent a vacation in supplying the congregation worshipping at Newington Chapel, Liverpool. His sermons excited very marked attention, and he was invited to the pastoral office. Accepting of this invitation, he entered upon his stated engagements on the third Sabbath of February, 1811, having just attained his twentieth year. His preaching attracted at once, such overflowing congregations, that in a few weeks it was found absolutely necessary to erect a much larger house, of which he laid the corner stone on the 15th of April, 1811. But it pleased Him whose designs are inscrutable to man, though always wise and good in themselves, to cut short the days of this most promising and devoted young minister. On Monday morning, August the 5th, he resolved to bathe in the river Mersey, thinking it might brace his nerves after the exertions of the preceding Sabbath, and prepare him for the duties to which he intended to devote the day. He had folded his paper and prepared his pen, in order to compose a sermon to be preached in the ensuing week, on behalf of the Religious Tract Society, of whose anniversary meeting he had just received a particular account, with copies of the addresses then delivered. Mr. Spencer left his paper and pen prepared for this purpose, and proceeded to the river, but soon after he had entered it, he was borne out by the current, sunk in the deep water, and was drowned. Thus suddenly was he called from his early labors on earth, to an eternal reward in heaven.

It is not pretended, of course, that the character of Mr. Spencer at that early age, had attained its maturity, and yet it must be admitted that in all its prominent features, there was evinced a development rarely witnessed in one so young. Experience would doubtless have done much toward confirming or chastening some of its peculiarities, and the varied circumstances of a longer life would have afforded ampler opportunities for testing its qualities and proving its strength—still, that character had already arrived at such a stage of progress, as to leave us in no difficulty in estimating its virtues as it *was*, or in conjecturing what it might have become with the discipline and habits of years.

As a man, he was generous, frank, independent, and sincere; and these noble qualities, having been brought under the influence and direction of a heart deeply imbued with the spirit of Christ, served to make him one of the most lovely and devoted Christians that the world has ever beheld. "With him," writes the distinguished author of his Memoir, "religion was no matter of mere profession and convenience; nor did it lose its impression by the frequent recurrence of its subjects and duties—he seemed to live under its abiding influence—it was wrought into the constitution of his nature—its principles were the springs—its precepts the rule—its objects the end of all his actions. To this he ever had respect; what opposed it he heartily abhorred—what clashed with it he cheerfully resigned—what injured it he conscientiously avoided. His love to God was ardent. In this I think he much resembled Mr. Pearce, of Birmingham; and, indeed, often, when contemplating the life of Spencer, my thoughts have involuntarily recurred to certain traits of character preserved in the memoirs of that glorified saint. His love to God shed a glorious lustre on his whole character and conduct; everything that came within the sphere of his influence or operation, was irradiated by it. But chiefly would I confine myself now to the influence of this noble principle upon himself. It inspired him with a love of piety: as a Christian he was eminent for *holiness.* He contemplated the character of God, and was attracted to it by its purity." "I shall not," says one of his friends, "easily forget the delight which sparkled in his eye, when conversing upon the divine attribute, holiness. 'How sweet,' said he, 'is that word *holy!*—*holy* Father—*holy* Saviour—*holy* Spirit —*holy* Scriptures. Surely, if there is one word dearer to me than another, it is the word *holy.*'" During his residence at Hoxton, the same individual observed to a friend in the institution, whose attention he wished to direct to the character of Spencer. "Perhaps, you perceive youthful levity in him?" "No," he replied, "I have remarked him particularly, but it was for his *spirituality.*"

Equally impressive was his *humility.* Never, perhaps, did one so young enjoy such friendships, or occupy such a space in the public eye. Admired, and ardently loved by all who knew him, he was, at the same time, the subject of a wide and unexampled popularity; and yet, he ever exhibited "the ornament of a meek and quiet spirit," walking in all lowliness, and in his conversation and conduct, evincing the most attractive modesty. So prominent a feature was this in his character that his ministry, no doubt, derived from it no small measure of its success. This it was that gave him such favor in the eyes of men, and this it was that led him, distrusting himself, to look to God for those abundant supplies of grace, which, while they beautified his life, gave peculiar effect and power to his preaching.

But, striking as were SPENCER's qualities as a Christian, that which constituted the chief ground of his popularity, was his distinguished ability as a *preacher.* His appearance in the pulpit was both interesting and commanding. His countenance had the fine bloom of youth. His action was graceful and appropriate, and with a beautifully distinct and clear voice, he stood before his crowded congregations, the very embodiment of manly dignity, displaying with spontaneous ease, all the characteristics of genuine eloquence. The justness of this representation is fully sustained in the high opinion expressed of his abilities, by that distinguished pulpit orator of England, Robert Hall: "I entertain no doubt," said he, "that his talents in the pulpit were unrivalled, and that had his life been spared, he would, in all probability, have carried the art of preaching, if it may be so styled, to a greater perfection than it ever attained, at least, in this kingdom. His eloquence appears to have been of the purest stamp, effective, not ostentatious, consisting less in the striking preponderance of any one quality, requisite to form a public speaker, than in an exquisite combination of them all; whence resulted an extraordinary power of impression, which was greatly aided by a natural and majestic elocution."

The *matter* of his discourses was always carefully arranged and eminently evangelical, while his manner is represented as having been peculiarly animated and solemn. With all the serious drafts upon his time, by the public engagements he performed, he made it a point to give himself to a diligent and thorough preparation of the important subjects intended for the pulpit. Most of his sermons, indeed, were written throughout, except the heads of application; here he usually trusted to the ardor of his mind, quickened by the train of remarks which he had pursued, and guided by a holy influence. Not that he slavishly committed his compositions to memory, and delivered them by rote, but he thus carefully wrought a channel for his thoughts, leaving room for such enlargements, especially at the close, as the fresh and holy promptings of his heart might dictate.

"The sermon in the study was completely formed—correctly arranged—and well connected—but to the lifeless form, delineated on his paper, and impressed upon his memory, in the pulpit he imparted a living soul; a principle of ardent piety, which operated as a charm, the power of which few were able to resist."

But while this was his usual custom, yet we are told that "when extraordinary circumstances conspired to render a departure from it necessary, he could with the greatest propriety and ease, delight and interest an audience from the rich treasures of his exalted mind. One instance of his powers, in extemporary and unpremeditated address, is related of him in Liverpool. Some important affair of a public nature engaged the general attention of the religious world, on a Sabbath evening, when as usual he had to preach; and, anticipating a thin attendance, he had prepared a sermon adapted to the supposed state of his auditory—but, when he reached the chapel, and saw it filled with anxious crowds, waiting to receive from his lips the words of life—his ardent mind seemed instantly inspired—he immediately fixed upon a passage more adapted to the scene, and with his pencil sketched the outline of a discourse, which, perhaps, in the whole series of his ministry, he never excelled."

The general cast of his preaching, perhaps, may be inferred from the texts noted in the following pages. His great absorbing aim seems to have been to win souls to Christ, and to accomplish this, he faithfully exhibited on one hand, the hopeless condition of men by nature, and on the other, the freeness and infinite value of that Salvation revealed to us in the gospel.

After a lucid exposition of his text, which was invariably marked by great simplicity, his whole soul would pour itself forth in a most impressive and impassioned application. "Here," says his biographer, "he wrestled with the people, with a fervor resembling that with which, in prayer, he wrestled with his God. He seemed to exhaust every argument which might be brought to bear upon his great object, and to these he often added appeals and entreaties, the most tender and affecting. *Then* he seemed to lose sight of every consideration, but his own responsibility, and his people's good—and as though the congregation before him were the only people remaining to be saved, and as though every time of preaching was the only opportunity afforded him of using the means of their salvation, he besought them as an ambassador for Christ, to be reconciled to God."

This intense earnestness, indeed, was with SPENCER, a prominent peculiarity. Hence, says the Rev. Mr. Styles, than whom no man, perhaps, was better able to form and express an opinion of his worth: "If I were to sum up Mr. Spencer's character in one word, comprehending in it only what is excellent and ennobling to human nature, I should say it was ANIMATION. His intellect was feeling, and his feeling was intellect. His thoughts breathed, and his words glowed. He said nothing tamely, he did nothing with half a heart."

But if this was a general trait in his character, it certainly appeared strikingly preëminent in his ministrations from the pulpit. Nor was his animation here to be regarded simply as a constitutional peculiarity. Active and ardent, he doubtless was in his natural temperament, but the source of his energy and the great impulsive power of his being was piety. With the Apostle, he acted under the influence of *constraining love.* This glowed in his heart—animated his countenance, sustained him in his labors, and gave him such power over the minds of his fellows. And the flame of this piety, let it be remarked, was not only kindled, but constantly supplied at the altar. It was invariably from communion with God in the closet, that he passed to what he described as that awful place—a pulpit." And those who heard him could never forget the devotional simplicity and fervor of soul which he manifested, when proclaiming the glories of the Redeemer, or when pronouncing that adorable name to which "every knee shall bow."

He was indeed—"A BURNING AND A SHINING LIGHT," and many there were who "*for a season*," rejoiced in his light. But suddenly he finished his course—his sun went down while it was yet noon, and, now, while we delight to cherish his memory on earth, he sweetly rests from his labors in heaven.

"O there was ONE, on earth awhile
He dwelt; but transient as a smile
That turns into a tear;
His beauteous image passed us by;
He came like lightning from the sky,
He seem'd as dazzling to the eye,
As prompt to disappear.

Sweet in his undissembling mien
Were genius, candor, meekness seen,
The lips that lov'd the truth;
The single eye, whose glance sublime
Look'd to eternity through time;
The soul, whose thoughts were wont to climb
Above the hopes of youth.

Of old, before the lamp grew dark,
Reposing near the sacred Ark,
  The child of Hannah's pray'r
Heard, midst the temple's silent round,
A living voice ; nor knew the sound
That thrice alarm'd him ere he found
  The Lord, who chose him, there.

Thus early call'd and strongly mov'd
A prophet from a child approv'd,
  SPENCER his course began;
From strength to strength, from grace to grace,
Swiftest and foremost in the race,
He carried vict'ry in his face,
  He triumph'd while he ran.

How short his day!—the glorious prize,
To our slow hearts and failing eyes,
  Appear'd too quickly won:
The warrior rush'd into the field,
With arm invincible to wield
The spirit's sword, the spirit's shield,
  When lo! the fight was done.

The loveliest star of evening's train
Sets early in the western main,
  And leaves the world in night;
The brightest star of morning's host,
Scarce ris'n, in brighter beams is lost.
Thus sunk his form on ocean's coast,
  Thus sprang his soul to light.

* * * * *

Revolving his mysterious lot,
I mourn him, but I praise him not;
  To God the praise be giv'n,
Who sent him—like the radiant bow,
His covenant of peace to show,
Athwart the passing storm to glow,
  Then vanish into heav'n." MONTGOMERY.

A. S. P.

HOBOKEN, *May*, 1855.

MEMOIR

OF

REV. THOMAS SPENCER.

MEMOIR

OF

REV. THOMAS SPENCER.

CHAPTER I.

Parentage and Early Years of Thomas Spencer—Love of Learning—Religious Impressions—His inclination to the Christian Ministry—Apprenticed to a Glover in London—Acquaintance with Thomas Wilson, Esq. commenced, under whose patronage he enters, upon his preparatory studies with the Rev. Mr. Hordle, of Harwich—Rapid Progress in Learning—Returns to his father's residence in Hertford.

SELDOM has a task so painfully arduous fallen to the lot of a biographer, as that which, in the mysterious providence of God, has unexpectedly devolved on me. The recollection of departed excellence, which a long series of years had developed and matured, is mingled with a melancholy feeling, and not unfrequently excites the tribute of a tear; but the individual who erects a monument to friendship, genius, usefulness, and piety, prematurely wrapt in the oblivion of the grave, must necessarily prosecute his mournful work with trembling hands, and with a bleeding heart. And yet the mind is soothed by the communication of its sorrow ; the bosom is relieved of an oppressive burthen, while it tells the virtues of the friend it mourns ; and the best feelings of the heart are satisfied with the consciousness, that instead of indulging in solitude, the luxury of unavailing grief, it has employed its powers to portray, in lively colors, for the improvement of the living, the excellencies of the beloved and pious dead. For myself, with mournful pleasure, I hasten to sketch the rude outline of one of the loveliest and most finished characters the present age has known :—pausing only to express my deep regret, that one so ripe for heaven, and yet so eminently useful upon earth, should be called from the important sphere he occupied so soon ; and that to hands so feeble should be committed—together with the solemn trust which he resigned in death, the painful duty of erecting this monument to his worth.

The Reverend Thomas Spencer, was born at Hertford, January 21, 1791. He occupied the third place out of four who surrounded his father's table, but shared equally with them in the tender and affectionate solicitude of parents, who, placed in the middle sphere of human life, were respectable for their piety, and highly esteemed in the circle in which a wise Providence had allotted them to move. It cannot be expected that any thing peculiarly interesting should mark the early childhood of a youth retired from the observation of the world, and far removed from the presence of any of those circumstances which might be considered as favorable to the excitation of latent talent, or the display of early genius. And yet the years of his infancy and childhood were not undistinguished by some intimations of a superior mind, from which a thoughtful observer might have been induced to augur something of his future eminence, and which his amiable father it appears did with silence watch. He himself observes, in a hasty sketch of his life, which now lies before me—"As far back as I can recollect, my memory was complimented by many as being very retentive, and my progress in knowledge was more considerable than that of my school-fellows ; a natural curiosity and desire of knowledge, I think I may say, without vanity, distinguished even the period of my infancy. I now remember questions that I asked when about four years old, which were rather singular, and which were confined chiefly to biblical subjects. No child could be more attached to places of worship, or could be more inquisitive about their concerns than myself ; and I may add, more given to imitate the actions of the minister and clerk."

When he had completed his fifth year, he suffered the severest earthly privation a child can know, in the loss of an affectionate mother. Though then too young correctly to appreciate a parent's worth, he deeply felt the stroke ; and in the liveliest manner he recalls the impression which at that early period this melancholy circumstance produced upon his tender mind. "When the funeral sermon was preached I could not help noticing the grief which seemed to pervade every person present. Deeply affected myself, I recollect, that after the service, as I was walking about our little garden with my disconsolate father, I said to him, 'Father, what is the reason that so many people cried at the meeting this afternoon.'—He, adapting his language to my comprehension, said, 'They cried to see little children like you without a mother.'" This event which shed so deep a gloom upon his family, seems to have excited emotions of a serious nature in his mind never totally effaced.

From this time he applied himself with diligence and delight to the business of his school. There was at this early age something amiable and engaging in his manners ; and this combined with his attention to his learning, soon secured the esteem and approbation of his respective teachers, and gained him, together with the first place and highest honors of his school, the character of a "*good boy.*" It is pleasing to mark the early combination of superior talent and sweetness of disposition in this extraordinary young man ; and it would be well, did the patrons of early genius more deeply ponder the reflection, that the graces of a meek and quiet spirit are far more estimable than the rare qualities of a prematurely vigorous mind ; and that the talents they cultivate with such anxious care, if unassociated with real excellence of soul, may render the idols of their fond adulation sources of anguish to themselves and incalculable mischief to mankind.

While a school boy, he became passionately fond of novels, histories, adventures, &c., which he devoured with the greatest eagerness in numbers truly astonishing. The perusal of these he always preferred to play and other amusements adapted to his years. He delighted much in solitude ; nor did he know a happiness superior to that of being alone, with one of his favorite books. He took no delight in the games of his companions, nor did he ever mingle in their little feuds. His natural levity, however, was excessive ; and his wit, fed by the publications he so ardently perused, would often display itself in impurity of language to the laughter and amusement of his fellows. Yet he was not without his moments of serious reflection, and that of a very deep and dreadful kind.—He was often overwhelmed with religious considerations, and the solemn sermons he sometimes heard, filled him with terror and alarm. So intolerable at one period were the horrors of his mind, that in an agony of despair, he was tempted, as many have been before him, to destroy himself. Thus at an early age he became intimately acquainted with the depravity of his nature ; and from the deep waters of spiritual distress through which he was called to pass, his soul imbibed an air of humility and a habit of watchfulness, which enabled him to meet with firmness the dangers of popularity, and to maintain a steady course, notwithstanding the press of sail he carried.

To these deep convictions of his early years may perhaps be traced the peculiarly pressing and impassioned manner of his address, when he strove to arouse the slumbering conscience, or direct the weary wanderer to the cross of Christ. The sacred poems and the passages of holy writ, which most he loved, were those of a cast similar to that of his own fervent mind ; and I have heard many tell, with tears, of the animation and rapture with which he would often repeat from that beautiful hymn of Henry Kirke White, his favorite author, whom in many shades of character he much resembled, and alas ! too much in his early and lamented fate—

Once on the stormy seas I rode,
 The storm was loud, the night was dark ;
The ocean yawn'd, and rudely blow'd
 The wind that toss'd my found'ring bark.

Deep horror then my vitals froze ;
 Death struck, I ceas'd the tide to stem,
When suddenly a star arose,
 It was the star of Bethlehem.

It was my guide, my light, my all,
It bade my dark forebodings cease:
And through the storm of danger's thrall
It led me to the port of peace.

Now safely moor'd—my perils o'er,
I'll sing, first in night's diadem,
For ever and for ever more
The star!—the star of Bethlehem.

The bias and inclination of his mind began at this early period to be disclosed; preachers and preaching seemed to occupy all his thoughts, and often he would exercise himself in addressing such domestic congregations as may be supposed to constitute the usual auditories of an infant. Thus in his earliest childhood he displayed his fond attachment to the Christian ministry, and the first efforts of his infant mind were directed to that sublime and dignified profession, in which the capacities of his maturer age were so brilliantly displayed. These infantine compositions were not unfrequently entirely his own; and when they claimed not the merit of originality, they were derived from hints collected from what he had heard or read. But his *preaching exhibitions* could not long be confined to the narrow circle and scanty congregation his father's house supplied; tidings of his early *pulpit talents* soon circulated through the neighborhood; many were anxious to listen to the instructions of this extraordinary child: and most regarded him, as he himself expresses it, "*a parson in embryo.*"

At this age, also, he wrote verses. He seems, however, to have had but a mean opinion of his talent for poetry. It certainly was not the art in which he most excelled. Though an individual may have a power of rhyming sufficient for throwing his feelings into tolerable easy verse, yet something more than this is required in a production which, under the dignified title of a poem, is to meet the public eye. And while most men of an enlightened mind and cultivated taste, have solicited the muses' aid for purposes of private instruction and amusement, and the domestic and social circle have been privileged to share in both, yet it is not necessary to the perfection of the pulpit orator, that he should be an exquisite poet, nor is it at all a detraction from the greatness of his character, that the world should hesitate to pronounce unqualified praise upon poetical effusions, on which the eye or the ear of friendship might linger with delight.

These observations will serve to account for the circumstance that none of Mr. Spencer's poetical productions are preserved in these pages. And while some partial friends, who saw with pleasure the pieces which circulated in private, may regret for the moment their entire exclusion here, his biographer hopes, that he shall render a more essential service to the memory of his departed friend, by occupying their place with extracts from his papers of a more solid and interesting kind.

These early displays of talent however introduced him to the notice and friendship of some individuals of wealth and consequence. This was doubtless considered by himself and his fond parent as no inconsiderable circumstance in the history and prospects of a child, who, if he rose into eminence at all, could have no facilities afforded him, by the auspicious omens of his birth, or the rank of his father's family. But, alas ! the fond anticipations which from this quarter he cherished, and perhaps with some degree of reason, were not all realized, to the full extent to which his sanguine mind had urged them. It was doubtless well for him, however, that they were not. The disappointments of childhood will give a sober cast to the else too glowing pictures and too anxious hopes of youth ; and while they excite a caution in respect to the confidence we should place in the prospects that unfold themselves before us, admirably prepare the mind for the event, when the pledges of friendship lie long unredeemed, and the fair blossoms of hope are blasted and destroyed.

In the mean time he applied himself with surprising diligence to the acquisition of knowledge. In his favorite pursuit he met with the most important aid, from the valuable friendship of the lato Rev. Ebenezer White, then the pastor of the Independent church at Hertford. For this amiable and pious man, so early lost to the church of Christ,* Mr. Spencer ever cherished and expressed the warmest affection; whilst he survived but a few weeks the melancholy pleasure of paying the last tribute of respect to his beloved remains, and giving utterance to the warm and authorized feelings of his heart, in a most impressive oration at his grave. From Mr. White he learned the rudiments of the Latin tongue; and though the early removal of that gentleman to Chester deprived him of his kind and valuable assistance, yet his father, who had discernment to perceive, and wisdom to foster the unfolding talents of his son, afforded him the means of more ample instruction, by sending him to the best school his native town supplied. Approbation cannot be expressed in language too unqualified of the conduct, in this respect, pursued by the parents of this amiable youth, who though surrounded by every circumstance of a worldly nature to check its progress, yet nobly determined to afford every degree

* Mr. White died Sunday, May 5th, 1811. An interesting memoir of his life (together with his select remains) has been published by the Reverend Joseph Fletcher, A. M. of Blackburn; with a recommendatory preface, by the Rev. Dr. Collyer, of London. In the melancholy but pleasing task of selecting these papers for the press, Mr. Fletcher was originally joined by the subject of these memoirs:—but whilst Mr. Spencer was thus engaged in rearing a monument to the memory of his departed friend—he too was suddenly removed, and it devolved upon the hand of friendship to perform the same office for himself.

of culture, which such sacrifices as they might be able to make would yield to a mind which promised to rise superior to the obscurity of its birth, and consecrate at some future period no common share of genius to the noblest and the best of causes. Nor must these expressions pass unmingled by regret, that many important accessions are lost to the interests of religion and literature by the neglect of *ignorant*, or the reluctance of *sordid* parents, who in the one case have not the capacity to discover talent, or in the other a disposition, where their worldly circumstances are narrow and scanty, to make any sacrifice of ease on their part, or expected emolument on that of the child, for its cultivation.

"Full many a gem of purest ray serene,
The dark unfathomed caves of ocean bear;
Full many a flower is born to blush unseen,
And waste its sweetness on the desert air."

At about the age of twelve years, Mr. Spencer considers himself to have become the subject of serious impressions of a deep and permanent kind, and to have felt something experimentally of the power of religion. This most interesting circumstance he simply states in the memoir of his life before referred to, but mentions no particulars respecting the mode in which these impressions were wrought upon his mind, or in what way they operated upon his character, his conduct, and his views. The *gen-*

eral effect, however, he distinctly records to have been that of heightening his desire of the Christian ministry, for which, it was strongly impressed upon his mind, God had destined him ; whilst it reconciled him to his present situation, which was most uncongenial to the bias of his mind, and most unfriendly to the accomplishment of his ardent wishes ; for the circumstances of his father's family were at that time of such a nature as to render his assistance necessary between the hours of school, and at length compelled his parent, however reluctantly, entirely to remove him. His removal from school, however, was not in consequence of his father's having abandoned the prospect of his one day entering on the work of the ministry, but an act dictated by prudence, which afforded him an opportunity patiently to wait, and calmly to watch the leadings of Providence, and the occurrence of any circumstances which might tend to fix the future destiny of his son. These prudential arrangements, however, were a source of keenest anguish to the mind of Spencer. He bowed at first with reluctance to the yoke of manual labor when but partially imposed—rapidly performed the appointed task, and leaped with joy from toils so repugnant to the elevated and ardent desires of his soul, to solitude and to books ; and when compelled entirely to leave his school and pursue from day to day the *twisting of worsted*, which he calls *the worst part of his fath-*

er's business, his grief was poignant and his regret severe. But religion in early life, assumed in him her mildest and most amiable forms. Its characters were those of uncomplaining acquiescence in the will of God, and cheerful resignation to his earthly lot. If, indeed, with patient submission to the arrangements of Providence he occasionally mingled a warm expression of desire, and suffered his imagination to dwell upon the bright visions of better days, and the animating promise of pursuits more congenial to the tone and inclination of his mind, which hope would give, till, for a moment, it seemed reluctant to return ;—it was natural ;—nor is it incompatible with the most perfect resignation to the Divine will thus to dwell on scenes of promised pleasure with delight. Such a combination of light and shade is beautiful in nature ; and not unfrequently in the history of a Christian's feelings does the sunshine of resignation break in upon the tears of sorrow, and produce a commixture of indefinable feelings, which, like the bow of heaven, are a pledge not unredeemed, of fairer scenery and happier days.

The writer, in thus recording the mingled feelings of his friend, has participated too deeply in circumstances and emotions similar to his, not to do it with the warmth of sympathy. He knows how hard it is to give a cheerful and undivided attention to one pursuit, though less repugnant than mechanical employ, when the heart is intently fixed upon another. Illy does the mind adapt itself to the narrow rules of business, the drudgery of manual labor, or the habits of commerce, when panting after study, devoted to the love of books, or eager to engage in the noblest work that can occupy the powers of man—the ministry of the gospel :—impressed with a consciousness, that if it is the will of God that the desire enkindled and cherished in the bosom should be fulfilled, some event will transpire to afford facilities and point the way—but day after day, expecting that event in vain, till *hope deferred makes the heart sick*, and all the visions with which she has charmed, seem gradually yielding to the influence of despair. Yet even here, religion has a power to soothe : she sheds the mild influence of resignation, when the glare of hope is gone—

> "Gives even affliction a grace,
> And reconciles man to his lot."

He continued working at his father's business and in his father's house, for about a year and a half, anxiously expecting some situation to present itself more congenial to his wishes, but no circumstance arose to interrupt the monotonous sameness of his every day's employ. It seems, however, that he still attended to the cultivation of his mind, and never wholly lost sight of the Christian ministry.—Meanwhile business languished, and his father was desirous of seeing him comfortably settled. Their mutual anxiety increasing to impatience, and his father reading on the cover of a magazine an advertisement for a situation which appeared to be suitable, they set out for London, but upon an interview with the advertiser they found insuperable difficulties in the way, and returned, with disappointment, to Hertford.

Some weeks after this fruitless journey, Mr. Spencer was recommended by a friend to place his son with Messrs. Windwood and Thodey, respectable glovers in the Poultry, who also introduced him to Mr. Thodey's notice. The first interview between the parties was satisfactory; every arrangement was made preparatory to his being bound apprentice, and Thomas soon after entered, in a new capacity, this worthy gentleman's house. The services connected with his new situation, the *better* part of which was far from grateful to the wishes of his heart, still panting for the ministry with unconquerable attachment, were some of them such as his spirit, at first, but reluctantly submitted to perform; yet aware that then the providence of God pointed out no other path, he cheerfully acquiesced, and exchanged, not without regret, the calm and tranquil enjoyments of an endeared domestic circle, for the bosom of strangers, the drudgery of a shop, and the bustle of the Poultry. But here, as formerly at school, his amiable manners—his modest behavior, and engaging appearance, soon won the affection of the family, (which was large,) whilst his fervent piety and superior talents, excited emotions of the highest order. An extract of a letter, obligingly addressed to me from Mr. Thodey himself, will best record his manner of life, whilst under that gentleman's roof:

"His appearance, his genuine modesty, diligence, and integrity, created an interest in our hearts, so as it were almost to identify him as one of our own children; he shared our privileges; united with us in family devotion; and I occasionally took the same opportunities of conversing with him on divine things, which I had been accustomed to do with all those under my care. I well recollect one Sabbath evening, being thus engaged with him alone, when from his pertinent replies to some questions I put to him about the concerns of his soul and the importance of an interest in the Saviour, I perceived he possessed an uncommon share of talent and intellect. This conversation gave me an impressive idea of his general knowledge of the doctrines of the gospel, and I saw in him the traits of a very strong and ardent mind."

Whilst at Mr. Thodey's, he conscientiously devoted himself to promote the interests of his employers, notwithstanding his natural aversion to business. He even became peculiarly attached to the family, and receiving from them tokens of affectionate attention, superior to any thing he had a right to expect, and of which he always spoke with gratitude, he became as happy as the circumstances of his lot could possibly allow him to be. He formed an acquaintance with several pious young men, who, though rather above his station, did not hesitate to respect genius and religion, even in a lad of inferior rank in life. Several times, also, he exercised his preaching talents at the house of a relation of the young man who was then his fellow-servant, but was afterwards a student in the same academy with himself.*

He describes the exercises of his mind, and the mode in which he passed his time, during his residence in the Poultry, with great simplicity and feeling.

"At this place my time was entirely employed, as it was fit it should be, in executing the will of my two masters; for the young man, who was active and friendly, I formed a great attachment, and was indeed interested in the welfare of the whole family. Marks of respect were shown me, which were I believe unusual to any of my predecessors. I made myself upon the whole tolerably comfortable: some difficulties and disagreeable circumstances of course fell to my lot, yet upon the whole I had many enjoyments. My acquaintance, whilst here, increased: with several young men, who indeed were rather above my station in life, I was particularly intimate, and more than twice or thrice did I give an exhortation at the house of a relative of the young man's, who was my fellow-servant.—The opportunities I had of hearing the word were very delightful, and a higher relish was given to them by the toils and business of the week."†

To youth who may be placed in similar circumstances with the amiable subject of these memoirs, his mild and cheerful deportment in scenes so un-

* Rev. Thomas Heward. † MS. Memoirs.

congenial to the bias of his mind, should prove a salutary and impressive lesson. Impatience and fretfulness are but ill adapted to the furtherance of any design, and a disposition to murmur, under the arrangements of our present lot, marks a state of mind most unfriendly to the patient sufferance of the toils, the anxieties and the disappointments inseparably connected with the ministerial life ; and whilst it is an obvious fact, that every young man possessed of piety cannot be employed as a preacher of the gospel, to such as conceive themselves endowed with talents for that solemn office, and yet are placed in circumstances which seem to forbid the indulgence of a hope they still cherish with an anxious pleasure ; to such, the subsequent history of Mr. Spencer will afford another striking proof in an innumerable series—that where God has actually called and qualified an individual for the ministry, he will, in his own time and by unexpected methods, make the path of duty plain before that individual's feet. Let no one, then, rashly attempt to break the connected chain of opposing circumstances by which his providence may have surrounded him ; but rather wait in patience till the hand that has thus encircled him opens up a passage, and by events, which may justly be considered as intimations of the Divine will, invites him to advance.

These remarks, the result of frequent observations on the ways of God in cases similar to this, not improperly connect the future scenes of Mr. Spencer's life, with those we have already contemplated. For the time was now arrived, that the cloud which had hovered over his future prospects should be dissipated, and another path—a path to which he had from infancy directed his attention with fond anticipation and intense desire—present its varied and momentous objects of pursuit for the cheerful, but, alas! the short-lived exercise of his superior powers. After a residence of about four months with his employers in the Poultry, circumstances occurred of such a nature as to render his services no longer necessary, on which account he left London and returned for a while to his parents at Hertford; but some time previous to the event which caused his departure from London, he had been introduced to the notice of Thomas Wilson, Esq., the benevolent and indefatigable treasurer of the academy for educating young men for the work of the ministry, at Hoxton. Mr. Wilson perceived in him piety and talents far above his years. His whole appearance and his engaging manners excited in that gentleman's breast an interest in this amiable youth, which he never lost, and he gave it as his decided opinion, (without elating him with a hope, of the ultimate failure of which, there was still a probability,) that his views should in some way or other be directed towards the ministry.

This revolution in Mr. Spencer's affairs was not

unnoticed or unimproved by Mr. Wilson, who wisely regarding it as a favorable opportunity for carrying into effect those generous designs respecting him, which from their first interview he had cherished, sent for him ; conversed with him upon the subject, and introduced him to Rev. William Hordle, of Harwich, a gentleman to whose care some of the young men were committed, whose youth or other circumstances did not allow of their immediate entrance into the academy, though they were considered as proper objects of its patronage. To this gentleman, at length, Mr. Wilson proposed to send Mr. Spencer for trial of his talents and piety, and for preparatory studies ; a proposition to which Mr. Spencer acceded with unfeigned gratitude and joy. The time fixed for his entrance into Mr. Hordle's family was January, 1806. The interval between this period and that of his departure from the Poultry, which was in October, 1805, he spent in his father's house, and for the most part in his father's business. Though this was repugnant to his feelings, he had yet learned, by five month's absence, in the bustle of a shop in the city, to appreciate the calm and tranquil pleasures of a domestic circle, to which he became more endeared as the lovely qualities of his mind unfolded, and the dignified and pleasing prospects of his future life were disclosed. But though considerable light was thrown upon his destiny, yet on leaving London, it was not finally determined ; and this pressed with peculiar weight upon his spirit, which, susceptible of the slightest emotion, must have deeply felt in leaving one scene of action, the uncertainty of which as yet partially veiled from him that which should succeed. Of the day of his departure he thus writes : "I anticipated it with mingled emotions ; a strong desire to see my father, mother, brother, and sisters, a sensation of sorrow at parting with my old friends, and the idea of uncertainty as to my future engagements in life, equally affected me. Although I had been absent from home but five months, the desire I had again to see Hertford was very great, nor do I suppose I shall often spend more pleasant evenings than the first one I spent at home, after the first time of being absent for any considerable season ; two or three days were spent in seeing other relations and friends, till—."*

Here the narrative, first referred to, and often quoted, written by his own hand, and evidently for his own use, abruptly closes ; and here for a moment his biographer will pause.——It is a charming domestic piece, which the hand of his departed friend, obedient to the warm and vivid recollections of his fervent mind, has sketched ; but scarcely has he pictured to himself the countenances of that interesting group which gathered around him again to bid him welcome to his father's house, and commit-

* MS. Memoirs.

ted the rude outline to his paper, than he is suddenly called off, and lays down the recording pen for ever! So did his life abruptly terminate; but the mysterious voice that summoned him from his endeared connections upon earth introduced his emancipated spirit to the bosom of a happier family above—not another family, but one most intimately connected with his own, for which whilst here he cherished such a warm affection. The sentiment this sentence breathes was familiar to himself, and often seen in the energy and fervor with which he would repeat these admirable lines of Kelly:—

"One family, we dwell in him;
One church above, beneath,
Though now divided by the stream,
The narrow stream of death.

One army of the living God,
To his command we bow;
Part of the host have cross'd the flood,
And part are crossing now.

Ten thousand to their endless home
This awful moment fly;
And we are to the margin come,
And soon expect to die.

Dear Jesus, be our constant guide;
Then when the word is giv'n,
Bid death's cold stream and flood divide
And land us safe in heav'n."

At Harwich, Mr. Spencer was completely in his

element. He commenced the year 1806 in Mr. Hordle's family, and was then about completing the fifteenth of his own life. At this interesting age, when the powers of the mind begin rapidly to unfold—when a tone is often given to the future cast of thought, and sentiments and habits are imbibed and formed, which constitute the basis or become the germ of the matured and finished character;—it was a circumstance peculiarly auspicious in the history of this lamented youth, that he was introduced to the pious and enlightened care of such a man as Mr. Hordle. In his preaching, in his lectures, and in his conversation, he saw most admirably applied, those elementary principles of theological science, the scholastic forms of which must else have been unintelligible or insipid to his mind. In the liberal and sacred current of his habitual thought, Mr. Spencer would find a safe channel for the yet infant stream of his own conception; whilst he would imperceptibly form his character upon that mild, correct, and amiable model, constantly before him.

It must be of incalculable advantage to a young man destined for the Christian ministry, as it evidently was to our departed Spencer, to pass a year or two beneath a faithful and enlightened pastor's roof—to be a spectator of his toil—a daily witness of the varied scenes of duty and of trial which the Christian ministry perpetually presents. It is true, that in academies, lectures on the pastoral care are read, and discourses on the duties of the Christian ministry delivered ; but one week of actual observation must impress more deeply on the mind all that such lectures can contain, and unnumbered other circumstances, equally important, but which no general analysis can include, than months or years of the most devoted study. And to the diligent improvement of this peculiar advantage, perhaps, may in part be attributed that early maturity at which Mr. Spencer's capacity for the sacred office had arrived. He had the seriousness, the reflection of the *pastor* while but a *student;* and when he actually entered on that holy office, the exercises of the pulpit, and the habits of his ministerial life, bespoke the knowledge of long experience, rather than of recent theory, and indicated the presence of a *master's*, not a *learner's* hand.

At Harwich his diligence was exemplary ; a judicious course of reading was marked out for him by his respected tutor, which he conscientiously and unweariedly pursued ; but besides this, he had the use of an excellent library, with rich supplies from which he amply occupied his leisure hours. He had made considerable progress in the Latin ; and soon after his introduction to Mr. Hordle, he commenced, under his direction, the study of the Hebrew. With this sacred language he was particularly pleased, and soon demonstrated his attachment and his diligence, by completing, with considerable labor, an abridgment of Parkhurst's Hebrew Lexicon. This work he accomplished in a small pocket manual, which proved of considerable use to him, and was almost his constant companion.*

Here, too, he first became acquainted with the principles of Moral Philosophy; and whilst from the lectures of Doddridge, and the essays of Locke, his mind derived vigor and energy, from the study of the Latin poets, and the classic authors of our own country, it gained amusement, and his compositions gradually assumed an air of elegance and ease.

But not only in literature and science was his progress conspicuous during his residence in Harwich; but he also made considerable advances in the knowledge and experience of divine things. That in the midst of all his studies, which yet he pursued with diligence and ardor, religion was the object of his chief regard and dearest to his heart, is evident from the uniform strain of his letters to his most intimate and beloved friend Mr. Heward, whose fellow laborer he had been at Mr. Thodey's, and the privation of whose society he seemed deeply to deplore. His views of the Christian ministry became

* Of this manual he made two fair copies, one of which is in possession of his tutor, and the other is amongst the papers from which these Memoirs are supplied. The design is honorable to his judgment, and the execution to his perseverance and his accuracy at that early age.

more and more consistent, and the impression of its vast importance more deep and solemn on his mind. The intense desire with which he panted for that sacred and honorable office became tempered, though never checked, by an awe of its vast responsibility, and a consciousness of incapacity for the full discharge of its numerous and laborious duties.

With Mr. Hordle he would sometimes indulge in the most free and unreserved converse on the state of his heart, and his private walk with God. In such conversations he was always much affected, and susceptible, from the constitution of his nature, of the most delicate impressions and the keenest feelings, it may be well supposed that in religion he would *deeply* feel. Hence the tenderness of his conscience, and the susceptibility of his mind would often overwhelm his bosom with convictions of guilt, and agitate him with unnumbered inward conflicts. Yet in the midst of all he evidently grew in spiritual strength—his mind acquired confidence—his principles became daily more and more confirmed—and he had advanced far in a deep and experimental acquaintance with the ways of God at an age when such advancement is rarely to be found.

Whilst at Harwich he regularly shared with Mr. H. the pleasing duty of conducting the devotions of the family, and frequently performed the sacred service with an enlargement of heart, a fervor and propriety of expression truly astonishing. But this was a circumstance he particularly wished should be concealed ; his modesty and diffidence shrunk from the observation of men, even of his nearest friends ; and in one of his letters to his friend* he writes, "My situation is comfortable, more so than ever; I am considered like one of the family ; of an evening I generally, by Mr. H.'s desire, engage in family prayer, he in the morning. *O tell it to no body on any account.* When he is out I always do."

To those who knew not the beloved original, the outlines of whose character these pages but imperfectly present, the detail of minute particulars may be uninteresting and insipid; but those who were familiar with him will dwell with pleasure on the faintest lineament that may be here preserved of a dear departed friend, so ardently, so deservedly, esteemed; whilst a combination of these varied and retired beauties may form a portrait on which the eye of a stranger may dwell with admiration, and the mind reflect with profit. It is in confidence of this that his biographer pauses to record another and a pleasing trait in his character at this early age—the peculiar warmth and constancy of his friendship. He seems, indeed, at this period to have had but one bosom friend, except those of his own immediate family; to him his letters breathe an affection the most glowing, spiritual and pure ; and perhaps no little incident more strikingly displays the tender

* Mr. Heward.

cast of his mind than that which he himself relates, with great simplicity, in a letter to his friend :—

"This morning we read (Mr. H. and myself) the second night of Young's Night Thoughts—the very place that treats of friendship ; I was rather affected at the reading of it ; and after it was finished, and we were alone, I told him (Mr. H.) I was no stranger to Young's sentiments in that place. He asked me 'If I had lost any friends ?' I told him no—not by death. He asked me 'if I had by treachery ?' O no, sir. 'How then ?' *Only by separation !*"

Thus in pleasant and familiar intercourse with one for whom he mingled veneration with affection, and of whom he never ceased to speak with all the rapturous energy of gratitude and filial love—in exercises and pursuits every way adapted to satisfy his ardent thirst of knowledge—in scenes and in society congenial to the tone and bias of his mind—in conscientious preparation for closer studies and severer labor, previous to his entrance on that sacred office long the object of his choice—and in deep communion with himself and God—did he pass the allotted period of his stay at Harwich.

As the term (a year) fixed for his residence with Mr. Hordle drew towards its close, his anxiety considerably increased ; he anticipated, with regret, a departure from scenes and society so much endeared to him ; and the trial through which he was to pass previous to his admission into the academy at Hoxton, when viewed in connection with his youth, excited in his mind considerable apprehension and dread. But the hope of success never entirely abandoned him ; whilst the pleasing prospect of being again associated with his friend, who had by this time entered as a student in the same academy, tended not a little to gladden and animate his heart.

In November he drew up a statement of his religious experience, his views of theological truth, and his reasons for desiring the Christian ministry, according to a standing order of the academy with respect to young men proposing themselves as candidates for its patronage. These papers, written in a style of dignified simplicity, and disclosing a knowledge and experience of divine things, which in a youth, scarcely sixteen years of age, must have excited the admiration of all to whom they were submitted—were duly presented to the committee, and passed, though not without some difficulty, arising from his age ; but the extraordinary qualifications he appeared to possess, and the strong recommendations of his friend and tutor, Mr. Hordle, overcame this obstacle, and the fifth of January following was appointed for his personal appearance before the constituents of that institution, in order to give them a specimen of his talents for public speaking.

Mr. Spencer left Mr. Hordle's family on the 18th of December, and spent the interval of time between his departure from Harwich and the day of his examination at Hoxton (which was postponed to the 7th of January) at his father's house at Hertford.

Whose imagination does not follow this beloved youth into the bosom of his family again ; who does not picture to himself the charming scenes of social and domestic joy his presence would inspire ! With what tenderness and affection would his venerable father bid him welcome to his paternal home again ; with what delight would he gaze upon the animated features of his countenance, smiling in all the ingenuousness of youth ; while with nobler feelings of delight he marked the unfolding graces of his mind, saw his improvement in the best of sciences—religion, and beheld him daily growing in favor both with God and man. With what adoring gratitude would they retrace together the scenes of his childhood, and the many alarming obstacles which once almost forbade the indulgence of a hope that the object of their ardent wish would ever be obtained ; and how, in the transport of those happy hours, would his family anticipate for him they loved, in the future stages of an honorable ministry, years of usefulness and comfort. Ah ! pleasing visions never to be realized ! Little did that interesting group conceive that it was his appointed lot but just to taste the joys and sorrows of a pastor's life, and then expire. Already they had seen the bud swelling with fullness—teeming with life ; now they beheld the blossom, and admired its beauty ; and they thought long to gaze upon the promised charms of the unfolded flower ; happy strangers of the melancholy and mysterious fact, that so soon as it had opened it must be suddenly cut down and die ! But such and so frail is man—"*In the morning they are like grass that groweth up, in the evening it is cut down and withereth.*"—Psalm xc. 5, 6. Such and so uncertain is human life—"*It is even as a vapor, that appeareth for a little time, and then vanisheth away.*"—James iv. 14.

CHAPTER II.

Letters written from Home—His Return to Harwich—Resumes his Studies—Interesting Correspondence—Papers submitted by Spencer to the Committee of Hoxton Academy.

At this interesting period of Mr. Spencer's life, it will be perhaps gratifying to the reader to pause, and gain a more familiar acquaintance with him than can be supplied by a narration of events and circumstances in his history, by perusing some extracts from his correspondence and other papers, which will throw much light upon the formation of his character, and afford a pleasing specimen of his early genius.

I have now before me a packet of letters addressed to his friend Mr. Heward, dated at various periods, from October, 1805, to December, 1806.—Though at the commencement of this correspondence he had not attained his fifteenth year, these letters breathe a spirit of the purest piety, and often express sentiments by which age would not be dishonored, in a style remarkably correct and vigorous. But the reader shall participate with me in the pleasure which the perusal of this interesting correspondence—this simple and unaffected utterance of early piety and friendship, has afforded me.

HERTFORD, *November* 12, 1805.

"——— I join with you in saying, 'how wonderful are God's ways.' We indeed little thought that Mr. H. was the person under whom I should be instructed, when we were at Hoxton, hearing him preach, or I, when I breakfasted with him; at the same time, I cannot forbear adoring that favor which is shown to me from God; ME who am utterly unworthy of the least of all God's mercies. Goodness and mercy have hitherto followed me, and, I doubt not, will through life. May that goodness which was so gloriously displayed in the salvation of sinners, and that mercy which has snatched so many brands from the burning, be our consolation all through life—our joy in death—and the burden of our song to all eternity."

The following observations are worthy of a much older pen, and display a judgment and discretion, rather unusual in a lad, not yet fifteen years of age.

"You informed me in your last, that your desires for the work of the ministry had not at all abated. I sincerely wish that they may be fulfilled, and that you and I may be fellow-laborers in the Lord's vineyard. God certainly can do this for us; let us pray that he may. You still appear dubious of your own ability for that important work. I would have you consider, that God works by whom he will work. He has many ministers in his church, real sent ministers, who have not those great gifts that distinguish many of his servants; and not only so, but these men have often been the means of doing more good than those of great talents—and what is the reason of this? *Even so, Father, for so it seemed good in thy sight*—is all that we must say. And you, my worthy friend, should also remember, that as yet, you cannot form any idea of your own abilities. As I have often told you, when I lived with you, I doubt not your abilities, when improved by application to study, &c. will be as fit for that employ, (if the will of God) as any other. God, you know, in every thing acts as a sovereign: '*I will work, and who shall let it,*' is his language—will work by the feeblest means, and the weakest instruments. I hope you will still be kept low in your own eyes, for, that, I am sure, is one quality, or rather property, of a gospel minister. At our best estate we are altogether vanity, and less than nothing. May the Lord keep us all truly humble. Luther used to say, there were three things made a minister—affliction, meditation, and prayer; that is, sanctified affliction, scriptural meditation, and earnest prayer; in which last particular I hope you are perpetually engaged. Pray, my dear friend, for direction of God—pray for grace, which is of more value, by far, than great gifts, and say in the language of resignation, hope, and faith—*Here am I, Lord, send me to labor in thy vineyard.*' You have appealed to me in saying, 'You well know I shall never rely on my own strength for success and usefulness'—I know you will not, (at least whilst in your present mind) and I pray that God would keep you still so determined. Let us then pray, that we may both of us be able, useful, and humble ministers of the New Testament.

"—— I am glad to find, that you generally hear three times a day. Young men who wish to be ministers, cannot hear too much of the gospel, provided they are anxious to improve on what they do hear——."

EXTRACT FROM A LETTER TO THE SAME.

HERTFORD, *November* 18, 1805.

"MY DEAREST FRIEND:—I expected to have heard from you before now, but as I have not, it becomes me to bear the disappointment with fortitude and resolution, hoping that it will not be long before I have a few lines from you. On Saturday last, I heard that that good and worthy man, Mr. Winwood, was dead.

It will, I doubt not, be a great stroke to the family; but I am well assured, that to him death was eternal gain. Truly, *the righteous hath hope in his death.* May you and I both be found at the last day on the right hand of the Judge with our respected master! While he is tuning his harp to the praises of a precious Jesus, we have to combat with many enemies; we have many trials to pass under

> Before we reach the heavenly fields
> Or walk the golden streets!

We shall, I am persuaded, feel our own depravity in many instances here below, ere we join with him in everlasting songs above; but if we are enlisted under the banners—the blood-stained banners of the cross, we shall certainly arrive there. Let us then seek, earnestly seek, after the one thing needful; and whilst earthly objects vanish and decay in our estimation; nay, whilst the world dies daily in our view, and its perishing things appear in their proper light—may we feel our hearts panting after the wells of salvation—our souls, with all their faculties, engaged in the noblest of all undertakings—our feet running in the good ways of God—our tongues making mention of his righteousness, and of his only—in short, may we be crucified to the world—risen with Christ—and transformed into his divine image and likeness. This, I trust, I can say is my desire, and I know it is the earnest wish of my dear friend.

"I am sensible that your attachment to me is as unshaken as ever. I hope you pray that both of us may be made ministers of the gospel; and in some future day, have our wishes respecting that completely fulfilled. I am very desirous that you may be shortly placed in a situation in which you will have more leisure for reading, writing, studying, &c. *O that you were going with me to Harwich.* Still continue to pray for one who feels his own unworthiness for the service of his God, and yet wishes to be an instrument of doing great good to souls: and if I should not be very successful in my ministry, methinks it would be reward enough to have labored for God, and not to have been employed in the drudgery of Satan."

The next letter, to the same correspondent, contains a specimen of his talent for the composition of sermons at that age. It affords a pleasing proof of his early skill in the practice of an art, in which he eventually so much excelled.

HERTFORD, *December* 3, 1805.

" ——— I have sent you my thoughts upon (or rather my way of discussing) that text Mr. Knight preached from. I hope your candor will excuse imperfections. I never read any thing upon it, and it is the production of a boy.

MATTHEW v: 20.—'*For I say unto you, that except your righteousness shall exceed the righteousness of the Scribes and Pharisees, ye shall in no case enter into the kingdom of heaven.*'

GENERAL HEADS.

1st.—EXPLAIN THE NATURE OF THE RIGHTEOUSNESS OF THE SCRIBES AND PHARISEES.

2d.—SHOW IN WHAT RESPECTS OUR RIGHTEOUSNESS MUST EXCEED THEIRS.

3d.—NOTICE THE CONSEQUENCES OF POSSESSING A RIGHTEOUSNESS NO BETTER THAN THEIRS.

1st HEAD.—EXPLAIN THE NATURE, &c.

It was self-righteousness.—Luke xviii: 9.

1st.—*This righteousness is founded in ignorance.*

Of God's nature,
Of the spirituality of his law,
Of the deceitfulness of the heart,
And of the true method of salvation.

2d HEAD.—SHOW IN WHAT RESPECTS OUR RIGHTEOUSNESS SHOULD EXCEED THEIRS.

The righteousness here termed 'yours' is the righteousness of Christ, which becomes ours by imputation, in the same manner as our sins became Christ's. This righteousness thus becoming ours, exceeds the righteousness of the Scribes and Pharisees.

1st.—*In its origin.* It is divine—the other human, or Satanic; as we doubt not, Satan first infused self-righteous thoughts into the minds of men, &c.

2d.—*Its nature and particular properties.*

This righteousness
Delivers us from bondage,
Saves us from sin,
Gives us holiness of life,
Makes us victorious in death,
Joyful in judgment, and
Happy through all eternity.

The righteousness of the Scribes and Pharisees cannot do this.

But our Lord might also allude to that righteousness which is implanted in us, as well as that which is imputed to us, and that far exceeds the righteousness of the Scribes and Pharisees in its effects, which are real good works, which

Spring from a good motive,
Are directed to a good purpose.
And have a good end.

These works are not meritorious, but serve for the justification of our faith, not of our persons, and they far exceed the legal performances of the self-righteous.

3d HEAD.—NOTICE THE CONSEQUENCES OF POSSESSING A RIGHTEOUSNESS NO BETTER THAN THEIRS.

Ye shall in no case enter into, &c.

1st.—Here we must necessarily dwell a little upon *the nature of the kingdom of heaven.*—Consider

1. The person of the King.
2. The happiness of the subjects.
3. The eternal duration of his reign, &c.

2d.—*How dreadful a thing to be shut out of this kingdom.*

3d.—*How peculiarly striking is the language of the Saviour—ye shall in no case, &c.*

Notwithstanding all your professions, long prayers, alms givings, &c., '*Ye shall in no case enter into the kingdom of heaven.*'

From this subject we draw a few inferences.

1.—We may learn from hence, *the evil nature of sin.* If all *self-righteousness* be so bad, what must *unrighteousness* be?

2.—We here see *the only true method of salvation*—the righteousness of Christ.

3d.—How necessary is *daily, serious self-examination*, in order to ascertain to which class we belong.

4.—We likewise infer *the necessity of prayer*, for instruction and grace.

5.—*How dreadful is the case of the self-righteous character.*

6.—*The believer may hence draw some comfort.* He is interested in Jesus Christ, and shall outride all the storms and troubles of life, sing the dear name of Jesus in the hour of death, and stand unmoved amidst the jarring elements, 'the wreck of matter, and the crush of worlds.'

"May the God of hope bless us both—fill us with all joy and peace in believing—enlarge our spiritual coast—give us to see more and more of the sinfulness of our nature—the depravity of our hearts—the imperfection of our graces—the smallness of our knowledge—the sufficiency of Jesus—the stability of our hope—the fullness of Christ. May he give us to see that our names are written in heaven—may he brighten up our evidences for glory—establish our faith—enlarge our desires—and give us hungerings and thirstings after righteousness. May we enjoy the blessings of salvation—the sweetness of communion with God—the peace bought and purchased for us by Christ Jesus—and that joy in the Holy Ghost, produced by his influences—and may we learn more and more of the heights, lengths, depths, and breadths of the love which passeth knowledge. May we dwell together in that happy land, where none but the righteous can enter, and where our worship shall be undisturbed.

"And now, my dear brother, I commend you to the hands of that God who doth all things well, and who taketh care of those who put their trust in him; and hoping soon to hear from you, I subscribe myself,

"Your truly affectionate friend,
THOMAS SPENCER."

HERTFORD, *December* 31, 1805.

"MY DEAR FRIEND.—I think myself very happy in having such a friend as you prove yourself to be. I know affection towards me is too deeply rooted in you ever to be erased by separation. Life's greatest blessing is a well chosen friend, and I do feel it so. You cannot imagine (only by your own feelings) what pleasure I take in recollecting past scenes, and recalling to the mind occurrences relating only to us, which never shall be forgotton. I hope we have the same 'friend that sticketh closer than a brother.' I am affected, peculiarly affected, when I read the solemn confessions you make of depravity, &c. You know Paul acknowledged himself the chief of sinners. When, therefore, you are bowed down under a sense of sin, *look unto Jesus*, there only salvation is to be found for those who, like you, are sensible of sin. But I verily believe my friend has already been washed in the fountain of his blood. Yes, I doubt not but you have passed from death unto life, and are called according to God's eternal purpose; therefore, instead of writing bitter against yourself, rejoice in Christ Jesus whilst you have no confidence in the flesh. Ah! my friend, you know not fully how I have lifted up my puny arm in rebellion against God; so that I cannot think myself a whit behind the chief of sinners. Young as I am, I am a great sinner; but blessed be God who has, I hope, given us both a good hope through grace: to him be all the glory.

"I shall, I expect, be in town a day sooner than was intended, viz: Wednesday, the 8th; my father will not come till the next day. Mr. F———, in his letter, mentions a desire that I would give them a lecture (*in the old way*) at his house in the evening. I am very willing to do it, and I hope we shall have your company.

His next letter is from Harwich, and contains a pleasing disclosure of the state of his mind on the accomplishment, so far, of his ardent wishes.

HARWICH, *February* 6, 1806.

"MY DEAREST FRIEND—I with pleasure embrace the opportunity which now offers itself, of writing you a few lines for the first time since I have been here. While I hope you enjoy your health, I can say I never was better in my life than I have been since I have been at Harwich. The air is very cold and healthy: I am sure I have felt the difference. In the town there are many inhabitants and a Methodist place besides Mr. Hordle's: by Methodists, I mean Wesley's people. Mr. Hordle preaches three times on a Sabbath day, and is very well attended, and on Wednesday evenings; prayer meeting on Monday night. I doubt not but you will join with me in returning thanks to the all-wise disposer of events for placing me in that comfortable situation which I now fill. I live with Mr. H. entirely; his study is where I pursue my learning, and in an afternoon I meet his boys (there are only nine) at his vestry to say a lesson or two with them. I learn *Latin*, *Geography*, and have got a considerable way in Doddridge's Lectures on *Pneumatology*, in which I meet now and then a *philosophical* subject; indeed, my dear friend, I really am very comfortable. *O! that my improvement may keep pace with the advantages I enjoy.*

"But, my dearest friend, what a separation between us. I often think of you when in this study pursuing my learning; think! did I say? I cannot help thinking of you, and I will cherish every tender thought of a friend I so much love. Oft-times I think of an evening, when we are surrounding the family altar, you are engaged in the busy concerns of life—whilst I am enjoying the advantages of a *kind teacher*, a good *library*, and various other blessings, you are behind the counter of a glove shop. You do not despair. I hope we shall some future day enjoy one another's company, and these advantages connected with it. When I walk out, as I in general do every day for exercise, I imagine you to be here—I converse with you—I see you—and fancy many other enjoyments, which perhaps will not come so soon. When I last saw you I was exceedingly vexed that we could not have half an hour together in private; but, however, I know you regard me still—and am sure I love you much; and it is some pleasure to think that we can yet pray for one another. O do not forget me, unworthy as I am, in your approaches to the throne of grace. Pray that I may not abuse my privileges; but that whilst I am here it may be manifest that I am possessed of a principle of divine grace in my heart. But I hope I need not mention this to you, for you do, I trust, still remember me in your best moments. I have not forgotten the pleasure I experienced the last time I saw you in London, nor the affectionate manner in which you conversed with me from Mr. F.'s to my cousin's the last evening.

"I had a very tedious journey here, as I could not sleep *all night* in the coach. But I think I am well repaid. I did not imagine that I should be treated with such care; I have a nice little bed to myself; and, in short, am surrounded with blessings. I take some pleasure in contrasting my present situation with what it was when at Mr. Thodey's; but after I have considered the peculiar advantages of this to that, I find that there was one pleasure I enjoyed there, which I do not here—that of your company and conversation; and thus is life made up of hopes and fears, pleasures and pains. May we be among those who are *strangers and sojourners* here, who seek a better country.

"The evening I generally employ in promiscuous reading, as the time is then as it were my own. As I come home from the vestry about an hour before the other boys, from that time till tea I am engaged in secret meditation, reading God's word, and prayer to him. Ah! Thomas, you are then more on my mind than during the other parts of the day, for I cannot but remember how often you have pressed on me the duty of private prayer; and indeed, my friend, you are then most remembered by me in the best sense. I do continue to pray for you; and I hope God will hear our petitions for one another, and send us answers of peace. I beg of you, I entreat you to be earnest in supplication for me, that if God has appointed me for the work of the ministry, I may be fitted for it, and have a divine blessing attending me in all I undertake.

"Mr. H. bids me write now and then the heads of a sermon of my own, and show it him. I have yet only done one: it met his approbation.

"Be so kind as to remember me to Mr. F., &c., &c. I suppose you like your business as little as ever; but I hope you will soon be put in a situation where you will yourself enjoy more—I mean in the best enjoyments. I still hope that we, formed for each other's comfort, shall yet be made blessings to each other, and that in a particular way. Then let the conceited, covetous worldling say, 'Friendship is but a name'—we know it is something more—it is a great blessing; and where the friends have grace in their hearts, it is so eminently and especially. David and Jonathan found it so. I often think of your noticing particularly that expression, *their souls were knit together*. Dr. Young thought so when he said, 'poor is the friendless master of a world.' I am thankful that I have had such a friend cast in my way that will be, I trust, a blessing to me all through life, and that will dwell with me in a better world. May the hope of that happiness stimulate us to more resignation to the divine will, and holy disdain of the vanities of time and sense.

"And now, my dear friend, my letter draws to a close; I can scarcely forbear tears while I write it. I hope you will overlook its very visible imperfections, and remember that it comes from one that loves you. Need I again beseech you to pray for me, that I may find mercy of the Lord, be blessed with every blessing here below, and crowned with glory hereafter.

"Write to me what religious intelligence you know I am ignorant of: I see the Magazine here, and other periodical works. And now I desire to commit myself, my dear friend, and all our concerns, into the hands of a covenant God; and wishing you every blessing, I rest your ever faithful and affectionate friend,

THOMAS SPENCER."

IN ANOTHER LETTER TO THE SAME, HE WRITES:

HARWICH, *April* 4, 1806.

"MY DEAREST FRIEND—I received, with the greatest pleasure, your letter of the 29th of February, together with my father's; and, as I was sorry you did not write to me before, so was I equally grieved at the cause; I sympathize with you in your afflictions, and hope that you are now quite recovered and—the rest of the family. I believe you when you say it affords you so much pleasure to hear of my welfare. O! *Thomas*, pray for me that my very comforts do not become snares. I should like to have had more of the heads, texts, &c., of the sermons you have heard in London; and hope that you find the ministry of Mr. K——, and those you hear at Hoxton, beneficial to your soul; for it is my earnest desire that, under the influences of the sacred Spirit, your soul may be like a well-watered garden. I (of course) hear Mr. H. three times on the Sabbath day, and I think I can say it has been to my profit: his sermons are indeed very *judicious*, *experimental and practical*, and I find it to be just the preaching I *want*. I keep a book, in which I put down the heads of most of his sermons, which, when it is full, I intend (if you would like) that you shall see. I suppose of an evening we have not less than four hundred and fifty people; in the day time not quite so many. There is a band of singers in the table pew, generally a bass viol is played, and Mr. H. preaches in a gown, and I think the people are more attentive than any I ever saw. Once in a fortnight Mr. H. preaches at the *work-house;* I have been twice, and I like it *very much.* In the week day I go to the Methodist chapel, and sometimes hear a good sermon there. I find by the Magazine that Mr. S—— is at Spa-fields chapel. I have spoken often about him to you, and have mentioned him in my letters, (though by the bye I spelt his name wrong.) He is a Cheshunt student—has preached very frequently at Hertford chapel. I would advise you, if convenient, to go and hear him, for he is a very bold and very faithful preacher. If you do, give me a little account of the sermon, &c. If I were you, I would try to hear Mr. B——'s missionary sermon.

"I am very glad that you informed me of Mr. F.'s and Mr. W.'s conversation. I liked it all very well, except that about my preaching, and, indeed, I had much rather that Mr. F. had not mentioned that for various reasons. If you have heard any more, pray tell it me.—'*He must not be put too forward.*'

"But you have raised my curiosity very much about the certain minister, who has, unsolicitedly, offered you his recommendation for Hoxton. But why this reservedness? I shall expect a friendly, satisfactory reason for your not telling me his name, &c. Do you think that I would abuse your confidence? I hope not—I think I should know better. As the month has expired, you *must* tell me in your next more about it, as whether you have seen this certain minister? what he said to you? &c., &c. I hope I have obeyed your request, and prayed for you; may God grant us both more of a praying spirit, and may he answer our petitions, one for another. I thank you for Mr. E.'s address. I have not yet written to him —*must*—though, Thomas, I think now I should be completely unhappy were I again to have anything to do with business, and I feel for you, as you say your time is wholly taken up in it every day, from six in the morning to eleven at night. I hope that while your aversion to the cares of the world increases, your spiritual affections are more animated, and your whole soul, from day to day, transformed more into the likeness of our lovely Jesus.

'*The effectual fervent prayer of a righteous man availeth much.*'—You seem peculiarly pleased with this passage, observe therefore,

1st.—That it is the *righteous* God regards; those who are redeemed by the Son's blood; loved by the Father's grace; sanctified by the Spirit's influence. Those who are weaned from the vanities of earth and time—whose affections are set on things above—in a word, who are born of God, and bound for heaven.

2d.—That they must *pray.* Prayer is the breath of the new born soul, a believer cannot live without it, for

Prayer makes the darken'd cloud withdraw;
Prayer climbs the ladder Jacob saw;
Gives exercise to faith and love,
And brings down blessings from above.

3d.—They must pray *fervently.* 'Cold prayers,' saith one, 'do but beg a denial.' In vain we offer up lifeless devotion to a heart-searching and rein-trying God.

4th.—These prayers are *effectual,* and avail much; they avail much in the sanctifying of our souls, and forming Christ there.

"Pardon this digression, as these thoughts have just sprung from my own mind.

"I hope you continue to enjoy your Sabbaths more than ever. How delightful it is '*to dwell in the house of the Lord all the days of our life, to behold the beauty of the Lord, and inquire in his temple.*'—That was Mr. H.'s text last Sabbath day morning and afternoon. In the morning he applied it to the church here below; showed what was meant by beholding the beauty of the Lord, and inquiring in his temple, and how desirable it was, &c. In the afternoon he applied all (with the greatest propriety) to heaven. Two very excellent sermons.

"I cannot yet give up the thought that we shall soon live together again; if we are to be so favored, how thankful should I be; if not, we must learn to know no will but God's, and acknowledge that the Judge of all the earth will do right. As yet let us not despair, but commit all our concerns into the hands of our covenant God and heavenly Father. We know he will do all things well. My situation is as comfortable, or more so, than ever, and I am considered like one of the family. We have a nice house, and here are only Mr. H., Mrs. H., the little child about eight months old—a sweet babe he is—the servant and myself. I read Virgil in Latin now, and what I do learn of anything serves to show me more of my ignorance. May the Lord keep me humble. I have theological questions to study, such as:

'Wherein appears the possibility of a divine revelation?

'Why it is desirable?' &c.

"I may consult books upon the subject, and here is a very good library. You will not forget your promise to write in your next about grace thriving in your heart. As for me, it is with tardy steps I creep, sometimes joying, and sometimes sorrowing. And yet without boasting, I think I can say I have known more of heart religion since I have been here than before; but it is very little altogether. I have experienced many happy moments in secret, such times as remind me of our last Sabbath afternoon together. But O! what a deal of pride, rebellion, carelessness, and all kinds of wickedness, is there in my heart; I tremble to think of what I deserve for my former levity, &c. But O, pray for me, that I may find grace in the eyes of the Lord, and live to some purpose in the world. I am afraid that there are yet improper motives in my desiring the work of the ministry. Since I have been here I have seen some little of its nature, &c. I am sensible that no learning, or human qualifications, are enough to fit me for that all-important work; and I hope that God will pour down showers of grace on me, instead of what I deserve, 'vials of wrath.' When you give me a little account of your 'growth in grace,' and how the lamp of religion keeps alive, I hope you will retrace some of the paths in which the Lord your God has led you, and tell me something of your former experience, present enjoyments, and future hope. If you wish to go on from one degree of grace unto another, which I do not doubt, commune much with your own heart, read the Bible as much as possible, and above all things pray *fervently*. I am perfectly well in health, as I hope you are. My father told me in his letter that Mr. M—— is still at ——, and that the chapel was still continued. I should like to have all the numbers of the Youth's Magazine, (but September and October last, those I have,) if I could have them sent conveniently; and it is not worth while to send by the coach, for you know the carriage will be more than the books are worth. Wishing you every spiritual blessing, I remain your affectionate and faithful friend,

"THOMAS SPENCER."

HARWICH, *June* 14, 1806.

"MY DEAREST FRIEND:—I received your parcel the morning after you sent it, and read your letter with the greatest pleasure. You judge rightly when you say, you suppose that I was anxiously waiting to hear from you. The providential dealings of God with you have (I hope) filled me with wonder and praise. Surely both of us have great reason to say, '*Bless the Lord, O my soul, and all that is within me bless his holy name.*' Let us not forget any of his benefits, but for these displays of his goodness, dedicate our bodies and souls to his glory, which is only our reasonable service. Let us both rejoice, that God has put this his *treasure in earthen vessels, that the excellency of the power may be of God, and not of man.* Little did you expect a few years ago, that you should be providentially called into the work of the ministry; but now you can rejoice, that unto you, who, *in your own view*, are less than the least of all the saints, is this grace given, that you might preach among poor sinners the unsearchable riches of Christ. Observe now the dealings of Providence in this circumstance. You are in a waiting frame, and when so God appears to grant you the desire of your heart. He has now made your path clear before you, and as to its being the call of God, I have not the least doubt; but, however, I hope you will recollect, that though your way has been thus shown to you, it may not always be so; difficulties, great and many, may await us both in our journey through life; but God has said, when thou passest through the waters, I will be with thee, and will prevent the floods from overflowing thee. Having such promises as these, my dear friend, let us press forward, and with holy resignation say, 'Where he appoints I'll go and dwell.' 'Tis true, we know not what a day may bring forth; but this we know, that God will never forsake those who put their trust in him, but will be their sun to illuminate them, their shield to defend them, and their God eternally to bless them. I do not at all wonder at your being perplexed in your mind about mentioning matters to ——. Had I been in your state, I should have dreaded it; but you did well in making it a matter of prayer before God, and God was very gracious in ordering it as he has done. You know that prayer to God is the best way of *making things sure*, so you, I trust, have found it. I should like to know the other circumstances at which you hint, but I dare say they are too tedious to mention; perhaps we may see each other soon, when *conversation* will settle it. I am much pleased, nay delighted, with the conversation you had with Mr. W. He is, I doubt not, a warm friend to the cause of Christ, and does all he possibly can to forward it in the world. I am like him in regard to zealous and earnest preachers, and like to see animation and life in a pulpit, and where the preacher's mind is fettered with notes there can be none."

HARWICH, *Oct.* 14, 1806.

"MY DEAREST FRIEND:—As it is now considerably more than a month since you wrote me a note from Hoxton academy, and I answered it, I conclude that a letter from me will be what you now desire; and yet I am not quite certain whether you should not have written first; but by way of compensation for my too long silence before, I am willing to converse with you on paper. And as Mr. Hordle is gone to Ipswich to-day, to an association of ministers, and I have nothing particular to be engaged in besides, I embrace the opportunity. You are now, I suppose, a little inured to study, and begin to find the difficulties of a student's life not so many as you apprehended they were. I long to know in what studies you are engaged, and how you like them. I have just begun the Greek language; so of course do not know much about it, my time having been of late principally employed in the Hebrew, of which I am very fond, especially as I now read it 'unsophisticated by Rabbinical points.' I please myself with the idea of seeing and conversing with you in the course of about *ten weeks;* but at that time there will be something else which I shall not so much admire. Do you ask me what it is? It is, my dear friend, nothing less than appearing before the committee of Hoxton academy. The thought of it makes me almost tremble. Yesterday morning Mr. Hordle told me that I must prepare the account of my experience, sentiments and motives for wishing the ministery, by November, to be then laid before the gentlemen of the committee. This you know must be done; and when I go to London about Christmas, I must go through all that painful task, which, as it respects you, is all over. He told me, too, that he supposed there would be some demur about admitting me merely on the account of my youth; but he does not know that it will be so as to hinder my admittance. Mr. Wilson has, it appears, written to Mr. H. about it; so, if the affair succeeds well, I shall be in the academy after Christmas *with you.* That one circumstance, your company and friendship, will make amends for all my trouble of mind on the occasion. You may be sure I shall communicate every circumstance to you, and keep nothing back, that so by one occurrence and another, our mutual attachment and sincere friendship may be increased and strengthened. What a *long* separation we have experienced: may we be brought together again to strengthen each other's hands, and be both engaged in the best employment. You must inform me in your next, how long you think it will be before you begin to preach, and tell me all your places of preaching, texts, plans, &c. I hope you have written to my father, as I requested you would. I believe they are going on as usual at Hertford. Mr. M. continues among them. May great grace rest upon them all. I do not doubt that I shall feel some degree of uneasiness when the time comes for my separation from my friends here at Harwich. I mean such as Mr. Hordle, &c, &c. But my satisfaction will be, that I shall see you who are still, and I hope ever will be, my dearest friend. We live in a world of changes. Life is indeed a checkered scene. And here we have no continuing city. May we seek one to come. May it be our happiness to enjoy the favor of Him who never changes, but is the same yesterday, to-day, and forever. When I consider my exceeding sinfulness and depravity, besides my inability, I feel almost *disposed to wish* my views had never been directed towards the ministry, but it does appear a call of Providence. How could I do any thing else than come here. And now, perhaps, a door may be opened even for my being a student at Hoxton; but I shall go there under several disadvantages; for, being so young, I may expect a good deal of contempt from some self-sufficient and arrogant students, (if such there are) and you know they stay no longer than four years, and after that I shall be but twenty years old, and what can I then say to old experienced Christians! I do indeed feel a deal of discouragement. 'O may the Lord encourage me,' &c. But I shall come under some advantages; for, as I am *not altogether* *ignorant* of many things taught at Hoxton academy, I shall find my studies easier than if I had to begin learning them, &c. I wish we could be in one class. Another disadvantage which Mr. Hordle has told me of is this—The students generally spend their money which they are paid for preaching, in books,* &c. Now, I shall be too young to preach for at least these four years, consequently I can have no books, &c. till that time. This appears a very great disadvantage. However, I would wish to leave all in the hands of God. He knows what is best for me. And if I am one of those who love God, and are the called according to his purpose, he will make all things work together for my good. I want that calm disposition which is careful for nothing, but in every thing by prayer and supplication, makes known its requests unto God. I often reflect on the dealings of Providence with us when I first came to Mr. T.'s. You, I suppose, had not the least prospect of being a student at Hoxton. And I could not see how my coming there to learn that business, could at all further my preparation for that sacred work. We there became friends. I was there just long enough to secure a worthy and affec-

* It may perhaps be considered as departing from the design of this volume, or descending too much to minute particulars---yet I cannot satisfy myself without directing the eyes of those gentlemen who may have the care of providing supplies for the pulpit in destitute churches, or in cases of the pastor's absence, to this important circumstance. But few of the students in our academies are overburthened with money---yet money is absolutely necessary for the purchase of books, without which their studies must be considerably retarded. Deacons, and others whom it may concern, should bear his in mind, in the compliments which they may make them for their occasional services; and remember, that there is no case in which they can with greater delicacy or propriety, display a generous regard to their wants in this respect, than when thus remunerating them for their acceptable labors. It is needless to express a disapprobation, which every candid mind must feel, of a conduct directly the reverse of this, which is perhaps too often practised when the consideration is diminished for the very reason on account of which it ought to be increased---it is but a *student.*

tionate friend, and to have the notice of Mr. Wilson. Now you, too, have left Mr. T. and are in the academy. I went, you know, home, not knowing what the event would be. Providence has sent me here; and O, 'what am I, or my father's house, that he has brought me hitherto.' We are now blind to futurity. We know not where we shall be placed in future life, whether far from, or near to each other. I hope you are happy in your own soul, and that you live near to God. There is a great danger of forgetting the concerns of our own souls, whilst we are constantly employed in studying divine things. I know a little of this from experience, and perhaps you do. I hope you continue to pray for me; that I may be kept from sin and evil, for you know '*the effectual fervent prayer of a righteous man availeth much.*' Does your brother David make progress in the divine life? You must, in your next letter, give me some account of the change which I hope is wrought in him, for I feel an affectionate regard for all who belong to you. I ought to write to Mr. E———. Is he well? When you see him, remember me to him, and also to your cousin T——. Tell him to write to me, if it will suit him. You may, likewise, if you please, tell him how my affairs stand, as I have stated to you. It will be needless for me to give you any advice respecting the composition of your sermons, or the prosecution of your studies, as you, without doubt have access to so many books on the subject. I hope you will read 'Watts' Improvement of the Mind.' I think it must be charming to attend Walker's lectures on philosophy. Do you attend them? I should like it very much. Mr. H. told me, that he did give lectures at the academy: of course you are there when he does. You know now when to expect me in London, a little before Christmas, cannot say the exact day; so that now, if you like, you may count the time. Do not be long before you let me hear from you; and when you write, write a good deal. I remain, with the tenderest affection, your sincere and faithful friend,

THOMAS SPENCER."

Such, at this early age, were the letters of this amiable youth. For the introduction of so large a number it is unnecessary to apologize, since that heart is surely in an unenviable state which can derive no pleasure or profit from their perusal. Their simplicity is not their smallest ornament; whilst for the many useful hints which they suggest, as well as for the fervent and exalted piety which breathes throughout the whole, they may be consulted with considerable advantage by youthful candidates for the sacred office. Let such as early feel the desires he felt, and pant with an equal ardor for the work of God, imitate his modest diffidence—his devotional temper—his jealousy of the motives which influenced his choice—his intimate communion with his own heart—his love of retirement—his habitual reference of his affairs to the will of God—his addictedness to self-examination and to prayer—and above all, that deep and solemn consciousness of the important work in which he desired, with fear and trembling, to be engaged!

CHAPTER III.

Spencer's call and qualifications for the Ministry in his fifteenth year—Enters at Hoxton—Diligence in Study—Vacation—Return to Hertford—First Sermon in Public—Continues to preach to the country people during his stay at Hertford.

In resuming the thread of the narrative, which the introduction of these extracts from his correspondence has suspended, it cannot but be gratifying to the reader, to be presented with that deep impression of Mr. Spencer's call and qualifications for the Christian ministry which his familiar intercourse with him had produced on Mr. Hordle's mind.

In a recent letter to a friend, that gentleman observes :—

"I have had but one opinion concerning our late young friend, which is—that he was born a preacher, and as much called to it, as Jeremiah to the prophetic, or Paul to the apostolic office. All the powers of his soul were evidently formed for it. While he was under my roof, preachers and preaching were the constant topics of his discourse; and those studies which had an immediate reference to them were his delight. His remarkable gift in prayer, though then just turned of fifteen, astonished and pleased all that heard him. He usually took his turn in leading the devotions of our little family; and in his attendance on my ministry, I have sometimes seen the feelings of his heart in the tears that gushed from his eyes."

In perfect accordance with these sentiments are those expressed by the same gentleman, in a letter to a friend at Liverpool, dated Harwich, 13th Dec. 1811 :—

"Of his genuine piety, his fine imagination, his early attachment to theological pursuits, his love of study in general, his amiable disposition, and the powerful bias of his mind to the work of the Christian ministry, I have repeatedly declared my firm conviction; and had Divine Providence spared his valuable life, I have no doubt, as his judgment ripened, his character, excellent as it was, would still have improved."

Whilst such were the impressions, so truly honorable to his character, left upon his tutor's heart, by the sweetness of his temper, and the vigor of his mind—it is pleasing also to observe the grateful and lively remembrance which the pupil cherishes of the kindness of his early friend.

In a letter, addressed to the Rev. Mr. Hordle, from Hertford, he observes :—

"The day of my examination is now fixed for the 7th of January. To that day, dear Sir, I look forward with trembling: may God grant me all that strength and boldness I shall then need. It is impossible for me to describe my feelings the night I left you. I tried to suppress my outward expressions of them as well as I could. But O! 'tis trying to part with friends who are become *very dear* to us; but is it not, also, comforting to look forward to a never ending eternity, when those who are cemented into one glorious body by the bonds of divine love shall never part?" Afterwards he adds:—" For my part, I desire to be entirely his, (God's) but still I find a heart of unbelief, ever prone to depart from the living God. I hope I feel my own unfitness for the important undertaking, for which it appears God designs me. May he keep me holy and humble, and fit me for all he has in reserve for me in the womb of Providence, whether prosperous or adverse."

In a subsequent letter, dated Hoxton, 25th March, 1807, he says:

"I am told S——, of Kensington, is going to Harwich: hope you will find him a blessing to your family, and when he shall leave you, may he review with as much pleasure the year 1807, as I do the year 1806. I trust I shall be constantly enabled to obey the kind advice which you gave me, and to lay every human attainment at the foot of the cross of Jesus; to dedicate all I have to him, of whom I would always esteem it my highest honor to learn; to give up every thing that I may be called to sacrifice for the promoting of his glory, and constantly to seek not my own things, but the things which are Jesus Christ's."

In another, towards the close of the year 1807, he writes:—

"I shall never forget the year I spent at Harwich; viewing one circumstance with another, I doubt not, but that it was as happy a twelve month as I shall ever live."

With such mutual feelings and expressions of affectionate regard, was Mr. Spencer's departure from Mr. Hordle's family attended. And this review of them will not be in vain, if it suggests to the young persons who may contemplate this imperfect portrait of one, whom living they so much admired, the vast importance of that impression, which the conduct of their childhood or their youth may leave in the scenes of their earliest association. For the most part, the character of the *youth* is the character of the *man*. If, on the circle of his earliest intercourse, an unfavorable impression of his disposition or his conduct is produced, there it is likely to remain; but, alas! there it cannot be confined; it not unfrequently travels further than the person with whom it is connected, and the character is familiar where the countenance is unknown. Who that has a respect, then, for himself, but must be anxious that the impression, upon which so much depends, should be a happy one; and that the correcter habits of maturer age should not be counteracted in their favorable operation by the injurious fame, or unpleasant recollections of his early years.

But we must follow the amiable object of our contemplation to a new scene.

The following are copious extracts from the papers which he submitted to the inspection of the committee at Hoxton, on his formal application for admission into that institution; they were accompanied by a note to T. Wilson, Esq.

"HARWICH, *Nov.* 10, 1806.

HONORED SIR:—With diffidence I present the following account of my short experience, doctrinal sentiments, and motives for wishing to engage in the solemn and important work of the ministry, to your judgment and that of the committee. I am with the sincerest gratitude for your favors, your humble servant,

THOMAS SPENCER."

"Harwich, *Nov.* 10, 1806.

"It was my happiness to be born of parents, who maintained a regard for real piety and the fear of God; by them I was, from my infancy, taught to read the Scriptures, together with other books of a serious nature. I think I may safely say, that from my childhood I felt some more than common impressions on my mind, with respect to the existence and perfections of God, the evil and awful consequences of sin, and the advantages of being religious; but alas! these impressions, though so frequently felt, had not that abiding influence which they have had on the minds of others, but were like the '*morning cloud and the early dew which passeth away.*' As I grew rather older, I began to perceive some excellencies in religion, and to envy the happiness, which I believed serious people enjoyed. I knew something of the form of religion and the doctrines of it, from having been taught catechisms, and lessons calculated to give youthful minds some ideas of the worship and conduct which God requires. Yet notwithstanding this, I gave too much (far too much) attention to the reading of novels and romances, the unhappy effect of which I lament to the present day. Many of these books I procured of lads, without the knowledge of my father. I felt a degree of pleasure in hearing lively, animated sermons; but I have reason to believe that this sprung from a desire to please my friends, and give myself an opportunity of imitating the preacher's voice and gesture. I also composed little pieces of poetry on sacred subjects, which I have since destroyed, because I then knew nothing of experimental, vital godliness, and of course was only mocking God in them; but I did not give up making verses. All this while, I was totally ignorant of that divine principle of grace in the heart, without which, I am sensible, nothing we can do is acceptable to God. I knew nothing of the Holy Spirit's work, in convincing me of sin, and leading me to Jesus Christ as my Saviour. I knew nothing of communion with God and with his Son. I hope some of the sermons of Mr. Ebenezer White, of Hertford, were not altogether useless to me, as well as some which I heard at Lady Huntingdon's chapel there; but from my conduct at that time, in various particulars, I cannot say that I had experienced what was meant by being born again. If you ask me from what time I date my conversion to God, I must say, that the exact time I cannot tell; but I think I may also say, that the Lord drew me gradually to himself, and by degrees I loved devotional exercises more and more; and I hope that I have, within these four years, experienced many refreshing seasons. How I wish to have my evidences brightened, as it respects personal interest in the Lord Jesus Christ! I desire to cast my all upon him, and wait his will concerning me. However short my experience in the divine life has been, can I not appeal to God, and say, '*Lord, thou knowest all things, thou knowest that I love thee?*'

"I hope that my reasons for wishing to be a laborer in the Lord's vineyard are sincere, and that they do not spring from any improper motives. If I should be called into it, I pray that I may be kept faithful, and never shun to declare the whole counsel of God. As I know something of the excellency of the ways of wisdom, I am anxious that my fellow-mortals may be partakers of the same grace, and that they may be brought to know God, and experience the riches of divine love and mercy in Christ Jesus: and if God should so honor me, as to make me an instrument in his hand of doing them real good, how happy should I be; how willing to endure hardships for Jesus' sake. As I trust God has given me a desire to act for his glory, and I know that he is glorified in the salvation of sinners, I am willing, if He should call me to the work, to engage in it. I am aware, that it is an arduous and a difficult work, yet from these principles, I would fain be a faithful minister of Jesus Christ. I would follow the leadings of Divine Providence. By the good hand of my God upon me, I am brought hitherto; and although some circumstances are against me, yet, 'where he appoints, I'll go and dwell.' I am not quite sixteen years old, yet young as I am, I have committed many sins, and experienced many mercies. Now, unto Him that is able to keep me from falling, and to present me before the presence of his glory with exceeding joy, be glory and majesty, dominion and power, for ever and ever. Amen.

"I believe in one God as the object of religious worship, that this God is from everlasting; and that in our Jehovah there are three distinct persons, viz.: the Father, the Son, and the Holy Ghost, and yet these three are one; that this is a mystery which we cannot explain, yet we must believe, because it is declared in Holy Writ. That man was created holy, but fell from his original rectitude, and sunk himself and all his posterity into sin and wo. I believe also, that God from all eternity elected and chose his own people unto eternal salvation; that men are in a lost state and condition, and are spiritually dead; that they cannot be saved by any merit or works of their own, but only by the righteousness of Christ the Saviour; that it is by the operation of God the Holy Spirit on the mind of man, that he becomes a sensible sinner; that his understanding must be enlightened before he can choose God for his portion, or the paths of religion as those in which he will walk. It was for this end and purpose that Christ Jesus came into the world, viz.: to save sinners by his own blood; and I am persuaded that there is salvation in no other but in him, and that '*he is able to save to the uttermost all who come unto God by him.*' I believe that he is the eternal God, '*the same yesterday, and to-day, and forever;*' that his grace is all-sufficient, his name, person, and all that concerns him, is precious to them that believe; that those who exercise a living faith upon him, are justified from all their sins—at the same time I know, that believers are called to be holy, and that it is by the consistency of their walk, that they are to evidence to those around them that their profession is sincere, for '*without holiness no man shall see the Lord.*' As I am fully satisfied with respect to the divine origin of the Scriptures, and the inspiration of the holy men who wrote them, so I believe that they are the unerring standard by which to try our faith, and upon which we are to rest our opinions. I believe, that the people of God should form themselves into separate churches, that they may enjoy the benefit of divine ordinances, such as baptism and the Lord's Supper, together with the hearing of the word, &c. I believe, that, notwithstanding all the Christian's enemies and dangers, he shall hold on his way, and grow stronger and stronger; and, though the doctrine of final perseverance has been much abused, as well as its truth much questioned, it is an article of my faith, because God's truth declares it. I believe in the approach of a judgment day—the eternal glory of believers, and the insufferable torments of the wicked in hell. I believe that God will have the whole glory of the salvation of those who are saved for ever and ever; and that through all eternity they will ascribe dominion, power, and glory to Him who loved them and washed them in his own blood—at the same time sinners will everlastingly blame *themselves* for their perdition and wo."

On the 7th of January he appeared at Hoxton, before the committee, and underwent the examination which he had so long and so anxiously anticipated—with success and honor: was admitted a student, and became immediately an inmate of the house. In a letter to his friend Mr. Hordle, dated Hoxton, January 21st, 1807, he says:—

"Two things make this day remarkable to me: one is, that it is my birth-day, as I am now sixteen years old; the other is, that I have been a fortnight in this house. On Wednesday, the 7th inst., that long dreaded day, I appeared before the committee. Your imagination may represent a little boy speaking before them. I felt a good deal of timidity, and waited the event with feelings of anxiety." "I hope I can say

I feel the importance of that work for which it appears God in his providence has designed me: but oh! I need larger degrees of grace to fill that station in such a manner, as that my own soul, and the souls of my fellow creatures may be benefited thereby."—"I recall to my mind occurrences which transpired when I was at Harwich. O may I have all God's dealings sanctified unto me. I want a deeper acquaintance with my own heart, and a more influential knowledge of God my Saviour."

That, on his entrance into the academy at Hoxton, Mr. Spencer was no novice in the knowledge and experience of divine things, is obvious from a perusal of the papers above cited. With a mind already the subject of considerable culture, and habits formed for the pursuits of science, he commenced his academical course under circumstances the most auspicious. The importance of such a previous preparation in candidates for the Christian ministry, and the patronage of our dissenting colleges, is not, perhaps, sufficiently considered. It is to be regretted, that so many enter without having previously obtained the lowest rudiments of general science, or even a tolerable acquaintance with their native tongue. The time allotted for a student's residence is, in the most liberal institutions, but short, compared with the immense labor and magnitude of the object to be obtained. But much of this time, short as it is, must be expended in the inculcation of those first principles of knowledge, which might be easily obtained elsewhere; and then when the student is somewhat prepared for studies more suitable to the dignity of a college, he begins to preach. Thus an attention which ought to be undividedly devoted to the labors of the study, and the exercises of the class, is partly lavished on preparations for the pulpit and public services. Hence arose the plan, so judiciously adopted in certain cases, in connection with the college of which Mr. Spencer was a member, and of the beneficial tendency of which he was so striking an example, of sending the candidates who may be defective in these radical points, or too young for admission, to some pious and able minister for preparatory instruction.

In the mean time, to remedy, as far as may be, by his own exertions, this serious defect, should be an object of conscientious regard to every young man whose views are directed to the Christian ministry. By a diligent improvement of his time—by a careful employment of those smaller portions of it, which in too many cases are suffered imperceptibly to slide away—aided by the friendly direction and advice of some prudent and well-informed minister, which may without much difficulty be in every case obtained—any one of tolerable capacity and perseverance might afford his own mind a considerable degree of cultivation, and attain a portion of knowledge, ere his entrance into an academy, most favorable to the facility and success of his pursuits whilst there.

These remarks more particularly apply to those young men, who, with views directed towards the ministry, are still engaged in secular employments, and to whom the privileges of an academy must be, in the first instance, regarded as a distant object.

Little of importance can be expected to have transpired, in connection with the early part of Mr. Spencer's residence at Hoxton. It appears, however, that here, as in the Poultry and at Harwich, his interesting appearance and amiable manners soon gained him the love and esteem of all. The tutors and the students alike felt an interest in this new and youthful member of their literary society —and he applied himself with diligence to the improvement of those advantages which he there enjoyed. He was now introduced to a wider range of observation and of study. But whilst a respect to the orders of the institution, and a desire to render himself, by useful acquirements, respectable in any circle in which it might be his future lot to move, induced him to apply with becoming diligence to the various occupations assigned him, he yet dwelt with peculiar attachment on such as were more immediately connected with the work of preaching. And with an ardent desire to be early and extensively employed in the ministry of the gospel, a desire strengthened and confirmed by time, it can be no matter of surprise, that to this darling object were directed all the hours of his leisure, and all the ardor of his soul.

At the vacation in June he returned to his father's house at Hertford. During his stay there he preached his first sermon in public. It was at the small village of *Collier's End,* six miles from Hertford. His auditory consisted of about thirty plain country people—and his text was 1 John i : 7. "*The blood of Jesus Christ, his Son, cleanseth us from all sin.*" Simple and unlettered, however, as his audience might be, they had sufficient penetration to discover the uncommon talents of their youthful preacher ; which, together with the novelty and loveliness of his juvenile appearance, excited in that little village an astonishment and admiration, which have since circulated through all the districts of the great metropolis, and almost every town in Great Britain. How beautiful is the progression which marks all the dispensations of nature, providence and grace. From the smallest springs the mightiest rivers rise, to promote the fruitfulness or waft the commerce of the world. From the grain of mustard seed, the kingdom of heaven gradually rises and expands, till it becomes a great tree, beneath whose shade all the nations of the earth repose ; and in the history of individuals—from the day of small things, has not unfrequently arisen a career, whose brilliancy has dazzled and surprised the world ; and from the remarkable concurrence of circumstances, events the most important to the interest of the individual, and the happiness of mankind, have sprung. It is for the most part denied to men, who move in a public and extended circle, to witness those early displays of genius, and that gradual development of talents, afterwards so eminent for their usefulness or splendor, upon which the eye of a philosopher would love to dwell. This is usually the privilege of a few obscure individuals in some retired spot. The new fledged bird first tries its pinions in its own sequestered bower ere it soars above its native glen, and courts the admiration of man by the boldness of its flight, or the sweetness of its song. And yet there is such a peculiar interest connected with the early efforts of a mighty mind, and the first stages of an eminent career, that we gather with diligence all that can be gleaned respecting them, and listen with delight to the narration of those who were spectators. But few perhaps who have heard of Spencer, but would gladly be transported to the peaceful village of *Collier's End,* and mingle with the auditors under his first sermon there. And it requires no uncommon acquaintance with the principles of our nature, and the doctrine of association in the human mind, to predict that the villages of *Halfway, Street,* and *Lewisham,* in Kent, will derive some celebrity in the religious world from having been the scenes of ministerial labor, when a youth, to a preacher, who for these twelve years past has held the delighted auditories of the metropolis the willing captives of his eloquence.* And surely such a principle as this, whilst in its gratification it yields an indescribable pleasure, may be cultivated to no small advantage. It banishes from the mind that despair of reaching it, which a contemplation of exalted eminence might inspire, by an assurance, that the object at which he aims is not unattainable, since its present possessor once occupied the same level with himself, and was attended by circumstances as unfavorable to his elevation as those which at present may encompass him.

Our amiable young preacher's first sermon excited a strong desire in his hearers for a repetition of his labors ; and his fame rapidly circulating produced an invitation also, from another quarter, for the following Sabbath. To these solicitations, we may suppose without much reluctance, he complied; and he preached again on the morning of July 12th, at a village called *Broughin.* His text on this occasion was Col. iii. 3, " *Ye are dead, and your life is hid with Christ in God.*" In the afternoon and evening of the same day, he preached again at *Collier's End.* In the afternoon from Acts xix. 2, " *Have ye received the Holy Ghost ?*" In the evening from Phil. iii. 18, " *They are the enemies of the cross of Christ.*" The attendance at *Collier's End*, was, on this second Sabbath, so much increased, that the room would scarcely contain the people

* Doctor Collyer.

who were desirous of hearing, and every one seemed still more deeply affected by the impressive manner, the solemn doctrines, and the surprising powers of this young divine. On the following Thursday he preached again at a place called *Brickenden*, from John iv. 29, "*Come see a man, which told me all things that I ever did; is not this the Christ?*" On Sunday, July 19th, he again resumed his labors at *Collier's End*, and preached in the afternoon from 2 Chron. xxxiii. 12, 13, "*And when he was in affliction, he besought the Lord, his God, and humbled himself greatly before the God of his fathers, and prayed unto him, and he was entreated of him, and heard his supplication, and brought him again to Jerusalem, and to his kingdom. Then Manasseh knew that the Lord he was God.*" In the evening the multitude that assembled was so great, that to gratify them all, he was under the necessity of preaching out of doors, which he did with great animation and effect, from Romans xiv. 12, "*So then every one of us shall give account of himself to God.*" It appears from the report of one who was present at the delivery of this sermon, that it was remarkably impressive. Although surrounded by so great a crowd, he seemed quite undaunted, and expressed himself with an ease and an energy which produced the most serious impressions upon many, and excited the astonishment of all. To see the old and grey-headed melted into tears beneath the simple touches and fervent appeals of a youth, but little more than sixteen years of age, proclaiming with the boldness and propriety of an experienced veteran the glorious gospel of the blessed God, must have been truly interesting. And it is also gratifying to know, that by the earliest labors of this excellent youth, happy and saving effects were produced, which remain to this day. On the evening of Thursday, July 23d, he preached at *Buntingford,* a town about ten miles from Hertford, from John x. 9, "*By me if any man enter in, he shall be saved, and shall go in and out, and find pasture.*" On Sunday, July 26th, he preached again, afternoon and evening, at *Collier's End.* In the afternoon from John vi. 44, "*No man can come to me except the Father which sent me draw him: and I will raise him up at the last day.*" In the evening from 2d Tim. ii. 19, "*Nevertheless the foundation of God standeth sure, having this seal, the Lord knoweth them that are his, and let every one that nameth the name of Christ depart from iniquity.*" On the Wednesday eʌening following he preached at *Hormead,* from Psalm iv. 6, "*There be many that say, who will show us ang good? Lord, lift thou up the light of thy countenance upon us.*" And on the Thursday evening again at *Brickenden.* At *Hormead* his congregation amounted to six or seven hundred persons, and the place where they were assembled was a barn. Indeed by this time his fame had so widely circulated, that where-ever he preached, numbers flocked from all parts to hear and see this wonderful youth ; and he might have preached every day in the week, had he been so inclined, so numerous were the invitations that crowded upon him. However, his vacation drew towards a close ; and his return to Hoxton suspended for a while these public exercises. He preached on the evening of Sunday, Aug. 2d, at *Roydon:* and we hear no more of his preaching till December. It certainly admits of doubt, whether these early exercises in public preaching are beneficial or injurious. That they are injurious, may be argued from the circumstance, that they tend to elate and dissipate the mind—to inspire it with conceited notions of its own superior powers—too soon, alas ! to familiarize the ear to the insinuating sounds of flattery, and, investing the youth with high conceptions of his present qualifications, to annihilate those humiliating views of his own ignorance and imperfection—and that ardent panting after knowledge in which lies the great source of respectability and usefulness in after life. Not to notice those practical errors into which the ignorance and incaution natural to youth may lead him, when engaged in directing men in affairs of infinite and eternal moment. If the aged evangelist—the venerable pastor, is heard so frequently to deplore his imperfection and lament the *possibility* of error in his public instructions—a young man may well proceed in his early labors with caution, and had need to be possessed of no common discretion and knowledge, to counteract the suspicions necessarily excited, in the breasts of the thoughtful, by his youth.

But, perhaps, on the other hand, there are peculiar advantages connected with an early entrance on the work of preaching. The novelty of the circumstance excites attention, and many are converted, who, but for the juvenility of the preacher, had never heard the gospel from his lips, and this is doubtless amongst the many *means* which an Infinite Wisdom has selected, for accomplishing, in the conversion of sinners, the purposes of an infinite love. Besides that on the preacher's own mind, his early employment in ministerial labor may have a most happy influence. By an early initiation into the difficulties and trials of the work, he may attain an ease and a skill in its execution, which is perhaps but seldom reached by the man who has commenced much later in the day. In youth the mind is all activity, and difficulties which are met with then are far more easily surmounted than when they are presented to the opposition of maturer age. But after all, much depends upon the peculiar circumstances of the individual case. Many a man is better prepared for the work of the ministry at sixteen than others are at forty ; and whilst the popularity and flattery which usually attend the course of youthful preachers would be the ruin of some, there are others indued with a prudence and a piety sufficient to resist their influence. And be it remembered, that the time allotted to every man for labor is at best but *short*, and that for many of our ministers—alas! that these should be, for the most part, the most eminent and useful!—is prepared an early grave! To be squandering away the precious time which ought to be devoted to the salvation of immortal souls, in the acquisition of profound and extensive erudition; to be immured for years in the walls of a study, and confined to the precincts of a college, impairing the physical strength by midnight application, and smothering the flames of holy zeal amid the ices of metaphysics and the lumber of heathenish philosophy, whilst thousands of immortal souls are perishing, to whose eternal interest those years might be successfully devoted—is certainly a conduct highly culpable, and not in the spirit of Him who said—"*work whilst it is day, for the night cometh, when no man can work!*" Far be it from the writer of this volume in any way to undervalue or decry that knowledge, which, in a minister of the gospel, the circumstances of the present times render so essential. These remarks only apply to those cases in which years are expended in adding to a stock already more than sufficient for present purposes, without beginning to apply to any practical use that which is so largely possessed; and may affect such institutions as, having for their object the preparation of young men for the work of the ministry, suffer the zeal for God, and the love of souls, which led them to its patronage, at least to lose a little of its fire by years of dry scholastic disquisition, ere they are suffered to go forth into the world and expend them on their proper object—the conversion of their dying fellow men.

With respect to Mr. Spencer, the world will judge whether he began to preach too soon or not. I believe that Liverpool, by far the most competent to judge in this case, will, without hesitation, decide in the negative. Perhaps there are, who may be disposed to say, "this was an exception." Granted; but in such exceptions, let a similar liberty be allowed. Where extraordinary gifts, attended by extraordinary grace, so early develop themselves, allow them a proportionably early exercise, nor rob the church of God of an useful minister, who, ere the period a cautious policy has fixed for the commencement of his labor is arrived—may be summoned to his rest.

CHAPTER IV.

His return to Hoxton—Christmas Vacation—First Sermon at Hertford—Appointed to assist in the pulpit at Hoxton—At the earnest entreaties of the people, allowed to preach—First Sermon at Hoxton in his seventeenth year—His success and popularity—Itineracy—Correspondence with Mr. John Haddon—Visits Brighton—Preaches with great Acceptance and Effect—Again at Hoxton—Preaches a Sermon on Fast-day—Appointed to deliver an Oration at the Academy.

On his return to Hoxton we find Mr. Spencer preaching occasionally in the work-houses, an admirable school for young divines. Surely this is no inconsiderable circumstance in which our dissenting colleges are superior as schools of practical divinity, to those of the establishment. There the student emerges at once from the retirement of private life, to all the publicity of the sacred office; which sudden transition, to a delicate mind, must often be attended with considerable pain, and may lead, in the first few instances, to a confusion and embarrassment most distressing to himself, and most unfriendly to his prospects of future respectability and usefulness. On the other hand, with us, the student *gradually*, almost *imperceptibly*, glides into the ministry, and by continued, but slow enlargement, of the sphere in which he is allowed to move, he rises from a few poor people in a work-house, to address the most respectable auditories.

On his return to his father's house, for the Christmas vacation, Mr. Spencer preached for the first time at Hertford. It did not happen to him, as is often the case, that he had no honor in his own country. Numbers pressed, urged no doubt, in the first instance, by curiosity to hear him ; and those who are accustomed to mark the influence of similar circumstances upon a susceptible mind, will enter a little into his emotions, when rising to address, upon the most solemn of all subjects, a vast multitude of his fellow-townsmen, amongst whom he recognised many of his juvenile companions—the several members of his own family—and, not the least interesting object in the group, the venerable matron who had early instructed him in the principles of his mother tongue, and whose lot it was to observe the first faint dawnings of a talent, then fast hastening to its fullest exercise and strength. But long after the influence of novelty may be supposed to have subsided, he continued to excite the admiration of his native town. His first sermon at Hertford was preached on the evening of Sunday, December 20th, at the Rev. Mr. Maslin's chapel, from Eph. v. 11, "*And have no fellowship with the unfruitful works of darkness.*" He preached again on the Wednesday evening following, and on the evening of Christmas day, on which occasion his text was, Mich. v. 2, "*But thou, Bethlehem Ephratah, though thou be little among the thousands of Judah, yet out of thee shall he come forth unto me that is to be Ruler in Israel, whose goings forth have been of old, from everlasting.*"

The passages of Scripture selected by Mr. Spencer, as the subjects of his earliest discourses, afford another demonstration, in addition to many others, of the general bias of his mind. They are such as one may well imagine a preacher panting for the salvation of his fellow men, would select for the commencement of his public labors. The topics which they suggest are of all others, the most solemn, as they are the most simple and the most important in the whole range of inspired truth, and hence they were best adapted to the preacher's age, and the unlettered character of his auditors. It seems, that in his earliest sermons there was nothing of that parade and glare—nothing of that excessive fondness of figures and love of imagery, which too often mark the first compositions of youthful preachers—preachers who, in a more advanced stage of their ministry, have not been less respectable or useful than he.

Whether this is to be considered as an excellence or defect, it is probable, with some, may be a matter of debate. Dr. Blair, (or rather Quintilian, from whom he copies,) in his remarks on the early compositions of public speakers, urges in favor of that exuberance of imagination and excess of ornament —that time and experience will prune all this away, and in proportion as the fire of youth declines, the glare of the composition will sink into the settled lustre of maturer age. And hence he argues, for an excessive indulgence of the imagination at this period ; since by the time the powers are called into full and steady exercise, they will have undergone a certain train of discipline, and have found their proper limits ; but if the composition has all the judicious sobriety of that maturer age, amid the vigor and vivacity of youth, what is it likely to be in the more advanced stages of its exercise, but cold, insipid, and dull !

But surely all depends upon the nature of the subject, and the source whence the public orator is to draw the energy which must give animation to his discourses. The fire of genius, the glow of imagination, must be the enkindling torches in the senate—at the bar ; but though not altogether useless in the pulpit, yet they are not the lawful sources of animation there. It is not the blaze of genius, or the glow of imagination ; but the sacred flame of fervent piety—the holy kindlings of a mind moved by principles derived from heaven, and the generous efforts of a soul impelled by an intense desire for the salvation of a dying world, that must impart life and energy to the correct, but glowing statements, the warm and impassioned appeals of the ambassador for Christ. Other sources of animation may be exhausted by exercise, and dried up by time ; but this can never fail. It will remain the same when the head of the venerable prophet is covered with hoary hairs, and the body is sunk in the decrepitude of age. Nay, as in the case of the apostle Paul, it will rise into brighter radiance as he advances to the termination of his course—a more ardent panting for the salvation of mankind will mark his dying hours, than that which attended his entrance on his labors ; and with David, the last prayer his spirit breathes will be for the universal diffusion of that gospel, which it has been the business and the honor of his life to preach—"*Blessed be the Lord God, the God of Israel, who only doth wondrous things. And blessed be his glorious name for ever; and let the whole earth be filled with his glory. Amen and Amen.*"

We now arrive at a period in Mr. Spencer's history, peculiarly critical and important. During the vacation of Christmas, 1807, the Rev. Mr. Liefchild, of Kensington, was supplying the pulpit at Hoxton chapel. One Sabbath afternoon, in January, Mr. Spencer being then returned to the academy from

Hertford, Mr. L. expressed a wish that he should assist him, in the public service, by reading the Scriptures and engaging in prayer. The request was granted, and an extract of a letter obligingly addressed by that gentleman to me, will convey a lively picture of the deep impression which his appearance and manner produced upon the large congregation before whom he stood.

"—— But when he appeared in the pulpit—after the first emotions of surprise were over, and after the mistakes of some, who supposed that he was a little boy belonging to the gallery, who, from ignorance or thoughtlessness, had gone up the pulpit stairs, instead of those leading to his seat, had been corrected, so sweetly did he read the chapter,* so earnestly, so scripturally, so experimentally, did he engage in prayer, that for the whole six Sabbaths afterwards he became the chief magnet of attraction to the place. The people now insisted upon it he should preach. I need not name his subsequent success."

The entreaties of the people having prevailed, Mr. Spencer, though contrary to the standing order of the institution, was allowed to preach. It was a delicate situation. Yet it was one to which he had long and anxiously aspired. Indeed, so strong was his desire for the public engagements of the ministry, that the fear of being long denied the gratifica-

* On the evening of the following Sunday, Mr. L. addressed young people; when Mr Spencer again conducted the devotional part of the service. The chapter which he then read was Ecclesiastes xii. A person since received into the church at Hoxton, dated her first serious impressions from the reading of that chapter, and the solemn prayer then offered up.

tion of his wishes, on account of his youth, actually preyed upon his spirits so severely as even to affect his health. But it was not from the love of fame or popular applause that he cherished this desire, but from the hope of being early and extensively useful;—as if urged by a presentiment of his impending fate—immediately to commence those honorable labors from which he was to be called so soon. When he appeared in the pulpit at Hoxton, a youth just seventeen years of age, he betrayed none of that distressing anxiety which marks the candidate for public approbation; but stood with all the dignified composure, and spoke with all the unembarrassed energy of an ambassador for Christ. His text was, Psalm xxxii. 6, "*For this shall every one that is godly pray unto thee in a time when thou mayest be found; surely in the floods of great waters they shall not come nigh unto thee!*" At the close of his discourse, the sentiments which dwelt upon the lips and countenances of his auditors were those of pleasure, admiration, and surprise. His excessive youth—the simplicity of his appearance—the modest dignity of his manner—the sweetness of his voice—the weight and importance of his doctrine—and the force—the affection—and the fervor with which he directed it, to the hearts and consciences of those who heard him—charmed and delighted, whilst they edified. And retiring from the sanctuary to the social circle, they dwelt alternately on the loveliness of the preacher, and the importance of the truths which they had heard from his lips.

Upon this scene the Christian student may, with advantage, pause and meditate. Looking forward, perhaps with considerable apprehension, to the period of his public entrance on the labors of the ministry, he may be anxious to ascertain what was the secret spring—the hidden source, of that calm composure and unfettered boldness, which characterised the earliest addresses of this interesting youth. To such then I can confidently say—it was not the proud consciousness of superior powers—of erudition—of genius, or of eloquence ; but it was the influence of a heart warmed with the love of Christ, big with the vast moment of his solemn theme, and panting with an ardor which no circumstances of difficulty could suppress, for the salvation of sinners. Such an influence as this will make the coward bold, and convert the most timid and feeble into valiant and successful champions of the cross. Before an influence like this, the love of fame—the glare of popularity, the opinions and the plaudits of mankind retire. No consideration remains but that of the worth of immortal souls, and the importance of their salvation. This, under the agency of the eternal Spirit, whose assistance every faithful minister may with confidence expect, will supply a closeness of appeal to arrest the attention—furnish topics of discourse to inform the judgment, and animated expostulations to warm the heart. When the blaze of genius and of oratory is extinguished, this will continue with a steady flame. And whilst many, his acknowledged superiors in talent and in literature, are left behind, the preacher in whose breast it glows will be conducted to scenes of extensive usefulness, and the enjoyment of an honorable renown.

Mr. Spencer now became the topic of general discourse—the subject of universal inquiry. His name spread far and wide. His danger became daily more and more imminent. Letters pressed upon him, filled with flattery—invitations arrived at the academy from all parts, for his services ; and he appeared, as a friend, who witnessed his sudden and extraordinary elevation, observed, like one standing on the brow of a precipice, amid the most violent gusts of wind. Disapprobation cannot be expressed in terms too strong of the conduct which is usually adopted by the religious public towards their favorite, and especially their youthful preachers. And the censure which may, in a lamentable degree, admit of universal application, falls with preëminent propriety on the professors of religion in the metropolis and its neighborhood. There, indeed, by the constant accession of fresh objects, to the sphere in which they move, such a love of novelty—such a fondness of variety—such a taste for something perpetually original—is excited and constantly fed—that whatever is uniform and solid, in the ministry of their established and experienced pastors, while it secures the attention and regard of the judicious and discerning, is too often neglected as stale and insipid by the more *lively* and *enlightened* class of hearers. A new name is announced on the cover of a magazine, or from the pulpit of some celebrated chapel, and thither the unstable multitude direct their steps. They sit in solemn judgment on the preacher's manner—his appearance—his action, and his voice; for amongst too many, alas! it is to be lamented, that the solemn truths which he delivers are but secondary objects of regard. If there should be nothing striking in his manner—nothing melodious in his voice—nothing singular in his appearance—nothing peculiar in his system—and nothing particularly favorable in the circumstances of his introduction to the pulpits of the metropolis, there he may continue his appointed period, and when it has expired, return to the peaceful village or the quiet town, where it is his lot to labor—

"The world forgetting—by the world forgot."

On the other hand, with this class of hearers the preacher who secures their admiration instantly becomes their idol. As if irresistibly impelled to extremes, they lavish on him the warmest eulogies and adulation, often too palpable to be endured. Forgetting that he is a man of like passions with themselves, they heap their honors on his head as though he could remain insensible to the plaudits they bestow, and perfectly superior to the influence of every principle of pride. The following lines of the inimitable Cowper too well express the sentiments which in these remarks must suggest themselves to every thinking mind, not to obtain insertion here:

"O Popular Applause! what heart of man
Is proof against thy sweet seducing charms?
The wisest and the best feel urgent need
Of all their caution in thy gentlest gales;
But swell'd into a gust—who then, alas!
With all his canvass spread and inexpert,
And therefore heedless, can withstand thy power?
Praise from the rivell'd lips of worthless bald
Decrepitude, and in the looks of lean
And craving Poverty, and in the bow
Respectful of the smutch'd artificer,
Is oft too welcome, and may much disturb
The bias of the purpose. How much more
Pour'd forth by beauty splendid and polite,
In language soft as Adoration breathes?
Ah, spare your idol! think him human still.
Charms he may have, but he has frailties too.
Dote not too much, nor spoil what ye admire."

But the preaching of Mr. Spencer, even in his earliest discourses, was not of that light and meretricious kind which may secure the temporary* ad-

* I believe that general experience will justify the observation, that however attendant circumstances may contribute, in the first instance, to render an individual popular, nothing but sterling

miration of the wandering and unsettled. It possessed much of the solid—the experimental, and judicious; and this secured him the attention and esteem of those, whose approbation any man would esteem it an honor to possess. But this only tended to heighten his danger. God, however, gave him grace equal to his day. His letters during his popularity in London breathe the same spirit of humility as that which marked his earlier correspondence; and a piety seldom surpassed in fervor and sincerity tended to preserve him steady in the midst of that tempestuous sea, upon whose billows, though young and inexperienced, it was his lot to ride.

Numerous and pressing however as were the invitations from different parts of the metropolis and its neighborhood, yet Mr. Spencer did not preach again in London (except in the work-houses, which the students regularly supplied, and also once in a small chapel in Hackney Road) until September.

worth can secure its perpetuity; and whenever the preaching of a popular minister has endured, without injury to his reputation, the ordeal of a ten or twenty years trial, he may safely be regarded as possessing an excellence superior to any thing his *manner* could exhibit. But I feel the delicacy of the topic I have thus ventured to introduce, and gladly refer to illustrations of the same subject by more experienced and far abler hands.—*See Fuller's Life of Pearce; and Jay's Life of Cornelius Winter.* Books in which examples, the one of more public, the other of more retired, but not less transcendant excellence, seem to live before us for our instruction. To every student for the Christian ministry they must prove an invaluable treasure.

In the meanwhile his talent for preaching had ample exercise in various parts of the country, which during this period he was allowed to visit. So that, from January 7th to September 8th he preached no less than sixty times. The following are the principal places which were then favored with his labors: —*Royden*, *Godmanchester*, *Ripton*, *Buntingford*, *Hertford*, *Dorking*, *Rumford*, *Harlow*, *Royston*, *Hadham*, *Hays*, *Chigwell*, and *Mill-Hill*. At all these places the attention he excited was considerable, and the impression he left remains with the people to this day.

Mr. Spencer's second sermon at Hoxton chapel was delivered on the evening of Thursday, September 8th. It confirmed the opinion of his excellence produced by the first. His text was, Acts x. 6, "*He is Lord of all.*"

The general sentiment of approbation and delight at first excited by his youthful appearance, and his extraordinary pulpit talents, was now deepened and established, and he began to preach pretty extensively in the pulpits of the metropolis and its neighborhood. On Sunday, September 18th, we find him in the pulpit in Holywell Mount chapel, and on the Sunday following, in that of Kennington chapel; and on the afternoon of Sunday, December 13, he supplied the chapel in Old Gravel Lane, Wapping. During the autumn of this year he also visited several parts of the country immediately surrounding

London ; and he preached, among other places, at *Upminster*, *Upsom*, *Guilford*, *Roydon*, and *High Wycombe.*

With respect to the wisdom and propriety of permitting such extensive public labors, in one so young, and at so early a stage of his academical course, there will be perhaps a diversity of opinion. On the *general* question, in which this is but an individual case, there can be but one sentiment. Nothing tends more to dissipate the mind, than much traveling and much society ; and particularly injurious to the fixed and laborious habits of a student's life is that kind of intercourse with society, which the young minister, in his occasional visits, usually obtains. The esteem in which, for the most part, the name of a minister is held, in the circles which he enters, secures him an attention and an ease by far too flattering not to be injurious ; whilst the refined and fascinating manners of some societies but illy prepare the mind for the imperatively severe characters of academic life. But perhaps a far more serious object of regard is the time which is thus necessarily and irretrievably lost to the great and avowed object of his pursuit. It is impossible to take a review of the past year of Mr. Spencer's life, and number up the several places at which he has preached—at some of them two or three times, whilst others he visited more than once, calculating their respective distances from Hoxton, and the time necessarily occupied in traveling, together with the many hours, perhaps days, which must have been consumed in preparing the discourses there delivered—without being struck with a conviction, of the immense loss which in a literary point of view he must have sustained ; and the pursuit of literature is, after all, the professed object of our dissenting colleges. Considering too, that this was but Mr. Spencer's second year of study, and connecting this with the shortness of the term he had to stay, and his exceeding youth, the impression is yet deepened. But Mr. Spencer's was an extraordinary case. His *forte* was the composition and delivery of sermons. He was at home and happy only in this sacred work. He seemed but to live for this object. Other objects he might contemplate, with respect and even esteem, excited by an impression of their utility and excellence—on this his heart perpetually dwelt with a fervent and impassioned love. It was evidently for this God had especially designed him; and for the work he had to accomplish, and the early account he had to render—all perhaps are now convinced that *he* was not suffered to begin too soon. For one whose day of usefulness has proved so short, and over whom the night of death so early and so suddenly has shed its gloom, we can not but rejoice that the first dawn was devoted to his honorable labor, and not even a solitary hour neglected, from the commencement to the termination of his career.

Mr. Spencer preached again at Hoxton chapel on Christmas day, morning and evening; and also delivered an address, on the following evening, at the prayer meeting. A day or two after he left London for *Brighton*, and preached his first sermon in that celebrated seat of gaiety and fashion on the evening of Thursday, December 29th, at the Countess of Huntingdon's chapel, from Zach. vi. 12, "*Behold the man whose name is the branch, and he shall build the temple of the Lord.*" On Sunday, 1st January, 1809, he preached in the afternoon at the Rev. Mr. Stiles' chapel, and again in the evening at the Countess'.

I am the more particular in marking the date of his first visit to Brighton, as it commences a new year, and forms also a most important epoch in his history. The interesting and endeared connections which he afterwards formed there, tend to throw a new and brilliant light upon his character; whilst they shed a softer air of melancholy around the circumstances of his early and lamented fate!*

Alas! of what moment to the Christian minister is the formation of connections such as these. Delicate as the subject may be, and illy qualified as I feel

* Those who knew Spencer, will enter fully into the meaning of this paragraph. I owe it, however, to those who knew him not, to say, that tenderness to feelings I should dread to wound, compels me to draw a veil over one of the most interesting scenes of his life.

I am to enter fully into its discussion, I yet cannot suffer it to pass without some observations on its vast importance.—By imprudence here, how many have destroyed, if not their *character*, yet to an alarming extent their *usefulness* and *comfort.* Upon the partner which a minister selects, much of his happiness depends. He must be indeed a child of sorrow, who with a heart broken by disappointment, and a brow clouded by care—such cares and disappointments as too frequently impart a character of gloom to many a pious pastor's life—finds no relief in his domestic circle, and seeks in vain for the soothing influence of sympathy in the individual whom he has chosen to be a "*help meet for him.*"

The important subject thus reluctantly though unavoidably introduced, distributes itself into many branches, each interesting in its kind, on each of which, age and experience might with considerable propriety descant; and however unwilling I might be to enter more largely into the discussion, yet did I think myself sufficiently possessed of either, I would certainly reprobate in the severest terms that rash and thoughtless haste which too often marks the decision of students and youthful ministers in this respect, and which too frequently leads to settled distress—final ruin—or shameful infidelity! To the honor of Spencer be it recorded, that his choice in the first instance displayed his *wisdom:* his uniform attachment until death, his *constancy!*

Mr. Spencer preached again at the Countess of Huntingdon's chapel, at Brighton, on Thursday evening, January 5th, and left that place on the following day. On the ensuing Sunday he preached at Holloway, morning and afternoon; and on the evening of Tuesday the 10th, addressed an immense congregation from the pulpit of that truly excellent man, the Rev. Rowland Hill, at Surry chapel. The subject of his discourse was Deut. xxxiii. 3, "*Yea, he loved the people; all his saints are in thy hand, and they sat down at thy feet, every one shall receive of thy words.*"

Between this date and the following midsummer, his labors appear to have been, in point both of number and success, truly astonishing. He now preached much in and about London, and wherever his name was announced, the crowd that flocked to his ministry, proved how extensive and deep the impression was which it had excited. Besides occupying many of the most respectable pulpits in the metropolis, during this period, he visited and preached in the following places: Guilford, Epsom, Worthing, Barking, Roydon, Dorking, Buntingford, Winchmore-Hill, Saffron, Walden, and Hertford.

During his stay at Worthing, which was in the month of February, he made several excursions to Brighton, which became more endeared to him by every visit. The attachment was mutual. His ministry excited universal attention ; multitudes pressed to hear him. The public prints declared their admiration of his powers; and the private circle forgot the trifling topics of the day, intent upon the discussion of his rare and extraordinary talents. More especially did he bind to him, in affectionate remembrance, the hearts of the young, by the warmth, simplicity, and affection of his addresses to them : and in no place which was honored by his labors, was his worth more fully appreciated in life, or his loss more deeply and universally lamented in death.

On the evening of Thursday, the 18th of May, he preached again at Hoxton chapel. His text on that occasion was Isaiah lxi. 10, "*I will greatly rejoice in the Lord, my soul shall be joyful in my God; for he hath clothed me with the garments of salvation, he hath covered me with the robe of righteousness.*"

But by so much preaching and fatigue, his strength became exhausted, and his health impaired ; and during the midsummer vacation, the committee superintending the stations of the preaching students appointed him to spend some weeks at Dorking, in Surrey, where the labor was but small, the retirement deep, the country beautiful, and the air salubrious. To this place he went in the beginning of July—having first paid a visit to his family at Hertford, and preached again in his native town. At Dorking he was committed to the care of Mrs. Alexander, a kind and pious matron, whose hospitable attention to all the servants of Christ who have had the happiness to repose beneath her roof, renders her worthy of the appropriate epithet of " Mother in Israel." The praises of such pious women are, and ought to be, in all the churches. Happy is that congregation which possesses one or two such valuable and useful characters. To the youthful preachers who may be commissioned from their respective academies to labor for a while in the congregations to which they belong, they often prove an inestimable blessing. By their timely assiduities, not unfrequently, diseases the most serious and alarming may be averted, by which valuable ministers might have been early snatched from the church and from the world ; and, at any rate, those little offices of unaffected kindness, in the performance of which they so much excel, will tend to soothe the anxieties by which, in early life, many a delicate frame is prematurely wasted and impaired.

For Spencer, too, the spot was admirably chosen. Nothing could better suit his fondness for retirement, and love of social or solitary walks. I am not a stranger to the scenery—I once visited it, like him, for relaxation ; and the remembrance of those happy days, in a thousand pleasing pictures and enchanting forms, crowds at this moment on my mind. The country is sufficiently bold and varied to inspire with ideas of grandeur and magnificence, though not so romantic and vast, as to excite astonishment and terror. From the summit of abrupt and lofty hills, clothed with luxuriant foliage, the delighted eye may roam at leisure over woods and valleys, that will not yield in fruitfulness and beauty to the fairest plains of Italy; and in deep embowered glens, made cool and fragrant by meandering streams, the mind may yield to melancholy musings, and to solemn thought—so unbroken is the silence—so profound the solitude!

During his stay at Dorking, it was his happiness to form a friendship the most intimate and endeared with Mr. J. Haddon, of London; and on the return of that gentleman to town, Mr. Spencer began an epistolary correspondence with him, which continued till his death. A valuable assortment of these letters have been kindly put into my hands, and with the greater part of them I shall enrich these pages. The following is, I believe, the first in the series:—

TO MR. JOHN HADDON.

"DORKING *July* 25*th*, 1809.

"MY WORTHY FRIEND:—I know no other way of expressing the pleasure your letters and your society have afforded me, than by endeavoring to repay your kindness, or at least by showing you that I am sensible of the obligations under which I am laid by you. The pleasant interviews, the truly social walks, and the various other enjoyments which we experienced together, have left an impression of attachment to yourself on my mind, which I am persuaded will not be easily obliterated. The country is indeed as pleasant in itself now, as it was the week before last; yet, believe me, it is not half so much enjoyed by me as it was then. The same streams indeed glide pleasantly along—the same hills majestically rise—the same enlivening prospects strike the eye, and pervade the soul, with admiration—and every thing around me seems to say, '*'Tis Surrey still;*' but there is a sad deficiency in all my perambulations—it is, 'that I am all alone.' Yesterday I went to Brockham; but there was no *Haddon* to meet me on my way thither, or to return with me any part of the way home. Last Tuesday evening Mr. Moore very politely offered to take me to Epsom, to hear Mr. Clayton the next day; which offer I most willingly accepted. On the whole, we had rather a pleasant day. Mr. George Clayton preached on Matt. xxi: 28. It may perhaps give you pleasure to hear, that I preached very comfortably last Lord's day from the new Bible, which is exactly the thing. I should know very little of the trials and difficulties of life, were I always to live as I now do. I really feel sometimes as if I needed something to quicken me to diligence, and put the graces of the Spirit in exercise, which, I am afraid, were I long to glide down life's stream so easily as I now do, would begin to die. Ease is a dangerous foe to the prosperity of religion in the soul, and opposition of some kind is essentially necesssry for us who profess a religion which is described as a race to be run; as a battle to be fought, and which is represented to us by every metaphor which gives us the idea of active labor and unceasing exertion. I hope to have the happiness of frequently meeting with you after my return to town; and I have the pleasure to inform you, that my appointments favor such intention. Mr. Wilson has written to inform me that I shall preach in town for five Sabbaths after the vacation. The manuscripts you sent highly delight me. Mrs. Smith wishes me to leave Herbert with her, to which I know you will not object. I continue about the same in health as I was when you left me; and am very thankful that here I have not to preach so many times as at several other places. That the good will of Him who dwelleth in the bush may ever countenance and console you; that the divine Spirit may ever lead you into all the truth; that you may possess every evidence that you have found favor in the sight of the Lord; and that Christ Jesus may be your eternal portion, is my humble, earnest prayer. Let us hope hereafter to behold his face together, in a world where we shall be liable to change and separation no more, but where we shall be enclosed in glory, changeless as his own. This is the desire of one who can truly call himself,

"Yours most affectionately,

THOMAS SPENCER."

"My kind hostess desires to be respectfully remembered to you. I expect I shall be in town next Tuesday."

Mr. Spencer left Dorking after the last Sabbath in July, and preached the six following Sundays in and about London. The places at which he labored during these six weeks were White-Row, Pell-street, Jewin-street, Camden chapel, Adelphi chapel, and Hoxton chapel. At Jewin-street he preached four Sabbaths, out of the six, afternoons and evenings. In the mean while his health still continued but indifferent, and indeed so much exertion both of mental and of physical strength was but illy calculated to promote its vigor. His mind, however, seemed every day to grow in activity and zeal. In the pulpit—in society, he was all animation and life. Like most who are the victims of much nervous irritability, his flow of spirits was excessive, which frequently led to ungenerous and merciless observations from those, who either had not the wisdom or the candor to attribute, what might appear as levity in him, to its real cause. It is indeed an unhappy circumstance, when such is the natural tendency of a man's mental constitution, and from nothing perhaps have young ministers suffered more than from this. At the same time, it is a shame and scandal to the Christian world, that there should be so many, who, professing to be the friends of students and youthful preachers, encourage and excite this unhappy bias, for their own amusement, and are then the first to censure the youth they have betrayed!

But where such is the *natural* disposition of a pious and devoted mind, its exercise in company is often followed by the keenest anguish and the deepest melancholy, in hours of solitude and reflection. The severe and malignant censurer should remember, that he is not omnipresent; and that there may be scenes in the retired life of the character he injures, which would put him to the blush! These remarks have been suggested by some passages in the following letter:

TO MR. JOHN HADDON.

"HOXTON, *August* 15, 1809.

"MY DEAR FRIEND:—I am sorry to inform you, that it is not in my power to gratify yourself, to please our friends, or to fulfill my own wishes, by devoting any evening in the week to visiting. I really cannot do it. My engagements this week are such as peremptorily to require my continuance at home, most likely till Sabbath day, at any rate till Saturday afternoon. I am obliged to those kind friends who expressed their concern about my exertions. I feel that I am not worthy of their sympathy. May their compassion lead them to pray for me, that I may be strengthened with all might by the Spirit in my inner man; and that He whose pleasure it is to increase strength to those that have no might, would help the infirmities of one who is weaker than a bruised reed, and yet has undertaken an office, to the discharge of which an angel is incompetent. My health is certainly in a better condition than it has been, but I am afraid I am still far from well: my head frequently aches, and I feel a sickness in my stomach. These are some of the miseries that flesh is heir to; but it is a joyful thought, that in the kingdom of glory our bodies will be no longer susceptible of pain, nor our minds of disquietude. Perfect health, composure, and joy, will be our happy lot when we see each other in a better world. And can we not hope that we shall do this; and that for ever we shall adore our common Saviour together? The leadings of his providence first brought us acquainted with each other; and the methods of his grace will, I hope, lead us on to glory, and in our way thither make us helps to each other. Pray for *me*, that my diligence may be excited; my levities checked; and my spirituality promoted. After all I say against the world, I must confess with shame that I am very like many of the men of the world in this respect; that I indulge in a lightness of disposition which is inconsistent with the character of a Christian, and makes us resemble those who never think of eternity and the solemnities of religion. Ah! my dear friend and brother, I have experienced in my short life many a bitter hour, occasioned by my own folly in this respect. But what a scandal is it to a professing Christian, that natural dispositions and surrounding temptations should overcome a principle of grace in the heart—a principle which ought ever to operate powerfully in weaning us from folly, and making us every day more and more serious and holy. Never do you be afraid of cautioning, or reproving me, but give me opportunity to prove that '*Faithful are the words of a friend!*' I have felt more, in reference to yourself, than I have ever yet expressed. More affection for you; more gratitude that Providence placed you in my way; and more determination to make you my counsellor and friend —than I have ever yet told you. The Lord help us to strengthen each other's hands in his good ways. I shall not like your letters so well if you do not direct them yourself. This you will say is folly, but I cannot help it. Adieu!

Yours affectionately,

THOMAS SPENCER."

"N. B. Saturday afternoon, if possible, I will see you."

The history of the following month is from the pen of his most intimate friend :

"At his return (from Dorking) he supplied Jewin-street meeting for a month, in the afternoons and evenings, where the attention he excited will not be easily forgotten. Before he left, numbers could not get admittance. The church were very anxious that he should settle among them, but their desire could not be complied with. I have heard him blamed respecting that business; but it was only by those who did not know the circumstances of the case. I was in the possession of his heart in that affair, and it would be unjust to his memory not to declare, that he was free from blame. His affectionate spirit keenly felt for them in their disappointment. 'The good people at Jewin-street,' said he, in a letter to me, 'have a strong claim upon our prayers;' and it was to soothe their minds that he composed his sermon upon Isaiah xxxiii: 20. The time of his supplying at Jewin-street was very pleasant to me. I claimed the whole of his time between and after the services, which inclined him to enjoy that retirement which was so congenial to his lowly soul. When going to preach no one saw him. I used to knock at his door—give in his refreshment—and watch the time for him. It was from the mount of communion that he always went to the pulpit, and this caused his sermons to shine gloriously. Frequently in passing to the house of God we kept perfect silence, while his mind has been so entirely absorbed, that I have found a necessity for guiding him ; and after worship he loved to stop as long as he conveniently could, that he might pass away unnoticed. But such was the character of Spencer—his deep humility—fervent piety—and amiable simplicity, that I am fully convinced it can not be fairly stated without suspicion of exaggeration ; and I must confess, that I should have found great difficulty in giving fallen nature credit for the excellencies, which, from the closest inspection, I saw resident in that truly illustrious and holy youth."

Having completed his engagements at Jewin-street, Spencer's labors became again miscellaneous and widely diffused. On Sabbath day, the 17th, he preached at Roydon, a village near Hertford, when he availed himself of the opportunity which this appointment afforded him of visiting his family. I cannot but conceive the bliss which such occasional interviews would cause in that little circle, which had once the happiness to call him theirs. To them the recollection of those happy hours devoted to social or sacred intercourse with their departed friend, must yield a soothing, though a melancholy pleasure. Nor is the reflection less honorable to his memory, than it is consolatory to their minds. In the midst of the unbounded popularity which he enjoyed—surrounded by new and splendid connections—the admiration of listening crowds, each eager to express his approbation; all ambitious of his friendship—he ever thought with the warmest affection upon those whom he had left in that obscurity from which he had himself emerged. Gladly did he seize the opportunity, when it occurred, of retiring from the public eye to taste again the tranquil pleasures of his home, and enjoy the interchange of all those sacred and delightful feelings which strengthen and endear the ties and obligations of social or domestic life. He was not unduly elated by his popularity. In his new associations he did not forget his kindred and his father's house. His family did not sink in his regard, in proportion as he rose to eminence.—The voice of universal praise did not drown the milder whispers of paternal love. But in a heart whose best affections were devoted to the noblest objects, and to which new scenes of exertion were perpetually unfolding, the family at Hertford held an honorable and distinguished place. The most extensive public engagements, are not incompatible with the retired duties of private life—and the cares and responsibilities of the most laborious ministry may be sustained and discharged, without absorbing those affectionate regards so justly claimed by parental kindness and fraternal love. 'Tis true, that as a Christian, and in his official capacity, every believer in Jesus is to the faithful minister a father—a mother—a sister—and a brother. But as a *man* the relations of life exist for him—and the feelings of humanity must be common to him too. A heart from which these ties are rudely severed, is but illy adapted to that soothing influence by which the

6*

office of the ministry becomes a source of comfort to the wretched ; and a man whose bosom is a stranger to the tender sympathies of human life—alike insensible to joy or sorrow—may with propriety administer the cold rites of a Stoical philosophy—but must ever be a living contrast to the religion of Jesus—a system whose characteristic spirit is that of the purest and tenderest philanthropy.

Before his departure for Roydon, the following letter was addressed by Mr. Spencer to his friend. The observations at the beginning upon Christian boldness are judicious—and, though ignorant of the particular circumstances which might have called them forth, cannot fail to prove interesting and instructive :

TO MR. JOHN HADDON.

Thursday evening, September 14, 1809.

"MY DEAR FRIEND :—I know you wish me to write you a great deal ; but I must plead the old excuse—want of time ; for I find that ——, instead of calling to-morrow morning, must have this directly, and I have but this minute left the chapel. You tell me your 'mind recoils from public duty, however plain and clear,' and you need not be told that this is a pity ; and in this respect you do not display that Christian boldness which is after all consistent with genuine humility—which the apostles displayed and enforced—which the Bible every where recommends—and which is well calculated to evidence our decided attachment to Jesus and his cause. It shall be my part, however, not to reproach you for the want of it, but to carry your wants before our Father's throne, and entreat him to fill you with all holy boldness and Christian courage ;

whilst at the same time I would most earnestly entreat you to consider the foolishness of your fears: the little need we have to seek to please our fellow-creatures, or to dread them, and above all the constant inspection of Him who said *whosoever shall confess me before men, him shall the Son of Man also confess befors his holy angels.* But I am persuaded that you are *not* ashamed of Jesus; yet there is great need for us all to ask ourselves repeatedly, 'am I fully on the Lord's side?' because this very examination itself produces the best effects, as it prompts us to give evidence before others of the reality of our hope, and it brings us near to God, who can make us strong in the grace that is in Christ Jesus, and faithful even unto death. Your letters always affect me; your company you know delights me; and what shall I say of your attachment to me, but *that it meets return.* I am often indeed induced to believe that you are too careful of me, and too much concerned about me. Expressions of gratitude on my part from my mouth or pen I know you do not want, therefore I shall not trouble you with them. My mind is perfectly at ease about the present or future laws of the house, as well as about any situation after I have filled it. O that I may be stayed on God! I often think what a pity it will be, if from our friendship there should arise no good effect; however, here I am wrong, because I am myself a witness that good effects have arisen to *me;* but I long that to us there may be opened fresh sources of comfort and joy in God, and that we may then be made abundant blessings to each other. I am going to preach next Sabbath at Roydon, a village near Hertford, where I have reason to hope God has owned and blessed my unworthy labors before. May he do so again. Perhaps I may go to Hertford to-morrow afternoon, as it was the place of my nativity, and is now the residence of my dear father, my sisters, brother, and mother-in-law. I could say much more, (though in the same feeble and desultory style) but you perceive my paper is full. I cannot expect to see you at all till Tuesday. The coach comes in town on Monday evening, about half-past six. If I can, I will walk then to Fleet-street.

Adieu, my dear friend,
THOMAS SPENCER."

From this period to that of his first visit to Liverpool, I am not in possession of any remarkable occurrences in Mr. Spencer's history. At any rate, I am aware of none which tend to illustrate any particular feature of his character, or of such a nature as to warrant their publication to the world. But there yet remain many interesting letters to his friend, Mr. Haddon, which will tend very much to supply the want of a connected narrative—and that friend who, during this period, enjoyed the most intimate acquaintance with him, and obtained a most accurate knowledge of his character, has furnished me with a series of anecdotes and observations, which will make the reader familiar with the man, and most strikingly exhibit the holy, humble, and fervent bias of his mind. For the present I shall content myself with making a selection from these letters, with such occasional remarks as may be necessary to illustrate their subjects or occasions; whilst the characteristic sketches above alluded to, will occupy some of the succeeding pages.

TO MR. JOHN HADDON.

HOXTON, *Oct.* 12, 1809.

"MY DEAR FRIEND—With pleasure it is that I inform you that I am appointed for *Vauxhall.* I feel pleasure, because this assignation gives us another opportunity of enjoying each other's society. I have not yet written to those friends in the country, but intend doing it to-morrow. May the young lady die in such a peaceful and happy state of mind, as shall, instead of suffering the survivors to sorrow as those who have no hope, rather give them to say—*Behold how he loved her!* I mentioned the circumstance to Mr. W., at the same time stating the wish of the Roydon people that I might supply them on Sabbath day. He told me it could not be complied with, assigning as a reason, that I was given out at Vauxhall. As the affair now stands, I am quite satisfied, because I wish to resolve all my appointments into the will of the Head of the Church. 'Where he appoints, I'll go.' Of all evils, I pray to be particularly delivered from leaning to my own understanding, and indulging my own wayward will. May obstinacy never characterize me. May grace always be given me to suppress it when it rises. To these requests I know, that from your inmost soul you say *Amen.* One of our fellow students has just delivered us a good sermon from—'*The righteous hath hope in his death.*' I enjoyed his sermon much more than I generally do those which are delivered to us on a Thursday evening. This was so experimental—so scriptural—so pious, that it found its way to my heart. May you and I, whenever we shall come to die, have a lively, a sure and a certain hope of reigning in life by Jesus Christ. Whilst so many are called away around us, surely we should recollect the uncertainty of our own continuance upon earth; and as death is still potent, still inexorable, and still delights to surprise, let it be our chief concern to have an interest in the affections of the heart of that Saviour, who shall destroy this last enemy, and give to his followers a crown of glory changeless as his own. On him may we now both live by faith, so that when we have served our generation according to his will, we may fall asleep in his arms.

"Adieu! Your's affectionately,

"Thomas Spencer."

The young lady to whom he refers in this letter, appears to have been one of the seals of his early ministry, and then at the point of death. One of the letters written by him on that occasion, I am able to lay before the reader.

TO MRS. ———.

"DEAR MADAM—Both your letters were safely and joyfully received by me. I say joyfully, because they show that God is putting honor upon my feeble and unworthy labors, and making use of them for your spiritual welfare—a circumstance that gives me more real pleasure than any other circumstance possibly could. You are much mistaken in supposing that I neglected to write to you because you had in your letters said anything improper; nothing could be more opposite to my ideas. Had this been the case, I should have felt it my duty to have set you right: but I can tell you what I can tell my God, when I say that I never heard or read an account of a young convert which appeared more satisfactory, or filled me with more delight, than that which you give me of yourself. I say this not to puff you up with spiritual pride, but to make you more thankful that you have obtained mercy, and to assure you that your suspicions of any dissatisfaction on my part are altogether groundless. Rather would I exclaim, '*what hath God wrought?*' and wrought too (well may I wonder) by his blessing upon my weak exertions. Oh! let the glory be ascribed to Him who gives testimony to the word of his grace. The excuse I have to plead for not writing to you before, is want of time and multiplicity of engagements—for in the academy my time is not my own. I have just been writing a long letter to Mrs. W———, stating my views, wishes and hopes for the welfare of her amiable and beloved daughter. May she be resigned to the Divine will, and ready when the heavenly bridegroom cometh! From all that I can learn, I have no doubt of her interest in the affections of that same Jesus who is now, I trust, all *your* salvation and all *your* desire. When I recollect that she, a seal to my ministry, is apparently going to join the heavenly musicians in singing that song which no man can learn but the redeemed, it is impossible to express my feelings. I am very desirous to hear from her own lips an account of the way in which the Lord met with her, and a statement of the sensations of her mind in prospect of the last conflict. I wished to come down to see her—I asked permission. This could not be granted me, because I was given out last Sabbath day at the place to which I am going. But I have the happiness of informing you that next Lord's day I shall preach at Roydon, and so shall have an opportunity of going to Thundridge Bury Farm. I hope that our covenant God is leading you in a plain path, and teaching you more of the corruption of your own heart and the love of Christ, by his holy Spirit. All I can recommend you to do, is to be much engaged in secret prayer to him. Oh! aim to get near to him in holy communion, then you will find a heaven begun below. You will have Christ for your constant companion, and you will obtain the desire of your heart. I view this as the time of your first love. May the zealous affection for Christ, which I hope you now discover, increase yet more and more. Live by faith upon the Son of God, who loved you, and gave himself for you. Commit your soul into his hands, and the souls of all the members of your family. It is my earnest prayer that you may grow in grace and in the knowledge of our Lord and Saviour Jesus Christ; that so I may have to rejoice that you received the gospel when delivered by me, as in deed and in truth the word of God and not of man. As for your request about a settlement for me at Roydon, I should recommend you not to expect it. I am always happy to come amongst you as an occasional supply, but I must venture no further. I have a variety of reasons for not considering it my duty to settle with any congregation as yet, or even to think of it, and I have thus far not engaged to do so at Roydon. Therefore I must request you not merely to check, but actually to eradicate the thought. Wishing you—your respected partner—and all your family the best of blessings, I remain,

"Your's sincerely,

"THOMAS SPENCER."

Had he then been sufficiently advanced in his studies to have cherished the idea of an immediate settlement—and had he been left to the free, unbiassed expression of his feelings—there is no spot on which he would have fixed as the scene of his stated and pastoral labors, in preference to a village so tranquil and retired as Roydon. He did not value popularity, except as it afforded him an opportunity of doing good. No one ever was more averse to pomp or to parade. He loved simplicity in all its forms. It was indeed a characteristic feature of himself; and had not the prospect of more extensive usefulness allured him to a wider and more public sphere, his passion for retirement would have guided him in his selection of a residence for life.

Talking with him on the subject of his health, which seemed declining, beneath the pressure of so much exertion, his friend said—"Do you wish to be early laid aside—or do you desire a premature grave?" "Oh, no," said he, "you know my wish—to have a meeting in the country, surrounded by trees—occasionally to see the shadows of the leaves quivering on the walls, in the reflection of the setting sun. A burial ground near, in which I and my people can together lie !* To live a long, honorable, and useful life, bringing many souls to the Saviour ! This is the summit of my wishes." Though it was denied him to enjoy the *first*, the *last* object of his desire, and by far the most important and dearest to his heart, he did possess ; for never was so short a ministry honored by the conversion of so many souls. Every week in Liverpool discloses some fresh instances of its success and one and another is perpetually rising up to say—" 'By the grace of God I am what I am,' but it was

* May I be indulged in another extract from the poems of Kirke White? It was a passage which Spencer often read with peculiar emphasis, and seems a melancholy comment on his own ideas :

"Beneath this yew I would be sepulchred.
It is a lovely spot ! The sultry sun,
From his meridian height, endeavors vainly
To pierce the shadowy foliage ;
'Tis a nook
Most pleasant."

"Yet may not undistinguish'd be my grave ;
But there at eve may some congenial soul
Duly resort, and shed a pious tear,
The good man's benison—no more I ask.
And oh ! (if heavenly beings may look down
From where, with Cherubim inspir'd, they sit,
Upon this little dim discovered spot,
The earth,) then will I cast a glance *below*
On him who thus my ashes shall embalm."

"Wishing he may not long be doom'd to pine
In this low-thoughted world of darkling wo ;
But that, ere long, he reach his kindred skies."

the ministry of Spencer that led me first a humble suppliant to the throne of mercy."

The situation of young ministers is peculiarly delicate and dangerous. The eyes not only of the religious public, but also of the world are fixed on them. And it is to be deplored, that where they have a right to expect the greatest kindness, they often meet with an undue severity; and those who ought to be the first to throw the mantle of love over their defects, are not unfrequently the most forward and exulting in their exposure. To an unhappy and inordinate love of scandal, many a fair and unblemished reputation has fallen the victim. The scattered wrecks by which they are surrounded, should inspire succeeding voyagers with caution. There is a cheerfulness, compatible with the deepest seriousness—the most fervent piety; and there is a levity, in which the dignity of the minister and the sanctity of the Christian, may alike be lost. Where this is witnessed, whatever claim the individual may have upon the *generosity* and *lenity* of the spectators, he has none upon their *justice*—they have a right to censure—and however we may deprecate their severity, none can deny them its exercise. And here it is perhaps that students are most exposed to danger. Fatigued and wasted by the close application and intense thought of many studious weeks, they enter, as they imagine, the circle of friendship, and instantly relax. Those who only see the effect, and are unacquainted with its cause, hastily form an unfavorable opinion of their character, and cruelly propagate the opinion they have rashly formed. These observations are not altogether inappropriate to the subject of the following letter :

TO MR. JOHN HADDON.

HOXTON COLLEGE, *Oct.* 27, 1809.

"MY DEAR FRIEND—The expression of affection your last letter, all your letters, and the whole strain of your conduct towards me evince, greatly affect me, and you will find my feelings upon the subject in Prov. xxvii. 19. Sanctified friendship appears to me to be one of the best sweets in the cup of life. It is what the Saviour recommended by his own example, and what the best of men have experienced benefical in every age. May this kind of friendship be exemplified in us, and may we mutually share in the affections of the heart of Him, who, '*having loved his own which were in the world, loved them unto the end!*' To his will in all things we must bow, and in his dispensations, however contrary to our inclination, acquiesce ; but '*not my will but thine be done,*' is language which requires a large degree of grace to use in all cases, and from the bottom of our hearts.

"Many eyes are indeed upon *me*, and much do I fear that they will see something in me ere long that will take them from me. Your warnings are faithful, but my heart is still deceitful, and Satan may, for any thing I know, be about to sift me as wheat. You are not ignorant of his devices. Oh! then, pray for me, that my faith fail not, so that, instead of the number of those who behold me, turning away from me with disgust and aversion, they may rather glorify God in me, and take knowledge of me that I have been with Jesus. The thought that affords me some degree of encouragement, is that Jehovah knoweth my path, and that *he is able to make me stand*, yea, to remove the suspicions of those who *'fear and wait to see.'* But really, I cannot help thinking that there are some people in the world who seem as if they wished for something to hinder one's usefulness; and who, by their too significant expressions on the subject, lead me to suppose that they would rejoice in such a circumstance, and say, 'Oh! so would we have it.' And why? Because then their clever prophecies would be fulfilled, and we should for the future put such confidence in their forebodings as to view them as certain omens of ill events. I do hope, however, that God will in great mercy either keep me from the snares that lie in my way, or take me to himself.

"I have to-day written to the Kidderminster people, referring them to the Doctor, or Mr. Wilson. I will try and be with you to-morrow by 12 o'clock. Do not be disappointed if I should not be able.

"I remain yours affectionately,

"THOMAS SPENCER."

On Sunday, the 5th of November, he was appointed to preach at Cambridge, in the pulpit lately occupied by the Rev. Robert Hall, A.M., a name dear to genius, as to religion. The day following, he spent in viewing the University. In a letter dated the 3d, he says: "Last night my surprise was excited by seeing that I am not appointed on the list for any place in town, but for *Cambridge*. I am to stay Monday over at Cambridge, to look at the colleges, &c. I shall think much of Kirke White;" and aware of the respectability, both in wealth and talent, of the congregation he was called to address, he adds, "the Lord make me prudent and faithful;

may it appear that he has some good end to answer by conducting me thither."

He was exceedingly attached to the poetry of Henry Kirke White. He could repeat a great part of it, and frequently quoted it with great emphasis and feeling. "And yet," said he in conversation with the friend to whom these letters are addressed, "there is a thirst for fame sometimes discovered, which pains me.

'Fifty years hence, and who will hear of Henry?'

Well, suppose *nobody* does, and what then? If Henry has served his day and generation, and is gone to glory, neither the church nor he will be losers; and the hearing of Henry will be too small a consideration to be brought into the account."

Public as Spencer's life had now become, and exposed as he was to the influence of every unholy passion which popularity might awaken, he yet maintained a close and holy walk with God. He courted solitude, and for the best of purposes. Of him it may be truly said, '*his fellowship was with the Father, and with his Son Jesus Christ.*' The holy and the heavenly tone his mind received in those retired hours, gave a peculiar unction to his ministry; and the knowledge which by deep communion with his own heart, and constant intercourse with God, he had obtained, rendered his preaching remarkably profitable to believers, and gave him a skill in administering instructions adapted to all the varieties of their experience. Of this the following is a pleasing specimen :

TO MR. JOHN HADDON.

November 9, 1809.

"MY DEAR FRIEND—Be assured that I, as well as yourself, have walked in darkness, and complained that there was no light. Fluctuations in experience are, I am sure, my lot, whilst my only consolation in such circumstances still remain—'tis the unchangeableness of Christ. Oh! what is so calculated to reconcile our minds to the way our Father calls us to travel, as the recollection, that whilst we are found in it, Jesus is the same, and that to the end of the journey ; and in every trying circumstance he is a present help. In darkness he will enable us to trust in the Lord, and to stay ourselves upon our God ; yea, he will cheer our desponding souls with visitation sweet. Seasons in which we experience darkness of mind, and depression of soul, are necessary : they form the analogy between us and those who through *tribulation* are gone to heaven : they render us fit subjects for the illuminating and refreshing grace of Christ ; they add a higher relish to the renewed enjoyment of the light and liberty of the gospel ; and they serve to prepare us for that world where the Lord shall be our everlasting life, and our God our glory.

"Reflecting upon deliverance from such times of depression should teach us to say—'*Return unto thy rest, O my soul, for the Lord hath dealt bountifully with thee!*' It should lead us to anticipate future favors, and rejoice that he that hath delivered us, can and will deliver ; and since the day has dawned, and the shadows have fled away, we should most cordially adore Him who has been appointed to give light to them who sit in darkness, and to guide our feet into the way of peace. May you and I ever enjoy the presence of Jesus, our best friend ; share in his tender sympathy ; his kind reproofs ; his excellent counsels. May he be our God for ever and ever, and our guide even unto death. Then we need fear no evil. If sensible that he is with us, we may pass through midnight glooms, and experience a season of great darkness, and yet look forward to a future time, when with pleasure we shall sing, '*The Lord is my light, of whom shall I be afraid.*' Oh! that I may be enabled to commit your soul and my own into the hands of Jesus as unto a faithful Creator. I can now add no more, than to say that

"I remain affectionately yours,

"THOMAS SPENCER."

About this time his health again declined. A severe cold for some days deprived him of his voice —and he was compelled to rest one Sabbath day from his public work. What were his feelings in prospect of that Sabbath, this letter will declare.

TO MR. JOHN HADDON.

December 6, 1809.

"MY DEAR FRIEND—It appears that your suspicions that I should preach three times to-morrow, will not, cannot be realized, for Mr. Western, as well as those around me are agreed, that I must not go to Hertford at all, judging it dangerous for me to go out, much more so to preach. Yesterday I passed a miserable day. The thought of the pain of mind the letter I sent home would occasion to my friends, hurt me much, and I was much worse than I had been before, as my lungs and throat felt more inflamed. To-day I think I am better, but still very far from well. I can scarcely bear the prospect of a silent Sabbath. I think I shall be quite out of my element to-morrow. Oh! that I did but more firmly believe, that he who is my Saviour does all things well, and that he who sustains the dread character of Judge of all the earth, must do right. If I am able, I shall hear Mr. Hordle in the morning. I have no voice yet. I hope it is not irretrievably lost. I need not say, that if you can call this evening it will give me unspeakable pleasure.

"Yours affectionately,

"THOMAS SPENCER."

Reflecting on this temporary indisposition in a letter to his father, he says :—I have reason to hope that the measure of affliction with which our heavenly Father thought fit to visit me, has been made a blessing to my soul. It gave me time for reflection and close self-examination. It gave a new zest to my feelings, and when it was removed, I hope I was inspired with fresh ardor to live for the glory of God."

Amid the constant bustle of a public life, the retirement which temporary indisposition affords, must be most beneficial to a pious mind. Then it can relax into a calm and intimate communion with itself. It can quietly indulge in such a review of the past, and such an anticipation of the future, as will tend not a little, under the sanctifying influence of the Holy Spirit, to curb its impetuosity—correct its levity—and regulate its principles. From the chamber of sickness, the exercises of the pulpit will be furnished with materials of the highest order ; and the beds of the diseased will be attended with a sympathy which experience of similar affliction only can excite.

The greater part of the Christmas vacation Mr. Spencer spent at Brighton, and on the first day of the year 1810, he preached at the Rev. Mr. Styles' chapel, to young people, from 2 Chron. xxxiv. 27, 28: "Because thine heart was tender, and thou didst humble thyself before God, when thou heardst his words against this place, and against the inhabitants thereof, and humbledst thyself before me, and didst rend thy clothes and weep before me: I have even heard thee also, saith the Lord. Behold I will gather thee to thy fathers, and thou shalt be gathered to thy grave in peace. Neither shall thine eyes see all the evil that I will bring upon this place, and upon the inhabitants of the same."

The good seed which he was the instrument of scattering in Brighton, very rapidly sprang up. In a letter to his father, written immediately on his return from thence, and dated Jan. 12th, 1810, he says, "a young person who heard me at Mr. Styles' last year, was called by divine grace under my instrumentality, and died before I went this time, bearing an honorable testimony to the religion of Jesus, and to her interest in it. Oh! what hath God wrought!"

During his stay at Brighton, he had occasion to solicit a favor of his friend in London, the performance of which was acknowledged in the following letter:

TO MR. HADDON.

BRIGHTON, *January* 1, 1810.

"MY DEAR FRIEND—However you may smile at the idea of my writing you a 'letter of thanks,' I assure you I think you have a claim upon it, for you have done for me what I should have liked few others to have done; but suffice it to say, it came safe to hand. Last Thursday I preached on Luke xxiv. 32. Yesterday morning at the Countess', on Eph. ii. 14. In the evening at Mr. Styles', it being the close of the year, on Exodus xxiii. 20. To-night I shall *only* preach, as one minister will commence and another close with prayer. It is said that I shall preach at the chapel on Thursday evening. You ask me, where I shall be next Sabbath. Many advise me to remain at Brighton; but it is my present intention to return home on the Friday, though I really feel myself in a difficulty about it. I hope I have, since I have been at this place, enjoyed the divine blessing—those with whom I associate are the excellent of the earth—with no others have I any occasion to be at all connected. In this respect I am like your good friend Mr. H. of Westminster. We certainly do not in general sufficiently estimate the worth of the society of those who discover the mind that was in Christ;—great is the benefit we may derive from their company. Oh! let those of us who fear the Lord speak often with one another; one may thus come at each other's follies, and stimulate each other to the performance of that good, acceptable, and perfect will of God. I think my cold is getting better. After I had preached last night, a valuable young Scotch clergyman who was there, wished I might live to preach many such sermons—what could I say, but '*all the days of my appointed time will I wait till my change come?*' It is a great satisfaction to know, that we are training up for heaven and 'ripening apace for the vision of God.' Pray for me, that this perseverence may be given me. You know my object is the glory of God in the good of souls—that this may be accomplished, by my exertions, is my prayer, my hope, my aim. Whether living or dying, may we be the Lord's. I have, however, at present, no other idea, than that I shall be spared yet, and *not die, but live and declare the works of the Lord.** Wishing you the enjoyment of the good will of

* Alas! how blind are we to futurity! A clergyman not long

Him that dwelt in the bush, and assuring you of my steady attachment,

"I remain yours affectionately,

"THOMAS SPENCER."

On Wednesday, the 28th of February, being a day appointed for a general fast, Mr. Spencer preached a sermon at Hoxton chapel, adapted to the occasion; his text was Ezk. lx. 4. "Go through the midst of the city, through the midst of Jerusalem, and set a mark upon the men that sigh and cry for all the abominations that are done in the midst thereof." The general scope and style of this sermon may be ascertained by the following extract from the communication of his friend :—

"A minister said to me, 'I don't know how a good fast sermon can be preached, without touching upon politics.'—'If you will hear Spencer to-morrow, I think you will find that it can be done.' When we met again, he told me that he had heard an excellent fast sermon, without a word upon politics. I remember, that in that sermon he said, 'when your ear is pained with oaths and imprecations as you pass the street, remember that that swearer is your fellow countryman, calling for vengeance upon *your* country, and do you, by ejaculatory prayer, strive to avert it.'"

To enter into a minute detail of the places at which Mr. Spencer preached between this period and the ensuing vacation, would be useless. Suffice

since, while uttering these very words in the pulpit, suddenly turned pale—his voice faltered—he fell back and expired! Little did the amiable Spencer think, that the hand which thus conveyed to his friend the pleasing anticipation of a long and useful life, should lie so soon in the impotence of death!

it to say, that his labors were unremitting ; that he visited several congregations in the country—particularly those at *Hertford, Reading, Henly,* and *Brighton.*

He was appointed one of the three students who should deliver the public orations at the coming anniversary—held at midsummer. This preyed with considerable anxiety on his mind, and although one should have imagined that by this time he had become familiar with large auditories and critical hearers—yet we find him shinking from the task, and expressing many fears respecting it. The subject allotted to him was, "THE INFLUENCE OF THE GOSPEL ON THE SPIRIT AND TEMPER." His colleagues in that trying service were, Messrs. John Burder and Stenner ; and to these gentlemen were given as topics of discussion, "THE DOCTRINE OF THE ATONEMENT," and "THE INFLUENCE OF THE HOLY SPIRIT." The day before that on which the discourses were to be delivered, he expressed his feelings thus :—

TO MR. JOHN HADDON.

HOXTON, *June* 19, 1810.

"MY DEAR FRIEND—Consonant with your request, I here transmit to you the notes of the sermon on Eutychus : if you can, let me have them again before I go into Lancashire. You mention *to-morrow*, and oh ! what anxiety do I feel in the prospect of it ; already it has cost me some tears, it may cost me many more. Would to God that I may experience the assisting grace of Him who has before proved himself able to do for me exceeding abundantly above all that I could ask or think. If the light of his countenance shine upon me, then

I shall shine in the sight of heaven, and in the eyes of his saints, who know and can recognize the reflections of the Saviour's glory. From what I can anticipate of the congregation, it will be terrific; but does not the promise, '*I am with you always*,' extend to particular occasions? Most certainly it does; then it takes in this trying service. May I have faith and trust in it, and be favored with an experimental confirmation of its truth. Believing that you do sincerely and constantly commend me to the kind care of your Father and my Father, of your God and my God, I remain

"Affectionately yours,

"THOMAS SPENCER."

CHAPTER V.

His first visit to Liverpool—Preaches at Newington Chapel. His popularity as a Preacher—Correspondence—Return to the Academy—Invited by the Congregation of Newington to become their Pastor—Calls from other Congregations—Acceptance of the call from Liverpool—Last Sermon at Hoxton.

We now arrive at the period of Mr. Spencer's first visit to Liverpool. Before we pass on with him to that new and interesting scene, it may be well to pause, and take such a general view of his mode of thinking and acting, while a student, as the following characteristic sketches from the hand of his most intimate friend, will furnish. I shall present them in a miscellaneous way just as they occur. Thus the reader will converse with him—hear his own sentiments, expressed in his own language, and imperceptibly become familir with the man.

"'That passage,' said he, 'is much upon my mind'—'Let no man despise thy youth.' I understand the apostle thus:—Let your walk and condnct be such, that no man *can* despise thy youth. And such shall be my own.'

"He was favored with peculiar facility in composition. 'Many a sermon,' said he, 'have I composed between Hoxton and your house.' His ideas flowed faster than he could write them, and when alone our conversation has met with frequent interruptions from his stopping to commit to paper, before they escaped him, the ideas crossing his mind. Turning to me privately, as I sat by his side one evening at the tea-table of a friend, 'Look at that,' said he, 'will it do?' It was the sketch of a sermon, which he had composed during the conversation. 'I don't know,' said he, (and those who suppose my friend was boasting, did not know him) 'I don't know,' said he, 'that for a long time I have had time enough for any one sermon: I was crampt in every head for want of time.' His sermons at that time were sixty-five to seventy-five minutes in preaching; though his hearers were not aware of it.

"In composing, he used to fold a sheet of foolscap paper in eight leaves, leaving the last side for the heads of application. However long the sermon might be, he never wrote more of it, and in preaching, varied the sermon every time he preached it. 'How do you obtain your texts?' 'I keep a little book in which I enter every text of Scripture which comes into my mind with power and sweetness. Were I to dream of a passage of Scripture, I should enter it; and when I sit down to compose, I look over the book, and have never found myself at a loss for a subject.'

"His memory was remarkably tenacious; he could regularly repeat every service in which he had ever engaged, with the chapter which he had read, and those of his acquaintances who were present. Returning from Halloway, after preaching, said he, 'Did you perceive any thing particular in me this morning?' 'No.' 'I was very ill in the pulpit; my memory totally forsook me; I could not recollect my subject, but having my notes in my pocket, I took them out and read them.' 'I am glad of it; I give you joy; you can no longer condemn assistance to an imperfect memory.' 'O no, I boast no more; from henceforth, I am silent upon that subject.'

"'The young man that has just passed my study door,' said he, 'is fearful that he shall not keep up *variety* in his sermons.

The best way that I find to attain variety is continually to ask myself 'What is there in the circumstances before me, that will benefit my sermon on Sabbath morning?' for a minister should turn every thing into gold. And by keeping my eye continually upon that point, I am seldom at a loss for variety.'

"Few persons have held pulpit eloquence in higher estimation than Spencer did, or in more contempt when it stood in competition with the interests of souls. I remember asking his opinion of an eloquent sermon which he had been hearing— 'Why,' said he, 'I could have wept over it—I could have wept to hear immortals so treated.'

"'Your morning sermon yesterday was approved, but not that in the afternoon.' 'No, I suppose not, and I will give you the reason. In the morning, when I preached on privileges, they were pleased; but when in the afternoon, I came to duties, they remembered their treatment of their late venerable pastor. I particularly respect aged ministers, and love to assist them, and generally add a trifle to the collection, when I have been preaching in behalf of a church which has an aged minister.'

"He was much tried by the envy of some little minds. Mr. S.—— said to him, 'You was very late, I hear at Walworth.' 'Yes, sir, and there you may see your own error; you know *you* say I am too eager for the pulpit, now you see your mistake.' At another time, 'Spencer,' said a person whose name shall be secret, 'Popularity is a dangerous thing.' 'It is.' 'No one is popular long.' 'Very true.' 'You are popular *now*, but you will not be so long.' 'That I certainly shall not, sir, if *your wishes* are accomplished; but I fully believe, that my popularity hurts you more than it does me.' The bell soon after summoned him to read (in his turn) a sermon for general criticism. The first person called upon said, that its *merits* were such, that he had nothing to say of its *defects*. That sentiment was universal. 'And,' said he to me afterwards, 'when I considered what had passed, I felt that that was a moment of gratification.'

"A lady who had misunderstood an idea in his sermon, wrote me a hasty letter, charging him with antinomianism, and me with gross impropriety in hearing him. It was a Saturday night, and he was to preach in the same pulpit the next day. I went to inform him of the circumstance, that he might take an unperceived opportunity of explaining himself. He held out his hand to give his usual affectionate squeeze, when I drew back. 'I don't know how to shake hands with an antinomian.' 'An antinomian! What is the matter?' 'Read this proof of it.' He read it; his pleasantry subside; and with a countenance which spoke the feeling of his noble soul, 'O,' said he, 'this letter does me good.—The attention of that congregation would have led me to suppose that they were pleased, and perhaps profited by what they heard; and yet you see that there were those present who not only misunderstood me, but supposed that I was a preacher of antinomianism. This letter does me good; for sometimes Satan claps me on the back, here in my study, and says, 'That sermon will do very well, and especially from one so young as you'—and then I begin to mount, and fancy that I *am* somebody; but such a letter as this clips my wings—and then,' said he, (with indescribable expression,) 'I drop into my place—the dust. Do bring me all the intelligence of this kind that you can.'

"One day mentioning to him an interesting text of Mr. Cecil's, preached on the last night of the year, said he, 'That will just do for me to preach at Brighton, to conclude the services of the present year. But don't show me Mr. Cecil's till I have composed mine. I would not borrow a single idea.'

"Preaching one morning at Hoxton, after he had prayed as usual at his entrance into the pulpit, I missed him; he bent forward for a considerable time so low, that I could scarcely perceive him from the gallery. When I afterwards asked him if any thing ailed him, said he, 'When I went into the pulpit, and saw that crowded audience, recollecting that they were all looking to me for instruction, and remembering my own youth and inexperience, I was overwhelmed, and leaning forward, implored more earnestly the divine assistance.'

"While preaching at Jewin-street, he one afternoon took the two lower steps at once, in ascending the pulpit stairs.—When we afterwards met, I asked, 'Did you notice the manner of your going into the pulpit?' 'I did, and thought that you would also—it was inadvertent; but it was wrong. It did not become the solemnity of the place.—I never remember such a circumstance before, and will be more guarded in future.' As a proof of the *necessity* of his watchfulness over the minutiæ of his actions, I mention that an aged Christian said to me some time afterwards, 'I loved Spencer's sermons, but there was a lightness about him.' 'A lightness! when, and where did he discover it?' 'At our meeting, in jumping up the pulpit stairs.' 'Did you see it more than once?' 'No.' 'Then I can tell you, that that once he felt and lamented as deeply as you could; and I am sure he never repeated it. Is not that satisfactory?' 'It is.'

"Spencer followed Cecil; he united deep humility with true ministerial dignity; nor do I conceive it possible for a youth to be less affected by popularity than he was; and as to flattery, if his flatterers had known the light in which he viewed them, they would have been silent. Coming from a vestry, where adulation had been offered—'Don't fear for me,' said he, 'on account of what is passed; it was too weak to hurt: my danger is when those, on whose judgment I depend, speak unguardedly!' At another time, after a young man had been very lavish in his praises, (who had several times been guilty of the same impropriety,) I told him I thought the next time he addressed himself to me, I should give him a hint of it. 'O no,' said he, 'treat it with the same contempt that I do. To mention it, would give too much importance to his judgment. I would not have him think that *his* judgment could *do any harm.*'

"Spencer was particularly happy in his choice of texts for particular occasions: 'I feel great difficulty,' said he, 'in preaching at Hertford, where I have to address many who walked with God before I was born. To-morrow will be the first Sabbath that I have regularly supplied there. I have chosen for my subject, Romans xvi: 7.' In which he showed what it was to be in Christ; and the duties which aged Christians owe to younger ones—faithful reproof and exhortation—prayer for them, &c. For his sermon on regeneration, he choose James i: 18, which, as he said, comprised the *whole* subject: the efficient cause—'The will of God,' the grand means used—'the word of truth;' the great end in view—that believers should be—'First fruits of His creatures.' A gentleman, who possesses a fine mind, said to me, 'I have heard so much of Spencer, that when I went to hear him, I expected to be disappointed; but I found the reverse to be the case. When he gave out his text it was with an emphasis which so forcibly laid open the apostle's argument, that my attention was rivetted, and I was perfectly astonished.'

"Mr. Spencer's simplicity in dress was well known. He avoided in that respect, the very appearance of evil, that his ministry might not be blamed. One Sabbath morning, when he called for me, he had a new coat on, which I told him I thought was more fashionable than he would approve. 'I did not know it,' said he, and on the next Sabbath morning, he asked me if I thought it more becoming *then:* he had had it altered.

"I was desired by several medical gentlemen to inform him, that unless he slackened his exertions, he could not live to see five and twenty. When I mentioned it, he said, 'that it certainly must be attended to, for that his hope was to live a long and useful life.' He therefore determined to alter the length of his sermons from an hour or sixty-five minutes to forty-five.

"'I am going,' said he, 'to preach at Vauxhall to-morrow, where you may come with a very safe conscience. You need not be afraid of a large congregation *there*. You do not like large congregations for me; but don't you remember how much more encouragement and satisfaction the man has who fishes in a pond which is full of fish, than he who fishes in a place where he knows there are but two or three.'

"Before S. left the academy, a gentleman, whose judgment, or piety, few are disposed to dispute, said to me, 'If it were not for the sound of his voice, with my eyes shut I could suppose him a man of seventy. He is ripening fast for heaven—I can fancy him an angel, come down into the pulpit, soon to return.'

"Another gentleman, possessed of undeniable critical skill, and difficult to please, after he had heard him, said, 'I stood the whole service—and I could have stood till midnight. I felt as under the influence of a charm I could not resist, and was rivetted to the spot. intent only upon the fascinating object I saw before me.'

"It was with sincere pity that he saw any young minister descend from the holy dignity of his station, by attention, as soon as the service was concluded, to the advances of females, who, had they really received the benefit they professed, would have shown it in a very different way."*

Mr. Spencer was appointed by the committee to spend the midsummer vacation in this year at Newington chapel, Liverpool, then destitute of a pastor, by the death of the Rev. David Bruce. The report of his extraordinary talents and amazing popularity had already, from various quarters, reached that place. And the congregation amongst whom he

* This is to Spencer's honor. Those who are accustomed to attend the vestries in London, after the sermons of popular preachers, will enter into the meaning of this observation. It would be well, if some whom it may concern would also take the hint it affords.

was for a few weeks to labor, had some pleasing expectations that they might find in him a future pastor, every way qualified for the important sphere of usefulness which so large and populous a town presented. But on the mind of Mr. Spencer far other impressions had been unhappily produced. From whatever sources he had drawn his information of the state of religion and manners in this place, it was certainly most incorrect—and such as led him to anticipate his visit with feelings of considerable uneasiness and reluctance. Nor did he seem at all anxious to conceal the fact, that his coming was the consequence of a necessity, to which he was compelled to bow. So deep was his prejudice against Liverpool, that it seems to have caused the only exception to that uniform submission with which he yielded to the arrangements made by his constituents for his labors. But on this occasion, he did not hesitate frankly to assure a gentleman, who meeting him in London, expressed a hope that they should soon have the pleasure of seeing him in Liverpool, that "it was not *his* wish to see Liverpool—and that although the committee had appointed him to go, he should do all in his power to prevail upon them to send some other student."

But a visit upon which so much depended, and whence such amazing consequences were to flow, could not be abandoned by a superintending Providence, to the obstacles of his prejudices, or the influence of his feelings. His destination was fixed. It was the voice of duty, and he obeyed. He arrived in Liverpool on Saturday, the 30th of June, 1810, and commenced his public labors on the following Sabbath.

Mr. Spencer selected for the subject of his first discourse, Luke xxiv. 32, "*And they said one to another, did not our hearts burn within us, while he talked with us by the way, and while he opened to us the Scriptures.*" In the afternoon he preached from Heb. xii. 24, "*And to the blood of sprinkling, which speaketh better things than the blood of Abel.*" And in the evening from 1 Cor. xv. 25, "*For he must reign till he hath put all enemies under his feet.*"

The impression produced by the labors of this Sabbath will be long remembered. The emotion then awakened has not subsided to this day. Every sermon that he preached tended to deepen the conviction of his piety and talents, and to endear him to the people. His lively, affectionate manner, and the simple but elegant style of his discourses, captivated all who heard him. Every sermon produced accessions to the congregation of such as, drawn by the report of his extraordinary powers, pressed to witness their display. The chapel soon became crowded to excess—and not alone the thoughtless and the gay, whom the charms of a persuasive eloquence and an engaging manner might attract, but pious and experienced Christians sat at his feet with deep attention and delight. There seemed to be indeed *a shaking amongst the drg bones.* A divine unction evidently attended his ministry, and such were the effects produced, that every beholder, with astonishment and admiration, cried " what hath God wrought !"

In his own views of Liverpool, too, a great change was wrought by the remarkable circumstances attendant on his ministry. The kind assiduities of the family under whose hospitable roof he resided, and an intercourse with the pious part of the congregation, which they carefully promoted, tended gradually to weaken his prejudices, and at length completely to turn the bias, and reverse the purpose of his mind. The period of his stay was limited to five Sabbaths ; but at the earnest solicitation of the people, he consented, after communicating with his friends in London, to add another to the number. And in the afternoon of the last Sabbath, he preached from Deut. xxxiii. 3, '*Yea, he loved the people,*' in such a style of endearment and affection, as seemed to warrant the indulgence of their warmest hopes. The last week of his visit was spent in the most delightful intercourse with Christian friends ; and on Tuesday, the 7th of August, he left Liverpool with reluctance and tears.

Very soon after his return to Hoxton, Mr. Spencer received from the church and congregation at Newington chapel, an unanimous and pressing invitation to accept the pastoral office over them. The call was dated on the 8th of August, 1810. After near seven weeks deliberation, Mr. Spencer returned an answer in the affirmative. In what exercises of mind these seven weeks were spent, those who knew the peculiar circumstances of his situation can well conceive. On the one hand—the unanimous request of a people to whom God had directed him contrary to his wish, and to whom he had become singularly endeared :—the imperious call of duty to a sphere of action for which his talents seemed every way adapted, in which his labors had been already remarkably successful, and which promised most extensive usefulness. These were circumstances of no common magnitude. But on the other hand, there were many powerful ties to bind him to the neighborhood of the metropolis. His family—his best friendships—his most endeared connections—the scenes of his early and honorable labors—all conspired in the prospect of his removal to so great a distance, to awaken the most painful and distressing feelings in his mind. And resolutely to resist the importunities of friends, the value of whose society we fully know—to rise superior to those local attachments which long and happy intercourse cannot fail to form—and to leave the circle to which time and frequent interchange of sentiment have rendered us familiar and endeared, for a land of strangers—involve a sacrifice which only the voice of duty can demand, or the hope of usefulness repay. Yet such are the sacrifices which the Christian minister must frequently be called to make; and whilst on his part they are with cheerfulness surrendered to the call of duty, and the cause of Christ, let those in whose particular behalf they are claimed, seek by every affectionate office of friendship, to blunt the edge of separation, and relieve as much as may be by kindness, the memory of distant friendships and endeared connections.

I insert a copy of Mr. Spencer's answer to the call which he received from the church and congregation at Newington; as it will afford to the reader an additional opportunity of obtaining an acquaintance with its amiable author.

TO THE INDEPENDENT CHURCH OF CHRIST, ASSEMBLING IN NEWINGTON CHAPEL, LIVERPOOL.

"MY CHRISTIAN FRIENDS—Being unwilling to keep you any longer in suspense than is absolutely necessary, upon the important subject of my settlement with a church and congregation, I feel it my duty to reply to your obliging and respectful invitation. You are well aware that I came amongst you influenced by the strongest prejudices against the place, and resolutely determined never to think of it as a sphere calculated for me. Whilst I was amongst you, however, several circumstances united to remove the strength of my prejudices, and I trust to make me determined by every appointed and lawful means to ascertain the will of God, and when ascertained, cheerfully to fulfil it, however opposed it might be to my private wishes and inclinations. A review of the partial degree of success with which my labors in Liverpool were honored, does afford me considerable pleasure, and I must say that I speak the real sentiments of my heart when I confess that the manner in which you, my respected friends and brethren in the gospel, have conducted this important affair, has raised you exceedingly in my esteem, and given me to believe that a preacher would find among you, as a people, those motives to diligenee and those sources of real happiness in the prosecution of his work, which, alas! are denied to many a faithful minister of the New Testament.

"When I regard you as a church and congregation, I feel anxiously concerned for your spiritual and eternal welfare, and indeed earnestly desire, if consistent with the good pleasure of His will, the great Head of the Church would make use of *me* to build you up in faith and holiness; but my motives for thinking favorably of your invitation arise also from other sources. I look at the state of thousands of inhabitants in that vast town, to many of whom I hope to be the instrument of conveying the 'joyful sound;' my soul longs that they may receive the salvation which is in Jesus Christ, with eternal glory, and influenced I have reason to believe by the direction of my God, I resolve to preach among them the unsearchable riches of Christ.

"I assure you, my fellow travelers to Zion, I can observe, with admiration, peculiarities in this dispensation which never before struck me in reference to any other situation. Oh, may it appear that this work and this counsel is of God!

'*Some* difficulties must be met, and some sacrifices must be made, *by me*, when I leave the scenes of my former exertions in the cause of Christ, for the sake of the people at Newington. But these are things which I must ever expect; these are circumstances which I resolved should never move me, when I first gave myself to God and His Christ!

"Truly believing then that I am acting under the direction of an all-wise Jehovah, and humbly asking that this may be made manifest in after days, *I accept the invitation* you have given me to exercise over you the pastoral office. I comply with your unanimous request, and shall from this day consider myself as solemnly bound to you, if you see it right to allow me the following requisitions:

"That I preach among you regularly but *twice on the Sabbath*, viz.: morning and evening. I mention this because I know that my constitution will not admit of three services in the day, and I am sure it is not consistent with your wishes, that I should prevent myself from future exertions by presuming on too much at first; and the plan I propose will, I am persuaded, after trial, prove beneficial rather than injurious to the cause at Newington. To preaching to you twice on the Sabbath and once in the week, I shall never have the least objection. My other wish is—

"That I may have in the spring of the year six weeks annually to myself, to visit my friends, and occasionally see other parts of the Lord's vineyard.

"I do not leave Hoxton academy till after Christmas, and perhaps may not be with you so early as you wish. It is my intention, however, to commence my labors among you, if convenient to yourselves, on the first Sabbath in February, 1811. Your sentiments on the subjects I have mentioned, you will be pleased to communicate to me as early as possible.

"And now just allow me, my respected friends, to request you not to form too sanguine expectations in reference to the pleasure you expect to enjoy when I become your pastor. You will doubtless find in me much to pity and to blame; yet it is my earnest prayer that you may never have to charge me with neglect in watching over you in the Lord; finally, I request your supplications for me at the throne of the heavenly Majesty, that a door of utterance may be opened unto me, that *on me* the communications of divine grace may ever be bestowed, that Christ may be magnified by my preaching and my life, that I may be preserved faithful unto death, and then receive a crown of life.

"Accept my cordial wishes for the prosperity of your own

souls, of your families, but especially of your Christian society and of the cause of Zion amongst you. Cease not to pray solemnly, fervently, and without intermission for me, and believe me yours, in our glorious Lord,

"THOMAS SPENCER."

HOXTON, *September* 26, 1810.

This official communication to the church was accompanied by a private letter to the friend, under whose roof he had resided during his occasional visit, and to whose care the preceding document was addressed.

HOXTON COLLEGE, *September* 19.

"MY DEAR SIR—If you wish immediately to know the purport of my enclosed answer to the respectful and pressing invitation I have received from Newington, turn to the 22d verse of the Epistle to Philemon.

"I hope you will forgive me for the long, the doubtful suspense, in which I have been obliged to detain you; in my own view I have acted rightly, and I have no doubt but you will say that it was all proper, when you come to hear my statement. It is astonishing what I have had to meet with through the *kindness* of my London friends—kindness you will think improperly manifested when I tell you that they, with very few exceptions, entreat, beg, and request, that I would not settle at Liverpool. I can only tell them that in this affair

'I hear a voice they cannot *hear;*
I see a hand they cannot *see!*'

And have the leadings of Providence lost their importance? or the direction of Heaven become merely matter of idle talk? I have not written individually to any person in Liverpool besides yourself: I should have found a difficulty in speaking of the business before I had made known my determination. By the first Sabbath in February next year I shall (God willing) be again in Liverpool, when I hope the presence of my covenant God will accompany me, and his Spirit grant me wide success. The prospect of leaving my friends and connections for so distant a place as Liverpool, and especially as many of them oppose the plan, sometimes fills me with melancholy gloom ; but 'thy will be done' is a petition that well becomes me in my situation; may I have grace given me to use it with a sincere and believing heart.

* * * * * * *

"I trust it will appear that the general good of the church of Christ, and of the inhabitants of Liverpool, is the object to which I have directed my warm and unremitting exertions. Farewell. I remain sincerely yours,

"THOMAS SPENCER."

To this may be added an extract from a letter dated September 1st, 1810.

"My mind still inclines to Liverpool, and that for the most substantial reasons. If I accept this invitation, I shall be obliged to make some sacrifices; but ought I not to make them cheerfully, when the honor of God and the happiness of immortal souls require them ? especially as I am bound not to count even my life dear unto me, so that I may finish my course with joy. The sacrifices to which I allude are chiefly, perhaps altogether, occasioned by absence from my friends and connections, and a removal from those interesting scenes of exertion which have witnessed my first efforts to disseminate divine truth, and in which I have been favored with some success."

Thus happily was a point of so much importance to the interests of religion in Liverpool determined. A consideration of the issue of *this* affair, together with many others perpetually occurring, should teach us to suspend our judgments of persons and places we have never seen—and should tend to weaken those unjust and injurious prejudices against them which we too hastily form—too tenaciously cherish. Often we picture to ourselves the most enchanting scenes, the most delightful associations, in connection with a spot we are about to visit, and are disappointed—and as often we find those charming scenes, and happy associations, in regions which our prejudices had invested with every thing gloomy and repulsive. Had Spencer yielded to the impulse of his feelings, he had never become pastor of a church in Liverpool. And although the memory of his lamented fate may induce, from feelings generally regarded as honorable to humanity, a wish that he had not—yet the *Christian* sees in this the hand of God—and, contemplating the mighty work which in his short ministry he was honored to perform, rejoices that, however mysterious the decree, it was ordered so. It is not for us to calculate whether he would have been *more* useful, or *less* useful, or *as* useful elsewhere—he *was* eminently useful in Liverpool—and though all must weep that he should be so soon, so suddenly removed—yet none who witnessed the extraordinary impression which his labors produced in so large and populous a town, but must rejoice in their success, and adore the Providence which brought him there.

Nor was it from the want of other calls that Mr. Spencer was induced to accept that which he received from Liverpool. Many were the churches which desired to enjoy his valuable ministry; amongst others, the following places may be named —*Kidderminster*, *Kentish Town*, *Jewin-street*, *Worthing*, *Southampton*, and *Tonbridge chapel*.

From the period of his acceptance of the call to Liverpool, till February, 1811, when he actually entered on the pastoral office there, his time was wholly occupied in the diligent pursuit of his studies, and the labors of the pulpit. Not a Sabbath passed, but witnessed twice or thrice his faithful publication of the gospel of peace. On Sunday, the 26th of August, he revisited Dorking—a spot endeared to him by the beauty of its scenery—but more by the memory of those happy hours, which introduced him to the knowledge and esteem of a most beloved and valuable friend.

The first Sabbath in November he spent at Brighton, where he preached three times in the pulpit of the Rev. Mr. Styles.

Returning to town he continued preaching in and about London till the close of the year, when he again visited Brighton, at which place he entered on the year 1811—the last of his life.

In what way his mind was exercised during this period—and how his principles as a Christian triumphed over his feelings as a man in the prospect of a long and painful separation from those he loved —may be seen by the following letter to a friend in Liverpool :—

HOXTON, *Dec. 5th,* 1810.

"MY DEAR SIR—I am persuaded that you will excuse my neglecting to write to you so long, when you recollect that the hope I daily entertained of seeing you in town appeared to represent my troubling you with an epistle as unnecessary. I am extremely pleased to hear of the increase and welfare of your family; I cannot but feel an interest in their prosperity and happiness ; may the Lord pour his Spirit upon your seed, and his blessing upon your offspring, that they may spring up as among the grass, as willows by the water courses ! I suppose I need not inform you, that I anticipate my journey to Liverpool with mingled emotions of mind. The idea of a long and painful separation from my connections does certainly at times overwhelm me with melancholy gloom ; I have not yet learned to conquer my feelings, nor am I particularly eminent for philosophic heroism. The idea that I am going where divine Providence has directed me, does occasionally impart to me strong consolation ; may my wishes as to extensive usefulness among you be answered; may they be exceeded in the prosperity of the church and congregation, and in the increase of spirituality and holy enjoyment in my own soul !

"I am glad you are successful in getting acceptable supplies ; this is a point which should be attended to. I should like the congregation to have the best of preachers. My books, &c. I must send from London before Christmas day, that I may have no trouble with them after my return from Brighton.

"I am extremely happy in the prospect of being with your family on my first entrance into Liverpool ; it will be far superior to my being with strangers. This half year has been a trying one as to preaching engagements, both on Sabbaths, and on week days. I continue supplying Hoxton, and the New

Chapel, Somer's Town, till Christmas: the day after Christmas day, I hope to go to Brighton, to stay there three Sabbaths, and to return on the 17th of January, to supply Roydon and Hertford the next week; and the last Sabbath in January, to take my leave of this part of the kingdom by two sermon at Hoxton. * * * * * * * * *

"Tell our friends at Newington chapel that I am tolerably well, and wish to be kindly remembered to them. Farewell, my valued friend. I am sincerely yours,

"THOMAS SPENCER."

The purposes expressed in this letter were accomplished according to the order in which they are stated. He visited Brighton, and preached on the last Sabbath of the old year three times, at Mr. Styles' chapel—in the evening a sermon adapted to the season, from 1 John ii. 17, "And the world passeth away, and the lust thereof; but he that doeth the will of God abideth for ever!" On the evening of the 1st of January, 1811, he preached an appropriate discourse at the Countess of Huntingdon's chapel, and on the following Thursday, and three times on the Sunday, he preached at Mr. Styles'. On the Monday evening, being the first Monday in the month, the missionary prayer meeting was held in Brighton, when he delivered a most animated and impressive address from Matt. xiii. 16–17, "Blessed are your eyes for they see, and your ears for they hear; for verily I say unto you, that many prophets and righteous men have desired to see those things which ye see, and have not seen them; and to hear those things which ye hear, and have not heard them." He continued another Sabbath in Brighton, and left that place some time in the following week. Passing through London, he went into Hertfordshire. On Sunday, January the 20th, he preached at Roydon, morning and afternoon, and at Hoddesdon in the evening. On the Tuesday evening he preached at Hertford, and slept again under his paternal roof. On Wednesday evening he preached at Stansted, and on Thursday evening again at Hertford. This was, I believe, his last visit to his native town, and to his father's house! The separation which then took place between himself and his beloved family was final. The farewell which he bade to the scenes of his infancy and childhood was eternal! I cannot suppress the melancholy feeling which this reflection has awakened in my mind. I am arrived at length upon the eve of a mournful detail, which all along I have anticipated with emotions of distress. Alas! that one so useful should be so soon removed! And that ere we enter on the solemn engagements of his pastoral life, we should be compelled to notice circumstances so closely connected with his death!

The following Sabbath, January 27th, was the last he spent in London. On that day he preached in the morning at Hoxton chapel, from Phil. iii. 8, "Yea, doubtless, and I count all things but loss for the excellency of the knowledge of Christ Jesus my Lord." And in the evening at Tonbridge chapel, from 2 Cor. iv. 3, "But if our gospel be hid, it is hid to them that are lost." The labors of this Sabbath completed his engagements at Hoxton and Tonbridge chapels ; but on the evening of the following day (Monday,) he took an affectionate leave of his beloved friends—the constituents—the tutors—the students—and the congregation at Hoxton, from the pulpit of that chapel. The crowd that pressed to hear his last sermon (for so it proved) in London was immense. One common sentiment of attachment and grief seemed to pervade the assembly. A friend charged him on that occasion not to play upon the passions. Not that he was in the habit of doing this ; but there appeared on this occasion a probability that he might. To that suggestion he replied, that "neither his feelings nor his conscience would admit of such trifling." He addressed the people on this interesting occasion from those memorable words of Paul—Acts xx. 24, "But none of these things move me, neither count I my life dear unto me, so that I may finish my course with joy, and the ministry which I have received of the Lord Jesus."

Thus were Spencer's labors in the metropolis closed for ever—labors, the renewal of which thousands anticipated with delight. But he was ripening fast for glory—and rapidly advancing to the termination of his course. Yea, the impression of his excellence—the feeling of regret at his departure—was yet strong and lively in the hearts of many, when the tidings of his death shed a deeper sorrow through the scenes and circles which he had edified by his public instructions, or enlivened by his private friendship!

It was on the 28th of January, that Mr. Spencer preached his farewell sermon at Hoxton chapel—and it was on the 15th of August, in the same year, in the same pulpit—and to nearly the same congregation—that his funeral sermon was delivered by Rev. Henry Foster Burder, one of the tutors of the academy. In that discourse, a just and elegant tribute was paid to the mingled piety and talent which formed the charm of his ministry. From the known endowments of the preacher, and from the opportunities which he enjoyed of obtaining a correct estimate of Mr. Spencer's powers, that tribute must derive considerable propriety and force: and as it chiefly regards his ministerial labors in London, I shall close these imperfect memoirs of them with an extract from it.

"During the last two years of our valuable friend's residence at Hoxton, he was very frequently engaged in preaching in London and its vicinity. As this chapel has been, on many occasions, the scene of his labors, and has been often thronged with the multitudes attracted by his ability and piety, I need scarcely attempt an estimate of his pulpit talents. That they were eminent—that they were brilliant—that they were captivating—will not, I think, be denied by any who witnessed their exhibition. He undoubtedly displayed no small degree of pulpit eloquence, and his eloquence was distinguished by characteristic features. It was not the kind of eloquence in which a youth of genius might be expected most to excel, and of which luxuriance of imagination constitutes the chief attraction; it was not a peculiar vivacity of fancy, which gave life to his addresses, although in this respect they were not deficient; but they rather owed their effect to the energy and animation infused by the ardor of his soul, and to the unaffected fervor of his religious feelings, the impression of which was aided by no small advantages of person, voice, and elocution. In endeavoring rightly to appreciate his qualifications for the duties of the Christian ministry, I must not omit to notice the truly edifying manner in which he conducted the devotional exercises of the pulpit. His gift in prayer was peculiarly excellent. The language of his petitions seemed to breathe the ardent aspirations of a heart alive to God, and accustomed to enjoy fellowship with the Father, and with his Son Jesus Christ.

That he was maturing fast for the enjoyment of his reward, even when he left London to commence his pastoral engagements, is a conviction indelibly impressed upon the minds of those who were accustomed to attend his preaching, or mingle in his society. They remember certain expressions, both of countenance and language, which seemed to indicate a tone of piety—a spirituality of feeling—too exalted for a long continuance here. And it is to be regretted, that such expressions, at the time so powerful in their influence, and so carefully preserved by a tenacious memory, no pen—no pencil can portray. Hence the sermons of animated and extemporary preachers, when introduced to us from the press, lose half their force and beauty. The scope of the discourse—the process of the argument—may be indeed preserved; but the unpremeditated, momentary flashes of holy fervor, and of brilliant genius, cannot. The eloquence of the eye—the expression of the countenance—the meaning which is sometimes thrown into every limb and muscle of the frame, are wanting. And though it is pleasing to possess a memorial of those whom living we revered and loved, yet the imperfection of the copy only deepens our regret at the loss of the original. In the preaching of Spencer, it seemed as though he saw before him every object he described—and felt the full force—the vast importance of every subject upon which he spoke."

Preaching one evening at Back-street, Horsley Down, and speaking of the reward of the faithful gospel minister, "Methinks," said he, "I already hear the melodious accents of the Saviour's voice, saying, '*Well done, good and faithful servant, en-*

ter into the joy of thy Lord.'" It was remarked, that he appeared as though he heard a voice, personally addressing him. His anticipation was in a very few months realized!

Anxious for the usefulness and variety of his ministry, he begged of his friend, upon his leaving London, to send him any useful pamphlets or works which might come out; "Let me know," said he, "when popular ministers are in town—the texts they take for particular occasions—festivals, &c., the settling or removal of my fellow students, &c."

The last time he was with his friend alone, prior to his setting off for Liverpool, their approaching separation was, as may be well imagined, the topic of discourse—when, with his own peculiar affection and energy, he said :—

"Through Christ when we together came,
In singleness of heart,
We met, oh Jesus! in thy name,
And in thy name we part.

We part in body, *not in mind,*
Our minds continue one;
And each to each, in Jesus join'd,
We happily go on.

Present in spirit still we are,
And intimately nigh;
While on the wings of faith and prayer,
We Abba! Father! cry.

Oh, may thy Spirit, dearest Lord,
  In all our travels still
Direct and be our constant guard
  To Zion's holy hill.

Oh! what a joyful meeting there,
  Beyond these changing shades;
White are the robes we then shall wear,
  And crown upon our heads.

Haste, Lord, and bring us to the day
  When we shall dwell at home;
Come, oh Redeemer, come away;
  Oh, Jesus, quickly come."

CHAPTER VI.

Mr. Spencer commences his pastoral labors at Newington Chapel —Suddenly called by affliction to Brighton—His fears relieved —Correspondence—Success of his ministry—Lays the foundation stone of a New Chapel for his Congregation—Correspondence—Ordination—His first administration of the Lord's Supper—Death—Funeral—Concluding Reflections.

On Sunday, 3d of February, 1811, Mr. Spencer commenced his stated, pastoral labors at Newington chapel, Liverpool. He was then just twenty years of age—possessed of every endowment that could render him eminent as a minister—and every amiable disposition that could endear him as a friend. The people of his charge, together with numbers who participated with them in their joy, hailed his entrance on his sacred duties with delight. From him they fondly anticipated a long series of varied and useful instructions—on him they gazed with admiration, as affording them no mean example of a holy and devoted life—and to him they looked with pleasure as their children's friend. That he was prepared to meet these high expectations, none who have contemplated the superior endowments of his mind can, for a moment, doubt—

his literary attainments, though not splendid, were respectable—his theological knowledge was considerable—his acquaintance with mankind indeed was scanty; he had only moved amongst the excellent of the earth; but this, while it might expose him to certain inconveniences, gave him this advantage—that he appeared in all the native ingenuousness of unsuspecting youth. His love of study was great, which insured a constant supply of interesting materials for his public ministry—whilst he possessed a facility, an ease, an elegance, in the communication of his thoughts, displayed by few. To all these, he added the graces of the Spirit in no common degree—the glorious attributes of a soul eminently devoted to God—a solemn awe of his sacred office—an habitual reference to the final account he should be called to render—and an ardent zeal for the Redeemer's glory! Such was Spencer when he entered on the duties of his stated ministry!

But I shall justify this sketch of his character by some extracts from his letters.

In one dated Brighton, January 9th, 1811, he says—

"I dread the termination of the happiness I now enjoy. It will be the commencement of a long and agonizing separation. Oh! that henceforth I may live more devotedly to God than I have ever yet done. I can truly say this is my desire; for to be a preacher of the gospel, and not to feel its *due abiding* influence on the heart, is awful indeed. Since I have been here

I have trembled for myself, when I have recollected the numerous follies of the four years I have spent at Hoxton. The Lord pardon me, and teach me to be more holy. Pray for me.

"Affectionately yours, ———"

The following letter was written the day after his arrival in Liverpool.

TO MR. JOHN HADDON.

LIVERPOOL, *February 2d*, 1811.

"MY DEAREST FRIEND—I am safely arrived at the scene of my future labors. My journey, though long, was far less irksome than any one I have before undertaken. The roads were bad; this made us late in our arrival at Liverpool. We did not reach it till a quarter before twelve last night. The short time that I have yet spent here has been quite *pleasant*—it has been *happy*. The serious people of the congregation have already paid me many kind and Christian attentions. With the blessing of the Master whom I serve, I expect to-morrow to spend a very delightful Sabbath. My best feelings for the glory of our Lord and the increase of his kingdom, will I hope be more strongly excited than ever they have yet been. I cannot but think that the Head of the Church has some great work to accomplish in Liverpool, and the desire of my heart is that I may be the instrument employed to effect it. Oh! for a large measure of the influence of the blessed Spirit to render me ardently pious, and to keep me zealous in my endeavors to do good to souls. I know *here* are numbers who *pray* earnestly for me, and whilst these pious people besiege the throne of grace on my behalf, I will not fear that my God will desert me. To be holy and to be useful at this moment, appears to be the first wish of my heart. Do you say, 'indulgent God, let it be accomplished!'

"I am tired with my journey and pressed for time. Believe me in the bonds of Christian affection, Sincerely yours,

THOMAS SPENCER.'

According to his anticipation, he did enjoy on the Sabbath a happy day, although in the morning he was considerably agitated by the peculiarly solemn circumstances of his new and most responsible situation. In the morning his text was admirably adapted to the occasion. Gen. xxviii. 22—"*And Jacob vowed a vow, saying, if God will be with me and keep me in this way that I go, and will give me bread to eat and raiment to put on, so that I come again to my father's house in peace: then shall the Lord be my God, and this stone which I have set up for a pillar, shall be God's house, and of all that thou shalt give me I will surely give the tenth unto thee.*" In the evening he preached from 1 Cor. xv. 49, "*And as we have borne the image of the earthy, we shall also bear the image of the heavenly.*" In the course of the ensuing week, he wrote as follows:

LIVERPOOL, *Feb.* 7, 1811.

"Oh! what a memorable day to me was the first Sabbath I spent in this place; every circumstance that took place appeared worthy of attention and big with events; never before had I entered a pulpit, with those awful, solemn feelings with which I was impressed that morning. The idea of appearing in a new character, of entering on a station which I have no view of relinquishing till the day of my death; the weight of responsibility which attaches to the ministerial character; the dread lest I should act in any way unworthy of my sacred office; all these things would naturally impart an unusual solemnity to the mind. ON THAT DAY heaven is my witness of the holy resolutions I formed. Oh that God may ever enable me to put them in execution."

The attention which his labors had excited, while an occasional supply, was repeated, now that he had commenced his stated ministry. Soon the chapel became again crowded to excess. The town was filled with his praise—the most respectable of the inhabitants were perpetually disappointed in their attempts to hear him, not being in any way able to gain admittance to the chapel, so excessive was the throng. His coming seemed to be the commencement of a new era in the religious interests of Liverpool—at least amongst the dissenters. The prejudices of many were gradually subdued. The tone of public sentiment, with respect to that class of Christians amongst whom he labored, considerably raised. Many, by no means anxious to conceal their opposition to his principles, were compelled to pay a just, though reluctant tribute to the fascinations of his eloquence ; and many whom the fame of that eloquence brought beneath the sound of his voice were savingly converted unto God ; and of these, some are at this moment honorable members of the church of which he was the pastor. So far from being elated by his popularity, and rendered vain by the uncommon attention he excited and received from all ranks—every Sabbath, while he grew in public estimation, he seemed to sink in his own esteem, in humble acknowledgments of his own unworthiness, and in a yet deeper sense of his awful obligations. The next is an extract of a letter to his father.

LIVERPOOL, *Feb.* 26, 1811.

"I assure you I have every reason to believe, that this is the sphere in which Infinite wisdom intends me to move. My congregation is vast every time I dispense the word of life. A general spirit of hearing seems excited in this large town—the prospect is in every respect encouraging, and I am induced to hope, that great good will be done. I feel the awful responsibility that attaches to my employment; and when I recollect the multitude of souls committed to my care, I tremble, and exclaim, '*Who is sufficient for these things?*' I often think how different is my situation now, to what it was when I lived at my father's house. I am called to an active and laborious scene. Once it was enough for me just to execute your wishes, and then in the quiet enjoyment of our own family circle to experience satisfaction and comfort. Now God has blessed me by making me a blessing to others. May he preserve me faithful and make me an honorable and holy Christian!"

Scarcely had Spencer entered on the full discharge of his public duties at Liverpool, when severe affliction in the endeared circle of his connections at Brighton called him to that place. A letter written about this period, displays the agonized state of his feelings—but abounds with expressions of holy acquiescence in the Divine dispensations. He left Liverpool on the 18th of March, accompanied by the valued friend under whose roof he resided, and whose guest he was during his first visit. Arrived in London, the following hasty note bespeaks the anguish of his mind:

LUDGATE STREET, *Tuesday night.*

"MY DEAR FRIEND—This moment I am within a few doors of you, but cannot reach you. Mr. H—— is with me: we have just got in from Liverpool, and start for B. to-morrow, at seven o'clock in the morning. I shall write to you from Brighton. Pray for me: I am in unutterable distress. Farewell. T. SPENCER."

The Sabbath after his arrival in Brighton, he did not engage in any public service. Much of the day doubtless was spent in administering comfort to the afflicted. The fears which he had sometimes been induced to harbor, were not, however, realized; health slowly returned. His friend was under the necessity of hastening to Liverpool, after the lapse of a few days—but Mr. Spencer remained at Brighton. His affectionate heart dictated the following letter, to welcome his friend on his arrival home:

TO MR. H———.

BRIGHTON, *Thursday morning.*

"MY DEAR AND VALUED FRIEND—I am pleasing myself with the idea that before this reaches Liverpool, you will have shared the hearty and affectionate welcome of a beloved and happy family: this is a blessing which you know how to improve and enjoy aright, and for which I am persuaded you will express the sincerest gratitude to the God of our mercies. May the same kind and watchful Providence which has, I trust, led you to your home in peace and safety, also preserve and defend me, that I may be again restored to the church and congregation at Newington, and be enabled to pursue a course of active and useful labor in the services of the Master whom I hope I really love.

"I frequently think that by this visit to Brighton on so mournful an occasion, I shall be better fitted to sympathize with the afflicted in general, and be taught how to commend them to God. Before this I had not been at all familiar with scenes of sorrow and distress. In the two sick rooms you visited last Monday evening, I have learned lessons which I shall never forget, and the benefit of which may probably be communicated to the church of Christ, as well as to myself.

"Our Redeemer himself, in order to be rendered a merciful and compassionate high-priest, was '*tempted like as we are;*' endured the various ills and sorrows that flesh is heir to; and hence (oh! blessed sympathy and kind relief,) he is able to succor them that are tempted.

"Next Sabbath morning I intend to preach at the Countess' chapel, and in the evening at Mr. Styles'; pray for me, that I may be supported and blest. It is still my design to reach Liverpool on Friday night: tell our friends that they may expect to see me in the pulpit on the following Sabbath. May I be there richly ladened with the good things of the kingdom; may I be animated by a mind fraught with rich and heavenly favors. I am sure that if my God restores those who are so dear to me to perfect health and strength, my heart, hard as it is, will not be insensible to the feelings of gratitude. No; it will leap as doth a hart; it will pant with the sensations of unutterable joy. I have received a very kind letter from our worthy friend, Mr. N. H——; do tell him it afforded me real pleasure, and give him my hearty thanks for his solicitude for my happiness. I hope you are going on well with the new chapel business; if possible, let us make Satan tremble; against the kingdom of darkness let us use the most active and unwearied exertions, and God shall bless us in our deed. I wish I could have attended the meeting of the Bible Society; my absence, however, was unavoidable. Give my affectionate regards to my dear friend Mrs. H—— and to your dear children. I hope I shall soon see you happy and well. Your unremitting kindness to me has produced impressions upon my mind which will never be obliterated. I shall be happy again to mix with your family circle, and to occupy my own pulpit.

To the hearers at Newington I intend to show my regard and best wishes by constantly laboring in their service.

"I am more than ever yours,

"THOMAS SPENCER."

The uncommon attention excited in Liverpool by Mr. Spencer's ministry, soon suggested the necessity of providing more accommodation than Newington chapel could afford, for the numbers who were anxious to enjoy the benefit of his stated labors. At first the idea of enlarging the old place of worship presented itself; but some difficulties arising, this was relinquished, and early in March it was resolved, that a chapel capable of accommodating two thousand persons should be erected—a committee of management was appointed—and an eligible spot of ground soon selected for the purpose. A most judicious plan for the building was proposed and adopted—the dimensions of which were thirty-two yards long outside, and twenty-one yards and a half broad outside. A liberal subscription was soon obtained, and the affair was in a state of such forwardness on his return from Brighton, that on the 15th of April, Mr. Spencer laid the first stone of the chapel, in the presence of an immense assembly—computed to consist of about six thousand persons. On that truly interesting occasion, he delivered an appropriate address, and solemnly dedicated the place to God by prayer.

About this time Mr. Spencer removed from the

hospitable abode of his early friend, with whom he had resided on his first coming to Liverpool, in order to lodge with Mr. Thurston Lassel, in the Park Road; a pleasant situation, about half a mile from the town. It was the lot of Spencer to be beloved in every circle which he entered—and none who were honored to behold his excellence, and enjoy his friendship, ever resigned him without feelings of the deepest regret. I cannot deny myself the pleasure of extracting a sentence or two from the willing testimony which that friend has borne to the sterling worth of his most amiable guest. I am the more anxious to do this, as it will unveil his character in private life, and show us what he was as the member of a family.

"We had the great advantage of Mr. Spencer's pious conversation and fervent prayers in the family for near four months, for he did not leave us till the latter end of April; it was indeed a pleasant and, I trust, a profitableseason, which we often review with great delight. With what pleasing emotions have we often surrounded our domestic altar and witnessed the fervor of his addresses to the God and Father of our Lord Jesus Christ. In this delightful employ he never seemed to engage with half a heart, his whole soul was alive to the service of his God: he was serious in a serious cause, nor did any circumstances that arose ever seem to unfit him for the discharge of religious duties. Morning and evening he generally engaged in prayer at family worship; the variety he produced on these occasions has often astonished us; it was impossible to trace anything like repetition; every prayer seemed quite new, and gave fresh proof of the powers of his mind and the ardor of his soul.

"Mr. Spencer naturally possessed an amiable disposition, and was innocently cheerful; no one could say that gloom or melancholy was connected with his religion. In his manners he was simple and unaffected; any thing like ostentation or parade he disliked exceedingly; he would always, if possible, avoid mixing with large parties. The company of serious, pious, plain Christians was his delight. He was kind, generous, and tender-hearted; the wants of the poor and necessitous he was ready and willing to relieve; 'to do good and communicate he forgot not, knowing that with such sacrifices God is well pleased.'"

But whilst all around him was prosperous and happy—whilst his ministry was successful beyond his most sanguine expectations, and hundreds were anxious to administer to his comfort; his heart was the victim of anxiety and grief. The continued and alarming indisposition of his friends at Brighton, inspired his delicate and susceptible mind with the most gloomy and agonizing fears. It was well. His Heavenly Father saw he needed some thorn in the flesh, under the circumstances of his unexampled popularity, to prevent his being exalted above measure, and to preserve his soul in a frame of holy solemnity, and humble reliance on himself. Lest the sun of his prosperity should dazzle him too much, these friendly clouds were permitted to intervene. Their salutary influence may be traced in the following letter:

TO MR. JOHN HADDON.

LIVERPOOL, *April* 16, 1811.

"MY DEAR FRIEND—The melancholy state of depression in

which I have been held so long must form my excuse for neglecting the sacred duties of friendship, in not writing before this to you. Oh! how soon can Jehovah blast our hopes of happiness from creature comforts, to convince us of the uncertainty of all earthly good! We *must* 'walk by faith,' and live in the exercise of a lively hope, that we shall obtain a better and more permanent rest. I scarcely dare, for my own part, anticipate any other kind of happiness on earth, but what may arise from communion with the Saviour, and the delightful work in which I am engaged, which, I must say, amidst all my trials affords me increasing happiness and pleasure. Thanks be to God, the work of the Lord is prospering in my hand; and though I may not have much pleasure in this world myself, I hope I shall be the means, in the hands of the Holy Spirit, of putting into the possession of my fellow creatures, real and substantial felicity; *this*, the gospel I am enabled to preach is sent to confer. The next week I expect to go to my lodgings. I shall reside in a retired, rural and delightful spot, with a family (three only in number) who belong to the congregation in which the Lord has graciously called me to labor; it is about half a mile from the town, away from all bustle and noise, commanding a most delightful and enchanting prospect of both land and water. My study affords a most extensive view of fields and hills, the river and the adjacent county, (Cheshire.) I am persuaded it is every thing I could wish for as a plan for my residence. In that pleasant study* I expect

* To me it is a melancholy reflection that I should so soon become the occupier of a spot in which he had fondly pictured to himself so many years of pleasure. In his own study; on his own table; in his own chair; I am now drawing up these memoirs of his life; around me are the fruits of his short but laborious exertions; and immediately before my eyes the path by which he descended to his grave! From every object within my view, I am admonished *"work whilst it is day, for the night cometh, when no man can work."* I would that every loiterer in the vineyard of Christ were attended by mementos such as these.

to spend much time, and enjoy some degree of pleasure ; and my dear friend will believe me when I assure him that amidst the afflictions which our righteous Father judges the best school for me, it would tend to alleviate my sorrows, and cheer my spirits, could he be in my new study, and as he did in my old one, occasionally spend an hour or two with me in social chat.

"Yesterday I laid the foundation stone of my new chapel—gave an address upon the spot, and dedicated the place to God in solemn prayer. The auditory consisted of not less than five thousand people, who were all fixed in their attention. May I, on that ground, often find a solace for my cares in the public worship of God! May he bless the undertaking! May his eyes and his heart be there perpetually!

"Farewell. I *must* break off by assuring you that I am sincerely yours, THOMAS SPENCER."

The week following that in which he laid the foundation stone of the new chapel, Mr. Spencer made an excursion into the country, and preached on the Tuesday evening at *Darwen*, and on the Thursday evening at a meeting of ministers at *Blackburn*.

During this journey, he suffered much from the complaint to which he was subject; but although laboring under the pressure of severe indisposition, in the pulpit he rose superior to the influence of langour and pain; and his exertions on that journey are still spoken of by those who witnessed them, and they were many, with delight.

On his return to Liverpool, Mr. Spencer received a melancholy summons to Chester, to attend the funeral of his early and amiable friend, the Rev.

Ebenezer White, and to deliver the oration at his grave. His obligations and attachment to that excellent man have already been recorded. When arrived at the scene of death, his delicate mind seemed overwhelmed in an agony of grief. He stood weeping in unutterable distress over the cold remains of his departed friend. His bosom formed for friendship, and even then the seat of no ordinary sorrow, was illy prepared to sustain the pressure of a stroke, by which he was suddenly bereft of one who had discharged for him the relations of the father, the tutor, and the friend! Mr. Walter White, who was the witness of his grief, has thus described it: —"I shall not easily forget this dear young man's behavior on the evening preceding my brother's funeral at Chester. We were standing together by the side of the coffin, viewing the corpse—he wept excessively, and clasping his hands with great emotion, exclaimed, 'Oh! that I may but finish my course like him!' and turning to me, he said with his usual energy, 'Oh! what a fine thought it is, that the *bodies* of the saints are purchased by Christ as well as their souls.' And then passing his friendly hand gently over my brother's face, he said, with great emphasis, 'This body is the purchase of Christ: it cannot be lost—it must revive again—all these limbs must resume their activity. Oh! with what fine sentiments and ideas does the Christian religion furnish us to what any of the heathen systems did!'"

Though excessively agitated in his whole frame, he yet sustained himself to deliver at the grave a funeral oration, characterized by tender and solemn eloquence—the eloquence of feeling and of piety.

His letters to his friends for some time after this event, contain occasional allusions to the death of Mr. White—and in a way which proves how much he loved him—how deeply he deplored his loss. In one he says—

"I have lately been visiting a scene of death at Chester; my worthy friend, Mr. White, is now no more in this world; but I doubt not he shines illustriously in another state of existence. When I was eleven years of age he came to Hertford, and used to spend a great deal of time with me; ah! little did I then think I should have to deliver a funeral address at his interment, and so far away too from the place with which we were then familiar. Peace to his ashes, and eternal joy to his departed spirit! and ere long may I meet him in that blessed state, where disappointments will no longer be his lot or mine."

On the Sabbath evening following, Mr. Spencer preached a funeral sermon for his friend, in his own pulpit at Liverpool, from Deut. xxxiv. 5, "*So Moses, the servant of the Lord, died there in the land of Moab, according to the word of the Lord.*" The sermon was solemn and impressive. Thus we record the mortality of others, and drop into eternity ourselves. On that Sabbath evening three months, his own funeral sermon was preached in the same pulpit.

Mr. Spencer seemed now to become more and more interested in his important work ; the scenes of every day appeared to present it to his mind in some new and interesting light. The powers of his soul were absorbed in its concerns. He could think and speak of nothing else. In the pulpit, or in the preparations for it—in serious conversation with his friends—or in the chambers of the deceased and dying, he was at home. He lived but for the discharge of his high obligations ; and in the prosecution of his arduous work he was both useful and happy. With astonishing rapidity his character and talents ripened. He seemed to grow daily in favor both with God and man. All that *saw* him, admired him, there was something so engaging in his manner—all that *heard* him, respected and revered him, so serious and important were the truths which he delivered—all that *knew* him, loved him, for his was every amiable quality that could excite and retain the best affections of the human heart.

Valuable as our public institutions for the education of students for the Christian ministry really are, they can afford but an inadequate conception of the complicated duties of the pastoral office. The work of the pulpit is perhaps, after all, not the most difficult or trying part of the pastor's employ —and the reason why so many fail when called into active service in the church of God, is probably this, that they never calculated upon one-half of the engagements which then press upon their regard. They had formed a most incorrect estimate of the numerous claims which the office of the ministry involves, upon their time—their talents—their patience—and their faith. They had imagined, that in the composition and delivery of sermons was the chief of their labor—and that when this duty was discharged, by far the heaviest burden was removed. The visitation of the sick, with all the peculiar delicacy, prudence, affection, and faithfulness which it requires—the consolation of the distressed, with all the caution and skill which the varieties of their grief demand—the reproof and admonition of the irregular, with all the mingled tenderness, constancy and fidelity, which, in such difficult cases, must be exercised—the care of the young, with that adaptation of temper and manner to their capacities which, in the work of catechising, familiar conversation or public instruction, is absolutely necessary—the advising, comforting and relieving the distressed, the embarrassed, and the indigent, who all press to him for counsel, solace and relief;—these, and unnumbered other duties connected with the pastoral office, are but seldom contemplated with sufficient seriousness amid the exercises of a college. And even in the *public* engagements of ministry, the circumstances of the *pastor* differ materially from those of the *student*. The pulpit compositions of the student are *general;* those of the pastor must be *par-*

ticular. The student has no individual case to suit; the congregation to whom he preaches are strangers to him; the pastor has as many cases as there are people committed to his charge. The student can select his topics, and adapt his preaching to the tone of his mind—or if peculiar reluctance should be felt, may enjoy the repose he wishes, and not preach at all; but the pastor *must* appear at the stated hours of worship, whatever be the frame and temper of his soul. Often he is called to the discussion of subjects but illy adapted to his feelings; and it becomes his duty to administer consolation to others which *his* bleeding bosom needs, but cannot take. He must sometimes cover with a smiling countenance an aching heart; and his lips must exhort to tranquillity and confidence in God, whilst over his own spirit broods the cloud of anxiety and sorrow! Happy shall I be if the perusal of these imperfect memoirs tend to excite in the breast of any a spirit of Christian sympathy and prayer for the ministers of the gospel; or if these statements of the labors and anxieties of their office, shall induce those to pause and count the mighty cost, who may be thoughtlessly pressing forward to the arduous work. Let such remember the worth of souls —the guilt of becoming accessory to their ruin— and the solemn account all must render at the bar of God, who have taken upon themselves the responsibility of seeking, by every possible method, to promote their eternal interests.

The considerations seemed ever present to the view of Spencer. The feelings of an affectionate and faithful pastor's heart breathe in every sentence the following letter.

TO MR. HADDON.

LIVERPOOL, *May* 31, 1811.

"MY DEAR FRIEND—You really must excuse my apparent neglect in not writing you before; but if you knew the number and pressing nature of my avocations, you would not wonder. I now feel, and deeply too, the dreadful responsiblity of my employment. I have sick beds constantly to attend—a numerous congregation committed to my charge—a character to sustain, which ought ever to appear *free*, even from the very *appearance* of evil—and all this with the most depressed state of feelings, and but little experience of the arduous duties the course of the Christian ministry embraces. Often do I exclaim, '*who is sufficient for these things?*' Oh! that I may find that my sufficiency is of God. I am led at times to derive encouragement from the good which I trust the blessed Spirit has accomplished by my feeble labors; but then I think again of my youth, my inexperience, my exposure to the fiery darts of the wicked one, and the *possibility* of my eventually becoming a '*a cast-away.*'

"Oh! there are many feelings of this painful class in my mind, which few can share, which I cannot dare frequently to communicate.

"All this and much more, do I daily feel. I wish you were with me. I could say a thousand things I cannot write, and you might console me with the comforts wherewith you yourself are comforted of God! Do pray for me, for I need it more than ever now. Often do I dispense to others that consolation I cannot take myself.

"Thank you a thousand times for Cecil. Oh! they are admirable; what a character was he. Oh! that the Head of the Church would but make me like him. The tracts are just what I wanted; may a Divine blessing attend the distribution of them. Farewell!

"I am yours affectionately,

"THOMAS SPENCER."

In another letter he writes:

"Cecil's works are a high treat indeed: you cannot think how I enjoy the perusal of them. There are such valuable hints for ministers—such inestimable directions, that I hope I shall evince the benefit of reading them to the last hour of the day in which I am appointed to work!"

The church and congregation at Liverpool now became anxious for Mr. Spencer's ordination, and Thursday the 27th of June was appointed for that solemn service. In the following letter he announced it to his early friend and patron, Mr. Wilson, whose presence on that occasion he earnestly desired.

TO THOMAS WILSON, ESQ.

LIVERPOOL, *June* 4, 1811.

"MY DEAR SIR—I am happy to inform you that Thursday, June the 29th, is the day appointed for my ordination. Will you allow me to expect the pleasure of your presence and society on that solemnity? If you were here you would be pleased with my prospect of usefulness, and you would be able to suggest some hints to our friends about the new chapel. Little things are apt to be neglected, and their neglect, though apparently trifling, would spoil the whole concern. We may well congratulate each other on the triumph the dissenters have obtained over an intolerant and oppressive spirit. They have imagined a vain thing: the Lord reigneth, let the people tremble. You know the great depression of spirits under which I have for some time labored; may the Lord appear a present help in this time of trouble. The walls of Zion are to be built, it appears, in troublous times, for such they are to me; yet I would submissively commit my cause to God; he may ordain that the benefit of his church, and the good of others, shall be promoted by the ills I endure. You know poor White, of Chester, has received the end of his faith—the salvation of his soul; I delivered the oration over his grave. Mr. Fletcher, of Blackburn, preached his funeral sermon. We are all dying creatures, hastening to the world of immortality. I think that lately the world has appeared to me in its true light—'*it passeth away.*' May we by every dispensation of Providence be rendered more meet for the inheritance of the saints in light: in due time may we be clothed upon with our house, which is from heaven. Present my kind respects to Mrs. and Miss Wilson. I hope you will try to visit Liverpool by the time mentioned. Wishing much to see you, I remain, dear sir, Affectionately yours,

"THOMAS SPENCER."

The day of ordination at length arrived. The chapel in which Mr. Spencer preached being but small, that service, which, amongst dissenters of the congregational order, is remarkably solemn, was performed at the chapel in Byrom-street, Liverpool, which was handsomely granted to the people at Newington chapel for that special purpose. It was indeed an interesting day. The services were commenced by the Rev. Mr. Evans, of Stockport, who read suitable portions of Scripture, and implored the Divine blessing upon the sacred engagements of the day. The Rev. Joseph Fletcher, M. A., of

Blackburn, then delivered an admirable introductory discourse, and received from Mr. Spencer his confession of faith, together with answers to the questions usually, on such occasions, proposed to the minister to be ordained; Mr. Spencer then kneeling down, surrounded by his fathers and brethren in the ministry, the Rev. John Cockin, of Halifax, offered up, with deep solemnity, the ordination prayer, accompanied by the imposition of hands. To this act of ordination succeeded a most impressive and affecting charge from the Rev. William Hordle, of Harwich, Mr. Spencer's former tutor and friend. The passage on which this excellent address was founded was Col. iv. 17, "*Take heed to the ministry which thou hast received in the Lord, that thou fulfill it.*" The Rev. Mr. Roby, of Manchester, preached to the people of Mr. Spencer's charge, upon the duties which devolved on them in the relation that day publicly recognized, from Gal. iv. 18, "*It is good to be zealously affected always in a good thing.*" The service was throughout most affecting and impressive; it was characterized by a peculiar solemnity, both in the feelings of the ministers and the people. The tender frame and delicate mind of Mr. Spencer was nearly overwhelmed by the awful considerations which then pressed upon him. Had the melancholy event which so rapidly succeeded this interesting service been at that time certainly announced, a seriousness more suitable to the occasion could hardly have been inspired; and indeed in Mr. Hordle's charge there were passages which in the sad sequel of this history appear most singularly appropriate—bordering even on the prophetic! One in particular deserves to be recorded :—

"You, my dear young brother, must die, and stand at the bar of God. Your ordination service may be only a prelude to your funeral service, for what is man? Man is but of yesterday, and his days are as a shadow. How often have we seen the sun go down while it is yet day! and while the church has been pleasing itself with the prospect of enjoying the pious, fervent labors of an endeared minister for years, has an unexpected stroke separated them forever! Mourning survivors wondering have said, '*Verily thou art a God that hidest thyself,* O *God of Israel, the Saviour.*' "

Too often such remarks as these are passed by unnoticed by the thoughtless—are merely considered as expletives to supply the want of other matter or splendid furniture to decorate and give effect to the address. The anticipation, though founded in reason, warranted by Scripture, and authorized by experience, is yet unaccompanied by any just assurance of the event it realizes; and its connection with any special decree of God is concealed from mortals. But there are seasons when the lips of holy men seem to utter something more than those vague admonitions of death, which, from their frequent recurrence, or the uncertainty of their immediate accomplishment, lose their power to impress. And to those who admit the doctrine of divine influence upon the minds of men, and more especially upon such as are appointed to state and enforce the solemn doctrines of revelation to mankind, it can be no source of astonishment that God should sometimes direct the thoughts and expressions of his ministers into a current adapted to certain ends he has to answer, or particular events he intends shall shortly come to pass. With respect to the passage above cited, and its corresponding event, persons will form their own opinion. I cannot, however, but regard it as adding somewhat to the force and propriety of observations such as these, since here was another instance, in which the event anticipated by the speaker as *possible*, though, at the time, perhaps, regarded by the hearers as highly *improbable*, was but too surely realized

Mr. Spencer was now fully invested with that sacred office, which from his infancy he had desired; and he set himself diligently to the discharge of its momentous duties. That he felt its importance, was evident to all. His habitual conduct and conversation proved it. To his most intimate friends he freely expressed his anxieties respecting it, and earnestly did he implore an interest in the prayers of his people and his brethren in the ministry. In the assurance that he labored amongst a praying people, he felt confidence : and no consideration is more adapted to relieve the mind of a faithful minister than this—while it pours unseen a thousand blessings on his head, it secures to his labors an affectionate attention, and an earnest desire rightly to appreciate and improve them. That which persons make the subject of earnest prayer, they will usually value; and it is hardly possible but that good must be uniformly the result, when both minister and people come from their closets, which have witnessed their fervent intercessions for each other, to the house of God. The apostle knew how to estimate the prayers even of the meanest Christians who enjoyed his labors. "*Brethren, pray for us.*" It is true that a people will for the most part take the cast of their religious character from that of their minister: if he be much alive to God, and zealous in the discharge of his ministry, he will communicate the sacred flame to all around him, and cause his people to reflect on every side the light his preaching and his example shed. But, on the other hand, are there no instances in which the reverse of this has been the case; the minister has been gradually disheartened and dispirited by a cold, supine, and worldly-minded people, who have continually thwarted him in his generous designs—counteracted his benevolent efforts—and quenched, by indifference and neglect, the ardor of his zeal.—Instead of assisting him in his glorious work, they have hung like weights about his garments; and instead of acting as pioneers to prepare the paths of

Christian benevolence for his willing feet to tread, they have clogged up the avenues with obstacles, and lined the way with insuperable difficulties. The spirit of the man has been broken by perpetual disappointment—vexation has gradually enervated his mind—and by slow and imperceptible degrees he has sunk into torpor and indifference—and the languor of the pastor has at length presented an unhappy counterpart to the supineness of the people. And even where neither the cause nor the consequences obtain to so alarming and fatal degree, still it is to be deplored that any approach to them should be suffered to exist. Here the stated attendants on a gospel ministry may often find a reason for that want of pleasure and improvement which sometimes they deplore, though most unjustly, at the preacher's cost. If prayer, special and fervent, for a blessing on their pastor's labors, has been neglected, the mystery is at once developed. For they have no right whatever to expect a blessing without prayer; and as they have no *right* to expect it without prayer, neither are they in a suitable frame to receive it; and thus it often happens, that where the prayerless soul departs empty away, the humble and earnest petitioner obtains a rich and suitable supply from the same table, and of the same food. It is *light bread* to the one, but it is life-giving and substantial provision to the other. *"Ask and ye shall receive."*

On the first Sabbath in July, Mr. Spencer dispensed, for the first time, the solemn ordinance of the Lord's Supper. It was a time of love—a season of refreshing from the presence of the Lord. The sweet impression of that happy day still remains, and its memory is yet dear to many. On the following Monday at the social prayer meeting in the evening, in the bosom of his people, he again solemnly dedicated himself to God, and renewed his vows to consecrate all his powers to their service in the work of the ministry. Indeed, all he wrote, or said, or did, indicated the holy fervor of his soul. Tenderly alive to the sacred delicacy of his character, he was anxious to sustain it well, that the cause of Jesus might not suffer by any spots it might contract.—Conscientiously awake to every call of duty which his most responsible station might involve, he was ready to obey them all, that the ministry might not be blamed. The following letter is from his correspondence about this time, and may be numbered with the last he ever wrote. The expressions which I have copied, are mingled with others sacred to the privacy of friendship. They promise pleasures never realized—unfold prospects suddenly destroyed—and record arrangements he was *not* permitted to fulfill.

TO MR. HADDON.

LIVERPOOL, *July* 8, 1811.

"MY DEAR FRIEND:—

* * * * * * * * * * *

"The ordination has for the last fortnight, occupied almost

the whole of my attention, and the impression, the solemn, the holy impression, of which I trust I shall never forget. Yesterday for the first time in my life, I administered the ordinance of the Lord's Supper, and found it to be indeed '*a time of refreshing from the presence of the Lord.*' My duties are more and more *important* and pressing. Conversations upon religious experience with candidates for admission into our church, and the calls of the sick and dying, must necessarily engage much of my attention. But I can sincerely bless God, that amidst all the depression of mind I have suffered, my work has been my delight. The duties of the ministry have often refreshed, instead of oppressing me. The pleasure of the Lord has prospered in my hands. I love the service of the Head of the Church better than ever I did: when I am watering others, I find that Jehovah the Spirit waters my own soul too! Oh! is not this an encouraging token for good?—— In great haste,

"I am ever your affectionate friend,

"THOMAS SPENCER."

But we must, however reluctant, pass on to the closing scenes of Mr. Spencer's life. As his death was sudden, I have none of those sayings or sentiments to record which occupy the last pages of most biographical sketches of departed saints; and yet his friends remember, with peculiar pleasure, in what a holy frame of mind he appeared to be during the whole of the week previous to his removal. If I should be more minute than may be deemed absolutely necessary in what remains of these important memoirs of this lovely youth, I trust that I shall be forgiven. I write for friendship; and to his friends it must afford peculiar gratification to follow him through all the scenes he visited, and mark the slightest movements of his mind during the last week of his residence on this earth.

On Sabbath day, July 28, being the day appointed for a collection for the new chapel, Mr. Spencer preached a most excellent sermon in the morning from Ezra ix. 8, "And now for a little space grace has been showed from the Lord our God to leave us a remnant to escape, and to give us a nail in his holy place, that our God may lighten our eyes, and give us a little reviving in our bondage." In the evening his text was Acts xiii. 26, "To you is the word of this salvation sent." On that day he exerted himself greatly, and complained much of a pain at his heart, but did not seem at night particularly fatigued. The following day he spent chiefly in conversation with his friends respecting the state of the church, and some candidates for communion who were to be visited and received during that week—he dined at the house of a friend—in the afternoon visited the sick room of one of his members—and in the evening attended the prayer meeting at the chapel, when he recapitulated the outline of a sermon which had been preached on the Wednesday evening preceding, by the Rev. Mr. Davies, of London. His memory was remarkably retentive, and he gave in that exercise a proof of its powers, which astonished all that heard him. That evening he slept in Liverpool, and early on Tuesday morning he went with a friend to Prescot, and laid the foundation stone of a new chapel there, and delivered an address adapted to the occasion, in the presence of a large assembly.

On Friday he was occupied until the afternoon in writing letters to his friends. I am able to present the reader with extracts from two of them.

August 2, 1811.

"I find growing pleasure in my ministerial employment; this evening I have to admit eight new members to church communion; indeed when I accepted this situation, I never conceived that I should have half the engagements or duties to attend to, which I now find must be accomplished, if I would merit the character of an active, useful minister of religion. I think my recent afflictions, and the solemn duties which now devolve upon me, have in a considerable degree chastened my character, and imparted, perhaps, a seriousness to my general deportment, which may prove highly advantageous to me in future life. How long this will *last* I cannot tell, but I think affliction adds a weight to a character nothing else does, and especially to young people and young ministers. I have lately been preaching in the villages round Liverpool. Oh! let us aim to glorify God, and then trust all our concerns in his hands, that so at the last we may be accepted of him."

In another, to his father, he says:

"I was much hurt at the account of my mother's illness; I hope no distressing circumstances have arisen, and by this time, perhaps I may indulge the idea that you are better yourself. Oh! how necessary that we should all seek a better country, since here there is so much change, affliction, and wo. May every trial be sanctified to us all, and we be meetened for the inheritance of the saints in light."

Having concluded his earthly correspondence with his distant friends, for ever, he left his residence and resumed his pastoral visits amongst his people and the candidates who were to be that evening received. At the church meeting he was particularly lively ; with holy joy he welcomed the new members into the communion of the church, and as he gave to each the right hand of fellowship, he addressed a short but most affectionate and solemn exhortation, admirably adapted to their respective ages, stations, and feelings. Indeed, all the duties of the pastor's office were conducted by him with a propriety and an ease, which years of experience are frequently unable to supply. With the unaffected simplicity of youth, he tempered the dignity of age —he seemed to be at once at home in the duties of his new and important station—never embarrassed or confused ; he appeared to have an intuitive perception of what belonged to his character and office, in every case as it arose ; and following the inward suggestion, he acquitted himself well, and discharged with undeviating consistency the high responsibilities he bore.

After the meeting, Mr. Spencer spent the evening in serious conversation with a few friends ; leading with great fervor the devotions of the family, and closing a day of sacred duties, with uncommon calmness and placidity of mind.

The following morning, Saturday, he spent in his

study, in preparations for the pulpit. In the course of the day he wrote to a young lady, one of the number received, the preceding evening, into his church—at the close of the note he said—

"I suppose you anticipate to-morrow with feelings of solemnity; you will appear in a new light to the church of Christ, and the spectators of our holy solemnities; we shall share to-morrow Zion's chief feast. May the blessing of the God of ordinances be upon us all. Wishing you the enjoyment of perfect health, and much communion with your best friend,

"I remain, &c.

THOMAS SPENCER."

After dinner on the Saturday, the conversation turned upon a passage in Ezekiel—"*I will cause you to pass under the rod, and I will bring you into the bond of the covenant;*" from which Mr. Spencer took occasion to speak much at large upon the nature and stability of the covenant of grace. In the evening he met the Rev. Messrs. Charrier, Lister, and Wray, the missionary, together with Mr. Laird, of Greenock, and others, at the house of a friend. It was a pleasant interview, and in reflection has afforded to the persons who composed that social party the sincerest pleasure. To his most intimate friends, it is a source of much satisfaction, that his pastoral engagements that week were such as every day to bring him into their society—so that they had constant intercourse with their departed friend—and passing with him from house to house can look back and say, "*Did not our hearts ourn within us while he talked to us by the way, and opened unto us the Scriptures.*"—Like the companion of Elijah, they walked with him in close connection from spot to spot, charmed and edified with the holy strain of his discourse, and the rising lustre of his character; but all unconscious, that whilst they were thus conversing with him upon earth, *the chariot of Israel and the horsemen thereof* were preparing to conduct him triumphantly to heaven. But the scene closes rapidly upon us. On the last Sabbath of his life, August 4th, he rose with unusual health and spirits. The family with whom he resided always beheld him with peculiar interest on the morning of the Sabbath, such an air of angelic mildness and composure sat upon his countenance—and so deeply did he seem absorbed in the contemplation of the sacred duties of the day. That morning he preached from Jer. xxxi. 3—"*I have loved thee with an everlasting love, therefore with loving kindness have I drawn thee.*" The way of his discussing the subject was simple and interesting: I have drawn thee to the CROSS—to the THRONE—to the CHURCH—were the leading ideas in the discourse. It was particularly adapted to the occasion, so many new members being that day added to the church. He afterwards administered the Lord's Supper in a most solemn and affecting manner. Such as witnessed the scene—and the number of spectators was about three hundred—bear an unanimous testimony to the deep solemnity by which it was characterized. His appeals to the conscience were so close and overwhelming—his invitations to the faint and weary were so pressing and tender—his countenance—his voice—his whole manner were so expressive of holy fervor, that every eye was fixed—every heart seemed moved. How long the impression will remain I cannot tell; but the emotions enkindled by the transactions of that day are yet lively in the hearts of many—and numbers love to converse upon it, as one of those rare and highly favored seasons, in which the distance between earth and heaven seems annihilated —and so transporting is the joy, that *whether in the body or out of the body*, the happy Christian can scarcely tell! To a friend who afterwards hinted that he appeared to be very happy in prayer at the Lord's Supper, he replied—" O yes; I thought I could have prayed, and prayed, and mounted up to heaven!" At the close of that memorable service —one, the ardor of whose feelings age had checked, observed, that " Mr. Spencer seemed that morning twenty years older in experience than he really was." At dinner he mentioned to the family, that he had received that morning a letter from a friend in London who had been formerly reluctant to his settlement in Liverpool, as though it were not the sphere designed by Providence for him. He then expressed the full conviction of his own mind, that he was precisely where he ought to be—under such an impression, he observed, that he was perfectly satisfied and happy; and adds, "if it had not been the will of God, I should never have settled here."

In the evening, in the midst of a throng, such as is rarely witnessed, and from which hundreds departed unable to gain access, he preached from Luke x. 42, "*One thing is needful, and Mary hath chosen that good part which shall not be taken away from her.*" His chief object in this sermon was to show, that communion with the Saviour is the one thing needful. Throughout the whole discourse, it seemed as if all the powers of his mind, all the ardor of his soul, were infused into his composition, and his delivery. In the application, he was uncommonly urgent with the young—earnestly exhorting them to an immediate decision on the side of Christ—representing to them the folly and the danger of deferring the important concerns of salvation and eternity to an uncertain futurity—and assuring them, that *very soon* he should meet them at the bar of God, and that there he should be a swift witness against them. By those who are best able to decide, it was observed, that his last sermon was perhaps the most adapted for usefulness of any he had preached—and this observation, which was made immediately after its delivery, has been since most amply confirmed, in instances perpetually presenting themselves, in which that sermon proved instrumental in effecting the happiest impressions, many of which have issued in a saving change.

After the labors of the day he went to the house of a friend to supper ; he did not appear to be unusually fatigued. With great fervor he led the devotions of the family. He read a portion of Scripture, and gave out the 165th hymn of the 2d book. He was remarkably copious and earnest in prayer —commending especially to God—the family—the church—the members who had recently joined—the missionary, (who was present) and every object to which his holy and benevolent mind recurred. At supper the conversation was pure and spiritual —such as the book of remembrance in heaven preserves—such as will not easily be forgotten upon earth. The subject was sudden death. The countenance of Spencer, always animated, was lighted up with holy joy as he discoursed upon the glory of departed saints—he seemed to realize the scenes he attempted to describe, whilst he expressed his own conceptions of the transport and surprise in which the disembodied spirit will be lost, when first admitted to the immediate presence of God. He spoke much upon the blessedness of putting off the garments of mortality in a moment, and being caught up unexpectedly and instantaneously to heaven! He seemed to lose the memory of the day's fatigue in the interesting theme, and frequently observed, that he had not for a long time felt himself so free from weariness. A little after eleven, he parted with his friends for ever. Never did they discover more of the warmth of his friendship, or the ardor of his piety, than in this last, happy interview. His countenance seemed irradiated with smiles of ineffable benignity—his whole deportment indicated a mind abstracted from the world, except so far as bound to it by the benevolent desire of doing good, and wholly devoted to communion and fellowship with God. So mature indeed did his character appear—so ripe did he seem for glory, that some of his friends could not but entertain a presentiment of his early removal. Though not then elevated to a higher sphere, he still appeared mysteriously weaned from earth. His loins were girt, and his lamp burning with unusual brightness, as though he expected the coming of his Lord. In its anticipations of future glory, his happy spirit seemed to try its pinions, preparatory to the glorious flight it was about to take.

On Monday morning, August the 5th, the last day that dawned for *him*, he rose rather later than usual ; his mind was too active for his body ; the exhausted frame required rest. After breakfast, he received a visit from a young lady, one of the members lately admitted into the church. He entered the room with a cheerful smile ; and the family having retired after some general conversation, he said, "Well, M——, you are now a member of a

Christian church ; yesterday you solemnly professed your faith in Christ, while the attention of many of our fellow creatures was fixed on you ; God also beheld your profession—all heaven and hell witnessed the solemnity." On her expressing some fears lest she should be unable to act consistently with the profession she had made, he replied, "Live near to Christ—be much in communion with your own heart—be very frequent in addresses at a throne of grace, and there is no fear of you." Then referring to the long and agonizing distress which he had suffered through the alarming indisposition of his dearest connections, and which seemed now happily removing, he said, "This severe affliction has not been sent, but for reasons the wisest and the best ; from it I have learned many lessons, and have enjoyed much of the presence of God under it. Oh, may my heart be filled with gratitude to Him who is the author of all our mercies." He frequently bathed ; he found it beneficial to his health. He purposed doing so that day, and had expressed his intention in the morning. He had just repeated the first verse of Cowper's admirable hymn—

"God moves in a mysterious way,
His wonders to perform;
He plants his footsteps in the sea,
And rides upon the storm,"

when one of the family came into the room, and said, that if he intended bathing, it was time that he should go, as it would very soon be high water. He assented; but whilst a towel was being procured for him, he turned to his young friend, and said, "I can't tell how it is, but I don't feel so much inclined to go, to-day, as usual." She asked if it was thought good for his health—he answered "Yes, it will brace my nerves after the exertion of yesterday." And, indeed, he had an immediate object in view, for he had folded his paper, and prepared his pen, in order to compose a sermon to be preached in the course of the ensuing week, on behalf of the Religious Tract Society, in London; and he was anxious that, by bathing, his mind might be invigorated for study, as he had frequently observed it to have that pleasing influence. Mr. Spencer and his friend left the house together, when turning towards the water, he said, "I must go this way." They parted. His friend sought again the bosom of her family—he went the way whence he never returned!

The following pages of this history must be filled with weeping, and lamentation and wo. They must detail as sad a catastrophe as ever humanity or religion mourned. With cheerfulness Mr. Spencer took the path which lead across the fields towards the Herculaneum potteries, a little above which it was his design to bathe. The eye of his friend, beneath whose roof he dwelt, followed him till distance hid him from his sight. Arrived at the spot which he had selected, not so much from a knowledge of the ground, as from the circumstance of its retirement, he asked a gentleman, who had been bathing, and who was then dressing, "if that was a good place to bathe at?"—he answered that it was, but that it was rather stony near the side, but better when further in. Mr. Spencer replied, "I rather think that it is a good place myself, and I don't like to bathe near the pottery, there are so many people." Mr. S. then asked again, "Is the tide nigh up?" to which he was answered, "About half past eleven." "Oh! dear," said Mr. Spencer, "it is near twelve." As this conversation passed, Mr. Spencer was undressing, and, at intervals, humming a tone. When undressed, he walked towards the water, and spoke to a workman belonging to the pottery, of the name of Potter, who also was bathing, and who directed him which way to come into the water. While walking in, Mr. Spencer observed, that it was very cold—to which Potter replied, "You will not find it so cold when in. Potter then plunged into the water about breast high, and when he next saw Mr. Spencer, he was swimming within his depth, but soon afterwards the tide swept him round an abrupt projecting rock, where the water was some six or seven feet. Potter himself, who was an expert swimmer, soon found the current driving him round the same rock; but he immediately, with difficulty, swam to the shore, when he looked about for Mr. Spencer, and, not seeing him, was much alarmed. At length, after the lapse of a minute or two, he saw the top of his head floating above the surface of the water. Potter could not tell whether he was amusing himself or drowning. He however cried out to him ; but receiving no answer, plunged in again, and swam to the rock, in order to render him assistance—but found it impossible—Mr. Spencer having sunk in seven feet water, and the currents being remarkably strong. Potter, with considerable trouble, and not till some time had elapsed, got up the side of the rock, and communicated the intelligence to Mr. Smith, of the potteries, who immediately ordered out two boats, which were directly manned and brought to the spot, when every exertion was made to find the body.

I have frequently examined the place ; indeed, I take a mournful pleasure in visiting the scene ; and I have sought the opinions of medical gentlemen respecting the *immediate* cause of Mr. Spencer's death. The spot is most unfavorable for safe and pleasant bathing. Whoever sees it at low water, is astonished that any person, acquainted with the nature of the shore, should venture there. There is a ridge of sharp and slippery rock, running in a curved direction, for many yards, into the water, and terminating abruptly ; on either side of this most rugged ridge the fall is instantaneous, and from one to two feet. It is highly probable, then, that

Mr. S. swimming, as was described, along by the shore, might bring himself up immediately on the edge of this treacherous rock, which being slippery, deceived him, and by suddenly precipitating him into deeper water, caused a spasmodic fear—a combination of instantaneous terror and spasm—which directly suspended the functions of life, and he sunk, without further agitation or conflict, in the arms of death.

"So sinks the day-star in the ocean bed,
And yet anon repairs his drooping head,
And tricks his beams, and with new-spangled ore
Flames in the forehead of the morning sky;
So Lycidas sunk low, but mounted high,
Through the dear might of him that walk'd the waves;
Where, other groves and other streams along,
With nectar pure his oozy locks he laves,
And bears the unexpressive nuptial song,
In the blest kingdoms meek of joy and love.
There entertain him all the saints above,
In solemn troops and sweet societies,
That sing, and, singing in their glory, move,
And wipe the tears for ever from his eyes.

In the meanwhile, the gentleman whom Mr. Spencer first addressed, returned, and, discovering the sad event, apprized them that it was Mr. Spencer, the minister, who was lost. Potter renewed his exertions to find the body, assisted by the people in the boats, in which they at length succeeded, after it had been under water about fifty minutes. By this time the melancholy tidings had spread abroad ; and happily some gentlemen of the faculty being in the neighborhood, and hearing of the event, hastened immediately to the spot, so that, ere the finding of the body, every thing was in readiness for instantly commencing the resuscitating process.

When drawn from the water, the body exhibited no symptoms of violence or struggle in the act of dying—the countenance was placid and serene—its features were perfectly undisturbed, and so lovely was its expression in death, that one of the medical attendants observed—a painter could not desire a finer object.

On the arrival of the body on the beach, the water was easily expelled, and being then wrapped up in flannel, it was immediately conveyed to the house of Mr. Smith, where, by the kind exertions of the family, every necessary arrangement had been made for its reception.

The apparatus having arrived from Liverpool, and three medical gentlemen being present to receive the body, the usual methods adopted in cases of suspended animation were instantly pursued. They were soon joined by three other gentlemen of the faculty, who rendered every possible assistance ; every expedient was, in the course of the afternoon, resorted to—but, alas, in vain ! and at five o'clock, in the opinion of all present, there remained not the faintest hope of restoring animation—the spark of life was totally extinguished.

Thus, in one sad moment, was lost to society and to the church of Christ, one of the loveliest of men —one of the most eloquent of ministers; upon whose lips, only the preceding day, hundreds had hung with delight, and the long continued and extended exertion of whose powers, in a larger sanctuary, the foundation of which he had but recently laid, thousands anticipated with eager desire! To tell how many hearts have bled, beneath this awful visitation, would require a fortitude which I do not possess—and constitute a volume, not surpassed in the anguish which it would describe, by any similar catastrophe in the records of human wo. The tidings spread through the populous town of Liverpool with a rapidity, such as, in cases of public calamity, is usually inspired. They circulated through all ranks, and excited one common feeling of regret in every bosom. They reached the exchange, and produced an extraordinary impression there; those who knew him, mourned the loss of one they loved—and those who knew him not, felt the agitation of that sudden shock, which the premature removal of such men occasions—they participated in the general sympathy, and deplored the loss of Spencer, as an event demanding general regret. Numbers hastened to the spot. Some incredulous, to obtain the sad assurance of the truth—and others to enjoy the mournful satisfaction of beholding that countenance in death, on which they had often gazed with transport, when kindled into radiance by the ardor of the soul that lately animated it. All was confusion and distress. Such a day has been seldom seen in Liverpool; a day of such dreadful gloom—such universal grief. From the countenance of every one to whom the tidings came, one might have imagined he had lost a friend; whilst many, to whom by intimate acquaintance he had become peculiarly endeared—petrified at first with mingled horror and surprise, when recollection and feeling returned, yielded, for awhile, to the influence of the deepest sorrow.

The estimation in which Mr. Spencer was held in Liverpool, was most decidedly marked after his decease. The public prints severally bore testimony to his worth, and pronounced a warm, but just eulogium on his extraordinary merits; the introduction of some extracts will not be unsuitable here:

"Mr. Spencer was about twenty years of age; in his person and countenance eminently prepossessing; and of manners most amiable, conciliating, and engaging. As a preacher his talents were held in a degree of estimation, or possessed of an extent of influence which have seldom been equalled in the annals of pulpit eloquence. His discourses were rather persuasive and hortatory than argumentative and disquisitive: they were addressed more to the imagination and affections, than to the judgment; and this, apparently, not so much from any deficiency of talent, as from a firm persuasion that, in matters of religion, the avenues to the understanding are chiefly to be sought in the heart. His sermons, thus constituted, were adorned with a felicity of expression, and delivered in an unremitted fluency of language, altogether surprising in extemporaneous discourses. These essential qualities of eloquence were assisted by an uncommonly distinct articulation, a tone of voice singularly melodious, and great gracefulness of action. Thus gifted by nature, and improved by cultivation, it is not surprising that he possessed the power of attaching an audience, in a manner that will never be forgotten by those who attended his ministry. Perhaps it scarcely ever before fell to the lot of any individual, at so early an age, to have diffused religious impression through so extensive a circle of hearers; and those who looked forward to the maturity of his powers, with the hope naturally inspired by his early excellence, will regard his loss as a public misfortune."

"The deceased was about twenty years of age, a youth of amiable and engaging manners; and his pulpit talents were so far above his years as to obtain for him a large share of public admiration and popularity. His premature death has most deeply affected the feelings of his numerous friends, who looked forward to the maturity of his early powers with the highest hope of obtaining in him a most valuable accession to the dissenting ministry."

But at the solemnities of interment, the strongest demonstration of public feeling was afforded. The concourse of people assembled to witness or assist in the last sad token of respect to his remains was never, perhaps, equalled in Liverpool. Religion, Humanity, Friendship, and Genius, mingled their tears at his grave.

All the streets through which the procession passed were crowded to excess, as also were the windows and balconies of the houses. But the greatest decorum was observed; and a seriousness, according with the solemn occasion, was manifested by all.—

The corpse was borne into the chapel, late the scene of Mr. Spencer's labors, and the Rev. Mr. Charrier of Bethesda chapel, read part of the 15th chapter of 1 Corinthians, and the 4th and 5th of 1 Thessalonians, and offered a most solemn prayer. At the grave an eloquent and impressive oration was delivered by the Rev. Joseph Fletcher, A. M., of Blackburn. The mournful service was concluded by a prayer from the Rev. Mr. Lister, of Lime-street chapel.

"The whole scene," a Liverpool journal observes, "was affecting—it could not be otherwise. Every idea which could be associated with the spectacle was such as to excite the deepest sympathy. The flower of youth, scarcely opened, snatched from the stem of life by a sudden and rude attack of mortality; a minister, who lately fixed the attention of crowded audiences by the power of his eloquence, conveyed to the house of silence and darkness; the fairest prospects of honor and usefulness in life blasted; the warm hopes of his friends wrecked in a moment; and the deep, the dreadful wound inflicted in the feelings of relatives, and the dearest connections. Such, however, are the appointments of a supreme governing Intelligence, to which human choice and wishes must bow with reverence, supported by the general principle of the justice, wisdom, and benevolence, which direct the affairs of men. Similar afflictions are of frequent occurrence in private life, though they there pass unnoticed. Public characters excite attention both in their zenith and fall; and so far as society is bereft of virtue, useful talents, and active zeal, their death is a public calamity."

On the following Sunday evening, a funeral sermon was preached at Newington chapel, by the Rev.

William Roby, of Manchester, from Heb. xiii. 7, 8, "Remember them who have the rule over you, who have spoken unto you the word of God ; whose faith follow, considering the end of their conversation : Jesus Christ, the same yesterday, and to-day, and for ever." This sermon, so admirably adapted to soothe the disconsolate congregation to whom it was addressed, has been presented to them, by its respected author, from the press.

But not in Liverpool alone was the shock of Mr. Spencer's death felt—or the loss occasioned by his sudden removal deplored. Scarcely was there a district in Britain to which the melancholy tidings did not reach. The universal esteem in which the beloved youth was held, was manifested by the numerous sermons which were preached throughout the country, to embalm his memory, and to improve his death. In London several were delivered—many singularly eloquent and appropriate ; several have issued from the press, and have been noticed in the preceding pages. The sympathy awakened for the mourning church, was as general as the regret occasioned by their pastor's death. Of Spencer it may be truly said, "*devout men carried him to his burial, and made great lamentation over him,*" whilst the situation of his bereaved people excited in every bosom compassion and grief, "*for they were left as sheep without a shepherd.*"

At first sight the event might stagger the strongest faith, for he was snatched away at a period when his life seemed of the utmost moment to the people over whom he presided, and the circle in which he moved. Scarcely had his talents reached their maturity; his character was even then unfolding; from the promise of his youth, his friends dwelt with rapture on the anticipations of his manhood, and every day added some strokes of reality to the picture they drew when suddenly, in the bloom of his youth—at the commencement of his course—just entered on his labors—he is arrested by the arm of death, and conducted to the silent grave. Was his death *untimely?* No—he had seen a good old age in usefulness, though not in years: "that life is long that answers life's great end." His end was fully answered, and he was gathered to the grave in peace. Was his death *severe?* No—to *him* it was tranquil and serene; he crossed the river of Jordan, singing as he went, and in an unexpected moment, found himself safely landed on the shores of immortality.

DISCOURSES

BY

REV. THOMAS SPENCER,

OF LIVERPOOL.

FROM HIS OWN MANUSCRIPTS.

DISCOURSES OF REV. THOS. SPENCER.

SERMON I.

ATONING EFFICACY OF CHRIST'S DEATH.

" The blood of Jesus Christ his Son cleanseth us from all sin."—
1 John 1: 7.

It has been the characteristic of really faithful ministers of the gospel, in every age, to speak of those blessed truths, the power of which they have felt in their own souls. This was the case with the apostles: they one and all declared the power of that divine grace which had melted their frozen hearts, enlightened their dark understandings, and renewed their stubborn wills. We see this in the first verse of the chapter from which we have read a text; in which the apostle says, " That which was from the beginning, which we have heard, which we have seen with our eyes, which we have looked upon, and our hands have handled of the Word of life;"—" that which we have seen and heard declare we unto you." Thus he puts the saints in mind of the gospel he had written, in which he declared to them that " Word of life" who had been with the Father, and was manifested to the world; and whom he now declares again unto them, that they might have fellowship with him, and all the true apostles;

assuring them, for a motive, that their fellowship was with the Father, and with his Son Jesus Christ. The fellowship of the saints is with the Father, as the source and spring of eternal life and happiness; and with the Son, as Mediator, who has opened the way, removed every obstacle, and given them an access by one Spirit unto the Father.

The design of the apostle in writing these things was, that their joy might be full. It was his earnest prayer, as well as the prayer of the apostle Paul, that the God of hope would fill them with all joy and peace in believing. He excites them to preserve fellowship and communion with God, by considering the transcendent excellence of the divine nature; "God (says he) is light, and in him is no darkness at all." How clear is his knowledge, for he is omniscient; and how unstained is his nature, for God is holy.

Our conduct then is awful, if while we pretend to holy communion with God, we walk in darkness. For there can be no communion between purity and impurity; heaven and hell; God and the devil. God hath fellowship with saints in affection and delight. They have fellowship with him in salvation and happiness. He gives himself and all he possesses to them, and they are enabled to give themselves to him. He bestows grace and pardon on us, and we resign our hearts, our affections, and our all to him. But in order to our doing this, some important change must take place in us; for by nature we are averse to God, prone to wander from him, and having the greatest enmity to him, yet there is a way by which man can be brought nigh unto God, have his natural enmity subdued, and be reconciled unto the Father of spirits. Therefore, lest any should be excited to despair, by a view of the enormity of their crimes, let them hear the consoling language of our text: "The blood of Jesus Christ his Son cleanseth us from all sin." When once our sins are pardoned by the blood of Jesus, we are admitted into communion with God, and with his Son. Oh! that our meditations on this passage may be profitable!

You will observe, that these words speak of the sacrifice of the Lord Jesus Christ, of the atonement of the Saviour; and we may consider them—as pointing out its value—as declaring its continual efficacy—and, as asserting its universal influence. Let us view the text—

I. As pointing out its value.

It declares the way of pardon to be by the blood of Jesus Christ the Son of God. By the blood of Jesus, in our text, we are to understand the last sufferings and the death of the Saviour. This blood is the ransom of our souls, the price of our redemption, and the expiation of our sin. This was the highest and most excellent part of his obedience. "Being found in fashion as a man he humbled himself, and became obedient unto death, even the death of the cross."

His whole life was a scene of suffering, but his death completed his obedience; in that he manifested the greatest love to God his Father, and men, his people. The expiatory sacrifices under the law were always bloody: death was to be endured for sin, and blood was the life of the creature; so the blood, the death of Christ, is the cause of our life, justification, sanctification, and glorification. The value of this sacrifice is infinite; and its value is plainly pointed out in the passage before us. It is the blood of Him whose name is Jesus; a name which is above every name; a name which is as ointment poured forth; and a name which causeth those who know it, to be joyful in Him that bears it. It is a name at which every knee shall bow, and every tongue confess that he is Lord, to the glory of God the Father. It is a wonderful, glorious, ineffable, and unspeakable name. The honorary title by which the Saviour is distinguished, stamps the greatest dignity on his sacrifice, and confirms its value. The blood mentioned in the text is the blood of a Saviour, as the name imports. It is the blood of one appointed and commissioned to save his people from the guilt, the power, the practice, and the love of sin. He rescues their souls from the power of Satan; and, having delivered them from all their vain expectations and false refuges, he saves them from the curse of the law;—to them there is no condemnation, because they are in Christ, by a living faith and vital union.

Jesus is a Saviour, because he finally delivers all his people from sinking into the pit of hell, being himself their ransom; and the blood of which we speak is the blood of one who has almighty power to save, even to the very uttermost, all that come unto God by him; and he has a full commission from God the Father to execute his eternal purposes of love to men, in saving them with an everlasting salvation; hence he is called Christ, having been anointed by the Father for this express purpose. The blood of which we speak is infinitely valuable, because it was shed by the Christ of God. Of him it is said, "Grace is poured into thy lips; therefore God, thy God, hath anointed thee with the oil of gladness above thy fellows:"—for him hath God the Father sealed. He himself said, "The Spirit of the Lord is upon me, because he hath anointed me." The priests, under the mosaic dispensation, were anointed; see Leviticus, the 4th chap. and 3d verse; Numbers, the 3d chap. and 3d verse; besides many other passages. Now Jesus is the anointed of the Lord, the Spirit was poured upon him without measure. Hence, when we pray for acceptance with the Father, we say with the psalmist, "Look upon the face of thine anointed." This anointing eminently qualifies him for the important office of a Saviour to his people. And must not that sacrifice be exceedingly valuable, which was made by the Christ of God? Must not that blood be precious which was shed by the Lord's anointed? The text then evidently points out its value, when it calls it the blood of Jesus Christ. It would be well for us, if our consciences were more and more assured of our interest in the salvation of Jesus Christ; then with what deep humility, unfeigned gratitude, and joyful praise, should we contemplate the subject.

Jesus is the Son of God, therefore his atonement is infinite; and, consequently, unspeakably valuable. It is the blood of Jesus Christ, the Father's Son, that cleanseth us from all sin. It is true that this blood was the blood of Christ's humanity, yet the merit of it was derived from his divinity. It was not his blood, as the Son of the virgin, which is the means of salvation, but his blood as he was the Son of God. We need not wonder then that it has efficacy sufficient to cleanse believers in all ages of the world from their vast load of guilt, when we recollect that it is the blood of Christ, who is God over all, blessed for evermore. Oh! how infinitely valuable does the sacrifice of Christ appear, on account of the divinity of his person! Let us all then highly value the atonement, the sacrifice of the Lord Jesus, for his was the blood of the Son of God.

What a privilege it is to belong to that church which he

has purchased with his own invaluable blood! Our faith is precious, inasmuch as it lays hold on the atonement of a precious Saviour, who shed his invaluable blood for sinners of the human race. It is the blood of Jesus Christ, the Son of God, which cancels the debt we all owe to God, which is the way by which we are delivered from condemnation, which insures our pardon, and by virtue of which we arrive at glory. Having considered the text, as pointing out the infinite value of the blood of Christ, we hold it up to your view—

II. As declaring its continual efficacy.

The blood of Jesus Christ his Son, cleanseth from all sin; it has a cleansing quality. And here it is evidently implied, that man by nature is defiled—is brought into such a state as to need cleansing—and who can doubt this solemn truth?—who, that studies his own heart, makes daily observations on mankind, reads the page of history, and peruses the sacred volume? There is not one who does these things, but will confess that man is by nature defiled. Sin is of a defiling nature, and it renders the subject of it impure in the sight of a holy God, who can never look upon sin with the least degree of approbation. It makes a man the disgust of angels and glorified spirits, the abhorrence of good men, and the fit companion for devils. Who can bring a clean thing out of an unclean? Not one. So none but God can new create the soul. All men by nature are defiled with sin; they come into the world polluted, and soon, by a long list of actual crimes, they render themselves more obnoxious to Divine justice, and expose themselves to eternal wrath. From the crown of the head to the sole of the foot, there is nothing but wounds, bruises, and putrifying sores. Sin has completely ruined us—made us defiled in every power and faculty of the soul, and left us without God, and without hope in the world.

Oh! what great reason have we all to lament the polluted state of man, and to put up the prayer of the Psalmist, saying: "Create in me a clean heart, O God; and renew a right spirit within me!" Or to say, in other words, "Lead us to the blood of Jesus Christ thy Son, which cleanseth us from all sin." Blessed be God there was a day when "this fountain was opened to the house of David, and to the inhabitants of Jerusalem, for sin and for uncleanness." But here we would observe, that the blood of Christ does not perfectly cleanse us from the sense of sin. The sparks of the fiery law will flash in our consciences—very often the smiles of God's countenance seem changed into frowns—Satan accuses, and conscience knows not how to answer. Unbelief very often starts in the mind of the believer, and he distrusts the Lord that bought him; but, however, the blood of Christ shall never lose its cleansing virtue—it shall be perfect in its effects—it has rent the veil between God and us—and it will rend that veil that is between us and conscience. The soul of a Christian shall be, ere long, presented before the throne of God, without spot or wrinkle, or any such thing.

Nor does the blood of Jesus entirely remove the risings of sin. The mind of a good man continues to be vexed, not only with abominations without, but corruptions within. We are not freed from the remains of sin, whatever some men may talk about perfection. Paul knew nothing of it, when he said, "Oh! wretched man that I am! who shall deliver me from the body of this death?" We may see an end of all perfection, if we are led into the wickedness of our own hearts, and the spirituality of the divine law; nevertheless, the blood of Christ will, in some future period, remove every stain, and make us holy as God is holy. It shall perfect what it has begun. The soul of a child of God shall be made pure as snow, and white as wool. Although the blood of Christ does not yet cleanse from the sense, nor the risings of sin, yet, adored be the name of Jesus, it removes the condemnation of sin—it frees us from its punishment. Although the nature of sin does not cease to be sinful, yet the power of it ceases to be condemning. Sin is not imputed to them that believe; and where the crime is not imputed, the punishment cannot be inflicted. Jesus having suffered, justice is satisfied, and God can demand no more. The cause and effect of Almighty vengeance are removed (as it respects those that believe) by the blood of Christ. The blood of Christ cleanseth them from sin. The pardon of sin properly consists in a remission of its punishment. It would be contrary both to the mercy and justice of God, to punish a man who had been cleansed by the blood of Jesus. Contrary to his justice—for he has accepted the sacrifice made by Christ, who paid the debt and acquitted the criminal, when he bare our sins in his own body on the tree. Contrary to his mercy—because it would be cruelty to adjudge a person to punishment who had been legally acquitted, and made innocent by the imputation of the righteousness of Christ. The believer, then, being freed from the charge of the law, is no longer obnoxious to its curse, for there is no condemnation to them that are in Christ Jesus. An accusing conscience, a violated law, a hostile world, and the enemy Satan, may bring their sentences of condemnation on others, but they cannot condemn believers; for there is nothing left that shall condemn them for sin, because Christ by his own sacrifice has condemned sin in the flesh. The blood of Jesus Christ the Son of God, cleanseth us from all sin. The cleansing efficacy of this blood shall be made manifest before an assembled world. Believers shall then be collected out of every nation, kindred, tongue, and people, to have their purification made known to all the world. That will be a time of refreshing, indeed—sin shall no longer distress—conscience no more reproach—and God no more correct. In the present life there is a secret grant of pardon to the believer, but then there shall be a solemn publication of it before men and angels. Christ will pronounce all his children righteous, and present them unblameable, and without spot to God his Father.

When the apostle says, "The blood of Christ cleanseth," it evidently implies that that blood is the only means of obtaining pardon. He joins nothing with it. It possessing the sole, the sovereign virtue of cleansing from iniquity, in vain do men expect pardon from mere mercy—from the intercession of saints—or from any righteousness of their own. None of these things can cleanse from sin. The types and ceremonies of the mosaic dispensation could never make the comers thereunto perfect, holy, or clean. They only prefigured the blood of the Lord Jesus Christ, which is the only way of pardon. Salvation is of grace from first to last, and you may depend upon it there is no fountain that can cleanse from sin but the blood of Christ; for it is that which cleanseth from all sin; and this blood cleanseth perfectly—removes every stain. The blood of the Redeemer being shed for his people, God looks on his church and says, "Thou art all fair, there is no spot in thee."

Thus does this text declare the efficacy of Jesus' blood.

Let us consider that this efficacy is perpetual, is continual. For it is said, "it cleanseth;" not, it hath cleansed, or shall cleanse at some future period, but it now cleanseth. And this may always be said of this precious blood, for it shall never lose its power, till every elect vessel is gathered in, and saved in the Lord with an everlasting salvation. There is a continued cleansing act; Jesus perpetually pleads it for us, and it constantly flows unto us. There is a stream of corruption always in our nature, so there is a constant flow of cleansing blood. It is a fountain now standing open for sin and for uncleanness. It was shed but once. It is often applied; and its virtue will be felt to all eternity. The blood of Jesus is never lost or congealed, like the blood of the legal sacrifices. It is, as a good writer observes, "as new and fresh for the work it was appointed to, as when it was shed upon the cross; as full of vigor as if it had been shed but this moment." The justification of a believer before God, stands upon as certain ground as the justification of Christ himself before God. He was accepted, because he shed his blood; and we are accepted, because we are cleansed by it. And the meritorious plea of this blood continuing forever, is not without the perpetual act of the righteous Judge, justifying them for whom it pleads.

Hence will follow our security at the last judgment. As his blood now cleanseth from sin, so his voice shall then absolve, completely absolve us from sin. Those poor sinners who are alarmed, as it respects their state, need not fear that the blood of Christ has lost its efficacy; for it continues to cleanse, and so it shall continue, whilst one elect character remains on the earth to be directed by the

Divine Spirit unto it for salvation. And after that, when all good men shall be safe in glory, every tongue shall be employed in adoring that sovereign grace, which directed them to this all-cleansing fountain. Since we contract guilt every day, this medicine can daily be applied. The pleas of this blood are renewed according to the necessity of our persons. Every time an Israelite was bitten by a fiery serpent, he must look up to the brazen serpent for cure; so we, upon every sting of conscience, must look up to Him who was raised on the cross, as for a remedy. Since the fountain is open every day, and we contract guilt every day, let not a day pass without fresh applications of this blood upon any defects in our walking with him, since the blood of Jesus Christ continues to cleanse us from all sin. But not only does our text denote the continual efficacy of the blood of Christ, but we would contemplate it,

III. As asserting its universal influence.

It cleanseth, not all persons, but from all sin. Since it was the blood of so great a person as the Son of God, it is as powerful to cleanse us from the greatest sin as from the least. It is a universal remedy. It absolves from the guilt of sin, and shelters from the wrath of God. The nature of our sins, and the defilement of them, are not regarded when this invaluable blood is set in opposition to them. Jesus was delivered for our offences, not for some few of our offences, but for all; therefore his blood cleanseth from them all—from all original transgression, and actual sin—from the guilt incurred, by omitting the good which God has commanded—and the commission of that evil which he has prohibited. God has laid on his

Son Jesus the iniquity of us all—the sins of all believers, in all parts, in all ages of the world; from the first moment that Adam sinned, to the time when the last sin shall be committed. As all the sins of the people were laid upon the head of the scape-goat, to be carried by him into the wilderness, so are all our sins pardoned and forgiven by the blood of Jesus. The greatest wickedness that was ever committed by men, was the murder of the Son of God; whom they took, and by wicked hands have crucified and slain. Yet, to the very persons who did this, pardon was offered. The Gospel was preached, " beginning at Jerusalem." Herein we behold an evidence of the inestimable value of this blood, and of its inexhaustible virtue. Oh! well might the apostle say, " It cleanseth from all sin." Do we come into the world obnoxious to the Divine vengeance, and hateful in the sight of God? Is the guilt of Adam's sin imputed to us? It is. Yet the atonement of Jesus extends to original pollution. Although born in sin, and conceived in iniquity, if he purge us with hyssop we shall be clean; if he wash us, we shall be whiter than snow. Have we omitted the performance of his holy law, and withheld that reverence which he so justly demands from us? We have. But the blood of Jesus makes full atonement for this—he has done more for us than we could have done for ourselves—had we a whole eternity to work out our own salvation. His blood cleanses us from sin; it removes all that guilt which is upon our consciences, for our not keeping the law of God. Although we have left undone the things which we ought to have done, yet Jesus hath done all things well. Again; by the atonement of Jesus, every actual sin is done away; for his blood cleanseth from all sin. We have sinned in thought, word, and deed. Our sins are heinous and numerous; yet they shall never be laid to our charge, if we are believers in Jesus. Should their number exceed the number of the luminaries that gild the arch of heaven, or of the particles of sand on the sea-shore, yet this precious blood removes the guilt of them from our consciences—their pollution from our hearts—the love of them from our minds—and, shall we add, the practice of them from our lives. Have we sinned in public? If we are believers on the Son of God, it shall be publicly declared at the last day, that God has pardoned all our sin. Have we offended him in secret? Alas! we have, in ten thousand instances. His Spirit shall secretly bear us witness, then, that our sins are all forgiven. Oh! let every believer unite in ascribing praise to Him—because he would love. Let each of us say—

"O! to grace, how great a debtor,
Daily, I'm constrain'd to be:
Let that grace, now, life a fetter,
Bind my wandering soul to thee."

From what has been said, we learn the infinite evil of sin, which required such a sacrifice as Jesus Christ; and should we not then detest it, and flee from it, as from the face of a serpent? Oh! let us beware of sacrificing the son of God afresh, and putting him to an open shame by our guilt and crimes. If there were nothing else to teach us the evil and damnable nature of sin, the blood of Christ loudly proclaims it. Let us not, then, attempt to excuse our sins; but whilst we are blessing God for the remedy, let us, as long as we live, lament over the disease. Sin must be hateful in the view of every good man; and, depend upon it, that that system of religion which allows sin, in any shape whatever, is a diabolical system—it is from Satan, and not from God—for he is of purer eyes than to behold iniquity with the least degree of approbation.

Need I say, that we learn from this subject the folly of self-righteous men, who attempt to find salvation apart from Christ. Oh! remember, that nothing but the blood of Jesus is sufficient to atone for the sins of men. All your legal performances amount to just nothing at all, as it respects obtaining your salvation. Oh! why will you not submit to the righteousness of God? Flee, sinners, to the Saviour's blood—wash there, and be clean—so shall you be made eternally happy, and shall be brought to join all the blood-bought race of ransomed sinners, in ascriptions of eternal praise to God and the Lamb forever. Then shall this triumphant language be the burden of your song —"Unto him that loved us, and washed us from our sins in his own blood, and hath made us kings and priests unto God, and his Father; to him be glory and dominion forever and ever." Amen.

SERMON II.

ALL MEN ACCOUNTABLE TO GOD.

"So then every one of us shall give account of himself to God."
—ROMANS XIV. 12.

THESE words were first addressed to the Romans by the apostle Paul: they spoke loudly to them, and bid them prepare for their final judgment. And are they of no importance to us, "on whom the ends of the world are come?" Do they demand no serious attention from us? Ought they not to lessen our attachment to present things, and inspire us with holy boldness and resolution in the cause of God our Saviour? They represent the great Eternal as our Judge, and we all, every one of us, giving an account of ourselves to him. And if the Judge is at the door, how careful should we be to live, not to ourselves; but whether we live, we should live unto the Lord, or whether we die we should die unto the Lord; so that, whether living or dying, we may be the Lord's. "For to this end," says the apostle, "Christ both died, and rose, and revived, that he might be Lord both of the dead and of the living." Why then, should we judge one another? "for we shall all stand before the judgment-seat of Christ." For it is written, "As I live, saith the Lord, every knee shall bow to me, and every tongue shall confess to God."

Oh, let the artful hypocrite, the openly profane, and the real believer, hear the solemn language of the text. It is language that concerns them all, and demands from every one of us earnest attention, close examination, and fervent prayer. " So then every one of us shall give account of himself to God." For a few moments, then, let us lay aside every other concern, and attend to this most important subject. From the text we shall make two plain observations—

I. That at the general judgment, we must give an account of ourselves: and

II. That this account will be rendered to God.

Oh! that the Holy Spirit would impress the subject on all our minds, and cause our meditations to be very profitable to all our souls. Observe then—

I. That at the general judgment we shall give an account of ourselves.

It is a subject which concerns us all, for it is said in the text, " Every one of us shall give account of himself to God." " The hour is coming in the which all that are in the graves shall hear his voice." " I saw the dead, small and great, stand before God"—that is, persons of all ages, states, and degrees of men, will have to make their appearance before the great white throne. The sea shall give up the dead which are in it, and death and hell (that is earth and the grave) shall give up the dead which are in them, and they shall all be judged, every man according to his works, even from the king on the throne to the beggar on the dung-hill. Then shall the rich and the poor meet together—the Lord shall be the Judge of them both: there will be no distinction made on account of former riches or poverty. Both the man of property and wealth, and he who in the sweat of his brow did eat bread, shall be judged at one tribunal. The man of learning and study will receive his sentence at the same tribunal, and from the same tremendous Judge, as the ignorant and illiterate man, who has neither opportunities to be wise, nor desire to be learned. All the various classes of men will stand before God on that solemn day. Then will the minister who labored, toiled, and spent himself in the service of God, give up his account. Being raised from the long sleep of death, with holy serenity and joyful triumph on his countenance, he approaches the Judge of all the earth. Accompanied with those who were called by his ministry, he exclaims: "Here am I, Father, and the children whom thou hast given me;" thou knowest that I aimed not at the great things of the world, though I was thankful for those conveniences which thou gavest me. I preached not to display learning or to acquire human applause, but, being washed in Jesus' blood myself, I longed to direct others to that blessed fountain: I preached in compassion to souls, and with an earnest desire to please and honor thee. Then shall the Judge say to this faithful laborer, "Well done, good and faithful servant; enter thou into the joy of thy Lord."

There also shall appear the time-serving loiterer in the vineyard of the Lord: and oh, what a dreadful sentence will be passed on that unhappy man who never faithfully warned of sin or of approaching danger! Many will rise up and accuse him in that day, because he did not warn them to flee from the wrath to come. Oh! in what unutterable anguish will he behold the Searcher of all hearts, and the Trier of the reins of the children of men, who will punish sinners with everlasting destruction from the presence of the Lord, and from the glory of his power! All that have believed through grace, and fled for refuge to Jesus, shall receive their acquittal before an assembled world. All whom everlasting love elected, sovereign mercy redeemed, and sanctifying grace made holy, shall hear their Judge saying, "Come, ye blessed of my Father, inherit the kingdom prepared for you from the foundation of the world." And every worker of iniquity, every enemy of the cross of Christ, shall then meet this Judge. And, oh! awful will be his sentence! Words cannot express the terror, the horror, the despair, which shall pervade his soul when that God, whose word, ways and people he despised, shall say to him, "Depart from me, thou cursed, into everlasting burning, prepared for the devil and his angels." Awful as this sentence is, it will be executed to its utmost extent, and the unhappy lost soul will to all eternity experience the weight of Almighty vengeance. In a word, our text says, "Every one of us shall give account of himself to God." Every one that has ever lived on this earth; every one that now inhabits it; every hearer of the gospel; every father of a family; every husband, wife, and child; every professor of religion; every enemy to God. Every one in this assembly will give up his account. All that the fire has consumed, that the sea has contained, or that the earth has inclosed, shall hear the trumpet sound, and awake either to everlasting life, or to eternal shame and confusion. The part allotted to us, our text informs us, will be to give an account of ourselves: we shall give an account of the talents which we possess

—the mercies which we enjoy—the judgments which we have abused—and the actions which we performed.

1. We shall give an account of the talents which we possess.

Our Lord represents our giving an account of the talents with which we are entrusted by a parable (you will find it in the 19th of Luke, 11th to 27th verses.) By this parable, he reminds us of that awful reckoning to which we shall be called, and which is mentioned in our text. He therein shows us that it will be in vain for us to approach the Lord of heaven and earth, saying, "Lord, behold, here is thy pound, which I have kept, laid up in a napkin." For why does God give men natural talents and abilities, but that they may improve them to his glory? There have been many who have been blessed with capacious minds and great abilities, who have prostituted that mind and those abilities to the vilest of purposes. These persons will all be summoned before the great tribunal to give an account of themselves to God, and will undoubtedly hear their tremendous Judge saying, "Those, mine enemies, which would not that I should reign over them, bring hither and slay them before me." And those to whom God gave but moderate talents, who yet improved them, and spent all their lives in that service which is perfect freedom, namely, the service of God, those persons shall be honorably acquitted, and, having been faithful in that which is little, shall be instantly received into the joy of their Lord.

Oh, let us never forget that we shall be called to give an account of our stewardship, and that we shall either be hailed to eternal glory, or banished to unutterable despair. Let us employ the abilities God has given us in the best of causes, in promoting the honor and glory of God our Saviour, by telling to all around us, the unsearchable riches of divine grace, that they may be encouraged to apply to the Friend of sinners, and find in him all that salvation which they need.

2. We must give an account of the mercies which we enjoy.

For what has God given us our time, but that we may catch the fleeting moments, and spend them all in wisdom's ways? Soon there shall be time no longer. Oh, then, let us not waste it but redeem it, because the days are evil: so shall time bear us away to a happy eternity. But, oh, what an awful reckoning will those have to give, who employ every art to kill time! We are favored with innumerable blessings of a temporal nature, of which we must give an account. God has given them to us, that they may lead us to repentance; and happy will it be for us, if they produce that desirable effect. And why does the trumpet of the gospel salute our ears with glad tidings of great joy? Oh, for how much more shall we have to answer than those who have never heard or known the joyful sound! Great is the company of those who preach the gospel of the Son of God: from time to time we hear them delivering their message; and for every sermon that we have heard, we must give an account. One Sabbath succeeds another, and one opportunity for meeting with the saints follows another; and for all these things we must give an account. In short, every mercy with which we are favored, whether temporal or spiritual, will pass before our eyes, and demand of us how we have improved it. Oh, for grace to keep this awful account in mind, that so we may highly esteem our privileges, and see to it, that we not only duly estimate, but properly use the mercies we enjoy, seeing the time is approaching when we shall enjoy them no more for ever.

3. We shall give an account of the judgments we neglect.

Sinners are often reproved, yet, nevertheless, they harden their necks, and will suddenly be destroyed, and that without remedy. How often does God display the terror of his frown to a nation by awful calamities, such as war, famine, or pestilence. He says to them, in these judgments, when he beholds their iniquity, "Shall I not visit for these things? and shall not my soul be avenged on such a nation as this?" Yet, though his hand is awfully lifted up, they will not see. But let the people of such a nation recollect, that they must give an account of that contempt with which they have treated national visitations. How often does God make irreparable breaches in families! visiting them for their impiety, he removes a darling son, a beloved daughter, a tender parent, an affectionate husband, or a much-loved wife, with a stroke! And yet, after all this, they are numbered with the families that call not upon his name. There is nothing short of efficacious grace that can cause the inhabitants of the world to learn righteousness. Oh! that the arm of the Lord might be revealed, in convincing men of sin, and forewarning them of the account they will shortly have to give of the little success attendant either on the mercies or judgments of God! And has not God already spoken to us by the loud voice of an awakened conscience? Have we never been exercised with personal trials, difficulties, or conflicts? Have we never known what it is to feel alarm in our own souls, and dreadful forebodings of the day of judgment? If we are not awakened by these evils to a sense of duty, our condemnation will be increased by them: for, for all these things we must give an account.

4. The righteous Judge will inquire into the actions which we performed.

"For God shall bring every work into judgment, with every secret thing, whether it be good or whether it be evil." The penetrating eyes of God will notice the motives from which our actions spring. Probably we have done numerous actions, well enough, in themselves considered, but which are rendered impious and unholy by the desires from which they sprung. All this shall be laid open before an assembly of angels, devils, and men. And for every idle word that men speak they must give an account. Oh! that before we shall be called to this tribunal, we may have our persons and services washed in the precious fountain of Immanuel's blood! Then the terrors of Sinai's fiery law will not molest us; nor will any one vial of divine wrath be poured out upon us. Then God will look upon us, and be well pleased for his righteousness' sake. They that have done good, shall rise to eternal life; and they that have done evil, to the resurrection of damnation. There is not even a wicked thought that will escape the notice of his eye, but they will be unto him like destruction, which is open before him, or hell, which is without a covering. Every thing will be noticed by God, the Judge of all, before whom we must all appear.

"So then every one of us shall give account of himself to God." Oh! that our account may be delivered with joy, and not with trembling; but a happy entrance may be administered to us, into his eternal kingdom and glory!

Having thus endeavored to show that, at the general

judgment, we shall give an account of ourselves, we proceed to remark—

II. That this account will be rendered to God. "We must give account of ourselves to God."

In the fifth chapter of the Evangelist John, and the twenty-second verse, it is said, "The Father judgeth no man, but hath committed all judgment unto the Son;" and again, in the twenty-seventh verse, he "hath given him (that is, Christ) authority to execute judgment also, because he is the Son of man." These passages seem to prove that God the Father will not appear as Judge, but God the Son, that is, Christ, in his now glorified state. And there are many other passages which confirm this idea, such as these:—"The Son of man shall come in his glory, and all his holy angels with him, and before him shall be gathered all nations," &c. "Behold, he (namely, Jesus Christ, the faithful witness, who loved us, &c.) cometh with clouds, and every eye shall see him, and they also which pierced him, and all kindreds of the earth shall wail because of him." And that this was the apostle's idea, is clearly deducible from the 10th verse of the chapter before us; at the close of which he says, "For we shall all stand before the judgment-seat of Christ." He uses similar language in the second Epistle to the Corinthians, the fifth chapter and 10th verse, where he says, "We must all appear before the judgment-seat of Christ." The apostle, in the text, says, "So then every one of us shall give account of himself to God." Now, can any one deny that this proves the deity of Jesus Christ? It is said, that God shall judge the world, and that act is ascribed to Jesus Christ, which plainly demonstrates that he is "God over all, blessed for ever." The godhead of Christ is the triumph of the christian, who can look up to him, and with filial fear, mingled with holy boldness, can exclaim, "My God!" And those who now deny that Jesus Christ is the eternal God, will, in the day of judgment, have sufficient evidence of his deity. He will appear in all the uncreated glories of his godhead to banish all his enemies to the gulf of perdition, the lake of fire and brimstone, whence the smoke of their torment will ascend up for ever and ever. Yes, they who now oppose the reign of Jesus, will then have to give up their account to him. All men shall appear before him, and he will give to every one according to his works.

We shall now observe, that our giving up our account to God, will heighten the solemnity of the scene—secure the impartiality of the sentence—and display the power and authority of the Judge.

1. It will heighten the solemnity of the scene.

It will be an awful thing to hear the sound of the angel's trumpet;—to behold the elements melting with fervent heat;—to see the graves opening, and the race of Adam shaking off the sleep of thousands of years;—to hear the doleful shrieks of souls lost for ever. Oh! it will be a dreadful sight to see unhappy thousands, standing at the left hand of the Judge, to be cast into the lake of hell, which already yawns to receive its new possessors! But, when we recollect that God himself is the Judge; that he who made heaven and earth, and is "glorious in holiness, fearful in praises, doing wonders," is to decide on the final state of every man, we are filled with solemnity and dread. Those who now treat the doctrine of a resurrection and future judgment with unconcern, nay, with contempt, who laugh away gloomy thoughts of an awful eternity, will then be serious in reality, when they behold God the Judge of all. For they must give an account of themselves unto God. Oh! what a solemn thought! to a God who knows all hearts, and has declared that he will by no means clear the guilty! Oh, that we could always feel the import of the solemn words of the text! for it will be an awful thing, a fearful thing, to fall into the hands of the living God. Not only will our rendering our account to the God-man Jesus heighten the solemnity of the scene, but it will also—

2. Secure the impartiality of the sentence.

That a sentence, final and irrevocable, will be passed on the actions of men in the last great day, is clear from the assertions of scripture. If our fellow-mortals had to pass this sentence, it might be adjudged with partial hands; but we have to adore God that this sentence will not be passed either by men, devils, or angels, but by God himself; for—

He deals to all the due reward,
Or by the sceptre, or the sword.

He only knows what an infinite evil sin is, and therefore he only can be the Judge to pass a final sentence on the bold transgressor. The excuses which men bring to their fellow-mortals, will avail nothing before the judgment-seat of Christ; and we may all rest assured, that God will acquit none in that awful day, but those who are clothed with the righteousness of the Lord Jesus Christ. How disappointed will those persons be, who are merely resting on the possibility of their doing as well as others! they should know that none will do well, but those who have fled for refuge to Jesus, the Saviour of sinners. Oh! that mankind would recollect that they must give an account of themselves to God, and that his sentence on their actions will be impartial: for he will not look on sin with the least degree of approbation, but will assuredly bid every worker of iniquity depart from his presence into the lake of fire and brimstone. We must appear before an impartial Judge.

3. Our giving up our account to God will display the power and authority of the Judge.

We have remarked before, that all power and judgment is committed unto the Son; and in that day he will display the arm of his power; his authority shall be displayed in sending his angels to rouse the dead, in calling them all to his bar, in giving them a sentence of impartiality and justice, in banishing ungodly sinners to remediless woe, and in receiving his favorites to the kingdom of eternal glory. And this power, majesty, and authority, will be displayed before the whole company of angels and glorified spirits; the race of man, from the first that was created to the last that died; and the host of wicked angels and condemned souls. Before all these our Jesus will display his eternal power and godhead, to the glorification of all his attributes and perfections; the justifying all his dealings; and the final happiness or complete and eternal misery of every individual. "Now consider this, ye that forget God, lest he tear you in pieces, and there be none to deliver." Remember, that he who will be your Judge is almighty,—that his power is uncontrolled,—and that the weight of his vengeance will be intolerable. Every one of you must give an account of yourselves to God. Oh, that his grace and mercy may be manifested, in welcoming us to everlasting happiness, instead of his vengeance being displayed, in banishing us from his presence and from the glory of his power!

This awful subject is calculated to alarm the sinner—comfort the believer—and instruct us all. When the apostle Paul reasoned of judgment to come, Felix trembled. And does not this subject, O sinner, affect thee? Can you be stupid and unaffected when you hear of the account you must shortly give? Those who at that awful day are found Christless, will also be speechless, hopeless, and helpless! How will their heads hang down, and their knees knock together! Oh, what pale faces, quivering lips, and fainting hearts! Oh, dreadful day! when the earth shall be trembling, the stars falling, the trumpet sounding, the dead rising, the elements melting, and the world on fire! Recollect the solemn tribunal before which you must appear, the impartial sentence you will receive, and the happiness or misery which will be your portion. What kind of account will you have to give of your talents, your time, or anything with which you have been favored? Oh that this subject might be properly impressed on your hearts and consciences, then you would never trifle with solemn things! You would be often examining yourselves, that you might know whether you had a good hope through grace. Remember that you have been warned of approaching danger, and of appointed death and judgment. Say not, with many of old, "Where is the promise of his coming? for since the fathers fell asleep, all things continue as they were from the beginning of the creation." There are sufficient proofs from reason and revelation, that there will be a judgment-day; and woe be unto those who are not anxiously concerned about the decision of their state on that important day.

We said, that the subject was calculated to comfort the believer. The second advent of Christ is to the christian a desirable event: he loves his appearing, and says, "Come, Lord Jesus, come quickly." At that day, when he shall give an account of himself unto God, all his woes will be redressed. No longer shall he have to mourn over a body of sin and death. No more shall he cry out, Deliver me from temptation. All his sorrows will be done away: the Lamb that is in the midst of the throne shall wipe away all tears from his eyes. Then the pardon of all his sins will be declared. God will show to angels, men, and devils, that he is well pleased for the righteousness' sake of Christ. All the angelic host will admire and adore the grace which has been displayed in his conversion; and the saint himself shall say, Amen, to all the praise. For he shall come to be admired in his saints, and to be glorified in all them that believe. At that day his soul will be taken to eternal glory, to dwell for ever in the contemplation of the Saviour's beauties, enjoying his eternal smiles. God will be his eternal all, and he shall be full of glory. But "eye has not seen, nor ear heard, neither has it entered into the heart of man to conceive, what God has prepared for them that love him."

To conclude:—This subject instructs us all: it teaches us to be concerned, to be always ready for our account; to walk humbly and closely with our God; to sit loose to all created objects; and to set our affections on things above: to improve all our mercies; to redeem every hour of our time; to hear the word of God, so that we may profit; to look for the mercy of our Lord Jesus Christ unto eternal life: and to keep in view the end of our journey, being constantly looking unto Jesus. In short, what our text first said to the Romans, it now says to us all,—"WATCH."

SERMON III.

SALVATION THROUGH CHRIST.

"I am the door; by me if any man enter in, he shall be saved and shall go in and out, and find pasture."—JOHN 10: 9.

ONE striking feature of the gospel of Jesus Christ is, its variety; for it makes known the same truths by various methods, and in various ways. In the book of God, our attention is arrested to consider the things that belong to our peace, by well-chosen metaphors and suitable language; and as it is God's own word it shall accomplish the end whereunto he has sent it, for which he has designed it, and to which he has said it shall prosper.

The chapter out of which we have read you a text, abounds with metaphors: in it God's people are represented as sheep, to denote their simplicity, patience, usefulness, and meekness. Jesus Christ speaks of himself as the good Shepherd who has laid down his life for these sheep; and the church of God is described as a fold, into which our Lord will shortly bring all his flock, so that there shall be "one fold under one Shepherd." In the beginning of the chapter, the Saviour shows the folly which those men manifest who seek to get into his fold by some other way, than by the door. The disciples understood not these sayings, yet without a parable spake he not unto them; but, having compassion on their infirmities, he told them, that he himself was the door of the sheep, that all who ever came before him were thieves and robbers, but the sheep did not hear them. "I (says he, in the words of our text) am the door; by me if any man enter in, he shall be saved, and shall go in and out, and find pasture." It is our design to consider these words—as affording a significant representation of Christ,—and as describing the blessedness of all his people. Praying therefore, for the divine illumination, and trusting that our meditations will be profitable to all our souls, let us consider the passage—

I. As affording a significant representation of Christ.

The name of our Lord Jesus is as ointment poured forth: as, in all his offices, relations, and characters, he is exceedingly precious to the believing soul, he must be at all times worthy of our attention, nay, deserving of our highest admiration, ardent love, and constant praise. Let us, then, laying aside every other concern, fix our minds on Him, who is the object of angelic adoration, the delight of God the Father, and the only foundation of human hope.

It is very remarkable that Jesus Christ is always spoken of in Scripture, in that manner which is best suited to the sinner's wants. Does he hunger and thirst after righteousness? Christ is that bread of life, of which if a man eat, he shall live for ever. Does he want a foundation on which to rest his eternal all? "Other foundation can no man lay than that is laid, which is Jesus Christ." Does he lament his ignorance? Christ is the great prophet and teacher of his church. Is he oppressed with sin and guilt? Christ is an atoning priest; "the Lamb slain from the foundation of the world." Does he groan under the power of his enemies? Christ is King in Zion, and shall subdue them all. Or, is he put to flight through terror? "The name of the Lord is a strong tower, the righteous runneth into it and is safe." Does he often forsake and wander from the Saviour? Christ is the good Shepherd that will bring him back to the fold. Are any of you desirous of entering into the state of believers here, and into the house where they expect to dwell above? "Christ is the door, by him if any man enter in, he shall be saved, and shall go in and out, and find pasture." This representation of Christ, therefore, is designed to teach us this one great and important truth: that Christ is the only way of entrance into the church militant below, and into the church triumphant above; yes, we say that Jesus is the door through which poor sinners of the race of Adam are admitted—

1. Into the privileges of the gospel church.

That this is the true literal meaning of the passage is evident, both from the design of the chapter, and from the latter part of the verse. From the design of the chapter, which represents Jesus as sustaining a character which he exercises in the church militant, and describes the people of his choice as scattered about, and shortly to be gathered together: from the latter part of the verse, which mentions blessings that are to be enjoyed in the present state, "He shall be saved, and shall go in and out, and find pasture."

The privileges of the saints are very great and numerous; and what renders them so infinitely valuable is that the possession of them is secured to all real believers, by the oath and promise of the Lord.

What excellent enumerations of many of them do we find in the book of God, especially in the eighth chapter of St. Paul's Epistle to the Romans: there you may find a list of the greatest blessings that God can bestow upon man, or that man can possibly receive. It would be in vain for us to attempt to mention all these inestimable privileges, but it may not be amiss to mention one or two of them, and see that they are all enjoyed through Christ; that he is the gate that leads to the garden of the Lord, where grow the choicest flowers; where spring the best delights. To approach unto God, to be favored with sweet access to the God of heaven and earth; to have fellowship with the Father, and with his Son Jesus Christ, by the means of prayer, and other exercises of religion, is the most honorable and satisfying employment in which we can engage. It is a privilege which we can never too highly estimate, and a duty which we cannot too frequently perform. "Let their money perish with them, (said a noble marquis,) who esteem all the gold and silver in the world worth one hour's communion with Christ." And to this there is no doubt, but every one who feels the power of real religion will heartily assent. But the man who is yet in his sins, who has not known Christ, or entered in by the door, knows nothing of this privilege; he knows not what we mean by communion with God, does nor see its necessity, and having never enjoyed it, cannot feel its advantages, for it is through Jesus, that "we have access, by one Spirit, unto the Father."

Wicked men often attend the means of grace, and some of them who are awfully deceiving themselves, fancy that their attendance upon the means will save their souls, not recollecting that Jesus Christ is the only way of entrance into such a state as that in which a man can properly enjoy the means of grace. When the man has had a view by faith of Jesus, and has been contemplating with wonder, love, and praise, the expressions of his tenderness, the dignity of his person, the riches of his grace, and the love of his heart, then it is that he can properly enjoy the means, or rather the God of the means. Without an entrance by Jesus the door, our prayers will be formal, our praises hypocritical, and our whole services adapted to make the Lord refuse to hear us.

The great and precious promises of the word of God, are only applied by the Spirit to those who are interested in the Saviour. To him who has passed through Jesus the door, are the promises of the Bible made; for they are all yea and amen in Christ Jesus, and heaven and earth shall sooner pass away, than one of these shall fail of its accomplishment. Whilst those who are in a state of nature have no solid satisfaction left when affliction seizes them, and outward circumstances seem to frown upon them, God keeps them in perfect peace whose minds are stayed upon him; their faith in God and in his Son is the best remedy for the troubles of human life, and they are blest with strong consolation. Having entered in by Jesus the door, they derive real, solid, and lasting happiness, from the source where alone it can be found, and in God himself are all the springs of their felicity.

In short, let it be remembered, that there is not one privilege enjoyed by the children of God, however great, but is enjoyed through Christ. It was in him they were chosen; through him they are freely justified, really sanctified, and graciously adopted; through what he has done we shall be safely conveyed over the troubles of life, sweetly consoled in the terrors of death, freely acquitted in the day of judgment, and finally admitted into the glories of heaven.

Do you want proofs of this? Read the sacred word, where you will always find that Christ Jesus is the Alpha and Omega, the first and the last, the all and in all in a sinner's salvation. "Blessed be the God and Father of our Lord Jesus Christ, who has blessed us with all spiritual blessings in heavenly places in Christ." Here you see the apostle plainly shows the source of all our mercies, namely, Christ Jesus; and, indeed, the volume of inspiration is filled with proofs, that Jesus is the only way by which we can obtain the enjoyment of any spiritual blessing. And if you ask any who have been enlightened by divine grace, whence it is that they are so happy, they will ascribe it all to Christ, and say, "By his grace we are what we are." Thus is Jesus the door by which we are admitted into the privileges of the gospel church.

2. He also is the way of entrance into the blessedness of the heavenly state.

It is lamentable to consider on what weak foundations many of our fellow-creatures rest their immortal concerns. Oh! what numbers build their eternal all on the absolute mercy of God, the external privileges they have enjoyed, or their own legal performances, and they look for salvation from no other source; they will not hear that Jesus is the only Saviour, but vainly attempt to save themselves; and, whilst the Bible asserts, and experience proves, that "there is no other name under heaven, given among men, whereby we can be saved, but the name of Jesus," they will apply to any other person for relief but to him from whom alone it is to be obtained. "Being ignorant of God's righteousness, they go about to establish their own righteousness, not submitting themselves to the righteousness of God." Jesus is the door to the regions of glory:

"Know ye not that the unrighteous shall not inherit the kingdom of God?" The foundation of all our preparation for heaven must be laid in our being washed, justified, and sanctified in the name of our Lord Jesus, and by the Spirit of our God.

The joys of heaven are unspeakable, complete, and eternal: "Eye hath not seen, nor ear heard, neither have entered into the heart of man, the things which God has prepared for them that love him." "In the divine presence there is fullness of joy, and at his right hand are pleasures for evermore:" but, however great the glory, or lasting the happiness of heaven, it must be well understood and remembered by us, that if we know not Christ as our only Saviour, we shall never see its glory, or enjoy its pleasures. Would we be partakers of the felicity of the heavenly world, we must enter in by Jesus the door; it is only he who can prepare us for that happy state. And do you ask, How it is that he makes us "meet for the inheritance of the saints in light?" the answer is, By imputing to us his own immaculate righteousness, whereby our sins are pardoned, and by affording us the sanctifying influences of the Holy Spirit whereby we are made holy. Without this blessed preparation for glory, where God is we never can come, "the gift of God being eternal life through Jesus Christ our Lord." Oh, let every one in the present congregation, lifting up to God the voice of prayer, exclaim, "Open to me the gates of righteousness, I will go in unto them and praise the Lord: this gate of the Lord, into which the righteous shall enter!" That Jesus is the way to heaven, is abundantly evident from the songs of the glorified, who ascribe all their felicity to him that "washed them from their sins in his own blood, and made them kings and priests unto God." Yes, my brethren, those who now stand round the throne of God, to hunger no more, nor thirst any more, are "they which came out of great tribulation, and have washed their robes, and made them white in the blood of the Lamb." Jesus is the only door, then try no other; he is an open door, then try him: bless the Lord, who, in his designs of love and mercy, and in his preached gospel, has set open this way to himself; adore him for giving you an assurance of your acceptance through Jesus, and for sweetly drawing you to himself, whilst others were left to perish in their sins. Thus have we considered the representation of Christ which our text affords: Let us now view the passage—

II. As describing the blessedness of all his people. They are here mentioned as entering in by the door.

What we have already said is sufficient to teach us that the language is metaphorical; that it implies their cordial reception of Christ, and their hearty belief in him; for, inscribed on this door, stand the soul-quickening words, "Believe and live." The blessedness of such as enter in by Christ is thus described:—"They shall be saved;"—"they shall go in and out, and find pasture."

Need we here observe that these promises relate to the present life, are great and unspeakable in their nature, as vast as God can make them, and as suitable to the exigencies of the soul of a poor sinner, as it is possible for them to be. To be a little more particular, three things are contained in the declaration of the text, namely, salvation,—liberty,—and provision.

1. Salvation.

By entering in through Jesus the door, you secure your

safety as it respects temporal calamities,—spiritual distresses,—and eternal woes.

Those who enter in by Jesus the door, are safe in temporal calamities; for, "They that trust in the Lord shall be as Mount Zion, that cannot be removed, but abideth for ever." What, though the nation in which they live is the object of divine displeasure and almighty wrath, God is saying unto them, "Come, my people, enter thou into thy chamber; and shut thy doors about thee: hide thyself, as it were, for a little moment, until the indignation be overpast." Yes, Jehovah has an ark, in which he shuts up all his Noahs in public distresses. For it shall be well with the righteous in what circumstances soever they may be placed. The name of the Lord is a strong tower, the righteous runneth into it, and is safe." Jesus is the believer's "rock, and fortress, and deliverer, his God, his strength, in whom alone he trusts, the horn of his salvation, and his high tower." "The eternal God is his refuge, and underneath him are the everlasting arms." "Happy are the people that are in such a case; yea, happy is that people whose God is the Lord." The Christian's way being committed to the divine care, and the Lord being acknowledged in all his ways, he shall not be destitute of domestic mercies; and although he may be tried in his family and circumstances, he shall be delivered out of his embarrassments, and all things shall work together for his good. Nay, though he is visited with bodily pains and afflictions, he shall be saved from their distracting influence, and blest with their purifying tendency. He shall glorify the Lord in the fires, and be made wiser and better, holier and happier, by all the trials he may be called to bear.

The saints, then, wherever they are, are safe as in the hollow of his hand: the Lord keepeth them as the apple of his eye. "The eyes of the Lord are always upon them, from the beginning of the year, to the end of the year," to notice their condition and to supply their wants. Oh, how great was his care of his ancient Israel! "In all their afflictions he was afflicted, and the angel of his presence saved them: in his love and in his pity he redeemed them; and he bare them, and carried them all the days of old." And we may rest assured, that as he is an unchanging God, the same care which was so remarkably exerted in behalf of Israel, shall be the protection of the saints to the latest age. "He shall deliver them from the snare of the fowler, and from the noisome pestilence:" "They need not be afraid for the terror by night, nor for the arrow that flieth by day; nor for the pestilence that walketh in darkness; nor for the destruction that wasteth at noon day; there shall no evil befall them; neither shall any plague come nigh their dwellings; for he shall give his angels charge over them to keep them in all their ways; they shall bear them up in their hands, lest they dash their foot against a stone; they shall tread upon the lion and adder, the young lion and the dragon shall they trample under foot." "I," saith the Lord, "will be with them in trouble, I will deliver them and honor them, with long life will I satisfy them, and will show them my salvation." And all this their security, is the happy consequence of their entrance in by Jesus the door. What, though they are persecuted by the world, they have to recollect that it hated Jesus the Master, before it hated Christians the disciples; they are assured that Christ has overcome the world, and by that assurance are encouraged to be of good cheer.

So also shall they be saved as it respects spiritual dis tresses. When assaulted by Satan, "the Spirit of the Lord shall lift up a standard against him," and "the God of peace shall bruise him under their feet shortly." Although they now groan under the wickedness of their hearts, and long to be delivered from the body of this death, their great Master has declared for their encouragement, that "sin shall not have dominion over them;" that "he will present them faultless before the presence of his glory, with exceeding joy; yes, they shall appear as a glorious church, not having spot or wrinkle, or any such thing." Sometimes they are distressed on account of the hidings of God's face, yet are they safe, because he will return unto them in mercy, he will not finally leave them, nor forsake them.

Once more, we say, they are safe from eternal woes. It is an awful truth, that "the wicked shall be turned into hell, and all the nations that forget God;" but it is a glorious fact, that to those who have entered in by Jesus the door, there is no condemnation, that they are safe from the avenging justice of an angry God, and from the direful effects of the divine displeasure, which the ungodly must endure to all eternity. They shall not fall into hell, because eternal love chose them, Almighty grace redeemed them, and the Holy Spirit sanctifies them for the enjoyment of heaven.

And is not this a great salvation? It is the salvation of which "the prophets have inquired and searched diligently, who prophesied of the grace that should come unto you." It is that which is the subject of the Scriptures, the joy of Christians, and the song of heaven. O then, let all beware of neglecting it; let those who have entered in by the door rejoice in their title to it, and let no presumptuous wretch dare to lay a claim to it, who, instead of being united to Christ, is dead in trespasses and sins. True believers are not only promised salvation, but—

2. Liberty. "They shall go in and out." Alas! they were once with the rest of mankind held in bondage and confinement, but "by the blood of the covenant, God has sent forth his prisoners out of the pit wherein there was no water." They were once the prisoners of the law, as they had all broken its righteous requirements; they were all exposed to its fearful curses; it demanded of them that satisfaction which they were incapable of giving; it therefore threatened them with eternal death, and held them in bondage; but when they entered in by Jesus the door, their debt was discharged by him, and he liberated them out of their bondage. "The prince of the power of the air, the spirit that worketh in the children of disobedience," the old serpent, the devil, formerly had them under his power, confined in his strongholds, bound in his chains, and employed in his drudgery; but God, having weakened his power, turned him out of his strongholds, broke the prisoners' chains, and has taken them into his service, and made them free.

Once they were tied and bound with the chain of their sins, but suffice it to say, that when they entered in by Jesus the door, they were made free from sin and every kind of bondage, in which they were held; no longer do they strive after the gratification of their own evil propensities, but yield themselves the servants of God, and bring forth the fruits of holiness. "Where the Spirit of the Lord is, there is liberty." "Stand fast, therefore, in the liberty wherewith Christ has made you free." "By me, if any man enter in," says Christ, "he shall go in and out." And how shall we describe or explain the liberty of the children of God? It includes real pleasure and holy boldness in communion with God. The saints shall go in and out. Their communion with the Father and the Son, through the Spirit, shall be constant and unwearied. They shall walk in all the ordinances of the Lord. That service in which they are engaged is perfect freedom. Their slavery is changed into the state of children, and their duty into choice; hence, their grateful enquiry now is, "What shall I render to the Lord for all his benefits?" So that the liberty of God's children is by no means a liberty to sin; no, they never court that liberty, but detest it as the greatest slavery. How awful must that system be which encourages sin under the idea of gospel liberty. Such a system is not from God, but from the devil, the father of lies. Avoid it then, fly from it, detest it; nor ever imagine, that God will countenance, or in the least way approve sin in his people. For holy are all his ways, and holiness becometh them that serve him for ever. That man who pleads for the commission of sin, and calls it the liberty of God's chosen, plainly proves that he is in bondage even until now.

There is one great and important blessing more mentioned in the text, and that is—

3. Provision. "He shall find pasture."

Real believers are the sheep of God's pasture. "The Lord," says the Psalmist, "is my Shepherd, I shall not want; he maketh me to lie down in green pastures, he leadeth me beside the still waters: he restoreth my soul; he leadeth me in the paths of righteousness for his name's sake." "Thou preparest a table for me in the presence of mine enemies, thou anointest my head with oil, my cup runneth over." The spiritual wants of those who have entered in by the door, are supplied with spiritual blessings: for your support and nourishment, ye children of God, there are the lively oracles of God, and Jesus himself. "Thy word," says one, "was found of me, and I did eat it, and it was the rejoicing of my heart." Make the Bible your constant study; by this blessed book you understand the will of God, your mouth is filled with arguments, and your soul derives fresh strength. Oh, let it be your meat and drink; live upon the glorious truths it reveals, and the glorious prospects it opens; let it be the man of your counsel: it well deserves your highest estimation, for it is the field in which the pearl of great price is hid; it is the pasture in which God appoints you to feed. Oh, then, "as new born babes desire the sincere milk of the word, that ye may grow thereby."

Our Lord, in the most charming accents exclaims, "I am the bread of life." "My flesh is meat indeed, and my blood is drink indeed." "Except ye eat my flesh and drink my blood, ye have no life in you." He then must be the support of your souls; live upon his almighty fullness, his rich grace, his abundant mercy, and overflowing goodness. We cannot enlarge here, but must just say, that the food of the christian is—divine in its nature,—and nourishing in its effects.

It is divine in its nature. The Bible is the word of God and not of man: the subject of the scriptures, the manner in which any thing is treated, their obvious design, the wonderful harmony of all their parts; the unblemished character of their writers; the wonderful way in which they have been preserved; the number of miracles by which they have been confirmed; the exact fulfillment of their prophecies; and above all, the application of them to the conscience by the Holy Ghost; are all incontestible arguments for the divine authority of scripture: and this divine word, christian, is to be your food. Jesus, too, is divine, for "he is the bread which came down from heaven: he that cometh to him shall never hunger, and he that believeth on him shall never thirst."

The believer's portion is also nourishing in its effects. The natural tendency of "the sincere milk of the word" is growth. "He that eateth the flesh and drinketh the blood of the Son of man shall live for ever." Christ gave his flesh for the life of the world, and he that partakes of this living bread, hath everlasting life, and shall be raised up at the last day.

Do we not learn from this subject, that Christ is the first and the last in a sinner's salvation?

Without him you are condemned, enslaved, starving, and in the road to hell. Oh then, look to Calvary for mercy, for salvation, for liberty, and for food.

Are we not taught by these considerations, that those who gain admittance into the church any other way than by the door, are in an awful condition? This is positively asserted in the first verse of the chapter before us. "He that entereth not by the door into the sheep-fold, but climbeth up some other way, the same is a thief and a robber." Oh, beware then, beware, of resting in a religious education, in your being members of christian churches, or any thing short of an approach to God through Christ; for if you profess to be in his fold, without passing through the door, you are accounted a hypocrite, and may expect a fearful looking for of judgment. Oh for grace to "strive to enter in at the strait gate; for broad is the way that leadeth to destruction, and many there be that go in thereat; and strait is the gate and narrow is the way that leadeth unto life, and few there be that find it."

Is it not clear, that gratitude to that God who has opened this door for sinners is our incumbent duty?

This is your way to Zion, O believer; sing of the goodness of God; sing to the praise of him who brought you into the good old way: and oh, "glorify God in your bodies and in your spirits, which are his." Glorify him in your hearts, lips, and lives.

Are we not to expect, that the time when Jews and Gentiles shall both enter by this door, will soon arrive? Read the sixteenth verse, where the Redeemer says, "Other sheep I have, which are not of this fold, them also I must bring, and they shall hear my voice; and there shall be one fold and one Shepherd." Blessed be God for such a declaration! O that he would bring in the Jews with the fullness of the Gentiles! He shall accomplish it in his time; shortly they shall be—

> All traveling through one beauteous gate
> To one eternal home.

Oh, let us pray that God would hasten the number of his elect, and bring them all through the door into the way to glory. Amen.

SERMON IV.

NO FELLOWSHIP WITH SIN.

"And have no fellowship with the unfruitful works of darkness."
EPHESIANS v. 11.

SUCH is the command of the God of heaven and earth, to all those who profess to love his Son, and enjoy the influences of his Spirit; who have espoused his holy and divine religion, and profess to be traveling through a world of trials and difficulties, to that rest which remains for the people of God. Our text is the voice of God himself through the instrumentality of his servant and apostle Paul, and therefore not only demands attention, but requires obedience, on pain of the displeasure of the Ruler of the skies.

Indeed we may suppose, we may say, that all the writers of the Scriptures, all the providences of God, all the heirs of glory, all the angels in heaven, all the damned in hell, are now saying to us, in the language of the text, "Have no fellowship with the unfruitful works of darkness." The text, my brethren, is the voice of every line of the Bible, of every poor backsliding soul, of every trembling conscience, and of every drop of the blood of Jesus. And shall these join their pleas in vain? Gracious God! enable us now to "cast off the works of darkness, and to put on the whole armor of God:" let it not be our condemnation that light is come into the world, and we love darkness rather than light because our deeds are evil; but may we do the truth and come to the light, that our deeds may be made manifest that they are wrought in God; and henceforth, may we have this testimony that we please Thee.

The perceptive part of the Bible is neither to be reckoned the ground of our acceptance with God, nor thrown aside as legal; for upon our obedience to that depends our recommending the gospel to others, our imitation of the Lord Jesus Christ, the evidence of our possessing the Holy Spirit, and the justification, not of our persons, but of our faith before God and men.

Our text is introduced just after the apostle Paul had been warning the Ephesians against being partakers with the children of disobedience, by avoiding their former condition and their present state. "Ye were," says he, "sometimes darkness, but now are ye light in the Lord; walk as children of the light, proving what is acceptable unto the Lord." Therefore might he say with propriety on this account, because ye were once darkness, but are now light, "have no fellowship with the unfruitful works of darkness."

May He who said, "I am the light of the world," illuminate our dark minds, and give us in his light to see light, that, in our meditations on this passage, we may not darken counsel by words without knowledge; but may be encouraged to proceed in our journey towards that place where the sun shall be no more our light by day, nor the moon by night, but where the Lord shall be our everlasting light, and our God our glory.

We observe that our text, I. Describes the sins of men; and, II. Cautions us against them.

I. This language of the apostle describes the sins of men —They are "the unfruitful works of darkness."

Man was at first created holy, placed in a happy situation by his Maker, and endowed with the greatest blessings; but, by his disobedience to the command of God, he rendered himself exposed to the death of the body and the soul, and, ever since, all his numerous posterity have been born in sin, and have continued to live and die under the influence of enmity to God, where divine grace has not changed the heart. The condition of every one in a state of nature is truly lamentable and awful: he is a sinner against God, an enemy to God, and at an awful distance from God; he is said to be alienated from the life of God. Sin is his element, his business, his study, his delight; and, if it be not pardoned, will prove his ruin.

Surely, it need not be proved to persons who have the least knowledge of their Bibles, that their sins are the unfruitful works of darkness, which are elsewhere called "the works of the flesh." "Now the works of the flesh are manifest, which are these,—adultery, fornication," and such like; "the deeds of the body." "If we, through the Spirit, do mortify the deeds of the body, we shall live." They are also called dead works. "How much more shall the blood of Christ purge your conscience from dead works?" And they are styled, the lusts of the devil. "Ye are of your father the devil, and the lusts of your father ye will do."

But, in our text, sins are called "the works of darkness, the unfruitful works of darkness;" to this description it behoves us now more particularly to attend. You see that they are described by their nature and tendency.

1. By their nature.

"The works of darkness." Good men are elsewhere said to be called out of darkness, and to be delivered from the power of darkness, and here the sins committed by the ungodly are expressly styled the works of darkness. Does not this denote the uncomeliness of sin? What is there, my brethren, in the vast creation of God, that is more filthy, more abominable, either in the sight of a sanctified soul, of a holy angel, or of the eternal God? As sin is the work of Satan, as it is the delight of those who never tasted the refined joys of Jesus's salvation, and as it proceeds from a heart deceitful above all things, and desperately wicked, it must be loathsome. Darkness itself is not half so uncomely; nay, that darkness which might be felt was but a faint shadow of the disagreeable appearance and odious nature of sin. Those whose minds have been illuminated by the divine Spirit to see the exceeding sinfulness of sin, need no other arguments to convince them, that it is uncomely: for, beholding it with eyes anointed with his eye-salve, they cry out, Unclean, unclean.

Again, does not the phrase, "works of darkness," denote the bewildering nature of sin?

And sin, my brethren, is the means of rendering men insensible to the voice of God and conscience; stupid, notwithstanding the loud calls of the ministers of the gospel, nay, hardened under its sound: having once set your foot in the broad way that leadeth to destruction, you find it no easy thing to turn back, to come to the way of peace; for, "Can the Ethiopian change his skin, or the leopard his spots? then may ye also do good, that are accustomed to do evil." It is really astonishing how men are led on from one sin to another, till, at last, they fall into the lake of fire and brimstone, to remain for ever with all the nations that forget God. Before they are carried down so low as others by the torrent of iniquity, could you foresee some of their future actions, and tell them of them, they would not believe themselves capable of performing such atrocities; nay, they would detest the thought. How strikingly do we see this exemplified in the conduct of Hazael, who, when conversing with the prophet Elisha, saw him weep, and said to him, "Why weepeth my lord? And Elisha answered, Because I know the evil that thou wilt do unto the children of Israel; their strong holds wilt thou set on fire, and their young men wilt thou slay with the sword, and wilt dash their children, and rip up their women with child. And Hazael said, But what, is thy servant a dog, that he should do this great thing? And Elisha answered, The Lord hath showed me that thou shalt be king over Syria." And afterwards he did those very things. Oh, then, see here the bewildering nature of sin; like a man in thick darkness, the sinner is led on he knows not whither. And here I cannot help mentioning the salutary caution of the Apostle Paul, "Avoid the very appearance of evil."

Again, does not this expression denote the awful state of those who commit sin?

They are in a state of ignorance. "They know not, neither do they consider the work of the Lord, or the operation of his hands." They know not whither to apply for happiness, and therefore seek it in improper directions. They are altogether ignorant of God, of Christ, and of themselves; for (O lamentable fact!) darkness has covered the earth, and gross darkness the people.

They are also in a state of unbelief. Numbers of them will not believe that the darkness of the Mosaic economy is past, and the true light now shineth. They will not believe, therefore, on Him whom the Father hath sent, but "This is the condemnation, that light is come into the world, but they love darkness rather than light."

Consequently their state must be a state of error.

In vain do they attempt to illuminate the darkness by natural religion, or systems of philosophy: one man professes to teach the way of heaven by the works of the law; and another sets up the false glare of human reason, as the true light of the world. "The blind lead the blind, and they both fall into the ditch." No reformation of their own has ever been sufficient to destroy in them the love and practice of the works of darkness. But the apostle in our text describes the sins of men—

2. By their tendency. They are "the unfruitful works of darkness." The apostle, addressing the Romans, says, "For when ye were the servants of sin, ye were free from righteousness; what fruit had ye then in those things of which ye are now ashamed? For the end of those things is death." By their being unfruitful, we are to understand that they are of no good tendency, but that they are hurtful, inasmuch as they now defile, and will hereafter damn the soul.

Men are dreadfully mistaken, when they suppose that they are in the road to happiness, whilst they are in the way of sin; for, saith the Scripture, Who hath hardened himself against God and prospered? Those who practice the works of darkness, expose themselves to want, to disgrace, to pain, to mental distress, to temporal calamities, and to hell itself. That some fruit is produced by sin we do not deny, but it is of the most awful kind. The direful effect and the sad fruit of Adam's transgression is felt by all. That brought death into the world, and all our woe; and let us for a few moments, look at the ill effects of sin, as strikingly displayed in a few instances in Scripture. For what, was the wife of Lot turned into a pillar of salt? It was that God might thereby display his hatred to sin: for you will remember that she had transgressed the divine command, and for that transgression was made an eternal monument of his displeasure. Again, I inquire, why was Gehazi struck with the leprosy?—why was his body made white as snow? My brethren, it was for sin; it was one of the fruits of the works of darkness; and to this day it remains recorded in the Scripture, that we may see that our God is the God of truth, and will manifest his displeasure against the workers of iniquity. Let me ask again, Why was Herod smitten by the angel of the Lord, and eaten up of worms? Scripture itself replies, "Because he gave not God the glory." He had long practised the works of darkness, and their awful effects he experienced in the pain of his dissolution. And why did Ananias fall down and give up the ghost after his conversation with Peter? Or, why did Sapphira, his wife, expire so soon after? Both these circumstances took place by the just vengeance of God upon sin; for they had not "lied unto man but unto God." And let me ask once more, Why were Nahab and Abihu fearfully devoured by fire from the Lord? This, also, was for sin: "for they offered strange fire before the Lord, which he commanded them not."

These, then, are a few of those temporal calamities with which God has visited the workers of darkness; but what are these to that dreadful doom which succeeds them? Compared with that, all these things are but as the small dust of the balance, without weight, and without regard; for we are told, "the end of these things is death." Yes, my friends, "Death is the wages of sin,"—death temporal and spiritual,—but chiefly, death eternal. Whilst the righteous are called to inherit "glory, honor and immorality, and eternal life," sinners "go away into everlasting punishment;"—are "turned into hell, with all the nations that forget God;"—are "punished with everlasting destruction from the presence of the Lord, and from the glory of his power;"—are doomed to endure the gnawings of "the worm that never dies," and to burn eternally, "in the fire that never shall be quenched."

And, oh sinner! can you call your life a life of pleasure? Will you not "die as a fool dieth, and will not your end be without honor?" Is God to be discarded, religion to be despised, and your soul neglected for this, for the torments of everlasting despair? Oh, sinner! consider your ways.

Thus you see that the apostle, when he denominates sin the unfruitful works of darkness, does not mean to say that it produces no effect—that it is followed by no consequences—that it is entirely a neutral thing, and makes a man neither better nor worse—but he shows us that it produces no solid, real, lasting good. Sin may and does afford momentary gratification to the minds of its unhappy and unhallowed votaries; but this gratification will not bear being reflected upon, and never lasts, but invariably makes a man discontented and dissatisfied. The works of the flesh are to every good thing unfruitful. Solomon, who had tried them all, gives us their amount, their sum total, in the following words: "Vanity of vanities, all is vanity and vexation of spirit." "There is no peace, says my God, to the wicked," exclaims one of God's favorites; and surely we must believe these holy and heavenly men; but, if this be not enough to prove that the works of darkness are unfruitful, you are called upon to witness the death-beds of those who have spent their whole lives in the commission of them, and we cannot refuse to believe their testimony; and they unite in showing us, that "The way of transgressors is hard;" that there is no peace in the conscience of an ungodly man; that they never have enjoyed any thing which it is worth living to enjoy, but that there was the rankest poison in their cup of pleasure; and that when dying they endure the awful anticipations of the pains of hell.

Will not this suffice for the discussion of the first part of our subject? we now hasten to the latter, and observe, that the apostle, in the text, not only describes the sins of men, but—

II. Cautions us against them.

"Have no fellowship with the unfruitful works of darkness," is his language.

Here observe, that he does not say, Partake not of such and such a sin, whatever you do of the rest; but condemns sin altogether, and says, "Have no fellowship with any of them, but rather reprove them."

The word fellowship, in Scripture, is used to signify joint-interest, partnership, and familiar intercourse; hence the saints are said to "have fellowship with God, and with his Son Jesus Christ;" and ministers and people are united in the fellowship of the Gospel. The Lord's Supper is the communion and fellowship of the body and blood of Christ; and we are commanded to "have no fellowship with the unfruitful works of darkness." We shall illustrate this exhortation by saying, Do not associate with those who commit them—do not occasion them by your evil example—do not defend them by aiming to extenuate them—do not partake with them, by not praying against them. And we will try to enforce these things by suitable motives—

"Have no fellowship with the unfruitful works of darkness;" then, that is,

1. Do not encourage them, by associating with those who commit them.

The saints are described in Scripture, as being "men much wondered at;" "as a peculiar people, a holy nation," and so on. God blesses them with peculiar nearness to himself, and loves them with a peculiar love. They are strangers and sojourners here; this is not their rest, it is polluted; it is only a wilderness through which they must pass, a place that lies in their road; an inn at which they must lodge; they are the friends of one another, and the heirs of glory; as such, therefore, it behooves them to conduct themselves wisely, discreetly, towards those who are without, who do not belong to their fraternity, and are not traveling their road. You cannot understand us as saying that you are to have no concern with the world; that you are to neglect your business and turn monks; or that you must not speak or deal with those who make no profession of religion; neither would we intimate, that you are supposed to have that faculty by which you can know who are real Christians, and who are not; or that, in every case, you can tell whether you are to be familiar with this or that man.

But there is great propriety in an expression which you have, no doubt, frequently heard, and which cannot be too often repeated: "Be in the world, but not of the world." Let it appear by your actions, that the sons of Belial are not your favorites, nor the votaries of pleasure your intimate friends. Seek to be delivered from the evil that is in the world. Let the language of David be uttered from the bottom of your heart, "I am a companion of them that fear thee, and of those that keep thy precepts."

For why should you associate with the persons from whom you will be eternally separated? And why should you not delight in the company of those, who, like yourselves, are traveling to that place,—

> "Where our best friends and kindred dwell,
> Where God our Saviour reigns?"

I think that one reason why every good man dreads hell so much is, because of the vile company it contains; and really, if you would have no fellowship with the works of darkness, you must not associate with the transgressors, and those who keep not the divine law. But again, if you wish and long to obey the command in the text, respecting the unfruitful works of darkness,—

2. Do not occasion them by your evil example.

The saints "are called to holiness;" "they are said to be the true circumcision, who worship God in the spirit and have no confidence in the flesh;" and God says to them, 'Be ye holy, for I am holy." "Let every one that nameth the name of Christ depart from iniquity." "Christ gave himself for us that he might redeem us, and purify us unto himself a peculiar people, zealous of good works." "Let your light so shine before men, that they, seeing your good works, may glorify your Father which is in heaven." The end of Christians in their walk and conversation should be to recommend religion; so that, by their attachment to one another, by the good fruit they produce, and the virtues they exhibit, men may be constrained to admire the blessed effects of the Gospel of Jesus.

But is this the case? Alas, alas, if it be it is but in a very small degree; as professors of religion, shame and confusion of face belongeth unto us, because so few of us "adorn the doctrine of God our Saviour in all things;" and so many cause the name of professors of religion to be hated by the men of the world. Oh, this is a serious charge; if our conduct is unholy and unclean, we are actually forwarding the devil's work, and encouraging men to continue to practice the works of darkness. Oh, for more of the influences of the divine Spirit! Oh, for more application of the blood of Jesus! Oh, for more enjoyment of the light of the divine countenance! These things would, undoubtedly, tend to the transforming our bodies and spirits into the likeness of Him, whose we are and whom we serve. But how often do we grieve the Spirit, think little of the blood of Jesus, pray but formally for the light of God's countenance! and then we need not in the least be astonished, that it should please the Lord our God to permit us to fall into sin. Oh, then, by all means, avoid the works of darkness, and,—

3. Do not defend the works of darkness by aiming to extenuate them.

The saints should exercise continued acts of repentance, should pray to see sin in its worst colors, in its blackest features, and in its exceeding sinfulness; that so they may be confirmed in their hatred to it, and their desire to be delivered from it. But very often it happens, that after a child of God has fallen into the snare of the enemy, he wishes to make his sin appear as little as possible, and tries to extenuate it; which shows that he still feels a desire after it, that it is yet hid in his heart, nay, it shows us that he has fellowship with the unfruitful works of darkness. Never, Christian, never contrive sin, assist in it, rejoice in it, share the profits or pleasures of it: never provoke men to it, never forbear to do all in your power to hinder men from committing it, never command it, nor commend it; never neglect to reprove it, and then you will not have occasion to endeavor to extenuate it.

Oh, how much of the spirit of the world do we, who call ourselves Christians, daily exhibit! When we come to look into our own hearts, and examine ourselves upon these points, does not conscience tell us that we have fellowship with the unfruitful workers of darkness; nay, that we are partakers of other men's crimes?

It would be an excellent thing for us, if we looked into the law of God more frequently; then should we, in discerning the spirituality of the law and the broadness of the commandment, see our own sinfulness and vileness. Then we should be obliged to confess our little conformity to the divine commands, and to acknowledge our little likeness to God and Christ.

Again, "Have no fellowship with the unfruitful works of darkness," that is,—

4. Do not partake with them, by not praying against them.

The saints are to be men of prayer, and, on every occasion, are to lift up holy hands to God, praying always with all kinds of prayer and supplications. The necessity of prayer arises from numerous and interesting sources which we cannot now examine. Prayer and intercession are to be made for all men, and certainly the ungodly part of mankind demand a share in our prayers as well as the righteous. Notwithstanding the assertions of men, respecting the propriety of limiting our petitions and not extending them to the whole world, we do assert that the man who does not pray for the pardon of the sins of men has fellowship with the unfruitful works of darkness. Oh, be not partakers with other men's sins by this. Believer, do Satan, sin, and the world, tempt thee by various allurements, to various crimes? the remedy is still before thee,—pray. The Divine Being takes pleasure in seeing you striving against sin, against spiritual wickedness in high places; and so shall you best show your aversion to sin, either in yourselves or others, even by praying repeatedly and earnestly against it; and here is a promise for your encouragement, "The God of peace shall bruise Satan under your feet shortly." And again he has said, "Sin shall have no dominion over you." But never forget that your great Master requires this of you, that you have no fellowship with the unfruitful works of darkness.

"Thus shall you best proclaim abroad,
The honors of your Saviour God;
While justice, temperance, truth, and love,
Your inward piety approve."

"Those that honor me," says the Lord of heaven and earth, "I will honor." "And they shall be mine," saith the Lord, "when I make up my jewels."

As motives to excite you to have no fellowship with the works of darkness, I would remind you that by so doing you obey the divine command,—follow the example of Christ,—answer the expectations of the world,—encourage your distressed brethren,—and yield comfort to the minister of the gospel.

We say, Do not have fellowship with the works of darkness, and then you will obey the divine command.

We need not repeat the numerous passages of Scripture in which God calls you to holiness; read your Bible, and then you will find them; but we wish you particularly to recollect, that God is your Father and your Friend. Christ Jesus is your Creator and Preserver, and therefore obedience to him is reasonable and equitable; and surely, if you have any reason to believe that God has called you by his grace, gratitude will lead you to show forth the praises of him, "who has called you out of darkness into his marvellous light."

If you obey the injunction of the text, you will also answer the expectations of the world.

Professors as well as preachers are as a city set upon a hill that cannot be hid, you are watched by the world: they readily expect more from you, than from those who never made a profession of the gospel. Do not then suffer men to say to you with contempt, "What do ye more than others?" But let them see that religion is a thing that not only affects the heart but influences the conduct, and makes a man what he formerly was not. And remember, that whilst you are doing this, you are glorifying God, and promoting the intents of him, whom you profess to love and serve.

Again, have no fellowship with the unfruitful works of darkness, and then you will imitate the example of Christ.

Of him it is said, that he was " holy, harmless, undefiled, and separate from sinners." " Follow me," was his own language; and we are told that he suffered, " leaving us an example, that we should tread in his steps." And surely it becomes us to grow up into Him who is our living Head in all things: to be made like unto Christ is an unspeakable blessing and honor. O, then, let that mind be in us, which was also in him. He had no fellowship with the unfruitful works of darkness. Then let not us.

Again, By a holy conduct and conversation you encourage your distressed brethren.

When a poor, doubting, weak believer, who is much afraid that he shall backslide from the truth, and disgrace his Master's cause, beholds your good conversation among the Gentiles, he will be comforted, and will reason thus: " There I behold an amiable christian, he walks circumspectly, redeeming tho time, he puts to silence the ignorance of foolish men by his actions; now naturally he is no more able to do this than myself, he is assisted by divine grace; that grace also shall assist me, shall shield and guard me from the power of my foes, shall make me hold out to the end, shall be my staff when I pass over Jordan, and my song for ever and ever."

Once more, By avoiding the works of darkness, you comfort the ministers of the gospel.

Alas, they need comfort. Theirs is an arduous employment, it is a work to which angels are incompetent; they study, preach, and spend themselves for you, and will you refuse to comfort their minds? And you must not think that going to them, and telling them you were comfortable under their ministry is enough, but let them see by your fruits that their labor is not in vain in the Lord, but that the truths they deliver have a blessed and lasting influence upon your life.

Reflections.

The man who yet works the works of darkness is in an awful condition.

The saints should cultivate fellowship among themselves, and with God, and with his Son.

The hypocritical professor will hereafter be discovered and condemned.

SERMON V.

Delight in God's Worship.

"Blessed are they that dwell in thy house: they will be still praising thee."—Psalm lxxxiv. 2.

This Psalm is generally supposed to have been penned by David at the time, when, by the ambitious and rebellious disposition and conduct of his son Absalom, he was driven from his city. The chief subject of it appears to be the sanctuary of God, and the ordinances of his house, for by their loss he had learned more highly to estimate their worth.

With the most animated language, the holy man expresses the amiableness, the loveliness of the tabernacles of the Lord of hosts; breaks out in ardent longings towards the courts of the Lord: represents his heart and his flesh crying out for the living God; envies the sparrow her house and the swallow her nest, because they were near the altars of his King and his God; and in the verse which we have selected as a text, pronounces a blessing upon those who dwell in his house. We are persuaded that this subject is highly interesting to every one in the divine presence, who is saying, " One thing have I desired of the Lord, that will I seek after, that I may dwell in the house of the Lord all the days of my life, to behold the beauty of the Lord, and to enquire in his temple." From the text then we shall attempt to raise, illustrate, and confirm these three propositions:—

I. That there is a place peculiarly distinguished as the house of God.

II. That there are persons who find an abiding residence in it.

III. That such characters are truly blessed.

We remark,—

1. That there is a place peculiarly distinguished as the house of God.

The whole creation is the workmanship of God; for he is the Former of all things visible and invisible; for his pleasure they are and were created; to him all beings bow, angels and archangels; men and devils submit to his control, and are subject to his disposal. He is the sovereign of universal nature, and the Manager of all worlds. He filleth all in all. This great God, in making known to us his mind and will, in order to suit our circumstances, and in compassion to our infirmities, has been pleased to represent the great things of his love in familiar language, and in terms with which we are well acquainted. Hence we read such language as our text, when mention is made of the house of God. The question then is,—What is intended by the expression, and what place is that which is so honored, as to be called Jehovah's house? For since "the earth is the Lord's and the fullness thereof," how can he be said to have any particular dwelling-place? The place of glorified spirits is in scripture called "a house;" hence, says our Lord, "In my Father's house are many mansions;" and the apostle, contrasting the future with the present state, exclaims, "For we know that if our earthly house of this tabernacle were dissolved, we have a building of God, an house not made with hands, eternal in the heavens." In that heavenly house, all the spirits of just men made perfect, all the angels of God, securely, happily rest and dwell; for that is a house which cannot be removed, but abideth for evermore. And justly may the words of the text be applied to its heavenly inhabitants; for they indeed are truly blessed, being for ever engaged in the worship, and employed in the service of a present Saviour. But to us, it does not appear, from the connection of the text, that heaven is here intended, but rather, reference is made to the house of God below, to the church militant, to the worshipping assemblies of the saints, to the tabernacles of the Most High. David refers evidently to the Jewish tabernacle, whither, no doubt, he constantly went up to worship, and the term, house of God, applies at large to the whole church, to every congregation of believers, and to every assembly of the people of God. The church of God, we say, is a house; it is called so in different passages of Scripture; thus, we read, that "wisdom hath builded her house:" that the spouse was "brought to Christ's banqueting house, and his banner over her was love:" that "Christ, as a Son, was faithful over his own house, whose house are we:" "that he was a High Priest over the house of God:" "that the mountain of the Lord's house shall be established in the top of the mountains, and shall be exalted above the hills, and all nations shall flow unto it:" that "holiness becometh the house of God."

With respect to this house, be it observed, that Jesus Christ is the foundation on which it rests: for "other foundation can no man lay than that is laid, which is Jesus Christ." The inhabitants of it are redeemed sinners, who have been taken from the ruins of the fall, and adopted into the family of God; here they reside and share domestic blessings, expecting, ere long, to be transplanted from this earthly residence, to the house of God above; where they shall all be made pillars, to go no more out for ever. Spirituality is the characteristic feature of the men who dwell in this house, of the code of laws by which every thing is regulated, and of the employments and engagements of all belonging to it. But the idea of our text is not merely that the church is a house, but that it is the house of God. Let us for a moment investigate the propriety of the term, and show the claims of God to this building. The psalmist calls it thy house, and it will evidently appear to belong to no less a person than Jehovah, if we consider him as the planner,—the former,—the furnisher,—and the inhabitant of the church. Observe then—

1. That Jehovah planned it.

In the councils of eternity, he determined to make man, foresaw his fall, and devised a scheme for his recovery. He was resolved, in his almighty mind, to rescue man from the pit of perdition, and frustrate the designs of hell, by sending his dear Son into the world, to lay down his life to redeem him. Hence he knew the number of all his saints, and determined on the objects of his sanctifying grace, so that those who really belong to the church of Christ are the chosen of God; thus saith David in another Psalm: "Blessed is the man whom thou choosest, and causest to approach unto thee, that he may dwell in thy courts." Nor less did the Almighty fore-ordain the means by which this church should rise in the world; for he beheld it from eternity, withstanding all opposition, and looking like the temple of God amidst all the attacks of his enemies; he so ordained it, that the gates of hell shall not prevail against it, and he well knows the time when its great Zerubbabel " shall bring forth the head stone thereof with shouting, crying, Grace, grace unto it." The Almighty, however, not only planned, but—

2. He actually formed the church.

" Every house is builded by some man, but he that built all things is God:" all the creation is the product of his infinite power and skill: " The heavens declare his glory, and the firmament showeth his handy work;" but in a more particular sense, in a spiritual point of view, is Jehovah the builder of the church: hence, says the apostle, " We are his workmanship, created in Christ Jesus unto good works, which God had before ordained that we should walk in them." He laid the foundation, and he erected the edifice: by calling men under the preaching of his gospel, he makes them members of the mystical body of Christ, and inhabitants of the church of the living God. Every man that is a christian, is so by the work of God: no human aid, nor will of man, can make a new creature; for the church of Christ consists of men that are " born, not of blood, nor of the will of the flesh, nor of the will of man, but of God." Whatever believers are, they are so by the grace of God. How mistaken then are those persons who imagine that they have always been in the church even from their birth; have been brought up in the house of God! whereas a man must be a new creature, must be born again of the incorruptible seed that liveth and abideth for ever, before he can say that he dwells in "thy house, O Lord of hosts." But once more we observe—

3. That it is by God that this house is furnished.

When we say that it is furnished, we mean that it is pro vided with every thing needful; and who can doubt that this is done by God? For the perusal, the instruction, the correction, the nourishment of his children, he inspired and conveyed to them his own precious word. The saints also are adorned with every gift and grace of the Holy Spirit: their faith, their love, their patience, their hope, their zeal, their humility, are all of the operation of the Holy Spirit: by these they are enabled to believe the promises of God; to entertain the highest affection for their great Householder, and for one another; to suffer the difficulties of the present state, and to bear them all with the prospect of a glorious immortality; to promote the cause of their Redeemer, and to wear the ornament of a meek and quiet spirit. Adorned with these graces they look forth as the morning, "fair as the moon, clear as the sun, and terrible as an army with banners." They are all glorious within; how wisely and how well are they provided in their spiritual house, with every thing that is necessary for their welfare! they are by no means left to themselves; for God "is their sun and shield: he will give grace and glory; and no good thing will be withheld from them that walk uprightly." O how "beautiful for situation is Mount Zion, the joy of the whole earth!" "Walk about Zion, and go round about her: tell the towers thereof. Mark ye well her bulwarks, consider her palaces; that ye may tell it to the generation following." But I must observe, lastly, and chiefly, that the church is called the house of God—

4. Because it is inhabited by God.

The Lord dwelleth in Zion: there in a peculiar manner

he displays the greatness of his glory, the wonders of his power, and the riches of his grace. Of the church he says, "This is my rest for ever; here will I dwell, for I have desired it." "This is the hill which God desireth to dwell in; yea, the Lord will dwell in it for ever." The apostle John says, "If we love one another, God dwelleth in us and his love is perfected in us:" and "Thus saith the high and lofty One that inhabiteth eternity, whose name is holy; I dwell in the high and holy place, with him also that is of a contrite and humble spirit." Here he constantly bestows his ordinances, and affords his gracious, supporting, and comforting influences. Oh, what honor does this confer upon us, to have God himself dwelling among us! Oh, what condescension does it display, that he should reside among those who have rebelled against him! Oh, what safety does it insure! for if God be for us, nothing can possibly hurt us! Oh, what happiness does it promote! for it is his presence that makes heaven; and surely no person is so happy as he whom God designs to visit and to bless by his constant presence.

Thus you see that the Lord's people is his portion; Jacob is the lot of his inheritance: thus you learn that the church is the house of God. This is the place so peculiarly distinguished; it is the church. Observe then,—

II. That there are persons who find an abiding residence in it.

"Blessed," says my text, "are they that dwell in thy house." The psalmist here has a reference to the priests and Levites, who were frequently officiating there, in their turns, night and day; and to the inhabitants of Jerusalem and Gibeon, where the ark and tabernacle were, who had frequent opportunities of attendance upon divine worship. Blessed then are the ministers, the priests, and the Levites, that have their residence about the temple, and are in their courses employed in its services. But the words are of larger import, and the blessing contained in them, belongs to all those who count it their happiness, and enjoy it as their privilege, to serve and worship God in his courts; who dwell in God's house, who are at home there, and therein transact their most important business. There are several passages of Scripture of similar import with our text: the saints are said to dwell in God's holy hill. David himself says, in another psalm, "I will dwell in the house of the Lord for ever:" and speaking of Zion too, in another place, he says, "They that love his name shall dwell therein."

What is it then to dwell in God's house? An answer to this question will form the whole of our discussion on this part of the subject; and you will bear with us whilst we remark that it includes in it—

1. The most ardent attachment to the house of God.

David himself is an evidence of this: hence you hear him saying, "Lord, I have loved the habitation of thy house and the place where thine honor dwelleth." His great love to the ordinances of God's house caused him to break out in such language as that of the Psalm before us; and his attachment to it arose from a renewed nature, without which no man can love God's house for its spirituality: it sprung from past experience of divine favor; it originated in a sense of the need of that blessed water which can only be drawn from the wells of salvation. And this disposition will never fail to characterize the persons alluded to in our text: those who dwell in God's house must necessarily possess a sense of the value of a station there; for would you choose a dwelling-place without some degree of attachment to it? David was king over Israel, and yet he felt a love to the tabernacle and temple. He might have employed himself in the business of the world, but still love to God's house predominated in his mind. And oh, how often do real Christians long for the Sabbath-day! they are frequently supported through the vicissitudes of the week, by recollecting that soon the day of rest will come, when they shall serve God in his temple. They hail the morning of that day with prayer and praise, and find it to be the "best of all the seven." But here I must remark, how very different is the conduct of those men who think a Sabbath a burden; and say, When will it be over, that we may set forth wheat, and pursue our callings! That man can never be said to dwell in God's house, who, when he attends it, comes only out of an idle curiosity, or sits and sleeps when he is there. None of you can be said to dwell in God's house who do not love the place; whilst those of you who know how to value divine ordinances, are the persons who, I have no doubt, find an abiding residence in the Lord's house. Dwelling in the house of God implies—

2. Constant attendance upon it.

Can that man be said to dwell in God's house, who visits it but once a year, but once a month, but once a Sabbath? Impossible! They that dwell in God's house, love as well one part of the sacred day as the other; and do not mind sacrificing a few trifles to be constantly there. Is it likely that the man who dwells in God's house, can content himself with coming in late, and thus disturb the worship of others? No: rather he will be one of the first that assemble in the sanctuary. He is always glad when it is said to him, "Let us go into the house of the Lord: our feet shall stand within thy gates, O Jerusalem." The worship and service of God is the delight of all the saints. And here lies the distinction between them and others: sinners *visit* God's house, but the saints *dwell* in it. They dwell there as a child dwells with his father; "for there they find a settled rest, while others go and come." It is their wish to obey their Lord, who tells them to "consider one another, to provoke unto love and to good works: not forsaking the assembling themselves together, as the manner of some is; but exhorting one another, and so much the more, as they see the day approaching." The good man is thoroughly persuaded, that the time cannot be far distant, when he shall go up to God's earthly tabernacles no more. Sickness may seize him and confine him to his bed, and hereafter death must arrest him, and remove him from this world; so that whilst he has to lament the loss of the outward ordinances, one consolation still remains, namely, the prospect of the better house above, and the hope of engaging for ever in the worship of Him, whose service is now his delight. How dear are the ordinances of the Lord's house to the believing heart! Whilst the men of the world constantly resort to the unhallowed haunts of pleasure, he as constantly attends upon God's house; his heart is there: there dwell all those who are united to him, by being partakers of the same heavenly calling with him; and it is there that God himself, that Jesus Christ his beloved Saviour, and the Lord the Spirit, peculiarly discover themselves to the child of God: hence, we remark, in the last place, that dwelling in God's house includes,—

3. The greatest enjoyment in it.

Where ought a man in the general to enjoy so much, to be so happy, as at home? the house of God then is the believer's home, therefore he is happy there. It would be in vain for me to attempt to mention all the privileges of the house of God, or to describe that blessedness which belongs to the pious, the sincere worshipper of Jehovah in his earthly courts. There his memory is refreshed in the things which he has heard, felt, and experienced, lest at any time he should let them slip; there the doubts that harass and perplex his mind, respecting his personal interest in the joys of salvation, are dispersed, and

> "Light breaks in upon his eyes,
> With kind and quickening rays."

The graces that are in him ready to die are strengthened, fresh life is put in his soul, and by the public worship of the sanctuary, he is inspired with courage to go on the remaining part of the journey of life, leaning on his Beloved. Believe me, my friends, the Christian's dwelling-house is a happy place: everlasting love secures the habitation of the just, and God, even their own God, delights to bless them.

The ordinances of the church are the glass, through which the face of our adorable Immanuel is beheld: they are the channels through which God is pleased to convey his blessings down to men: in short, they are, in every point of view, calculated to promote happiness in the minds of the children of God. O Christians, whilst you dwell in the house of the Lord, never despair of enjoying the blessings of grace. You know that he never said to any, Seek ye me in vain: be diligent then in the use of the means, that God may therein be precious to your souls. Never think of relinquishing your situation in the house of your God, because you have not always immediately found what you wanted: you recollect, no doubt, that when our Lord appeared after his resurrection to the disciples, Thomas was not there: now had he been there, he would never have had occasion to disbelieve that Jesus was raised from the dead. God loves them that loves him, and dwells with the humble and contrite spirit. You have reason, you are bound, to expect the greatest of favors in the church of God; and you may depend upon it, the great Head of the church has not raised your expectations to disappoint them, but will supply them, nay, will do exceeding abundantly above all that you can ask or think. Still then make the church of Christ your abode, your residence, your home, for it was for that purpose that it was designed: it was intended by God to be an earthly tabernacle, in which you should pass the years of your minority; to be the place of your abode antecedent to your entrance into the better house above. How well is it observed by the admirable poet,—

"The saints on earth, and all the dead,
But one communion make;
All join in Christ, their living Head,
And of his grace partake."

It is wisely and well adapted for a residence for you, furnished with every thing necessary, having the most glorious, the great Householder to superintend all its concerns, and every member of the family being a subject of the King in Zion. In short, it ever has been, now is, and shall continue to be, the dwelling place of the saints; for they are they that dwell in this house. Let me show you—

III. That such characters are truly blessed.

For on them a blessing is pronounced in our text, and wherein does their blessedness consist? Is it in an increase of worldly prosperity? Are we told that they shall be more respected by the world than their fellow-creatures? or are they to expect that their attendance upon divine worship procures the favor of God, and by it they merit heaven? No, beloved, no such things are mentioned, and I will venture to assert, that none such are expected by the sincere believer. But their reward is in their work, their blessedness is in their employment; for, says my text, "They shall be still praising thee." It is true that there are numerous privileges insured to the attendants upon God's house, mentioned in various other parts of Scripture, but we shall confine ourselves at present to the idea of our text: their blessedness then arises from the nature, and from the perpetuity, of their engagement.

1. The nature of their employment is a source of their happiness.

Their work is praise. "Praise waiteth for thee, O God, in Zion: unto thee shall the vow be performed." "In the midst of the church will I sing praise unto thee." "Let them exalt him also in the congregation of the people, and praise him in the assembly of the elders."

When Christians properly consider the glories of the divine nature, and the wonders God has wrought for them in their election, calling, adoption, justification, redemption, and sanctification, they cannot forbear bursting out in songs of praise and thanksgiving; and truly "praise is comely for the upright." The Lord Jehovah himself is the object of their praise and adoration: and what is he?

he is the source of all true knowledge, the author and donor of every good and perfect gift, with whom there is no variableness, nor the least shadow of a turn; with him is the fountain of life. In him are all the supplies that we need, and from him proceeds every blessing, both temporal and spiritual. Viewing God then in this light, the saints make his temple echo with his praise: and must it not be blessedness itself to engage in such a delightful employment? While many think it their happiness to fawn and cringe to their fellow-creatures, my brethren, be it our happiness to worship the King, the Lord of hosts. He must be blessed that praises God, because he is led to see that excellency and glory in the Divine Being, which must engage the adoration of those who are favored with the enjoyment of it. Ask the true Christian why he praises that God whom others neglect and slight: he will tell you, "Because I am enabled to see him engaged on my behalf, and all his perfections are on my side; and I know that if God be for me, nothing that others are able to do against me can do me any injury."

The believer praises God for the blessings of his grace, for all the mercies he enjoys, and for the prospects he has of eternal life and blessedness; then who can doubt that those who dwell in God's house are truly blessed? Their employment comes the nearest to that of glorified saints in heaven, and has, connected with it, the most distinguished favors. Tell us no more then of carnal amusements, of sensual joys, which never yield any solid satisfaction: be it our happiness to dwell in the temple of God, and by Jesus Christ to "offer the sacrifice of praise to God continually, that is, the fruit of our lips, giving thanks unto his name." But if the blessedness of the saints arises from the nature of their employment, much more will it do so—

2. From its perpetuity. "They will be still praising thee." Similar to this is the resolution of the psalmist, contained in the 146th Psalm. "While I live will I praise the Lord: I will sing praises unto my God while I have my being." The pleasures of the followers of the Lamb are not transient, but lasting; they are never to be interrupted: by day and by night they warble the praise of their Creator and Redeemer. Thanksgiving to God shall check the mourning sigh, to which they are liable to give vent under trouble: all through life the divine praise shall employ their tongues, nay, when the powers of language fail in the article of death, their streaming eyes shall intimate the joys they cannot speak. And what think you shall be their employment after the last conflict is over, and the chains which confined them to flesh and blood are broken? Then shall they rise to join the heavenly musicians, to sing that song which none can learn but the redeemed. Nor shall the glowing troops that surround the throne of God and the Lamb, sing more loudly than those who have been brought out of every nation, kindred, and tongue, and people, to shout for ever, "Unto Him that loved us, and washed us from our sins in his own blood, and has made us kings and priests unto God and his Father, to him be glory and dominion for ever and ever. Amen."

The sweet work, the glorious theme of praise to Jesus shall occupy eternity itself, and when unnumbered ages have rolled away, yet it may be said, "They shall be still praising thee."

Such is the employment of those who dwell in the Lord's

house; it is a perpetual engagement, and therefore they are truly blessed to whom it belongs. If there are any believers here in the house of God at this time, let me tell them never to be dumb in the praise of their great Lord. Praise him, Christian, with joyful lips. Praise him, by reviewing and acknowledging his goodness; by speaking to those around you of his greatness; and by acting before all to his glory. Praise him in your families, praise him in the world, praise him in your closets; but more especially praise him under the sacred roof, within the temples of the living God: so shall he grant you the light of his countenance, and the visits of his love; so shall he meeten you for the rest that remaineth for the people of God.

Having gone through what I proposed, I will close this discourse with one remark, which is this:—

Regularity of attendance upon the house of God is a pleasing sign, but no decisive evidence of a man's being a real Christian.

We cannot tell the motives that bring you to the temple of God. You may come, for aught we know, from custom, or because you feel a curiosity to know what is done there: we are not acquainted with the feelings of your mind when you are there; they are only known to that God, whose prerogative it is to judge the heart. Examine yourselves to know whether your after conduct is influenced by anything you have heard from the mouth of God's servants in his temple. See whether you are the characters that dwell in God's house, and have any right to claim their privilege, or any taste for it. May God bless his word, through Jesus Christ. Amen.

SERMON VI.

DEITY OF JESUS CHRIST.

"He is Lord of all."—Acts 10 : 36.

The ardor of that affection which the apostles and primitive Christians felt for the Saviour, is truly remarkable, and well worthy of our imitation, upon whom the ends of the world are come. When they were addressing their fellow-mortals on the important concerns of the soul, if his name did but come under their notice for a moment, they left their subject to speak of some of his distinguished excellences. In many instances we behold this in the discourses and epistles of the apostle Paul; and can it not be perceived in the language of Peter, which now lies before us? "The word," says he, "which God sent to the children of Israel, preaching peace by Jesus Christ;" and then, as he had formed the highest ideas of his character, he adds that sentence which we have selected for a text, and which, in the New Testament, is enclosed in a parenthesis, "He is Lord of all."

The honor of the Saviour cannot be an unwelcome or an unpleasant subject of consideration to those among us to whom "his name is as ointment poured forth:" our hearts are inditing a good matter, when the things concerning the King are our subject; for "He is fairer than the children of men, grace is poured into his lips; therefore God hath blessed him forever." His name shall be remembered in all generations; the people shall praise him forever and ever. The glories of Jesus are the objects of angelic research: why should they not be the theme of our meditations? for "He is Lord of all." We will attempt, then, to illustrate the honor this text confers on the Saviour; to prove its truth; to show its propriety; and to point out its influence. Let us, then, briefly, in the first place—

I. Illustrate the honor this text confers on the Saviour, that so we may understand it.

It represents him as "Lord of all;" and does not this intimate his right of creation, possession, and dominion over the inanimate creation, the whole church—yea, all things in heavenor on earth? When our Redeemer is styled "Lord of all,"it includes—

1. His creation of all things.

It is the Lord that made heaven and earth, the sea, and all that in them is; Jesus made them, therefore he is Lord. "All things were created by him, and without him was not any thing made that was made." "He is the image of the invisible God, the first-born of every creature, for by him were all things created that are in heaven and that are in earth, visible and invisible, whether they be thrones or dominions, principalities or powers. All things were created by him and for him, for he is before all things, and by him all things consist:" so that when the believer surveys the beauties of nature, he can say, "My Jesus made them all!" The sun that rules by day, the moon that shines in the night, "that great and wide sea, wherein are things creeping innumerable, both small and great beasts," and this earth which we inhabit are all the work of his fingers. The heavens declare his glory, and the firmament showeth forth his handy work. The whole universe was made by him, and formed, when as yet it was not; the glory of his perfections is displayed in the works of his hands; his power in producing them; his wisdom in arranging them, and his goodness in preserving them. But some will say, Do we not, in ascribing the work of creation to Jesus, wrong the Father and eternal Spirit? By no means; for the acts of the three that bear record in heaven are, like their nature, one. But this doctrine is thus represented in the sacred volume, especially in the New Testament, and it is well said to be a truth which imparts an unutterable dignity to Christianity; a truth which lays a foundation for the comfortable hopes of a Christian; a truth which will render the mystery of our redemption the wonder and delight of eternity.

Oh! that we may all experience the new-creating power of Christ; for all believers are his workmanship, created in him unto good works, which God has before ordained, that we should walk in them. He that formed the universe, can create in us a clean heart, and renew in us a right spirit. Grace has made a new world. Oh! that we may dwell in it! for "He that sat upon the throne said, Behold I make all things new!" and "He is Lord of all."

Again, does not the language of our text intimate—

2. His universal possession. For he not only made all these things, but he now holds them in the hollow of his hand. All are his, and this appears to be the meaning

of the term "Lord" in various passages of Scripture. Every thing is the property and right of Jesus; for has any one taken them out of his hands? or, has he lost his power to uphold and preserve them? Both these things are impossible. He possesses all glory in his own nature, for he is the Lord of glory; he only has life, and it is he that animates every living soul: all things subsist by his bounty. But oh! how extensive are his riches of grace! how large the store-house of blessings he commands! how abundant that fullness which it hath pleased the Father should dwell in him! Not only does he possess these blessings, but he hath promised to communicate them to us, for "He will give grace and glory, and no good thing will he withhold from them that walk uprightly." As he possesses all things, he has said, "Whatsoever ye shall ask the Father in my name, I will do it." And the saints may rejoice that all are theirs, whether the ministers of the gospel, or the world, or life, or death, or things present, or things to come; all are theirs, for they are Christ's, and "He is Lord of all." But the honor that our text confers on the Lord Jesus includes in it—

3. The extent of his dominion. For the term "Lord," in Scripture, very frequently signifies one that has rule or authority. And does not Jesus govern all? Angels, men, and devils, are all either his willing or involuntary subjects. It is his to say to this man, Go, and he goeth; to another, Come, and he cometh. He maintains an uncontrolled sway over heaven, earth, and hell, but most eminently is he Ruler in Israel, and King of saints. He exercises a spiritual government over his church; and of the increase of his government there shall be no end. It behooves us to submit to his will, for his commandments are not grievous;

to conduct ourselves as faithful subjects; to be jealous of his honor; to place on his head many crowns; to shout for joy saying, "Hallelujah, for the Lord God omnipotent reigneth;" and to expect to be ourselves kings and priests unto him forever, where there shall be no enemies to him or us, and opposition shall have fled forever. As Lord or Governor of all, it belongs to him to communicate his blessings just as he chooses, to send men to preach his Gospel wherever he will, and to bestow on his faithful subjects a crown of glory, brilliant, like his own.

The language of our text then does imply that he first formed all things, that he still possesses them, and that whilst earthly honors totter to the ground, and states once illustrious fall to rise no more; his is a kingdom which cannot be removed, but abideth forever, for "He is Lord of all." Having thus attempted to illustrate the text, that so we may understand it, let us—

II. Prove its truth; that so we may believe it. And if it be asked, How do we know that Jesus is Lord of all? we answer, by referring you to the language of infinite wisdom—the universal assent of all the saints—the confession of his most inveterate enemies—and the songs of the glorified in heaven. As the law and the testimony should ever be the arbiter in cases like these, we will adduce—

1. The language of infinite wisdom, as a proof that Jesus is Lord of all. And here he is called a Saviour, Christ the Lord, Lord both of the dead and the living, the second Man, the Lord from heaven, the Lord of lords, and King of kings, the Lord of hosts, God over all blessed forever. These honorable titles distinguish the Saviour above all the sons of men, or all the angels of God; they bid us view

him as Lord of all. Jehovah himself has universally declared him as such; that word which is true and faithful, one jot or tittle of which can never fail, that word, which is the word of God, and not of man, plainly shows that he is invested with the greatest honor. Had he been so denominated only by our fellow-men, we might have called it in question; but when we recollect that it is the voice of God, and not of a man, which distinguishes him as the Creator, Possessor, and Governor of the ends of the earth, this must satisfy us. We may attend in the next place—

2. To the universal assent of all the saints.

Was there ever one of the redeemed of God, who would refuse to crown him Lord of all? Has there ever been a single instance of a Christian not loving the Saviour, or not feeling the tenderest concern for his honor and glory? Have not might, majesty, and dominion, been ascribed to him by all really enlightened men? The sound of "Thou art the King of glory, O Christ," now reverberates on my ear, as proceeding from the whole church throughout all the world. This, indeed, ever characterizes the children of Zion, that they love to glorify their king; Abraham, David, Isaiah, Daniel, Micah, and all the patriarchs and prophets, entertained these views of the Saviour And were these fools or madmen? No: rather say, they were enlightened to behold his glory, and divinely taught this grand mystery of the kingdom.

Who is there that has believed through grace, that does not view the Saviour as thus glorious, or find his name, person, work, and office, to be precious? Not one of God's redeemed ones in the present assembly, will refuse to acknowledge Jesus, and to ascribe to him great glory. All of you who have felt the power of his grace, in renewing and changing your hearts, now unitedly exclaim, "He is Lord of all." Observe,—

3. The testimony of his most inveterate enemies.

When he was upon earth, the Jews, his persecutors, could not help confessing, that never man spake like him,—and that even the winds and the sea obeyed him: they saw the miracles he wrought, and were filled with astonishment. A centurion, at his remarkable death, exclaims, "Verily, this man was the Son of God!" Nay, Satan himself must acknowledge his power, and say, "I know thee who thou art, the Holy One of Israel;" and again, the foul fiends whom he overcomes, cry, "Art thou come to torment us before the time?" Thus confessing his remarkable power over them, and saying, in effect, "He is Lord of all." And how often is there, even now, a conviction on the minds of his enemies, that the same Jesus with whom we have to do, is an awful Judge, and that there is no escaping the fierceness of his anger! But oh, how much they concede to the honor of the Saviour on a death-bed, when they exclaim, "Oh, Galilean, thou hast overcome me!" The judgment day, too, will disclose his terrors, and terrible indeed will be their sensations, when the pit of hell has enclosed them, and they are left as eternal monuments, everlasting instances of the justice and terror of his power. Those who denied his authority on earth, must, with doleful lamentations, confess it in hell, "For he must reign till he has put all enemies under his feet:" being, even by the acknowledgments of his foes, "Lord of all."

Let us then urge for a further proof of the dignity of the Saviour's character,—

4. The songs of the glorified in heaven.

They being no longer vexed with a body of death, nor

liable to form imperfect ideas of the glory of the Saviour, are exclaiming to him, "Thou art worthy, O Lord, to receive glory, and honor, and power; for thou hast created all things, and for thy pleasure they are and were created." They sing the song of Moses the servant of God, and the song of the Lamb, saying, "Great and marvellous are thy works, Lord God Almighty, just and true are thy ways, thou King of saints: who shall not fear thee, O Lord, and glorify thy holy name? for thou only art holy: for all nations shall come and worship before thee, for thy judgments are made manifest." They ascribe to him alone the complete and final victory over the beast and his followers, and over Antichrist at large, and sing "Salvation to our God that sitteth upon the throne, and unto the Lamb forever." To him that "hath on his vesture and on his thigh, a name written, King of kings, and Lord of lords," are all their praises directed; for they own him as over all, God blessed for ever, and celebrate his praises whilst eternity rolls along, for "He is Lord of all."

Having thus briefly endeavored to prove the truth of the text, that so you may believe it, I would now endeavor—

III. To show its propriety, or equity, that so we may admire it.

Here we intend to investigate the claims of the Saviour to this preëminence, and see that it is right that he should be "Lord of all." And we say that it is altogether equitable that he should be so, because of the divinity of his nature—the appointment of his Father—and the merits of his sufferings. Jesus "is Lord of all,"—

1. On account of the divinity of his nature.

It is well known, that some maintain that our Lord

Jesus Christ is but a mere man, like ourselves; that he had no existence prior to his being born of the Virgin Mary; and that he is the Son of God merely by office; but we have every necessary proof from Scripture, that he is God: for the Father has testified that he is such, saying, "Thy throne, O God, is forever and ever:" as such the angels adore him; his miracles attest it; and his own declarations put it beyond the possibility of a doubt. In believing that Christ is God, we have not followed cunningly devised fables, and in asserting it, we speak forth the words of truth and soberness. And if it be so that his nature is divine, ought he not to be acknowledged as Lord of all? He "is not a man that he should lie," and therefore, when he says that he and his Father are one, we must confess, that the high honor conferred upon him in the text, does most properly belong to him. He is "the man that is my fellow, says the Lord of hosts:" therefore divine honors are most justly his due, and who are we that we should refuse to render him the honor he demands? for he is Lord of all. Let no bold blasphemer dare to murmur at the distinguished honors of the Son of God; but let every one of us fall prostrate at his feet, saying, "My Lord, and my God!" Whilst cursed is the man that trusteth in man, and maketh flesh his arm, blessed are all they that put their trust in him: for he is God, and beside him there is none else; and justly has he ordained that "they who despise him shall be lightly esteemed." He will be acknowledged as Lord of all,—

2. On account of the appointment of his Father.

Here we must particularly regard the honor of the Saviour in his mediatorial character. Has not the Father exalted him with his own right hand to be a Prince and a

Saviour, to give repentance unto Israel and the remission of sins? Has he not highly exalted him, and given him a name which is above every name; that at the name of Jesus every knee should bow, and every tongue confess that he is Lord to the glory of God the Father? Jehovah has, indeed, conferred the highest possible honor upon his Son Jesus, and made his kingdom stand firm as his own eternal throne; he has glorified him with the glory that he had with him before the foundation of the world. He has passed a decree, that all men shall honor the Son, even as they honor the Father. He has committed all judgment into his hands, and views him as his coequal Son, now he appears before him in heaven. And shall we dare to question the right of the Saviour to this title, when it is given to him by God himself? The Father views his own honor and that of his Son as intimately connected. Whatever God appoints is right. The honor of the Saviour is of divine appointment, therefore he may well say to us, "Be still, and know that I am God."

That day which shall burn as an oven: that day for which all other days were made, shall reveal to us the uncreated glories of the Saviour; till then, let us rejoice that he is by the will of the Father "Lord of all."

We argue the right of this honor belonging to the Saviour—

3. From the merit of his sufferings.

"For we see Jesus, who was made a little lower than the angels, crowned with glory and honor for the suffering of death." The promise of God the Father to his Son Jesus was, that he should see his seed, that he should prolong his days, and that the pleasure of the Lord should prosper in his hands; that he should see of the travail of his soul and be satisfied; that he should divide a portion with the great, and the spoil with the strong; that he should have the heathen for his inheritance, and the uttermost parts of the earth for his possession; that he should break them with a rod of iron, and dash them in pieces like a potter's vessel. Verily, Jesus was made perfect through sufferings, and these expressions of his glory are the consequence of his abasement: for, because he endured the cross, despising the shame, and overcame principalities and powers, therefore "He is Lord of all."

Having just glanced at the import, the truth, and the equity of the text, let us now—

IV. Point out its influence, that so we may be affected by it.

Observe, then, that it warrants in us the most ardent attachment to him—it bears an unfriendly aspect on the enemies of the cross of Christ—it teaches us all to lift up to Jesus the voice of prayer and praise—and it gives us every reason to believe, that all things will terminate in the benefit and glory of the church.

1. Our text warrants in us the most ardent attachment to the Saviour. Because it represents him as invested with every excellence, and possessed of all possible power; and whilst we have this thought, that he is the Friend of mortals, as well as "Lord of all," surely we cannot help admiring and loving him.

He has exhibited undeniable proofs of his attachment to us; and shall the Lord of all be a "Man of sorrows and acquainted with grief," and we not be filled with attachment to him? Does his life of suffering and death of infamy, produce no effect on us? Remember, his love to us was great indeed, was prior to ours, was from everlasting, and as unmerited as it was unsought; and shall it meet no return? His glory, when viewed in connexion with his regard to sinners, is enough to make every heart flow with gratitude and burn with love. Who is so proper an object of our affection as the "Lord of all?" Whilst every thing else changes, he is the same. O, say to him then, "Whom have we in heaven but thee, and there is none upon earth that we desire beside thee."

2. This subject bears an unfriendly aspect to the enemies of the cross of Christ.

For if "he is Lord of all," none can oppose him with impunity, or reject his claims, and go away unpunished. As soon as Judas's band heard him say, "I am he," they fell immediately to the ground: and since his arm is so strong, I tremble for those who deny his divinity, despise his atonement, laugh at the influence of his Spirit, and will not have this Man to reign over them. He never will clear these guilty characters, but has threatened them "with everlasting destruction from the presence of the Lord, and from the glory of his power:" and as "Lord of all," he is able to execute every threat, and to perform that awful word which is gone out of his mouth. Oh, what will the despisers of Christ do in the day of their visitation? How can they escape the damnation of hell? He will soon appear as the Alpha and Omega, the beginning and the ending, the first and the last; and his glories will be viewed by these very persons with astonishment and confusion of face. As no honor was ever ascribed to him by those men, no glory shall be conferred on them by him; for he is able to cast them, both body and soul, into hell! Let them all then bow with submission and "kiss the Son now, lest he be angry, and they perish from the way, when his wrath is kindled but a little. Blessed are all they that put their trust in him."

3. Our text teaches us all to lift up to Christ the voice of prayer and praise.

For if he be "Lord of all," he ought to be adored, worshipped, and had in reverence by all the creatures he has made. "Let all the angels of God worship him," is the high command of God himself: and whilst the angels are paying him their adoration, shall the proud mortal man refuse to do so? It is not idolatry to worship our Jehovah Jesus, it is only rendering him the homage he deserves, requires, demands, and expects. O Christian, recollect, that in every time of trial you have to look up to him, who "is Lord of all," for support: supplicate then the help of his hand, adore the wonders of his love, praise him for the assistance he has already afforded you, nor ever imagine that you can be too lavish in adoring him who is exalted far above all blessing and praise. As "Lord of all," he is able to answer every petition that is put up to his throne, and will take no excuse for our neglecting to pray to him. His very nature, too, induces him to hear and answer prayer, so that this consideration ought to bring us low at his footstool, to implore of him the blessings of his grace. Had he indeed been but a man like ourselves, he could have no authority to demand our worship; but as he is God over all, blessed for ever, it is at the peril of any one to refuse rendering honor to him.

4. Our subject gives us every reason to believe that all things will terminate in the benefit and glory of the church.

Because the honor of Christ and the interests of his saints are closely connected, and he cannot fail to attend to the interests of those whom he has purchased with his own blood. Amongst them peace shall be published by Jesus Christ, who "is Lord of all:" it shall be dispensed to one nation as well as to another: he will be a wall of fire round about his saints, and the glory in the midst of them. The power, wisdom, and goodness he possesses, shall all be displayed in the behalf of that ship of which he is the Pilot, and of the family of which he is the Householder. And as he is the Head of the church, and "Lord of all," her walls shall be called "Salvation, and her gates praise:" by his blessing upon her, she shall become the Zion of the Lord, the city of the Holy One of Israel; and "the praise of the whole earth shall she be called." Even the machinations of our enemies shall be overruled for our good, and the divine glory shall be effectually promoted by every individual member of his family: so greatly will he distinguish his faithful servants from an ungodly world, that he will finally receive them to himself, and place them near his throne; where his glory shall be seen, his presence felt, his influence communicated, and his virtues sung, for ever and ever: for "He is Lord of all."

Brethren, what think ye of Christ? Is he all your salvation, and all you desire? or, are you despising and refusing to adore him? Is this Lord of all, your portion, your treasure, and your hope? or, are you yet ignorant of his glory, and destitute of his grace?

There is one passage of Scripture which I would wish might make an impression upon your minds, and then I shall have done; it is this: "No man can call Jesus Lord but by the Holy Ghost." Now the influences of this Spirit are essentially necessary to give Christ a throne in your heart. Has he testified of Jesus there, and taught you to say—

O that with yonder sacred throng
We at his feet may fall!
We'll join the universal song,
And crown him Lord of all!

312

SERMON VII.

THE FELLOWSHIP OF THE SAINTS.

"Then they that feared the Lord spake often one to another, and the Lord hearkened and heard it; and a book of remembrance was written before Him, for them that feared the Lord, and that thought upon His name: and they shall be mine, saith the Lord of hosts, in that day when I make up my jewels; and I will spare them, as a man spareth his own son that serveth him."
MALACHI iii. 16, 17.

It has often been remarked, and certainly with truth, that in the most abandoned ages of the world, the Lord has had a remnant according to the election of grace; he has preserved a seed to serve him; he has had numbers that have not bowed the knee to Baal. The chapter out of which we have read our text, gives us an account of deplorably wicked times, records the rejection of divine ordinances, the robbery of the honor of Jehovah, and the general impiety which were chargeable upon the Jewish nation: and yet it makes honorable mention of characters, whose holy zeal, and active endeavors to revive religion, should stimulate us, who hear things they never heard, and see glories their eyes never beheld, to be doubly concerned for the honor of Him, in whose hand our breath is, and whose are all our ways. Blessed be the God and Father of our Lord Jesus Christ, that there are now many in our own land, as well as elsewhere, who are cleansed in the blood, sanctified by the Spirit, and passing to the enjoyment of the presence of Jesus Christ; and who, like the faithful worthies, whose pure religion is noticed by Malachi, and approved by Jehovah, fear the Lord, speak often one to another, and think upon his name. Let us consider—

I. The excellences of good men which are here celebrated.

II. The approbation of them which God here testifies.

I. The excellences of good men which are here celebrated. And you will observe that they are more particularly distinguished by their holy fear of God; their pious meditation upon him; and their Christian fellowship one with another.

1. The first excellent trait which we behold in their character is their holy fear of God.

They are said to be "they that feared the Lord." And "who shall not fear thee, O Lord, and glorify thy name?" The Divine Being, brethren, claims your reverence, and "blessed are they that fear the Lord, that greatly delight in his commandments." The persons mentioned in our text were like Obadiah, who feared the Lord greatly: they were like Abraham, of whom the angel testified after his trial, saying, "I know that thou fearest God." They were like the churches mentioned in the Acts of the Apostles, who "walked in the fear of the Lord." They were like Cornelius, who was "a devout man, and one that feared God with all his house."

This divine principle, far from being the produce of the barren soil of nature, must be wrought in us by the power of the Spirit; for one of the promises of the new covenant is, "I will put my fear in their hearts, that they shall not depart from me." It springs not from a sense of guilt, for this fear is cast out by divine love; but it induces love to Jesus, it teaches us to hate evil, it prompts to ready obedience, and it leads to the throne of God; for where he is, there shall also his servants be.

2. These Old Testament believers were noted for their pious meditation upon God.

We are told that they "thought upon his name." Ah, how unlike those who have not God in any of their thoughts! how unlike many (must I not say most of us?) who suffer our minds to be so employed with earthly things, as to let our God, our Saviour go! These men of God, while some trusted in chariots, and some in horses, remembered the name of the Lord: in the multitude of their thoughts within them his comforts delighted their souls; their meditation of him was sweet; they were glad in the Lord; their minds were stayed upon him: the desire of their souls was to him and to the remembrance of his name; and do you know any thing of this? Have you ever enjoyed much of God in the secret silence of the mind? Do you daily, hourly, in your desires and contemplations, rise to the heavenly world? Isaac went out into the fields to meditate; upon whom do your thoughts delight to turn? There is enough in the name of God for contemplation. Review what he is in himself, and especially what he has done for you; frequently contemplate that work of redemption, which is to be your wonder for ever and ever; think of Jesus with thoughts of affection and desire; let your minds trace his actions; let the eye of faith behold him in glory pleading your cause; let it penetrate the cloud that separates between him and you; let it realize the happy time when you shall come before him. And if these are your contemplations, the effects of them will appear; the world will behold you as the Israelites beheld Moses, when he came from the mount, with his face shining exceedingly. Your whole deportment will savor of it, and your conversation will be in heaven, from whence you look for the Saviour.

3. These men, of whom the world was not worthy, were remarkable on account of their Christian fellowship one with another.

"They spake often one to another;" and, no doubt, they spake of the best things; they considered one another, to provoke one another to love, and to good works, and so much the more as they saw the day approaching. We can imagine them saying, "Come unto me all ye that fear God, and I will tell you what he has done for my soul." Methinks I hear them together reviewing the divine dealings towards them, till their hearts burn within them, while they talk to one another by the way. They were to one another what Jonathan was to David, when he strengthened his hands in God, thus proving that two are better than one. And do we not know that "He that walketh with wise men shall be wise, whilst a companion of fools shall be destroyed."

How truly deserving of imitation was the conduct of Anna the prophetess, who came into the temple when Simeon was blessing Jesus, "and spake of him to all them that looked for redemption in Israel." We see also fine instances of the same communicative disposition in the disciples who conversed together about Christ, and brought one another to him. So let us, then, comfort ourselves together, and edify one another, and exhort one another daily, "looking diligently, lest any one of us fail of the grace of God."

We know that men, like Simeon and Levi, are brethren in iniquity; but, "O my soul, come not thou into their secret; unto their assembly mine honor be thou not united." *They* invite one another for the worst of purposes: why should not we for the best? They say, "Come with us, we shall fill our houses with spoil; cast in thy lot with us; let us have one purse." But let us turn our eyes from them to the select society of Christians, and "behold how good and how pleasant a thing it is for brethren to dwell together in unity of love." They are all loved with the same everlasting love, all united to the same precious Jesus, all traveling to the same glorious heaven; surely, then, those communications ought to be, must be sweet. Learn to bear one another's burdens, to pity one another's faults, to pray for one another's best interests; so shall you copy the example of the best of men, and evidence that there is no bond in heaven or in earth so uniting as the love of Christ, which begets, preserves, and powerfully constrains to love.

While infidelity prevailed over many in those days, yet the grace of God influenced some: the Spirit of Christ dwelt in them, the presence of Christ was enjoyed by them, even that presence which turns mourning to joy, and death to life; which cherishes our weak faith, and illuminates our dark understandings; which adds new life to fainting hearts, and would make a heaven of hell. It is our mercy, that whenever two or three are gathered together in his name, there his presence is, to chill our corruptions, and bring heaven into our souls.

Having considered the excellences of good men, which are here celebrated, let us now notice—

II. The approbation which God here testifies of them.

And, taking up the ideas of our text, we observe, that this approbation appears, in his paying kind attention to their employment,—in his granting them a share in his affectionate remembrances,—and in his promising to own and spare them in the day of judgment.

1. Let us see how God evidences his approbation of them, in paying kind attention to their employment: for "the Lord hearkened and heard it."

God, indeed, has searched us and known us, for there is not a word in our tongues, but lo, O Lord, thou knowest it altogether! and so vast is his notice, that "for every idle word that men speak, they shall give account in the day of judgment." But in a peculiar manner, in a gracious way, does he attend to the groanings of the prisoners, to the cries of the needy, to the conversation of fellow-pilgrims. When you, brethren, unite in enquiring, What has God wrought for our own souls, for our families, for the churches to which we belong, or for the world at large? the Lord hearkens and hears it.

With real pleasure he sees, he listens to the public testimonies you give of the excellences of his cause, for, O glorious truth! the Lord taketh pleasure in the prosperity of his servants. Think not that the heavens are brass against you, or that he takes no notice of your actions, for he knows and he approves the way of the righteous. What real consolation does this convey to our minds! for though our spiritual conversation may be neglected by most, and held in the greatest contempt by many, the Lord hearkens and hears it. As God could remonstrate with the ungodly in the days referred to in the text, so his eyes were upon the righteous, and his ears were open to their cry. Satan, your subtle and too powerful enemy, cannot, after all, prevent the approbation of your God in covenant, and your God in Christ. O, then, go forward to sing in the way to Zion: "Be of one spirit, and of one mind, striving together for the faith of the gospel," and the Lord will hearken and hear it.

2. Jehovah manifests his approbation of them, by granting them a share in his affectionate remembrance; for "a book of remembrance was written before him" for them.

"Remember me, O my God, for good," was the prayer of Nehemiah: "Lord, remember me, when thou comest into thy kingdom," was the petition of the dying thief; and an interest in the Divine recollection is indeed a great blessing; and great as it is, it is granted to them "that feared the Lord, and that thought upon his name." "A book of remembrance was written:" this language is metaphorical, and is used to express the particular, the abiding, the never-to-be-forgotten recollection, which God has of the honor his saints put upon him. "He tells even their wanderings, and puts their tears into his bottle; are they not in his book? Of every thing, you, Christians, are enabled to do, to the glory of his grace it may be said, "It is written before him." The deeds of Bigthana and Teresh were written in the book of the Chronicles before king Ahasuerus, to their infamy and disgrace; but yours are inscribed by an immortal pen in the book of God's remembrance, to your joy and the lifting up of your head.

It is evident, from the following verse, that this is one of the books which shall be opened in the day of judgment;

and do you not recollect in what approving strains "the King eternal, immortal, and invisible," speaks of the acts of his saints, as recorded in the 25th chapter of Matthew's gospel? But remember, these deeds are by no means spoken of as approved by God as meritorious; no, but only as testimonies of their real religion, as evidences of their possessing faith, without which, none of these things could be acceptable in the sight of God; and as proofs of their superiority to those on the left hand of the Judge.

And what are we that God should think of us? Say, brethren, are we not altogether unworthy of his notice? Have we not indeed merited his wrath? And yet he gives us every blessing, and records our names on the palms of his hands, yea, prints them on his very heart.

3. God gives an evidence of his delight in their services, by promising to own and spare them in the day of judgment. "They shall be mine, saith the Lord of hosts, in the day when I make up my jewels."

Yes, he accounts them his jewels; despised as they are by men, they are chosen of God and precious. They are dear to him; he has rendered them comely by the righteousness of his Son, and in them he magnifies his bright and glorious perfections.

There is a day coming when he will make them up; when he shall send his angels to gather his elect from the four winds of the earth, when they shall have his name written on their foreheads in legible characters, and when Jesus shall say, "Well done, good and faithful servants, enter ye into the joy of your Lord." Come, subjects of my conquering grace, ever children of my love, and partakers of my Spirit, "inherit the kingdom prepared for you from the foundation of the world." Then shall all believers, the poorest not excepted, be owned before an assembled world, be dignified with the blessings of heaven: when Christ, who is their life, shall appear, they also shall appear with him in glory; crowns of honor shall be placed on their heads; palms of victory shall be held in their hands; robes of glory shall adorn them; and hymns of praise shall be heard from them, to the sovereign grace of Jesus; then they shall be ever with the Lord of hosts.

"And I will spare them, as a man spareth his own son that serveth him." They are his sons, begotten by his grace, adopted into his family, and distinguished with all the privileges of the children of God; whilst on earth they were active for him: they love him with the affection, the zeal, and the constancy of a son: and "like as a father pitieth his children, so the Lord pitieth them that fear him." I will spare them (as the passage may mean) till that day; I will preserve them from every evil, to the enjoyment of myself; they shall be kept by the mighty "power of God, through faith unto salvation." And then, when the last trumpet shall sound, and the dead shall be raised, I will spare them according to the multitude of my mercy; since I did not spare my Son for them, I will spare them for him. "When he shall appear, they shall be like him, for they shall see him as he is:" grace shall be brought to them at the revelation of Jesus Christ: they shall find mercy of the Lord in that day: they shall have no part in the fury of God's wrath, in the fire of hell, which is the second death; they shall be delivered from going down to the pit, for he has found a ransom. Oh, then, Christian, lift up your head, for your redemption draweth nigh.

Sinner—this subject proclaims your misery: instead of fearing God, you hate and disobey him; instead of meditating on him, your mind is occupied on what you shall eat, what you shall drink, and wherewithal you shall be clothed. You never stretch a thought half-way to God; instead of going with others in the road to heaven, the conversation in which you mingle is sensual and devilish. Your friends are the enemies of God, and you delight to confirm one another in your opposition to Jehovah; he sees you, but it is with indignation; he marks it down, but it is that it may appear against you another day; you shall be consigned over to the devil; instead of being spared, you shall be damned.

Oh, believer, live up to your character as delineated in the Bible; rejoice in the prospect of eternal life; when called to it, pass the river Jordan with a hope full of immortality, and so shall you be ever with the Lord. "Wherefore, comfort one another with these words." Amen.

SERMON VIII.

THE BELIEVER'S JOY IN CHRIST.

"Whom having not seen ye love; in whom, though now ye see him not, yet believing, ye rejoice with joy unspeakable, and full of glory."—1 PETER, i. 8.

THE second appearance of the Son of God is an event for which every Christian, when in a proper frame of mind, ardently longs, and earnestly prays; it is his employment and delight, to be "looking for the blessed hope and glorious appearing of the great God and our Saviour Jesus Christ:" it behooves him always to be hasting unto the coming of the day of God, and to hope to the end for the grace that shall be brought to him at the revelation of Jesus Christ. On that day a display will be given of the grandeur and glory of the God we worship: those dispensations which appear to us at present irreconcilable with his perfections, will then strike our admiring minds as being altogether right, yea, absolutely necessary, to accomplish his own designs, and illustrate the depths of his infinite love. This mortal shall then put on immortality, and this corruptible be clothed with incorruption; a final termination will then be put to all those fiery trials, which are now sent to try us; the Christian shall, both in the glory of his body and in the purity of his soul, resemble his Redeemer; and, in fine, the kingdom of heaven will be opened to all believers, and a loud voice shall proclaim, "Blessed are they that have done his commandments, for they have a right to the tree of life, and may enter in, through the gates, into the city." Since these shall be some of the grand transactions of that illustrious period, the saints cannot forbear exclaiming, "Come, Lord Jesus, come quickly."

But whilst the high expectations of the redeemed are directed towards the Saviour's second advent, it is worthy of remark, that he is not an uninteresting character to them now. Although they glory in the thought (which is so beautifully expressed in the verse preceding our text,) of "the trial of their faith being found unto praise, and honor, and glory, at the appearing of Jesus Christ," still there are present enjoyments in religion, and the believer has all good things in possession, as well as all glorious things in reversion. They have earnests given them of the happiness of that day; and do not Christians feel an anticipation of that rapture which will then begin, when they are enabled to say, in the words of our text, which immediately follow an allusion to the day of judgment, "whom having not seen we love: in whom, though now we see him not, yet believing, we rejoice, with joy unspeakable and full of glory?"

From the passage then, thus introduced, we shall endeavor to show you two things: That Jesus Christ is yet invisible;—that notwithstanding this, he excites the Christian's best sensations.

I. Jesus Christ is yet invisible.

"Whom," says the apostle, "having not seen," and "in whom, though now ye see him not."

No doubt Peter here refers to a sight of Christ in the flesh; since the greater part of those to whom he wrote, had not "beheld his glory, the glory of the only-begotten of the Father, full of grace and truth:" it was his design to comfort their minds, and to inform them that, although Christ lived no longer on earth, there is a possibility of enjoying the blessings of his undertaking in our own souls, and that this shall be the case till time shall end.

But the idea of Jesus being unseen, must not only be viewed in reference to those to whom the apostle wrote, but in its bearings upon us; for the words of our text are as applicable to us, upon whom the ends of the world are come, as they were to those who lived a short time after the ascension of the Saviour. And we may contemplate our Lord Jesus Christ as invisible in two respects, namely: in the glories of his person—and in the mysteries of his providence. We would consider our Lord Jesus Christ as an invisible Saviour, as it respects—

1. The glories of his person.

He, my brethren, is "that blessed and only Potentate, who alone hath immortality. Dwelling in light, to which no man can approach; whom no man hath seen nor can see."

Formerly, indeed, he was beheld, arrayed in human nature; and we might have addressed those who were familiar with him: "Blessed are your eyes, for they see what many prophets and righteous men desired to see, but saw not:" but you remember that, before his resurrection, he said, "A little while and ye shall see me, and again a little while, and ye shall not see me, and because I go to my

Father." Now the heavens have received him out of our sight, "till the times of the restitution of all things:" the eye of sense cannot trace his glory now; we cannot soar to the third heavens, and say to the angels of God, "Sirs, we would see Jesus:" it is impossible that his beauties should ever be viewed by mortal eyes; the sight would dazzle, would confound us. He is inclosed in a veil of glory which we cannot penetrate, appearing in the presence of God for us: a miracle must be wrought before we can discover him on earth: this was done in the case of Stephen; for, when standing before the council, he, looking steadfastly into heaven, said, "Behold I see heaven opened, and the Son of man standing on the right hand of God;" and the animating sight caused him to leave the world with a holy calmness, yea, to die like Jesus, imploring forgiveness for his enemies. Instances like these, are, however, very rare; for, as to the state of the church in general, and as to the discharge of his mediatorial office, he is not seen of any. The high priest, you recollect, was not to be seen after his entrance into the holy place until he returned again; so you, Christian, must live by faith, and not by sight: faith is the evidence of things not seen. And should not this consideration, namely, that ye have not seen the glory of the person of Christ, urge you, stimulate you, as a powerful motive, to run with renewed alacrity, toward the mark, in the road to heaven, the chief pleasure of which place will be to see him as he is? Is it not worth dying for, to contemplate his excellences? to see that glory which has been hid from ages and from generations, but which will catch the gazing eyes, and employ the eternal adoration of the saints of God for ever? But till that day when "this same Jesus, who is now taken up from us into heaven, shall so come in like manner, as he went into heaven;" I say, till then we must speak of him as one whom we have not yet seen.

But in another sense Christ is invisible, and that is—

2. In the mysteries of his providence.

We know not his designs in his dealing with us, and could we know them, yet we cannot see how his methods of acting tend to accomplish them; our blindness, as creatures, is one thing that prevents us from searching and finding out God, or tracing the Almighty to perfection. "His ways are in the deep, and his judgments past finding out;" he is unsearchable in all his deeds; nor man, nor angel can give any account of some of his ways. His reasons are known only to himself; and it is enough for us, that the Judge of all the earth will do right. What is the reason that, under afflictive dispensations of providence, when perhaps God is taking from us those comforts of which we are but stewards, we murmur, and complain, and grieve? It is because we cannot see how these things are uniting with other occurrences, to promote our holiness and happiness. Here then Jesus is unseen, even in the designs of his mind, when he tries us in this way. We cannot sound his judgments with mortal lines, we cannot view them by feeble sense.

A believer cannot walk by sight; Jehovah has seen fit to render it impossible; yet, amidst all the storms of life, however driven upon seas of distress, it should always afford us consolation, that our Father is at the helm, and that ship is well conducted of which he is the pilot.

Is our life a journey? It is an unseen hand that guides us, that prevents our foes from overcoming us, that shields us by night and by day from innumerable dangers; and it is the part of faith to rejoice that however obscure the dealings of God are now, they will all be made clear hereafter; it shall be shown that the great chain of events most wonderfully illustrates the character and perfections of God. That wisdom which led us through every danger that kind hand that even robbed us of our comforts, for the most beneficial purposes, shall be viewed with unutterable pleasure when we are blessed with strong immortal eyes. God will be his own interpreter, and every mystery will be made plain; so that we shall no longer worship an invisible Saviour, but be filled with gratitude for a view of the deep things of God.

Jesus is invisible then, as to the glories of his person, and is not now beheld by us; and as for his judgments, we have not known them: but though he is unseen by the saints, we observe—

II. That notwithstanding this he excites their best sensations.

This he must do because he is their all and in all: from him all their mercies flow, in him all their happiness centres, and to him all their exertions are directed; hence his religion engages in its service the best passions of the human soul: the finest feelings of the mind are called into exercise, by him who is yet unseen; and particularly is the Saviour the object of strong affection,—lively faith— and unutterable joy. Jesus Christ has attracted, though he is invisible—

1. Strong affection.

"Whom having not seen ye love." You have no doubt often heard that Jesus possesses the greatest possible excellences, that he is perfectly amiable, and altogether lovely. As God he possesses every perfection, being equal with the Father: "In him dwells all the fullness of the Godhead bodily." As man he had every thing that can adorn human nature, and make it more honorable than it was before our first parents fell; and, as our Mediator, he has every thing suitable and necessary for us men, and for our salvation: his countenance is as Lebanon, excellent as the cedars, it is as the sun when he shineth forth in his strength; so that he has united in himself all human and divine beauties: this is our Beloved and this is our Friend.

The saints, having discerned this, are ravished with his excellences, the flame of divine love is kindled in their souls, and they esteem it the heaven of heavens only to see his face. All the beauty of creation is deformity itself when compared with the person of Jesus: angels are not half so fair, nor the stars half so bright; and, if this is the case, no wonder that he is the object of attachment to all enlightened minds. And they love him too, let it be remembered, because he first loved them; therefore it was that he revealed himself unto them, because he had set his love upon them: the fullness of grace that is treasured up in him, the offices he sustains in the economy of their salvation, and the relations he bears to them, all endear him to their souls: hence they love him with a superior and peculiar attachment, with a love that is shed abroad in their hearts by the power of the Holy Spirit, and which is distinguished for its constant duration. All that belong to him, that bear his image, and are conformed to his lovely likeness, have a share in their affections, even for the sake of Him, who alone is worthy of the highest place in our affections: the members of his family, the truths of his gospel, the ordinances of his appointment, and the precepts of his love, are all beloved by Christians, because of their connexion with the Lord Jesus Christ, "of whom, and through whom, and to whom, are all things." They love him with all their souls, and hearts, and mind, and strength; the affection that they feel for their friends in the flesh, great as it is, and ought to be, is coldness, when compared with the glowing ardor of their love to a Saviour, for whom, if called to it, they would cheerfully suffer the loss of all things, yea, rejoice and be exceeding glad that they are counted worthy to suffer for his sake. It was divine love that animated them in the prospect, yea, in the very feeling of the flame, and that gave them joy in the most critical period, causing them to leave the world rejoicing in that everlasting attachment, the pleasing effects of which they so clearly displayed.

Oh, how this holy principle deadens the warmest passions to the things of time and sense! with what holy contempt it enables us to look down upon the pursuits of those who are unacquainted with the joy of loving Jesus! and at the same time that the Christian dwells on this delightful name, the angels are surrounding him with pleasure, rejoicing to hear the name they love, from a mortal tongue. He is the bright morning-star, before which all the twinkling sparks of night begin to die away. The greatness of the Godhead, and the sweetness of the creature, meet harmoniously in him: neither the shades of the night, nor the business of the day, must hide the image of Jesus from the sight of the Christian. Yea, the company of the saints in heaven, and the brilliancy of the place, would be all nothing, if Jesus removed: the Christian would be tired of life, would long to die, would find immortality a curse, if he were placed far from Jesus. When he is brought very near to him, even here upon earth, when glory is introduced into his soul here, he begs of God to stay his hand, for he can bear no more happiness whilst he is in the body of sin and death; he feels the great yet delightful pressure of glory, and he cries, "Turn away thine eyes, for they have overcome me." The inhabitants of the heavenly world can sustain the vision; its joys are too intense for a mortal, the glare overcomes us. Yet love me still, and translate me whenever thou choosest to the place where I shall behold thee with strengthened sight, and my heart shall be all love, and thou all my joy!

2. Jesus is the object of the saints' lively faith. "In whom, though now we see him not, yet believing."

This expression shows us the very nature of faith, or at least its peculiar characteristic, which is, to regard invisible things; in this way it acts upon Jesus the Son of God, for "Blessed are they that have not seen, and yet have believed:" those who are regenerate and love Christ, have their faith drawn towards him: and it is not merely a notional, historical, or temporary faith, which they are enabled to exercise upon him, but a scriptural, heartfelt and constant act. It is not merely crediting the truth of his assertions, but our text has a reference to a perpetual looking to him as the Author and Finisher of faith, a quitting self for his sake, a leaning upon him as the only Saviour, a casting our all into his hands, and an expectation of grace and glory from him; and all this is done whilst he is unseen. Now to make a man believe in this way to the saving of his soul, divine influence is essentially necessary; it belongs to the same Spirit of faith, who taught sinners in former days to believe in Jesus, to work this gracious principle in our hearts at the present time.

The saints have faith now instead of vision; but shortly their faith shall be changed for the sight of God; and they shall be satisfied, when they awake up in the divine likeness: the use of faith is to give them to know all this, for they believe that they shall behold him, whom now they see not; they must exercise faith in the second appearing of Christ, because he has himself asserted its truth; the dispensations of providence are paving a way for it, and they have in their own breasts the earnest of it, and now in their possession the Holy Spirit.

This principle is, however, liable to change, it has its different degrees; there is such a thing as little faith, and we may be strong in faith, giving glory to God; this consideration should teach us to say, with the disciples of old, "Lord, increase our faith!" Faith is always acceptable in the sight of God; an implicit reliance upon the atonement of Jesus is the best sacrifice we can offer to the Searcher of the hearts, and Trier of the reins of the children of men: whilst without faith it is impossible to please him. Great and many have been the exploits performed by it; what wonders it did for Abel, Enoch, Noah, Abraham, Sarah, Isaac, Jacob, Joseph, Moses, and the Israelites in general! and what shall I say more?

The last sensation which we mention among those which Christ excites in the minds of his people, is—

3. Unutterable joy. "Ye rejoice with joy unspeakable and full of glory."

The covenant engagements of Jesus, his very name, his incarnation, his blood, his promises, his work, and intercession, all seem to say to us, "Rejoice evermore." They have introduced grand, solid ground for joy; and heartfelt pleasure is connected with faith and love. This is a transport that is better experienced than described; for when God lifts up the light of his countenance upon a soul, that soul has more joy than the men of the world have, when their corn, and wine, and oil increase; strangers intermeddle not with this joy, they know nothing of it, it entirely surpasses their understanding: saints themselves cannot tell it half, they have not language to express it, they cannot convey proper views of it to others; for it is unspeakable, being excited by a participation of God's unspeakable gift: it is full of glory. There is a rejoicing in iniquity, an evil and a scandalous triumph; but the joy alluded to in our text, makes the subject of it appear truly honorable in the eyes of angels, good men, and God; it is a pleasure that maketh not ashamed, that leaves no sting behind, for it is substantial; whilst the joy of the hypocrite is but for a moment, and the laughter of fools is like the crackling of thorns under a pot: this holy sensation, increasing more and more, is the beginning, the pledge, the presage of eternal happiness; it is glory begun below; it is a kind of first fruits of the new life, which we shall pluck from heavenly trees in the kingdom of glory above: the saints can tell something of the happiness of the world of spirits, by the bliss which a discovery of divine love causes in their souls, even in the midst of the greatest calamities. Such was the rapture which Peter, James and John felt, when in the mount of transfiguration, with the Son of God! and far greater will be the rapture of the glorified spirits round the throne of God and of the Lamb for ever.

That mount, how bright, those forms how fair!
'Tis good to dwell for ever there;

Come death, dear envoy of my God,
And bear me to that blest abode.

Oh, let us never forget that Christ Jesus is the proper, the appointed, the only object of religious joy. Whatever the Christian rejoices in must have some connection with him. Are the promises the matter of his rejoicing? These were all made by him, are all ratified, " are all yea and amen in Christ Jesus to the glory of God by us." Is it any spiritual blessing? It comes to us only through his mediation. Oh, then, Christians, joy in God, by whom you have now received the atonement; " rejoice and be exceeding glad, for great is your reward in heaven:" " rejoice in hope of the glory of God:" let your heavenly inheritance be the matter of your triumph, " though now for a season, if need be, you are in heaviness through manifold temptations." While the rich man glories in his riches, and the mighty man in his might, do you rather rejoice that your names are written in heaven: declare his works with rejoicing; go to God your exceeding joy; with joy draw water out of the wells of salvation; shout for joy, all ye that are upright in heart; joy in God, the God of salvation: finally, my brethren, rejoice in the Lord; rejoice in the Lord always, and again, I say, rejoice. So shall the Lord your God rejoice over you with singing, yea, rest in his love.

Let me remark, by way of conclusion, that these sensations, from various causes, are not always felt; but our love is cold, our faith dying, and our spark of joy quenched, so that we go daily mourning; but these things ought not so to be: they indicate that religion is at a low ebb in our souls; and if this be the case with us, we may cry, " O, my leanness! my leanness!" But must we not lay the blame of our little enjoyment of religion upon ourselves? Surely we must. O that the Spirit of true faith and joy would fill us with all joy and peace in believing!

Let me ask, how many of us, in the divine presence, can appropriate the language of the text to ourselves, and say of Jesus, "Though now I see him not, I love him, I believe in him, I rejoice in him with joy unspeakable and full of glory?"

Let me tell the sinner who has no interest in the bliss of which we have been speaking, the fearfulness of his character, and the certainty of his punishment.

Oh, Christian, go on to glorify Him who having not seen you love, and in whom, though now ye see him not, yet believing ye rejoice, with joy unspeakable and full of glory. Amen.

SERMON IX.

ETERNAL LIFE, HOW GAINED.

"Lay hold on eternal life."—1 TIMOTHY 6 : 12.

WHAT a peculiar solemnity is there in the advice of an aged Christian to a young convert : to hear one whose hopes of a happy immortality are strong and lively, whose prospects of eternal glory are sufficient to make him long for the cold embrace of death, and look with triumph on the ghastly horrors of the tomb ; to hear such a one instructing those who are just commencing their journey to heaven is truly affecting, because we know, that at such a time, the most important truths will drop from his lips ; and hard indeed must be the heart of that man, who can think of them without an awe upon his mind, without a determination to fulfill the best wishes of a dying friend. So Moses addressed the children of Israel, just before he died in the land of Moab, according to the word of the Lord. So Jesus, when his hour was not yet come, discoursed with his disciples and cheered their minds, which experienced the sorrow of disappointed expectations and terminating friendship. And so such a one as Paul, the aged, gives the kindest and best advice to Timothy, his own son in the gospel, while he shortly after presents him with his own situation and the feelings of his own mind, saying, " For I am ready to be offered up, and the time of my departure is at hand."

One of his last exhortations to Timothy, before his rapt spirit was borne to God, was, "Lay hold on eternal life;" and permit me to say, that obedience to this injunction is as all-important to us, as it was to the young evangelist to whom it was addressed. I intend, then, to offer a few thoughts upon—the object presented to our view,—and the exhortation concerning it.

I. The object presented to our view. Eternal life.

By this expression, the happiness of the heavenly world is evidently intended; and when it is called eternal life, we are not merely to understand that it will have no termination, that there will be no more death; but we are taught that every thing that can render life desirable or delightful, will be there enjoyed, without interruption, in rich abundance, so that God's people will be eternally satisfied with his goodness. It is impossible for me to describe to you eternal life, or to tell half the glory which is felt in that happy land from whence no traveler returns. Had I, like Paul, been caught up to the third heaven, and heard unspeakable words, and seen its inconceivable excellence, I could not, even then, tell it you: there are glories which it is not lawful to utter: eye has not seen it, ear has not heard it, the heart of man cannot conceive it; the tongue of Gabriel, the favorite angel, could not describe it: yea, nothing short of the full possession of it, can give us an adequate idea of its excellence. Hear what you may of eternal life, and conceive of it to the utmost stretch of your powers, when you arrive at the threshold of heaven, you must exclaim, with the astonished queen of Sheba, "The half has not been told me!"

All we can do is, to form some ideas of it, from the

views under which it is represented in the divine word; and lest we should darken counsel by words without knowledge, we shall deduce our observations upon eternal life, from that unerring source; and we remark, for the sake of distinction, it especially includes in it, a perpetual enjoyment of—divine favor,—divine knowledge,—and the divine presence.

Eternal life comprehends—

1. A constant enjoyment of the divine favor. This idea is founded upon the following passage in the Psalms, "His anger endureth but a moment; in his favor is life." As the favor of God runs through our natural life, and is the source and support of our spiritual life, there is no doubt that it will be the felicity of our eternal life. For ever, brethren, will believers rejoice that it was through the free favor and unmerited grace of God, that they arrived at the kingdom of glory: the song of the redeemed is, "Not unto us, not unto us, but unto thy name be all the praise." They will acknowledge in devout exclamations, that they owe all their purity to Him that loved them, all their conquests to him that died for them, and all their happiness to him that rose again, and thus begot them again unto a lively hope. The favorable smiles of God, too, will delight them for ever and ever; they shall be approved by him, and acceptable in his sight, through the mediation of the Son of his love.

That must be eternal life, which embraces the complete enjoyment of the lifting up of Jehovah's countenance, and the everlasting smiles of a covenant God. Even now, the consciousness of interest in the benevolence of the God of the whole earth, puts more joy into the mind of a Christian, than the men of the world receive when their corn, and their wine, and their oil increase: but what will be their pleasures when they arrive at the shores of that peaceful land, where doubts and fears are known no more, but the full assurance of divine favor is enjoyed for ever and ever.

2. Eternal life includes divine knowledge.

This is evident, from these words, "This is life eternal, to know thee, the only true God, and Jesus Christ whom thou hast sent:" and this knowledge is eternal life; not only as it prepares us for the enjoyment of it, but as it contributes the very essence of its felicity and joy. "Whoso findeth wisdom findeth life." O, take fast hold of instruction, let her not go, for she is thy life. In heaven we shall know even as we are known. Our ideas of God will be clear and consistent, our eternal life will be a life of intelligence, and the divine character will unfold and open to us a wide field for active enquiry and diligent research. Hence we may well be so anxious to enquire in God's temple, to be perpetually making new discoveries, under the teachings of God himself, of his own character and dispensations, and to be learning the manifold wisdom of God for ever and ever. Thus shall we eternally possess an understanding that we may know him that is true, and we shall be in him that is true, even in his Son Jesus Christ. And who amongst us all, that knows any thing of the Saviour, would not wish to know more, and to see more of his excellent greatness through the countless ages of eternity? Lord Bacon would say, "knowledge is power." But the Bible gives us to see that true knowledge is life, is nothing short of eternal life.

3. The last ingredient in our eternal happiness, that we mention at this time, is the divine presence.

Jesus Christ is, indeed, the life of his people now, his ordinances delight their minds, and his spiritual presence removes all thoughts of solitude; but hereafter their eyes shall see the King in his beauty, even in the land that is yet afar off. It is the principal part of the glory of the inhabitants of the new heaven above, that the Lord God shall dwell amongst them; thus they behold his beauties, and have him as their kind companion forever and ever. Innumerable passages of Scripture that represent Christ as the life of his people, suggest the idea that his presence, his constant presence, makes eternal life. And what a glorious life is this, existence and complete felicity unite in the land of Canaan above! Judge, if you can, what a redeemed soul experiences the moment it enters into the midst of the heavenly city; and think too highly, if you can, of that most wonderful of all subjects, "eternal life."

Having thus briefly reflected on the object presented to our view, let us now turn our attention—

II. To the exhortation concerning it. "Lay hold on it."

We may lay hold on eternal life—by embracing the Gospel which reveals it—by believing on Jesus, who bestows it,—by relying on the promises which ensure it,—and by pressing towards the full enjoyment of it.

1. Lay hold on eternal life, by embracing the Gospel which reveals it.

In what a benighted state was the world before the diffusion of the Gospel: what vague, uncertain, and confused ideas were entertained by the most enlightened men of that day, of a future state: all was wild conjecture and mere speculation. Hence arose the absolute necessity of a light to lighten the Gentiles, and to be the glory of Israel, the need of a day-star to visit us, and to guide our feet into the way of peace. For this the Gospel was inspired, and to accomplish this it is evidently calculated; for by the Gospel our Lord Jesus hath abolished death, and brought life and immortality to light. The Bible, brethren, discovers eternal life. This mystery is concealed in the Gospel of Jesus, from carnal eyes, while it is revealed unto babes. Hence appears the superiority of the Gospel to the volume of creation: "The heavens indeed declare the glory of God, and the firmament showeth his handy work; but the law of the Lord is perfect, converting the soul; the testimony of the Lord is sure, making wise the simple; the statutes of the Lord are right, rejoicing the heart; the commandment of the Lord is pure, enlightening the eyes." The Gospel reveals a heaven to come; shows us that by nature we have no title or claim to it; and teaches us where it may be found. Hence it is called the word of life. Oh, what a treasure is contained within the covers of the Bible! This is the field where the pearl of great price is hid, and eternal life is brought to view. And shall this Gospel be neglected by you? rather bid farewell to every other system, call it vanity and lies, and bind the Gospel to your heart. Where the truth is received in the love of it, where the Gospel is esteemed as invaluable, and that kind epistle which assures us of pardon and glory, is not only perceived there, but actually believed and embraced; there eternal life is laid hold of.

2. Lay hold on eternal life, by believing on Jesus who bestows it.

"This is the record, that God hath given unto us eternal life, and this life is in his Son. He that hath the Son hath life: he that hath not the Son shall not see life, but the wrath of God abideth on him." "The gift of God is eternal life through Jesus Christ our Lord." He, brethren, is the only medium through which this blessing can be communicated to us, as is evident from the language of the glorified themselves, who are now singing that song which no man can learn but the redeemed. We shall be eternally indebted to Christ for our felicity; then lay hold on eternal life by faith in him; let it not appear that there is "none of us that stirreth up himself to lay hold on God." Oh, take hold on God's strength that you may be at peace with him, and you shall be at peace with him.

If Jesus is the life of the Christian, and the very sum and substance of eternal glory; and heaven the enjoyment of him; how concerned should we be to apprehend him by faith. Jacob laid hold on eternal life when he wrestled with the man Jesus till the break of day, and said, "I will not let thee go, except thou bless me." The church laid hold on eternal life, when she said of Jesus, "I held him and would not let him go, till I had brought him to my mother's house." Simeon had hold on eternal life when he took Jesus in his arms and blessed him. The afflicted woman in the Gospel had hold on eternal life, when she said, "If I touch but the hem of his garment, I shall be whole." Go ye, then, and do likewise. Believe in the name of the only-begotten Son of God, and because he lives, ye shall live also; yea, as long as he exists, shall you remain in the mount of glory; for your faith itself shall prove that a union subsists between himself and you, more intimate and inseparable, than that which subsists between the firm foundation and the stately edifice; the fruitful vine, and the living branch; the influential head, and the active members.

Faith in Christ, and eternal life, are always inseparably connected in the word of God. Oh, may they be so in our experience, that the abundant grace may, through the thanksgiving of many, redound to the glory of God.

3. Lay hold on eternal life, by relying on the promises that insure it.

You are to spend your days in hope of eternal life, which God, that cannot lie, promised before the world began. Eternal life is the grand, the best promise contained in the Scriptures: it is that to which all the rest are subordinate. Oh, then, live by faith upon the promises, so shall you lay hold on eternal life.

Who were they "whose carcasses fell in the wilderness, concerning whom God sware in his wrath, that they should not enter into his rest?" They were those who believed not. So we see that they could not enter in, because of unbelief. And unbelief will ever be a barrier to our possession of the heavenly Canaan, for it is a virtual rejection of God himself. The accomplishment of the promises of God is certain; why, then, will ye not enjoy those blessings which are so intimately connected with a firm expectation of that eternal life, with which the promises of God are fraught?

Lay hold of eternal life in the promise: your Father's legacy, Christians, secures it for you; read with pleasure your title to it, and look upon yourselves as no longer strangers and foreigners, but fellow-citizens with the saints, and of the household of God. Rejoice in the security of your claim to eternal life, dwell upon it with pleasure, and this thought will cheer the rugged path of life, and reconcile you to your present condition.

"Seize the kind promise while it waits,
And march to Zion's heavenly gates;

Believe and take the promis'd rest,
Obey, and be forever blest."

4. "Lay hold on eternal life," by pressing toward the full enjoyment of it.

This appears to be the principal idea of the text; for in the expression there is an allusion to the active exertions of racers to gain the prize. We are not to count ourselves to have apprehended; but this one thing we are to do, forgetting those things which are behind, we must press forward towards those which are before, aiming at the mark for the prize of the high calling of God in Christ Jesus. You are not laying hold on eternal life if you rest satisfied with present attainments, and are inactive in religion. You should daily become more and more animated in your pursuit of the prize, by faith's view of its glory. If the famous Carthagenian general, Hannibal, could inspire his troops with so much courage, by a prospect of the fertile plains of Italy, from the barren Alps over which they were passing, how much more courageous should Christians become, by a prospect of that glory which Christ exhibits to their view, and promises in his word!

You can have no better proof of sincerity than that which will be afforded by constant exertion: you are only safe in this way. O that the Holy Spirit may enable you to lay aside every weight, and the sin which doth so easily beset you; and to run with patience the race set before you, looking unto Jesus as your example, who, in obtaining our redemption, persevered through difficulties, even to the end.

To excite you to such a conduct as I have been recommending, I might mention the two motives subjoined in the verse whence our text is taken: to lay hold on eternal life, namely,—as the end of your calling,—and the language of your own profession. This is the end of your calling: "Lay hold on eternal life, whereunto thou art also called." We are called, brethren, to glory and honor; but as preparatory to our possession of it, we are called to warfare and unwearied exertion in the divine life. This is the language of your own profession: "Lay hold on eternal life, whereof thou hast professed a good profession before many witnesses." When you entered on the cause of Christ, you engaged yourself by a solemn pledge to war a good warfare. The vows of God are upon you; O, then, lay hold on eternal life; if you do not, you belie your own profession, and give those of us who behold you reason to suspect that you have no part or lot in the matter.

By way of inference, I would remark,—

Of how many things may a man lay hold, and yet come short of eternal life. You may amass riches, till they take to themselves wings and fly away: you may pursue your own gratification, and prove yourself "a lover of pleasure more than a lover of God," till your delights are exchanged for insufferable torments: you may have a large share of honor, till that puff of noisy breath, gives place to indelible infamy, and everlasting confusion of face: you may fill a conspicuous station in the church of Christ, till the Master of assemblies declares you to be one of those whom he never knew. All these things, and many more, may be possessed by you on earth, and yet you may fail of the grace of God, and see eternal life, as Balaam said he should see Christ, afar off. O, then, be concerned to let your treasure be in heaven, that you heart may be there also.—Again—

How essentially necessary is the influence of God's Spirit, and grace, to enable us to possess so vast a treasure, and hold so valuable a possession. Heaven, may one say, is too great a prize for me to seize: so it is, if you are possessed of mere mortal power; but, "I can do all things through Christ which strengtheneth me," is language which becomes the most weak and humble Christian. True it is, that unless we are "strengthened with all might by his Spirit in the inner man," the hand of faith will become palsied, so that we shall not be able to lay hold on eternal life; but if the same glorious Being who says, Stretch forth thy hand, at the same time gives us power to apprehend the blessing, we may rejoice that heaven and all its glory properly and inalienably belong to us.

Men and brethren, suffer the word of exhortation: those of you who have yet never heard the heavenly voice of Wisdom, nor entered the society of believers, let me faithfully tell you, that you are daily making the wrath of God, which is the second death, more and more certain; you are advancing rapidly to hell, the mouth of which is open to receive you. Ah! you may wish to lay hold on eternal life, when it will for ever shrink from your touch.

O, let those of us who have a good hope through grace, endure unto the end, so shall we be saved: let us persevere, in hope of understanding more of the heights, and depths, and breadths, and lengths of this subject in the kingdom of glory.

To all of you, sinners or saints, professors or profane, young or old, I would say, The voice of God's ministers, of dying friends, of opening graves, of the Holy Scriptures, and of Jehovah himself is,—"LAY HOLD ON ETERNAL LIFE."

SERMON X.

THE RAINBOW ABOUT THE THRONE.

"And there was a rainbow about the throne, in sight like unto an emerald."—REVELATION iv. 3.

AMIDST the chequered scenes of life, the insignificance of the pursuits in which mankind in general are engaged, and the prospects of mortality and death, which must sometimes strike our minds, it is the privilege and happiness of the real Christian to look beyond the grave; to summon all the powers of his mind to contemplate the glories of a future world; to bid farewell to earth; and inspect, yea, anticipate for himself, the happiness of the glorified in heaven. The vanity of the creature is made use of as an impulse to drive him elsewhere to seek for solid joy; and finding that beneath the skies there is no proper satisfaction for the vast desires of an immortal soul, he looks beyond; above them he soars within the veil; beholds his ever-loving Saviour scattering the best of blessings on all the happy tribes; hears them recounting the wonders of his grace; and feels the animation in his mind which the sight of the joys of heaven ever more inspires.

O, my brethren, let us aim to do this: the things of time and sense have engaged by far too much of our attention through the week; on God's own day then, let us rise "to the general assembly and church of the first-born, whose names are written in heaven:" let us, in spirit at least, join the spirits of the just made perfect, in their admiration of Jesus, in the homage which they pay him.

The highly favored apostle John shows, in the chapter before us, how, in vision, a door was opened in heaven, and a voice calling him, promised to show him things that must be hereafter; immediately, he says, he was in the Spirit; his mind was supernaturally impressed with those ideas which he had to reveal to us: the objects which he beheld must not be thought by us to have a real existence in the world of spirits, for the language is altogether metaphorical; and we are presented with hieroglyphics; the meaning of which may be developed, and will instruct us much in our views of the kingdom. Like Paul, then, not knowing whether he was in the body or out of the body, in his own apprehension; he was admitted into the presence of God, and he was favored with a vision of a glorious throne, on which sat One whom it was utterly impossible for him fully to describe: for glory, to look upon, he was like a jasper and a sardine stone; the throne itself, however, was surrounded by a phenomenon, which may well attract our notice at this time; for, says our text, "There was a rainbow round about the throne, in sight like unto an emerald."

You ask, what this rainbow is? The bow which God set in the clouds after the flood, was a token of the covenant he had made with man, that he would never destroy the earth any more by water; and there is no doubt, brethren, that the rainbow spoken of in my text, is the better covenant, the covenant of grace, far exceeding any other covenant whatever. The manner in which a rainbow illustrates this well-ordered covenant, and the several other ideas of it contained in our text will now come under our notice; and let us, my brethren, all pray earnestly, that the God of creation, providence and grace, would give us to see how one part of his works illustrates another; and how they shall show forth his eternal power and Godhead, while they are calculated to excite our admiration, joy, and praise.

Permit me then, my friends, to ask you—

I. Is the rainbow a reflection of the rays of the sun upon a thin watery cloud? The covenant of grace owes all its excellences to Jesus Christ, the "Sun of righteousness."

That beautiful appearance in nature, the rainbow, is never seen but when the sun shines, and is evidently formed by a refraction of his rays on a watery cloud. It has often been asked, whether there was an appearance of this kind before the general deluge: it seems most likely that there was not; and therefore the rainbow is a more certain proof of the truth of the divine promise than it otherwise would be: every disposition of a rainy cloud will not produce a rainbow; and it is asked, who knows, but before the flood, the God of creation might have so arranged the clouds that they should not form any: but be it how it may, it is evident, the sun is the cause of the rainbow's beautiful appearance.

So, brethren, in that covenant which the rainbow represents, Jesus our Sun is all in all. Did he not submit to all the conditions of this covenant, and appear before his Father, as ready to lay down his life for his sheep? Yes, brethren, he declared his determination to fulfill the law, and make it honorable, and to bring in an everlasting righteousness. The whole administration of this covenant was committed into his hands; he is the surety, the trustee of it; all the blessings of it are lodged in his hands: so also is he the testator of this covenant, for he, in the promises of his gospel, has bequeathed all these mercies to us sinful men: as an Intercessor, he pleads for us, and obtains the full possession of all those favors; yea, in his offices he reveals and applies them to our hearts. There would never have been any covenant of grace at all, if it had not been for Jesus: "For of him, and through him, and to him, are all things; to whom be glory for ever and ever." No wonder, then, that he is represented to us in another part of this book, as having a rainbow upon his head; for the covenant of grace is his, and we must all give him the glory of its existence, stability, and blessings. On this account it is that we must crown him with honor; and through eternity we shall be praising him for the weight of sufferings that he endured as its condition; for his divine perfections which he has displayed in it; for his administering its rich mercies to us on earth, and causing them to flow uninterruptedly into our souls for ever and ever. The covenant of grace is a reflection of the glory of the Sun of righteousness, and owes all its beauty to him: therefore, whenever we look upon the rainbow, let it serve to remind us of the covenant made with Jesus; and thus let us look from nature up to nature's God.

II. Are our minds struck with the diversified colors of this beautiful phenomenon in nature? Let them remind us of the numerous blessings which are treasured up in the everlasting covenant.

The beauty of the rainbow consists in its various and well-disposed colors; and, oh what a grand variety of blessings is there in the covenant of grace! What clusters, what heaps, what numbers of favors are contained here! Blessings for time and for eternity; temporal and spiritual good; our election, calling, justification, sanctification, comfort, righteousness, possession of the Spirit in all his influences and operations, and the security of eternal glory, are all covenant mercies: hence, you know, they are called "The sure mercies of David." Yea, the believer may look upon the food he eats, the raiment he wears, the air he breathes, and all the common blessings of life, as tokens of covenant-love, and sanctified to him as much through the mediation of Jesus, as his everlasting consolation and good hope through grace. Oh, with what distinguishing privileges is this covenant fraught for all the chosen seed! the blessings of the saints are numerous: "This is the heritage of the servants of the Lord; and their righteousness is of me, saith the Lord."

There is nothing that the child of God can possibly want, but is secured to him here; the blessings that proceed from infinite wisdom, infinite power, and infinite love are promised to the true Israelites; their "God will give grace and glory; and no good thing will he withhold from them that walk uprightly." On account of this covenant, all things are for our advantage; whether the world, or life, or death, or things present, or things to come, all are ours, for we are Christ's, and Christ is God's. Upper and nether spring blessings are secured to us here; support under trouble, calmness in the prospect of death, a lively hope at the very moment of nature's dissolution, an open acquittal before an assemblage of all worlds, and a triumphant admission into the society of the blest, are all included in this rainbow. "There is none like the God of his saints, who rideth upon the heavens for a help, and in his excellency on the sky: the eternal God is thy refuge, and underneath are the everlasting arms; and he shall thrust out the enemy from before thee, and shall say, Destroy them. Israel, thou shalt dwell in safety alone; the fountain of Jacob shall be upon a land of corn and wine, also his heavens shall drop down dew! Happy art thou, O Israel! Who is like unto thee, O people, saved by the Lord, the shield of thy help, and who is the sword of thy excellency: and thine enemies shall be found liars unto thee, and thou shalt tread upon their high places." These blessings then form the various colors in the bow round about the throne, in sight like unto an emerald.

III. Was the rainbow an emblem of peace between God and man after the flood? The covenant of grace declares reconciliation, and secures the redeemed for ever from the deep waters of affliction, which had often before overwhelmed them.

That the rainbow is to be regarded by us, as a security against another universal deluge, is evident from God's language to Noah immediately after the flood: "I do set," says he, "my bow in the cloud, and it shall be for a token of the covenant between me and the earth. And it shall come to pass, when I bring a cloud over the earth, that the bow shall be seen in the cloud; and I will remember my covenant which is between me and you, and every living creature of all flesh: and the bow shall be seen in the cloud; and I will look upon it, that I may remember the everlasting covenant between God, and every living creature of all flesh, that is upon the earth." The covenant of grace, brethren, reconciles man unto God; it is the source of all Scriptural and divine peace; indeed, its character is, that it is the covenant of peace; through its influence we shall "dwell in quiet habitations and sure resting places" for ever. Yea, God, giving his own account of it, says, "For this is as the waters of Noah unto me; for as I have sworn that the waters of Noah should no more go over the earth, so have I sworn that I would not be wroth with thee, nor rebuke thee: for the mountains shall depart, and the hills be removed, but my kindness shall not depart from thee, neither shall the covenant of my peace be removed, saith the Lord, that hath mercy on thee." This rainbow, then, that surrounds the throne of God, is a sign that the happiness of the saints shall be no more interrupted, that they shall be no longer subject to the inundations of trouble of any kind: seas of tribulation, and floods of distress, shall be known no more: the former things will be passed away. Here, indeed, they were liable to torrents of temptations, to persecutions, to famine, to sword, and nakedness; but, over all these things they shall be "more than conquerors through Him that loved them;" and the bright rainbow will make known to them the designs of God; will show them their unfading felicity: Jesus their Sun shall display his beams of glory, and thus gild the clouds with the most beauteous rays: the saints of God then will have to be thankful for so peaceful a sign, when sun and stars shall be extinguished for ever. Deluges of woe shall never overspread the city of our God, which is the New Jerusalem: there, there shall be no more pain, no more iniquity, no more death. Violence shall no more be heard in that land, wasting and destruction within its borders: the heavenly inhabitants shall hunger no more, nor thirst any more, neither shall the sun light on them, nor any heat; but the Lamb which is in the midst of the throne shall feed them, and shall lead them to living fountains of water, and God shall wipe away all tears from their eyes.

Remember, then, Christians, that for all this you are indebted to the free grace of God, and that it is all secured to you in the covenant of grace; it is because your names are enrolled in the record of the skies, because you are given into the hands of Christ by the Father, that heaven and all its glory will be revealed to your view, and possessed by you forever and ever. Oh, with what delight will you survey this significant bow; what rapture will fill your minds under the pleasing idea, that the wild dismaying scenes of life are over forever; and that, instead of anarchy and confusion, the Prince of peace reigns, dispensing quietness and assurance forever: the wearied spirit will weep no more, but will wear an eternal smile of joy, since its communication with its God will be without interruption, and its holy pleasures without an end.

"Oh, may I bear some humble part
In that immortal song:
Wonder and joy shall tune my heart,
And love command my tongue."

IV. Is the rainbow said to be round about the throne of God? The covenant of grace includes in it, and glorifies, all the persons in the Trinity, and is ever in their sight and remembrance.

Our text says, "There was a rainbow round about the throne:" the throne of God is enclosed in it: so the covenant of which we speak, interested the whole Deity; the powers of the eternal mind were engaged in the salvation of poor and miserable sinners; and herein he thus displayed and harmonized all his perfections. What wisdom there was in devising a scheme like this, which could never have entered into the mind of any but The Eternal! What goodness, what power in putting it into full execution; and what faithfulness in consummating the scheme of human redemption! Not one of the adorable persons in the Trinity, but was engaged in this covenant: the agreement was peculiarly entered into between the Father and the Son; and the Holy Spirit brings home all the blessings of this covenant to the consciences of sinners; he applies the work of Jesus to our hearts, and herein glorifies abundantly all that the Father and the Son hath done before.

More of God, too, let it be remarked, in his character and designs, is developed to us by the covenant of grace, than could otherwise ever have been known, and by this covenant a revenue of glory will redound to his own great name.

And if this rainbow is round about the throne, it must be always in the sight of God; he beholds it, and is well pleased for his righteousness' sake. Amidst our backslidings, a sight of the rainbow caused our covenant God to say, "For a little moment I hid myself from thee, but with everlasting mercies will I gather thee." It is our mercy that he cannot be unmindful of his covenant, and that, because "he is of one mind, and none can turn him;" and never can he cease to be mindful of the welfare of those whom he chose out of the world, and whose names are continually before him.

This rainbow will be before Him forever and ever; he will delight in his covenant; it will never repent him that he saved sinners; with complacency will he behold the glorified spirits of his saints, who will be enjoying more largely than ever they had done before, the distinguishing favors of the covenant of grace: being made thus accepted in the Beloved, he will bless them with the smile of approbation, and the lifting up the light of his countenance. Finally,—

V. Are we informed that the rainbow was in sight like unto an emerald, green, beautiful, and durable? How delightful to contemplate and enjoy the blessings of the covenant of grace! it is always new and lasting as the throne which it surrounds.

An emerald is a precious stone, next in hardness to the ruby, and its green color much refreshes and strengthens the sight. The rainbow of the new covenant then is like unto an emerald. What beauties meet in it! what order how admirable to consider its nature and institution! and is it not like that faith which apprehends it? like the promises with which it is fraught, exceedingly precious? David of old could testify its value to his mind amidst domestic trials, saying, "Although my house be not so with God, yet he hath made with me an everlasting covenant, ordered in all things and sure; for this is all my salvation and all my desire, although he make it not to grow."

This covenant may animate us in the greatest depressions; it may cast a lustre upon the dark dispensations of providence, because it teaches us that they will all end well: a knowledge of an interest in it disarms death of its terrors, yea, bids him lay our ruins in the grave; seeing that death and hell combined cannot interrupt the repose of a saint in the bosom of his covenant God. No emerald is so beautiful, so precious, or refreshing, as this rainbow; this covenant claims the last accents of our poor faltering tongues, and will employ the first notes of our celestial harmony.

It is also more durable than an emerald: hard and lasting as precious stones may appear, they are mouldering dust and perishing atoms when compared with the designs of God. This is styled an everlasting covenant; it endures as long as its Author; the blessings of it are enjoyed through the unnumbered ages of eternity; it was first entered into never to be broken, and it will remain immutable. This rainbow will surround the throne of God, as long as God will have a throne for it to surround; for, "Hath he spoken and will he not do it; hath he commanded, and shall it not stand fast?"

"My God, the covenant of thy love
Abides forever sure;
And in its matchless grace I find
My happiness secure."

"The Lord loveth judgment, hates robbery for burnt-offerings, will direct our work in truth, and has made an everlasting covenant with us: so that all that see us shall take knowledge of us, that we are the seed which the Lord hath blessed."

By way of inference—

Let believers be always mindful of this covenant. Since God has done so much for you, can you let his favors be buried in unthankfulness, and die without praise? Shall it be said of you, "They remembered not his holy covenant?" Shall this bright rainbow display its beauties all in vain for you? O! let it be the ground of your triumph, the foundation of your prayers for yourselves and others, and let it always influence you to be joining yourself to the Lord in perpetual acts of self-dedication, in an everlasting covenant that shall never be forgotten: nor be discouraged that you are at present perplexed with trials and difficulties; but evermore boast that the rainbow still is nigh, and that it as much secures your admission into heaven, as it prevents any storms or deluges there. This covenant is a proper subject for investigation; in it lies a mine for you to dig in; it contains pearls of great price, such as will well repay your labor, and delight your soul. View yourselves as redeemed by the blood of the covenant, and rejoice that you shall admire it forever and ever.

The sinner should think of this subject with the greatest awe; for God says to him, "What hast thou to do that thou shouldst take my covenant in thy mouth?" Not interested in it, you cannot share its blessings.

This subject points out the necessity of self-examination.

Shall we ever behold the glory of this rainbow? Be ever enclosed in it? If it be the case,

"Then will he pour salvation down,
And we shall render praise;
We, the dear people of his love,
And he our God of grace."

SERMON XI.

THE GLORY OF CHRIST IN THE WORK OF REDEMPTION.

"And he shall bear the glory."—Zechariah 6: 13.

Of whom speaketh the prophet this? of himself or of some other man? It is spoken, brethren, of Him who is clothed with a vesture dipped in blood, and whose name is called the Word of God. Whilst the second temple was erecting, the voice of the prophet Zechariah was directed by the Spirit's inspiration to that glorious building which this but prefigured. Divinely directed, he adorned Joshua with crowns of silver and gold, and was commanded to behold him as a type of the man whose name is "The Branch," who was to grow up out of his place, and who alone was appointed, and about to build the temple of the Lord, and who is well described in the words I have read you as a text, as having all possible power, for "He shall bear the glory."

These words intimate, that all the honor of the erection, preservation, and completion of the spiritual temple, properly and solely belongs to Jesus: they show us that the whole glory of our salvation, from first to last, must be ascribed to him; and they lead us to view him as having on his head many crowns. God forbid that this should be an unprofitable subject for our meditation at this time.

We may remark then, that all blessing, and glory, and might, dominion, and power, must be ascribed to Christ, in opposition to the idea of any praise belonging to man: since his hands laid the foundation, and raised the superstructure of this edifice, the honor belongs not unto us, not unto us, but unto his venerable and adored name. Neither Zerubbabel nor Joshua, were to be looked upon as the prime causes of the erection of this temple at Jerusalem; for it might well be said of it, "This is the finger of God!" and surely the kingdom of universal nature, the fullness of almighty power, and the whole glory of our salvation, must alone be ascribed to the man whose name is "The Branch." Indeed no others could bear the glory but himself; it would be a weight too heavy for them, and a burden intolerable to sustain; but "the government shall be upon his shoulders:" since "of him, and through him, and to him, are all things; to him be glory for ever and ever."

Permit me, then, to call your attention to the different ways in which Jesus is glorified, on account of his mediatorial work; and to view him as receiving abundant honor from both the other divine persons in the Trinity;—from the plaudits of the angelic world;—from the ministry of the gospel;—from the conduct of all his saints;—from the dispensations of his own providence;—and from the acclamations of the glorified spirits in heaven.

Our text is true, which declares that Jesus shall bear the glory, because he has borne it, and still is abundantly honored and glorified,—

I. By both the other divine persons in the Trinity.

That there are three that bear record in heaven, the

Father, the Word, and the Holy Ghost; and that these three are one, is explicitly taught in the pages of inspiration, which are true and faithful: being one in essence and dignity, they also unite in glorifying each other, and by the different offices which they have been pleased graciously to discharge in the economy of our redemption, they show us that the Lord our God is one Lord. The Saviour of sinners, the second person in the Trinity, always delighted when on earth in glorifying the Father, by discharging his will, fulfilling his law, and reflecting his honor in all his perfections; as well did he make honorable mention of the Holy Spirit, in his diversified operations upon the human mind, and intimate that his own work would be incomplete, without the work of the Holy Spirit. And shall not both the Father and the Spirit unite in causing him to bear the glory, who had so wonderfully glorified them on earth? God the Father has "glorified his Son, with the glory which he had with him before the world began:" and he has done this by acknowledging, accepting, and exalting him.

He acknowledged him, as the man that was his fellow, as his servant whom he upheld, his elect in whom his soul delighted: he testified of him, saying, "This is my beloved Son, in whom I am well pleased, hear ye him." He never left him without witness of his entire and hearty approbation of himself, and of the work in which he was engaged. Of no other did he ever say, "Thou art my Son, this day have I begotten thee;" and again, "I will be to him a Father, and he shall be to me a Son." The voice from the excellent glory recommends only Jesus as the Saviour of the ends of the earth. Again, he accepted him, and thus made him to bear the glory. He received him into the highest honors, when he had by himself purged our sins; he looked for no more than what Jesus had accomplished, and could not but admire his finished work; yea, he was well pleased for his righteousness' sake. The Lord smelled a sweet savor from his oblation and death, and smiled with divine benignity upon his victorious Son, in whose work he rejoiced, as it was the frustration of hellish schemes, the effect of heavenly counsels, the fulfillment of inspired prophecies, the glorification of divine attributes, and the salvation of immortal souls.

The Father glorified him too, for he has exalted him. "He has set him on his own right hand, far above all principality and power, and might, and dominion, and every name that is named, not only in this world, but in that which is to come." We speak of Him "whom God raised from the dead, and gave him glory." "Wherefore God also has highly exalted him, and given him a name which is above every name." He has placed him far beyond the reach of his enemies; and vowed, that upon himself shall his crown flourish. The Father's exaltation of his Son, shows us that he has glorified him above all his name, while it teaches us to sue for the blessings he has appointed him in that state to bestow.

But the Holy Spirit also comes forward to place honors upon his head, and to "anoint him with the oil of gladness above his fellows." "He," said Jesus himself, "shall glorify me, for he shall take of mine, and shall show it unto you." He glorifies him then, by witnessing of his person, as being lovely and amiable; adorned with every grace, and shining more illustriously than the sun in his strength. He testifies too of his work, as being suitable and complete, as it is essentially necessary for the salvation of our souls: it is the office of this Spirit to direct the eye of the mind to him, taking it away from every other refuge. So also does he glorify him, by witnessing of his fullness, for the supply of all our wants; he leads us to him for every thing we need, and teaches us to cry to him mightily for spiritual blessings. Thus do both the Father and Holy Spirit unite in giving glory to the Son. O, how true is the text then, which says, "He shall bear the glory!" Let us now view him as honored and glorified

II. By the engagements of the angelic world.

Of angels we know but little; suffice it to say, that they are superior to man in the scale of being, as they are invested with strength of intellect and activity of mind, which we do not possess; and remember, especially, that whatever they are in their nature, their employment is to glorify that same Jesus, who is all our salvation and all our desire. They promote his honor, and cause him to bear the glory, as they constantly adore him,—and as they invariably execute his will.

Observe, he is glorified by angels, because—

1. They constantly adore him.

"Let all the angels of God worship him," is the mandate which they have to obey; and as he is the Lord of angels, they readily offer him that homage which a sight of his glories evermore inspires. For Him, brethren, "the morning stars sing together, and the sons of God shout for joy." Those active intelligences can exclaim, "Worthy the Lamb," though they cannot add, "He was slain for us." At his feet they cast their crowns; before his glory they veil their faces with their wings; to him they cry, "Holy,

holy, holy, Lord God Almighty." He bears the glory too, because—

2. The angels invariably execute his will.

They are ministers of his, and do his pleasure: commissioned by him, they wait on his saints; witness their devotions; preserve them from danger; and watch affectionately over them till they arrive at glory. From Jesus it is, brethren, that they receive their orders: to one he says, Go, and he goeth; to another, Come, and he cometh. He is the Captain of this host of the Lord. He marshals them; they are altogether in subordination to his will; and with pleasure they fly through his vast empire to fulfill his orders. And whilst they do all this, are they not glorifying him? Are they not crowning him with honor and glory? The highest archangel glories in the thought of being a servant of Jesus of Nazareth. The angels of God may all be heard to say, "He shall bear the glory." We remark once more, that the Saviour of sinners receives a revenue of glory and honor

III. From the ministry of the gospel.

This promotes his glory by revealing—exalting—and applying him to the heart.

1. The gospel reveals the Saviour. True it is, that he needs only to be seen to be adored and loved; and it is the excellency of the Bible, that it exhibits Christ; holds him up as the only Saviour; and presents him to our view in almost every page. In fact, every part of the Bible should be viewed in its bearing upon him: he is the substance of the promises, the prophecies, the types, the narratives, and the epistles. By testifying of him in this way, the gospel glorifies him; and every faithful minister

is enabled to say to him, "If I forget thee, O Jesus, let my right hand forget her cunning; if I do not remember thee, let my tongue cleave to the roof of my mouth." The gospel glorifies Christ—

2. By exalting him.

Oh, in what high terms does it speak of Jesus! what figures, what metaphors, what language it employs, to set forth "his eternal power and Godhead," his rich grace, and his wonderful love! Who is so highly spoken of in the ministry of reconciliation as Jesus Christ, who "shall bear the glory?" Here he is styled "Lord of all," "King of kings," "The image of the invisible God," yea, "All in all." The writers of the Scriptures seem at a loss for words to communicate their ideas of his infinite glory, and seem sensible that they can but lisp out a few broken expressions to his honor and praise. Every leaf of this book seems to say to us, "He shall bear the glory." The gospel glorifies him further, as it is the means in the hands of the Spirit—

3. Of applying him to the conscience.

When this gospel is viewed, as it is indeed and in truth, the word of God, and not of man, then Christ Jesus is all the confidence and boast of the sinner. By its influence the sinner's eyes are enlightened to behold his glory; his prejudices are removed; so that he contemplates him "as the Son of God with power:" his will, which before resisted, and would not submit to the righteousness of God, is so subdued, the bias of it is so turned, that he desires earnestly and humbly to be saved in God's own way. In short, through the instrumentality of the gospel, Christ Jesus is formed in his heart the hope of glory; and so is he abundantly honored.

Thus, you see, that the grand design of the gospel, in its inspiration and diffusion, is to recommend and glorify the Saviour, and promote his praise, who alone shall build the temple of the Lord.

Once more, Jesus shall bear an exceeding weight of glory—

IV. From the conduct of all his saints. "They shall hang upon him all the glory of his Father's house." The saints honor him when they believe on him,—imitate him, —obey him,—and suffer for him.

They testify his honor when they believe on him to life everlasting: a poor sinner is enabled to put honor upon Jesus, by simply taking him at his word, and relying on him for life and salvation. Yea, we are bold to remark, that this is the best way to glorify him; that by faith we honor his attributes and perfections, and cause a revenue of praise to be rendered to his own great name; and, "whoso offereth praise," we know, "glorifieth him, and to him will he show the salvation of God." He that believes, honors the plenitude of his redemption, the riches of his grace, the efficacy of his blood; and this is the glory which he alone shall bear, since "there is salvation in no other; neither is there any other name given under heaven, among men, whereby we must be saved."

Further, Christians glorify the Saviour when they make him a model for their imitation; when they endeavor so to walk even as he also walked; to mark the footsteps that he trod; to be holy as he was holy; and to evidence the same mind that was also in him. Hereby they honor the holiness of his nature, and the rectitude of his life: in his service below he must ever have the preëminence. You are not called to be like heroes, philosophers, or politicians, but to be conformed to the image of the Son; so "shall he bear the glory."

You will honor him, then, by obeying from the heart, "that form of sound words which he has delivered unto you." "His commandments are not grievous;" then let them be your study, your delight, your path in which you shall go. "If ye love me," says he, "keep my commandments:" nor is there any better evidence of strong attachment to his person, than prompt and steady obedience to his precepts. In your different spheres of action, in all your engagements and pursuits, in your intercourse with the world, as well as with the saints, never forget you are bound to glorify the Saviour, and to put honor upon his name, by living not to yourself, but to him that loved you, and died for you, and rose again.

Nor should you forget, that you must glorify him by all that you endure. Here I am reminded of the remarkable testimony that is borne of the sickness of Lazarus, of which it is said, that "His sickness was not unto death, but for the glory of God, that the Son of God might be glorified thereby:" by your patient submission to the divine will; by your earnest desire that your afflictions may be sanctified; and by your preparedness for glory; you honor his love, his goodness and his grace.

Christians are to live only to the glory of Jesus; they are bound to promote his honor, in all their thoughts, words, and actions; and we know that their death promotes his glory; so that he is honored in them, whether by life or by death: and in that great day, "for which all other days were made," he shall come to be admired in his saints, and to be glorified in all them that believe. The noble army of martyrs praise him; the goodly fellowship of the apostles praise him; the whole church, throughout all the world, doth acknowledge him as God's honorable, true, and only Son. Once more, "He shall bear the glory,"—

V. From the dispensations of his own providence.

"All his works praise him." His great design, in governing all things, is to secure to himself abundant glory. It is evident that the government is upon his shoulders; that without his permission not a sparrow falls to the ground; and that "by him it is that kings reign, and princes decree justice." In all the events, then, of a providential nature, that have taken place in the world, Jesus Christ is honored; but he is especially so, in the guidance and direction of the saints to Zion's holy hill. They are, indeed, the children of providence, peculiar favorites of Heaven; and no wonder that Jesus glorifies himself on their behalf. Do you ask, what in him does providence glorify? I answer, much every way. It glorifies all his attributes and perfections; but peculiarly does it honor his power, his wisdom, and his goodness. The power of his arm is herein abundantly displayed, seeing we are led to understand that there is nothing which he cannot accomplish; that there is no work too hard for him; that he can very easily tread a monarch down, or dash a world to pieces: he can raise the poor from the dunghill, and set them among princes; he effects whatever he chooses: and does not all this glorify him? especially when we recollect that he produces all things by a word, or by the mere volition of his own mind. Yea, very often for this cause doth he raise men up, that he may show his power in them. His peculiar providence glorifies also his wisdom, which appears in his causing all things to work together for good: every pin of this tabernacle is, indeed, in its proper place: there is not a trial borne by a Christian, but is absolutely necessary for mim. At the day of judgment, when the dispensations of his providence shall be unravelled, we shall see him to be the only wise God, and trace that inimitable skill, which had been displayed in the construction and government of the world. These things also glorify his goodness, which is over all, and his tender mercies which are over all his works. Every thing he does is done well; and what we know not of his dealings now, we shall know hereafter. O, then, speak of the glory of his kingdom, and talk of his power; make known to the sons of men his mighty acts, and the glorious majesty of his kingdom; "For his kingdom is an everlasting kingdom, and his dominion endureth throughout all generations:" all his providential dealings say, "He shall bear the glory." We hasten to remark, that Jesus will receive abundant glory—

VI. From the acclamations of the glorified spirits in heaven.

That Christ Jesus is the theme of heaven is abundantly evident, from the representations given us in the word of God, of the employments and songs of those who appear before God in the new Jerusalem. It is Jesus's name that sounds so melodiously upon their harps; it is his love which excites their triumphant praise; it is his unrivalled, uncreated beauty, which strikes them with admiration, and fills them with delight. Jesus must be considered as greatly honored by their acclamations, if we recollect, that they are unquestionably sincere, united, uninterrupted, and eternal.

"He bears the glory" of their triumphs, for their homage is sincere. Here, indeed, men profess to know, him, but in works deny him; with their mouths they acknowledge him, but by their conduct they betray him; they call him Lord, Lord, but do not the things which he says: and suppose ye, for a moment, that Christ owns himself honored by such characters? I tell you nay; but he will appoint them a portion with hypocrites and unbelievers. But the language of a glorified soul is the expression of its pious feelings; there is no formality in worship there, nor is there any hypocrisy or deceit, for the former things are passed away. Whilst they exclaim, "Worthy is the Lamb," they feel that he is exalted above all blessing and praise. Jehovah himself, who searches the heart and tries the reins of the children of men, testifies of them, that they are Israelites indeed, in whom there is no guile. Amidst all the numbers of the blood-bought throng, there is not an individual but feels his obligations to the grace of Jesus; and who, when he pronounces his charming name, does not glow with sincere affection towards him. He himself knows, then, that he alone bears the glory of their praises; because, when they adore him, their hearts are not wandering after other good.

Large is the revenue of glory which Christ receives from the spirits of the just made perfect, because their adorations are united. In praising him they all agree; not one refuses to join the song, not one wishes it to close. Jesus himself is the delightful bond of union to them all; they are all united in Christ. Those that were redeemed from different tribes, and tongues, and people; that were called by grace at different periods of their existence; that were separated from each other, when on earth, by different sentiments, or by other once existing circumstances; now all join in one common hallelujah, and in one loud amen. The Saviour has the satisfaction of finding himself to be the joy and wonder of them all, for " He shall bear the glory."

Their acclamations, too, will be uninterrupted. They will honor him, then, not with frail, but with incorruptible bodies: they will never feel languor or weariness; being so glorified, that every thing in their constitution, when on earth, which was calculated to impede their devotions, and to control their holy pleasures, shall be known no more. Wandering thoughts, cold affections, and earthly desires, shall not break in upon their solemnities, or cause them any more to render an unacceptable sacrifice, or to present to Jehovah the blind and the lame. And there, too, " the wicked will cease from troubling, and the weary be at rest." How great, then, must be the honor which they will present to the Saviour, if it were only from the consideration that it will be uninterrupted.

He will also bear surprising glory, because the acclamations of his redeemed will be eternal. As they see fresh wonders in him; they will present to him fresh praise and new honor: they will not grow weary of adoring the name of Jesus: but whilst unnumbered ages pass along, they will adore him, and cause him to " bear the glory." For ever and ever will they adore his wisdom in conducting the affairs of his church; his triumph in completing that spiritual temple: and while immortality endures, all their harps, and all their songs, will be employed in praising Jesus, the God of Zion.

Let me tell those who do not love to praise the Saviour now, that they are totally unfit to join the grand assembly above, and that they cannot be admitted into heaven, till they have higher thoughts of Jesus Christ, and lower thoughts of themselves: yea, till they are divinely taught to hate sin, and live here with that holiness without which no man can see the Lord. Let me beg of the obstinate sinner, for his own sake, not to go on insulting this lovely, this glorious Redeemer, because he will certainly slay his enemies, with the sharp two-edged sword that goes out of his mouth; he will consume them with the brightness of his coming. Let me excite you all to join in praising Jesus: your obligations to him, Christian, are infinite: diffuse then the savour of his name in every place; ascribe to him the kingdom, the power, and the glory: say, "Now is the Son of man glorified, and God is glorified in him." Blessed be his glorious name for ever; and let the whole earth be filled with his glory. Amen and Amen.

SERMON XII.

THE WILFUL OBSTINACY OF THE IMPENITENT SINNER.

"As for the word which thou hast spoken to us in the name of the Lord, we will not hearken unto thee."*—JEREMIAH xliv. 16.

UNDER Johanan, the son of Kareah, the Jews fled into the land of Egypt, contrary to the expostulations of the prophet Jeremiah, and dwelt in the country of Pathros. When they were there, he delivered his own soul of their blood, by faithfully setting before them their idolatry and impenitence, and clearly prophesying their utter destruction from the presence of the Lord, and from the glory of his power; declaring to them, that God would take this remnant of Judah, who had set their faces to go into the land of Egypt to sojourn there, and cause them all to be consumed, and fall in the land of Egypt: "That they should even be consumed by the sword, and by the famine; and that they should be an execration, and an astonishment, and a curse, and a reproach."

You are, perhaps, ready to suppose, that when the mourning prophet had delivered this heavy burden of the

* During the vacation, Mr. Spencer preached at Dorking; on closing his labors there, he repeated all the passages from which he had preached, and then announced this text.—*Ed.*

word of the Lord, they, like the inhabitants of Nineveh, clothed themselves in sackcloth and ashes, and cried mightily, saying, "Who can tell if God will turn and repent, and turn away from his fierce anger, that we perish not?" No such sentiments pervaded their minds; no such expressions dropped from their lips; and judge what hard hearts they must have possessed, when you hear that our text contains their impudent reply to the word of God by his servant. "For all the men and all the women that stood by, even a great multitude, yea, all the people that dwelt in the land of Egypt, in Pathros, answered Jeremiah, saying, "As for the word which thou hast spoken to us in the name of the Lord, we will not hearken unto thee. But," say they, "we will certainly do whatsoever thing goeth forth out of our own mouth; and then they acquaint him with their decided determination to pursue their idolatrous and impious course, notwithstanding all that the prophets of the Lord could say against it. And since the unrenewed heart is still hard and impenitent; since the will of man, by nature, is obstinate and perverse; and since the love of sin predominates in the hearts of the unregenerate; mankind frequently pay no better attention to the messages of the heralds of salvation, than these deluded Jews did to the warnings of Jeremiah. Faithful ministers are frequently obliged to return to their closets with an aching heart, under the idea that many are saying in their hearts, and by their conduct, "As for the words which thou hast spoken to us in the name of the Lord, we will not hearken unto thee." These words, then, lead me to show,—that it devolves upon ministers to address sinners in the name of the Lord;—and to point out the unpleasant reception with which their message often meets.

I. We will show, that it devolves on ministers to speak to sinners in the name of the Lord.

These impious Jews, in our text, mention the word which Jeremiah had spoken to them in the name of the Lord. We said, that it devolved on ministers to speak to sinners in the name of the Lord. Yes, brethren, to sinners. Foolish, and inconsistent with the tenor of Scripture and apostolic preaching, is the idea, that the people of God only are to be addressed from that awful place called a pulpit. The messengers of Christ have to alarm, exhort, and reprove: their embassy is calculated to interest those who are in the gall of bitterness, and in the bond of iniquity, as well as those who have believed through grace. The watchmen upon the walls of Zion are to endeavor to dissuade those who are without from living and dying ignorant of the way of salvation, as well as to tell the church that her warfare is accomplished, that her sin is pardoned, and that she shall receive of the Lord's hand double for all her sins. Those ministers who are held as stars in God's right hand, lead men to avoid the blackness of darkness for ever, as well as guide our feet into the way of peace.

We find that the prophets addressed the vilest of men: the voice of Wisdom itself is directed to the foolish, and those who have no understanding. John the Baptist calls upon those whom he terms a generation of vipers, to "repent, for the kingdom of heaven is at hand." Jesus Christ himself expostulates with, and exhorts, and weeps over sinners: to sinners the apostles preached, whose danger affected their hearts, and excited their earnest prayers; so that no wonder they cried, "Why will ye die!" and, Ye fools, when will ye be wise? Ministers of the present day, endued, we hope, with the same Spirit, and inspired with the same sentiments, adopt the same conduct, and cry aloud, not sparing, but earnestly addressing those, to many of whom (awful thought!) they are a savour of death unto death.

To sinners they have particularly to declare the mischief occasioned by sin. They represent to them their deplorable situation; they describe to them the horrors of the pit wherein there is no water, in which they lie; the miseries of that prison in which they are closely confined; the unprofitableness of the drudgery in which they are engaged; and the tribulation and anguish which they have to expect. Knowing the terrors of the Lord, they persuade men; and sensible, that if they are unfaithful, the blood of souls will be required at their hands, they are instant in season and out of season, if by any means they could persuade them to flee from the wrath to come. Hence, to sinners they have to exhibit the compassion of the Saviour; to them they cry, "Now is the accepted time, now is the day of salvation:" they are earnest in exhorting such to flee to the Saviour's open arms, and to apply instantly to him who never casts out those who come to him. They tell them, that the Saviour's heart is made of tenderness, and that his bowels melt with love. The servants of Christ say continually, "Ho, every one that thirsteth, come ye to the waters; yea, come, buy wine and milk without money, and without price;" and they direct them to Him who hath said, "If any man thirst, let him come unto me and drink."

The ungodly part of a congregation must never consider themselves as uninterested in the truths of the gospel; for, like the Jews of Pathros, they can call the message of their minister, when they address him, "The word which thou hast spoken to us."

But what we wish you particularly to notice is, that they do all this in the name of the Lord. They speak in the name of the Lord; for they speak in obedience to his command. They remember that the Head of the church, the Governor of Zion, and the Owner of the golden candlesticks said, "Go ye into all the world, and preach the gospel to every creature." They recollect too, that when the blessed and holy Trinity cried, saying, "Whom shall I send, and who will go for us?" they replied, "Here am I, send me." They call to mind a period, when they, led by the providence of God, devoted their talents and their lives to him, and conferred not with flesh and blood: do they not then, when the path of duty is made so abundantly plain to them, speak in the name of the Lord? Jehovah calls them his prophets, his servants; (for he is never ashamed of those who, in an abandoned age, show to men the way of salvation,) and says to them, "Be not afraid of their faces, for I am with thee to deliver thee."

They speak in the name of the Lord, too, because they speak in perfect agreement with the divine word.

"To the law and to the testimony, if they speak not according to this word, it is because there is no light in them." The ministers of the gospel have to declare among the churches, "the manifold wisdom of God;" and "This is the word, which, by the gospel, is preached unto you." No minister can be said to speak in the name of the Lord, who does not make Jesus Christ, who is the subject of the Scriptures, the sum and substance of his ministry; or who does not view the Bible as the unerring test of truth, and never-failing fountain of light and life. Faithful ministers do speak in the name of the Lord; for they are chosen vessels, and they go their ways to bear his name unto the Gentiles. The authority of Heaven is stamped upon all they say, when they speak, as led by the Spirit of truth into the truth contained in the Bible. They speak to sinners in the name of the Lord also, because they address them in a firm dependence on his Spirit. The Spirit shall direct them in their studies, shall give the enjoyment of the gospel in their own souls, and shall animate their hearts, by taking of the things of Jesus, and showing them unto them. This Spirit they depend on for illumination, for power, and for success; and if they have so divine a teacher, and derive help from so blessed and exalted a source, do they not speak in the name of the Lord? Because God pours out his Spirit upon them, therefore it is that they prophesy; and because the power of the Highest overshadows them, their words are often "quick and powerful, sharper than any two-edged sword, piercing even to the dividing asunder of the joints and marrow;" their tongues are like the pens of ready writers; and their own souls rejoice within them, when they testify the glorious majesty of Jesus's kingdom.

Do they not speak in the name of the Lord, lastly, since they preach in the hope of promoting his glory?

From a sincere desire to honor him, ought they ever to dispense his glorious gospel; nor have we any reason to think that that man preaches in the name of the Lord, who preaches himself and not Jesus Christ. If the motives of the company of preachers are right ones, they are to glorify God by debasing the sinner, exalting the Saviour, and aiming to promote holiness of heart and life. If these are their aims, brethren, they speak to you in the name of the

Most High God. And well may they ask, "Who is sufficient for these things?" The faithful ministers of Christ can say, "We are not as many who corrupt the word of God, but as of sincerity, as of God, in the sight of God, so speak we in Christ." It is a work that might fill the heart of an angel, and has occupied the hands of the Saviour. When I consider what it is to speak in the name of the Lord, I tremble for myself, I tremble for my brethren, but, most of all, I tremble for those time-servers, who love the praise of men more than the praise of God, and do not commend themselves to every man's conscience in the sight of God.

Having endeavored, then, to show you that the ministers of the gospel, like Jeremiah, speak to sinners in the name of the Lord; I would now—

II. Point out the unpleasant reception with which their message often meets. Their hearers say to them, "As for the word which thou hast spoken to us in the name of the Lord, we will not hearken unto thee."

We hope that there are but few who would plainly say this in words; who are so hardened as to glory in their shame; or so incorrigible as to tell God's ministers that they cast his words behind their back, as unworthy of attention, and beneath their notice: yet we are persuaded, that there are many professors who say this in their hearts, and who will not see when the hand of God is lifted up: for, if this were not the case, would ministers so often have to lament over them, saying, O that they were wise; and O that there were such a heart in them, to keep his commandments and do them? To show that there are many, who in their hearts say, "As for the word that thou hast spoken to us in the name of the Lord, we will not hearken unto thee," let us inquire, whether mankind in general hear the word of God attentively, believingly, and obediently. Many there are who seem to say, We will not hearken unto thee attentively. God has written to these characters the great things of his love, and they account them small things: hence, his ministers have to address "a disobedient and gainsaying people." Are there not some of you who never think of engaging the powers of your mind to hear the word of God; who think his service long and tiresome, and say, "When will the Sabbath be over, that we may set forth wheat;" who think so lightly of God's ordinances, as to come in late, and disturb the worship of others; or who, as if you wished us to believe that you have no couch at home, make God's house of prayer a place of repose, and the time of worship an opportunity to indulge in sleep? Careless hearers, then, all say, "We will not hearken unto thee." And oh, how few are there that will hear believingly! The word does not profit, "not being mixed with faith in them that hear it;" men often reject the counsel of God against themselves, and disbelieve the record that God has given of his Son. Their conduct shows that they believe not in the name of the only-begotten Son of God. There are many hearers of the gospel who view the atonement of Christ as unnecessary; the evil of sin as greatly exaggerated; the influences of the Spirit as nothing but enthusiasm; and the doctrines of original sin and imputed righteousness, as cunningly-devised fables. To such we would say, "O fools, and slow of heart to believe all that the prophets have spoken!" Jesus Christ is set forth crucified among you; but this is your condemnation, that light is come into the world, but you love darkness rather than light, because your deeds are evil. Nor will they hear obediently. For there are many who profess to admire the truths of the gospel, but do not the things which his servants say: their temper is not reformed; they are as idolatrously covetous as ever; not one single alteration is produced in them by the gospel. God says to one of his ministers concerning them, "And lo, thou art unto them as a very lovely song of one that has a pleasant voice, and can play well on an instrument: for they hear thy words, but they do them not, with their mouth they show much love, but their heart goeth after covetousness." Thus, they do not hear, so that their souls may live; and their minister is obliged to say to them, "I am afraid of you, lest I have bestowed on you labor in vain;" and he is confirmed in his suspicions, by their rooted self-righteousness and unabated love of the world.

They really seem to have formed the resolution contained in my text, and to say, "We will not hear thee." They have made a covenant with their eyes, to behold nothing but vanity; with their ears, to refuse to listen to the voice of the charmer, charm he ever so wisely; and with their hearts, never to receive the engrafted word of truth, which is able to save the soul. And, let me ask, Why is all this? What is the reason that they will not attend to those things, which, it is evident, belong to their peace? I firmly believe, that the reason why they say, "As for the word which thou hast spoken to us in the name of the Lord, we will not hearken unto thee," is,—because they are in league with sin,—and what ministers teach, loudly speaks their condemnation. It is, we remark,—

1. Because they are in league with sin.

This is what you love, sinner; and therefore you cannot

bear to hear it represented as an evil and a bitter thing. What your ministers represent as amiable and lovely, is diametrically opposite to your carnal taste; and being like these impudent Jews at Pathros, determined to fulfill the desires of your own heart's lusts, you refuse him that speaketh on earth by the authority of Heaven. You hear, perhaps, without much regret, the holy name of the Lord continually blasphemed: you hear, with satisfaction, any thing else, but the things pertaining to God and to his church. Because the works of darkness are your delight, you set at naught all his counsel, and will have none of his reproof. You scorn the messages of his grace; despise one of his servants after another; and your hearts say of Jesus, whom the Father sent, saying, "They will reverence my Son;" This is the heir, come, let us kill him, and the vineyard shall be ours.

It is sin that hardens your heart against the impressions which the Gospel should make upon you; it is sin that shuts your eyes against the heavenly light. It is Satan who teaches you to say, "As for the words which thou hast spoken to us in the name of the Lord, we will not hearken unto thee." You say so, too, because,—

2. What your ministers preach loudly speaks your condemnation.

No debtor more unwillingly looks into his books, which show him the extent of his arrears, than you examine your own hearts, when your consciences are roused to attend to the words of the law of God, as repeated by the ministers of the sanctuary. Ahab, the king of Israel, is a striking instance of this: you remember, that when Jehoshaphat asked him, if there was not another prophet of the Lord of whom they might inquire; he replied, "There is yet one man, Micaiah, the son of Imlah, by whom we may inquire of the Lord; but I hate him, for he doth not prophesy good concerning me, but evil."

See here, then, sinners, the reason why you will not hearken to your ministers. You know that they show you your own truly awful characters; they tell the exceeding sinfulness of your lives; and represent to you the terrors of the Lord; they must prophesy evil concerning you, whilst you continue in your present state: for living and dying unconcerned about the word, they tell you in the name of the Lord, that all the curses that are written in this book shall lie upon you, and God shall blot your name out of the book of life forever.

Two or three remarks shall close the present discourse. I would say, by way of inference, in what an awful state are those persons who are making the resolution contained in the text. They are evidently exposed to the loss of their privileges, to hardness of heart, and contempt of God's word and commandments: and to utter and eternal destruction. For, "if he escaped not, that despised Moses' law, but died without remedy, under two or three witnesses, of how much sorer punishment, suppose ye, shall he be thought worthy, who (by rejecting the Gospel) tramples under foot the Son of God, and counts the blood of the covenant an unholy thing?" "He that hath ears to hear, let him hear." "Hear, and your soul shall live." The voice of God demands attention. Listen to the Friend of sinners, as he speaks in his word, and great advantages will result: so shall it appear that the word has not fallen by the way-side, upon a rock, or among thorns, but upon good ground.

How blessed are they to whom faith cometh by hearing!

What reason have they to be thankful for the preaching of the Gospel, and the news of salvation! What prejudices it has opposed; what ignorance it has enlightened; what consolation it has afforded; and what blessings it has diffused! Live, then, as those who have received the Gospel. And now, brethren, I commend you to God, and to the word of his grace, which is able to build you up, and to give you an inheritance among all those who are sanctified.

SERMON XIII.

GOD THE DEFENSE AND GLORY OF HIS CHURCH.

"Look upon Zion, the city of our solemnities; thine eyes shall see Jerusalem a quiet habitation, a tabernacle that shall not be taken down; not one of the stakes thereof shall ever be removed, neither shall any of the cords thereof be broken."

—Isaiah xxxiii. 20.

It is probable, that when this prophecy was delivered, the city of Jerusalem was threatened with an immediate siege; but Jehovah engages to defend it from the attacks of its enemies, the Assyrians, and to render it at once quiet and secure: but yet the text which I have read to you, appears to have a direct reference to the privileges and stability of the Gospel church; for Jerusalem, after this period, was never long preserved from hostile invasions; therefore our attention is turned from it, to that glorious city against which the gates of hell shall never prevail. We shall therefore, without any further introduction, proceed—To take those views of the church of Christ, which our text recommends, and—Enforce that attention to it which it demands. Let us,—

I. Take those views of the church of Christ which our text recommends.

And we are led to regard it in a three-fold point of view: as a solemn city—as a quiet habitation—and as an immovable tabernacle.

We have the church of Christ represented to us,—

I. As a solemn city. "Look upon Zion," says my text, "the city of our solemnities."

The church of the Lord on earth is called, "The holy people,"—"The Redeemed of the Lord,"—"Sought out, a city not forsaken." It is that great city, "the holy Jerusalem." It is "Mount Zion, the city of the living God." It is "the holy city, which is the mother of us all." The orders and laws necessary for the city of Zion, are contained in these lively oracles, which may also be considered as the charter of the privileges of its happy and active citizens. Peace is within its walls, and prosperity within its palaces; and every thing is conducted well, being managed by him who is the God of order and not of confusion. Its great King ever dwells in the midst of it, and its walls are continually before him: the immunities, for which its inhabitants are distinguished, are numerous and inestimable; including deliverance from the bondage of corruption and sin, together with a full enjoyment of a right to the tree of life, and to all the blessings they can need: these they obtain by pleading the name, blood, and righteousness of Jesus, the King's Son. Watchmen are set upon its walls, to assure the citizens that their iniquity is pardoned, and that their sin is covered; as well as to promise a sanctuary to the weary and distressed, who yet remain without the gate.

Its walls are called salvation, and its gates praise; its streets are all pleasant, and its towers may well strike the eye with admiration. We, however, briefly sum up its excellences, when we say, that it is "the city of the Lord, the Zion of the Holy One of Israel." But we particularly wish to notice the solemnities for which this city is distinguished: it is well called in my text, "The city of our solemnities." This name may be applied to Jerusalem, on account of the most solemn feasts that were there made; the solemn assemblies that were there held; and the solemn sacrifices which were there offered. Nor is the term at all inapplicable to the church of God, which consists of serious believers, who enter into the most solemn engagements with Jehovah; who are employed in the most solemn exercises of mind that can be possibly imagined; and whose minds are peculiarly affected with the solemnities of death and judgment.

Real religion, brethren, is altogether a solemn thing; its exercises are abused, when they are not entered upon, and pursued with real devotion of heart: nothing trifling can be viewed with approbation by the Father of the spirits of all flesh.

Oh that when we entered the church of God, we were more impressed with the idea, that it is the city of our solemnities; then would our levities be checked, our minds be prepared for the devout service of God, and he would, indeed, cleanse the thoughts of our hearts, by the inspiration of his Holy Spirit. In the church of God, we are called solemnly to give ourselves up to him, saying, Lord, I am thine; here we are, with all seriousness, to aim to promote the best interests of our immortal souls; here we are, with reverence and godly fear, to offer the sacrifice of a broken and contrite spirit. Never look upon Zion, then, without remembering, that there the most solemn transactions pass between God and the soul.

2. Our text views the church of God as a quiet habitation.—"Thine eyes shall see Jerusalem a quiet habitation."

It is "builded together for an habitation of God, through the Spirit;" for he hath chosen the tribe of Judah: the Mount Zion, which he loved: and he built his sanctuary like high palaces, like the earth which he hath established for ever. God himself is the householder, for he hath chosen Zion, and desired it for his habitation; and here, too, dwell all the faithful. There is something very consolatory in the idea, that all the worthies now in glory, that ever trusted in Christ, were all members of that church which is one; and that all real believers are considered by Jehovah as forming a part of it, as united in Christ. It is a habitation that incloses all real believers, by whatever name they may be called amongst men, and however far they may be separated from each other on the wide earth, or wider seas; they are, in a spiritual sense, all lodged under the same roof, and all inhabit the house of God, whose house are we. This dwelling-place of the just, then, is remarkable for the security which is there enjoyed, and the peace which pervades the whole. It is a quiet habitation; here the Prince of Peace takes up his residence, and dwells, and reigns: here the work of righteousness is peace, and the effect of righteousness, quietness and assurance for ever; and God's people dwell here in a peaceable habitation, and in sure dwellings, and in quiet resting-places. Those who reside in this habitation need not be afraid of evil tidings, but should rather have their hearts fixed, trusting in the Lord, and thus be quiet from fear of evil. Peace is the legacy which the Saviour left to all the members of his family; and it is promoted in and among us, by the benign influences of the sacred Dove. Blessed then are the people that are in such a case; yea, thrice blessed are they whose dwelling is Mount Zion. What a happiness it would be, if those of us who profess to be Christians, evidenced more of that pure affection to each other, which is "like the precious ointment upon the head, that ran down upon the beard, even Aaron's beard, that went down to the skirts of his garments."

3. The church is described as an immovable tabernacle. "A tabernacle," says my text, "which shall not be taken down; not one of the stakes thereof shall ever be removed, neither shall any of the cords thereof be broken."

The church of Christ may here be described as a tabernacle, in opposition to the superior glories of the New Jerusalem in heaven: for it is true, that the church militant is but a tabernacle, when contrasted with the inconceivable excellences of the paradise of God. Divine glory is manifested to us, and known by us here, but in part; but there we shall know even as we are known: there are grand discoveries reserved for us in heaven, and church-privileges laid up for the redeemed ones in the house not made with hands. As a tabernacle, brethren, the church of God may often change its place: this is shown us by the state of those cities in which once the cause of our Redeemer prospered, but where now his name is never heard. Here, Asia, I cannot but think of thee; for I behold the glory which once distinguished thy solemn assemblies, now shining in the churches of the saints in the British isles. Yes, brethren, though the place of the church militant may be changed, its situation altered, yet its privileges can never be taken away, nor can its stability be ever shaken, or its duration ever cease; for, as the mountains were round about Jerusalem, so the Lord is round about them that fear him, to show himself strong on their behalf. The Jerusalem church, though it might verify the promise in the text, by experiencing a long space of peace, and season of rest from war, together with the restoration and continuance of their sacred privileges, has now lost all its excellence, and Ichabod (the glory is departed) may evidently be seen inscribed upon it. The true church typified by it, the tabernacle referred to in our text, shall never be taken down whilst the world itself remains. A seed to serve him is secured to the Redeemer, as the reward of the travail of his soul, and a generation to call him blessed shall never be wanted whilst he is called Head of the church. The promises of the covenant, which declare that Zion cannot be removed, but abideth for ever, confirmed by the invaluable blood of Christ, and the ordinances and institutions of his gospel, never can be shaken whilst they rest not only on the authority, but on the preserving power of Christ. These are things which cannot be shaken; and we may even rejoice, that, notwithstanding the rage of a hostile world, or of the enemy Satan, still the church's foundations are in the holy hills; the Highest himself shall continue to establish it; and to the end of time it shall be said of this and that man,—that They were born there.

Having endeavored then to place before you the church of God, as described in the text, I would now,—

II. Enforce that attention to it which it demands.

My text says to all, "Look upon Zion." Here I may say,—

1. Look upon it, angels, with complacency and delight. We know that your exalted minds rejoiced at the idea of the erection of this temple of God; you saw the plan and

admired it: nor less were you struck with amazement at the great grace which the blessed and Holy Trinity displayed in putting it into execution. You have, with pleasure, often beheld our Jesus, from time to time, taking men, one of a city and two of a family, and bringing them to Zion. Still then let its increasing honor be the subject of your investigation; surround its walls night and day; and minister for good to all its individual members: but ye need no exhortations from mortals on a subject like this; we know that you, with desire and praise, still look upon it; and this moment I hear you all unite in saying, "Zion is a place which we all desire to look into." Then leaving the angelic host to gaze upon the Zion of God, we would say,—

2. Look upon it, sinners, with astonishment and desire.

To you who know not God, I would address myself, and say, Look upon Zion; behold real Christians, in the union they experience, and in the temple where they worship, and remember that Zion stands, though you have endeavored to oppose it. Look upon Zion, sinner, and there you will see the arm of the Lord exerted in the success of a cause which you seem determined to oppose. Look upon Zion, and recollect, that though you have often said, "Let us break their bands asunder, and cast away their cords from us," yet the Lord holds you in derision; and that your attempts against his cause are feeble and vain, and that your hope of success is an idle dream. But we would excite you to look upon Zion, that you may long to join its holy society, and unite in the solemn vows that are therein paid to the mighty Maker of heaven and earth. Can you behold its order, happiness, and joy, and not feel a wish that you might exchange the dissatisfaction and the melancholy you often experience, for the good of God's chosen, and the felicity of his heritage? Do not you think that "it will be an honor to appear, as one new born and nourished here?" Go then, and express your wish to the great Head of the church, that he would write the name of the Lord on your foreheads, and invest you with the privileges of the inhabitants of Zion. Again,—

3. Look upon it, Christians, with wonder, love and praise.

Of all characters in the world, it behooves you to "walk about Zion, and go round about her, to tell the towers thereof, to mark well her bulwarks, and consider her palaces; that ye may tell it to the generations following." Surely, as you reside in it, you ought ever to admire it, and call it the city of your solemnities, a place to which you are no strangers, but which is the place you have chosen to dwell in. O, let your eyes ever see Jerusalem a quiet habitation. Gaze on it with pure affection towards all your fellow-citizens: you shall be blessed if you love Zion: look on it then as the lot of your inheritance, and the place in which your soul delights; and ever praise, magnify, and bless Him, who constituted it what it is, who made you to dwell in so quiet a habitation, so secure a resting-place: be it your glory to be joined to the saints, and near to the Saviour.

All of us, in the presence of God, should look upon Zion; should contemplate the solemnity, the peace, and stability of the church; and this will inspire us with contempt of the world. For what is the world and all the glory thereof, compared with Zion, the city of our solemnities? Our worship is serious; they are fools, who never raise their thoughts above the ground they tread on: they sport now, but their laughter will be turned into sorrow, and their pleasure into the bitterest pain: all around them is serious, but they are without consideration, and consequently without hope. We have a quiet habitation; but "There is no peace, saith my God, to the wicked:" the church of God is secure; they are exposed to every evil in the world, and in that which is to come. Looking upon Zion, too, will direct our attention to its great Original. It will teach us to ask, Who formed all this? And thus from Zion our thoughts will pass to Zion's God, and our meditation upon him shall be sweet, yea, we will be glad in the Lord. Looking upon Zion will show us God's chief work; for here he is seen, and here he is great in Israel; so that we shall be led to rest in him, whose workmanship we are.

I have already anticipated the idea, that looking upon Zion will also fill us with desire to be inclosed within its walls. For who can look upon it without suing for a residence in it, if the saints are so quiet from fear of evil, and so secure, notwithstanding the number, power, and situation of their enemies? A child of God, must be a name better than that of sons or daughters; who can survey it without saying, Lord, bring me, keep me there?

And, finally, looking upon Zion will tend to strengthen our confidence and faith. For we shall say, If God has already defended his church so long, he will continue to do so; will be a wall of fire round about it, and the glory in the midst of it; yea, will raise the members of the church militant to the glories of the church triumphant. O, then, "turn away your eyes from beholding vanity," and "look upon Zion, the city of our solemnities; see Jerusalem, a quiet habitation, a tabernacle that shall not be taken down, not one of whose stakes shall ever be removed, not one of whose cords shall ever be broken."

SERMON XIV.

CHRIST THE ANGEL WHO GUARDS HIS CHURCH.

"Behold, I send an Angel before thee, to keep thee in the way, and to bring thee to the place which I have prepared."
—EXODUS xxiii. 20.

AT the period when these words were spoken, the children of Israel were about to leave Sinai, and proceed on their journey towards the land of Canaan. The Sovereign, Judge, and Lawgiver of his saints, had already given them plain directions for the regulation of their conduct, and now encourages them by a promise of the care of infinite love and by an assurance that he would commission an angel to go before them, to keep them in the way, and to bring them to the place which he had prepared.

And who was this angel? certainly not a created one: true indeed it is, that the whole host of angels are ministering spirits, sent forth to minister to them who shall be heirs of salvation; and that it is their perpetual employment and delight to guard the saints of God from danger, or to bear them up in their hands, lest at any time they dash their feet against a stone. It is most evident, that the sons of God, the children of the light, those who are Abraham's seed and heirs according to the promise, are the objects of their peculiar charge; yea, the angels of God are powerful guardians, to whose care we are partly committed during the time of our minority, previous to our possession of our heavenly inheritance. Yet it is not one of these who is referred to in our text, because this great and mighty Messenger from heaven possesses more honors than they can claim, and is invested with authority and power which they could never hold. This Angel has God's name in him; this Angel can forgive sins: for the next verse to my text says, "Provoke him not, for he will not pardon your transgressions:" this Angel was ever to be present with them, and to conduct them safely to the land of Canaan, a land flowing with milk and honey. See, then, his superiority to those who, notwithstanding the powers they possess, are but the creatures of God; and ask, Who this Angel is? It must be evident, that he is a divine person, if it were only from this consideration,—that he pardons transgressions;—for, as the Jews justly asked, "Who can forgive sins but God?" But surely you have frequently heard and read of the Angel of the covenant; and you remember Him that dwelt in the bush. It is far more than probable, that this Angel, then, is no less a person than our Lord and Saviour Jesus Christ. He is that Angel of whom dying Jacob testified, that he had redeemed him from all evil, and whose presence and blessing he wished ever to accompany the lads upon whose heads he laid his hands. We know that he attended the children of Israel, for "the Angel of his presence saved them; in his love and in his pity, he redeemed them; and he bare them and carried them all the days of old." It is the same that wrestled with Jacob; that kept the burning bush unconsumed; that did wonders before Manoah and his wife; that struck the admiring eyes of Daniel; and that explained the mystery of the vision to Zechariah: and so here he engages to keep

God's chosen ones in their way, and to bring them to the place which he had prepared.

The glories of the Saviour are the same in every age; he being subject to no change, but subsisting, as the Father of lights, with whom is no variableness, nor the least shadow of a turn. Every thing that may be of use to lead us to his glory and excellence, should be the subject of our contemplation and delight; nor should we refuse to take any view of him, which the Bible warrants, or recommends: wherefore, let us turn our attention to him as the Angel of the Lord. He still performs for his church what he accomplished for Israel; for the Lord has given him for a Leader and Commander to the people; yea, he is our God for ever and ever, and our Guide even unto death; so that we may safely view him as conducting his chosen tribes through duties, dangers, and trials, till they all appear before him in Zion. Let us first then view the Lord Jesus under the representation of an angel; and secondly, contemplate that office mentioned in our text, for the discharge of which he is so eminently qualified.

We will endeavor—

I. To view the Lord Jesus Christ under the representation of an angel.

"Behold," says God, to those who have turned their backs upon the world, and go in quest of a happier state, "Behold, I send an angel before thee." We would observe here, that it is utterly impossible fully to represent his excellence, either by this or any other allusion; but the idea of an angel may serve to show us somewhat at least of His loveliness, of whom we hope to be learning for ever and ever.

From the language of scripture we are led to connect an idea of personal glory with that of an angel: we read of men being astonished at the brightness of their appearance; and by several other expressions to the same intent, are led to conceive of their superiority to man in point of form and comeliness: this may at least remind us of the beauty and heavenliness of the person of Christ. This Angel of the Lord is, indeed, "fairer than the children of men, grace is poured into his lips, and God hath blessed him for ever." Glory and majesty ever characterize him; nor is it any wonder, that when the beloved disciple had a view of him, he fell at his feet as dead. No tongue can tell, heart conceive, or imagination represent, the personal glory of this Angel of God's presence, for "he is altogether lovely."

Strength also appears to be a scriptural idea when considered as applied to angels. Hence, says the Psalmist, "Ye angels, that excel in strength." All their power is evidently communicated to them from above; but it is clear that it is very great. The power of angels is intimated, when our Lord says, "Thinkest thou that I cannot now pray to my Father, and he shall presently give me more than twelve legions of angels?" leaving us to infer that they, by their power, could deliver him from all his foes. And, speak we of strength, the Angel of the covenant is mighty,—"the Lord of Hosts is his name;" let the deliverances he has wrought for his favored people teach us "his eternal power and Godhead," and show us that his arm is all-powerful, and that he can accomplish whatsoever he pleaseth in the worlds of nature, providence, and grace. An angel could loose Peter from the prison, and set him free. Christ Jesus has delivered us who were tied and bound with the chain of our sins, and has demolished the strongholds of Satan.

Intelligence is another property of angels, and may serve to form a resemblance between them and the Captain of this host of the Lord. Their active minds are ever employed in investigating the things of the kingdom, and in looking with reverence and desire of perpetual instruction into the ark of God, and in learning from the churches the manifold wisdom of God. But what is their information when compared with that of him, "in whom are hid all the treasures of wisdom and knowledge?" their knowledge is indeed great, but not infinite; they cannot search the hearts of men, nor know future events in any other way than as they are taught by the Lord of hosts. But he tries the reins of the children of men; nor do we ever speak a greater truth than when we say to him, "Lord, thou knowest all things."

Holiness must also ever be viewed by us as one grand characteristic of the angels of God; hence in Scripture they are so frequently called, "his holy angels." Living so near Jehovah as they do, no wonder they reflect his image: they were first created pure, and they have ever been preserved so; they are the angels that sinned not, and therefore never fell. And the idea of their sanctity should impress our minds with shame, when we recollect that they watch our conduct, and inspect our devotions. But the Angel of whom we speak, here lays a sole claim to the title of "He that is holy, and he that is true." When we bow before him, let us cry, "Holy, holy, holy, Lord God Almighty!" and desire to see him as the eternal God, as a real man, and as our Mediator: he has ever maintained unspotted holiness.

The last excellency which we shall mention as existing in the angels is, concern for our welfare. For they are all ministering spirits, sent forth to minister to them who shall be heirs of salvation. They lose no opportunity of doing good to the saints, by suggesting good thoughts; by restraining Satan; by averting dangers; and by assisting and providing for them. But, as it regards benevolent deeds, Jesus has far outdone them all; he flew to help us, he ran to save; how ready was he to lay down his life in our behalf! how well pleased was this angel of the Lord to acquit us, when we stood before him justly charged with numerous crimes! how gracious is he to the present moment, in supplying our wants, and doing for us what no angel in heaven could ever accomplish! Our interest lies near his his heart; yea, he is not ashamed to call us brethren: there is mercy in all his dispensations; nor have any of us ever had reason to complain that he has been unfaithful to his promise, or unkind to us. These, then, are the characteristics of the Angel spoken of in my text, who befriended the Israelites of old, and who ever encampeth round about them that fear him. He possesses personal glory, unlimited strength, universal intelligence, untainted holiness, and a benevolent disposition. May his glory be the object of our admiration and study; his strength be exerted in delivering us from evil: his understanding be in a measure communicated to us, that we may be wise and understand the fear of the Lord; his holiness be the means of leading us to aspire after personal sanctity, and his benevolent actions excite our gratitude and praise forever.

Having admired the character of the Angel who was sent before the children of Israel, let us now—

II. Contemplate that office, for the discharge of which he is so eminently qualified.

Observe his divine commission. "I," says God, "send an angel before thee." He has been divinely dedicated to the office of Guide and Leader of his people; and hence, as he was present with the believing Israelites, and glorified their families, and their assemblies, with his heavenly grace, and conducted them forty years in the wilderness; so will he guard us from danger; the Lord himself shall be our Sun and Shield, we shall go whithersoever he leads us, and where we reside, there shall he also dwell. He shall lead, direct, and advise us: the rising generation shall cry after this glorious Angel, and say, "Be thou the guide of my youth:" and, to those in the decline of life, he says, "Even to old age I am he, and even to hoary hairs will I carry you." Oh, how happy ought we to be under the conduct of so divine a guide! he goes before us, then, for two purposes specified in the text: to preserve us all through our journey, and—to administer to us an entrance into the wealthy place.

1. This Angel of the Lord goes before us so preserve us all through our journey. "I send an angel," says God, "before thee, to keep thee in thy way." He preserved them from wandering, for he led them forth by a right way, that they might go to a city of habitation: he keeps them in the way marked out by unerring skill; the way that has been trodden by the whole host of the redeemed, and, consequently, the way that leads directly to our Father's house. And if this great and mighty Angel goes before us, surely our safety is made abundantly certain; for what enemy can withstand him, if he slew Sihon king of the Amorites, and Og the king of Bashan for the Jews?

surely an army of corruptions, shall be by his power laid level with the ground, and the world, sin, and the devil, be trampled under the feet of his followers, while they shout, "The Lord God of hosts is with us, the God of Jacob is our refuge." If he goes before us to keep us in his way, how animated should we be by his conquests; and while he says, "Fight on, my faithful band," let us wage war with every spiritual foe, and have respect to the recompense of the reward. This Angel goes before us to keep us in the way, and thus displays his infinite perfections: his goodness, wisdom, condescension, ability, and holiness, are manifest on every occasion; and whilst he plants fear in the hearts of his foes, his grace and love will never fail to delight those who are chosen, called, and faithful. In conducting them through this world, he makes use of the directions of his word, the excellences of his own example, the influence of his divine Spirit, and the hand of his providence: these things say to us, "This is the way, walk ye in it." Having then such a glorious Companion, let us not fear the difficulties that lie in our way, but forget our troubles; and in the strength of the Captain of salvation, who leads us in paths of righteousness for his name's sake, "Let us run with patience the race set before us, looking unto Jesus, the Author and the Finisher of our faith."

2. The Angel of the covenant, too, goes before us to administer to us an entrance into the wealthy place.

"I send an angel before thee, to keep thee in the way, and to bring thee to the place which I have prepared:" thus he did for the Israelites when he introduced them into Canaan: but, oh, what will he do for believers when he brings them to the place which he has prepared!—a place of which Canaan, after all, affords but a feeble representation: a place prepared for our reception before the world began, and taken possession of by Jesus as our forerunner, who has entered within the veil for us: to this place our exertions are directed, and at this place we shall all eventually appear; whilst to bring us thither is the part of our adorable Leader, the Angel of the covenant.

He shall cause us to loose our anchor from the earth, to pass into eternity, a gallant vessel, with every sail set to the favoring breeze, and entering into the harbor of eternal peace, amidst the plaudits of redeemed men and waiting angels. Jesus shall be the medium of our access to God in heaven, and through him, we shall have an abundant entrance administered unto us into his eternal kingdom and glory. He shall receive our disembodied spirits to himself, and at the end of our journey, open to us the door of everlasting bliss, and show us the regions of glory; yea, say to us, "Come in, ye blessed of the Lord: why stand ye without?" Yea, he will present us to his Father, "blameless before him in love;" he will glory over us as the objects of his love, and the purchase of his blood: yea, through his mediation and death, we shall be forever "holy, and unblamable, and unreprovable in his sight, being presented faultless before the presence of his glory with exceeding joy." Oh, what a distinguished part in the economy of our salvation does the Angel of the covenant bear! He first leads to the road that will conduct us to his kingdom and glory; and he finally introduces us into the august presence of God, even the Father, and so brings us to the place which he hath prepared. This shall be the portion of all his saints, for in glory they will all finally appear, though some on boards and some on broken pieces of the ship, yet it shall come to pass that they shall all escape safe to land.

Who is our guide?

Reason? passion? or the Angel of the Covenant?

Sinners, destitute of a guide, &c.*

What is the object of our hope?

It is being brought to the place which God has prepared, or are we yet attached to earth? If we now have our conversation in heaven—

> "See the kind angels at the gates,
> Inviting us to come;
> There Jesus the forerunner waits,
> To welcome travelers home."

IMPROVEMENT.

Our text suggests a motive to obedience: a test of examination, and a ground of hope.

* No doubt Mr. Spencer enlarged on these subjects in delivering this Sermon, and also, as usual, in the improvement.

SERMON XV.

SINNERS ABUSE THE LONG SUFFERING OF GOD.

"Because sentence against an evil work is not executed speedily, therefore the heart of the sons of men is fully set in them to do evil."—ECCLESIASTES viii. 11.

How dreadfully depraved is human nature! How abject is the condition in which the fall of our first parents has placed us! What a sink of pollution is the heart of man! Considered, indeed, as creatures in the eye of Deity, we must appear meanness itself: of the dust of the earth we were formed; and as soon as our sovereign Creator says, "Return, ye children of men," we mix with our original, we are obliged to say to corruption, "Thou art my father; to the worm, Thou art my mother and my sister." But, oh, viewed as sinners, how offensive must we be in the sight of the God of infinite purity and immaculate holiness! Alas, for us, for we have fallen! fallen low indeed from the state of rectitude in which we were created: being in honor, we did not abide: now darkness overspreads our understanding, perverseness distinguishes our will; earthly mindedness characterizes our affections: the path of folly, is that we choose; the course of impiety, the resolution of living in direct enmity against God, is that which we decidedly adopt. We need not go far for proofs of the truth of these assertions: that man is depraved, is written in his countenance, is discovered in his conversation, is betrayed in his deportment.

I have now before my eyes one of the most striking evidences of human depravity, that can ever be produced; it is in my text, which declares, that "Because sentence against an evil work is not executed speedily, therefore the heart of the sons of men is fully set in them to do evil." Which passage justifies four observations:—that sin is an evil work;—that sentence is gone out against it;—that the execution of this sentence is often deferred;—that this circumstance, through the depravity of men, frequently produces the worst effects.

I. Sin is an evil work.

Our remarks upon this part of our subject will, indeed, be very brief; and they must be regarded as only introductory to the rest. But I would charge home upon all my hearers, the guilt of sin; I would, as in the presence of God and his elect angels, tell every individual in this place, that he has, ever since he had a being, been doing an evil work. Our text may, perhaps, directly refer to some particular sin; but it will do us no harm to consider the expression, "an evil work," as descriptive of sin in general; sin, brethren, to the commission of which our constitution is prone; sin, in the practice of which some amongst us have lived long; sin, which, perhaps, many in this congregation roll as a sweet morsel under their tongue, is "an evil work." A moment's reflection may show us,—that it is evil in itself,—and in its consequences.

1. Observe, it is evil in itself. For what is sin? It is the transgression of the law; it is the breach of the commandment which is holy, just, and good. The law of God is divinely excellent; it is the line of human conduct, marked out by infinite wisdom and unquestionable authority; now sin is a departure from it, and therefore is evil: it is a violation of the wholesome and excellent injunctions which are stamped with the broad seal of Heaven. To see that sin is an evil work, you need only contrast it with what the Bible recommends, and with that at which the most enlightened and holy men ever aim: in its nature it is exceeding sinful; it is alienation from the divine life; it is opposition to the divine will; it is enmity to God, the Judge of all. Surely that which satan brings into action, by influencing an already depraved and abandoned heart, must be evil. It is the abominable thing which God hateth. The reason why man is filthy, is because he drinketh in iniquity like water. Hence,—

2. Sin is evil in its consequences; for it was the cause of pain to the Saviour, and of wo to man. I say, it occasioned pain to the Saviour: but for this evil work, he never would have become destitute, afflicted, tormented; but for this, he never would have had to toil up Calvary's hill, bearing the weight of his own heavy cross; but for this, he never would have endured the burden of the Father's wrath, or the insults of his inhuman foes. This evil work, too, introduced the whole train of calamities amongst mankind; gave being to wretchedness and despair; gave a sting to conscience, and a sting to death. It is this that is now training up so many for hell, and preparing them for the endurance of the fiercest pains. Oh, is not sin then an evil work? Ought you not with holy haste, and deter-

mined aversion, to flee from it? Cry mightily to God, saying, Deliver us from evil? So vile a thing is sin. Let us show,—

II. That sentence is declared against it. And a sentence which, permit me to say, is divinely announced,—awfully severe,—strictly just,—and certain of its accomplishment. The sentence against an evil work is,—

1. Divinely announced. Who can, who should, sit in judgment upon it, but the God against whom it is committed? He now decides on human actions, and he will hereafter publicly investigate them at his dread tribunal, before an assembled world. He has sworn in his wrath that iniquity shall not stand in his sight; he has declared that he will, by no means, clear the guilty; that sin shall not go unpunished, is one of the fixed principles of the moral government of God, a rule of which he has never yet lost sight, nor will till the great burning day. On the account of this evil work he has kindled a fire in his anger, which shall burn to the lowest hell: all the curses contained in this book against sin, are affixed to the commission of it, by God the Judge of all; so that we speak of no trifling thing when we describe the sentence against an evil work. It must strike you, too, if you think at all, that the sentence adverted to in my text is,—

2. Awfully severe. God has shown us that we commit a great evil in forsaking him, the Fountain of living waters; he has intolerable pains for the workers of iniquity: the sentence is severe, for it condemns the miserable offender to the torments of conscience, to restless uneasiness, to insatiable desires, even in the present life; and we know that death is the wages of sin; that a painful separation of

soul and body, that a dreary lodging in the house appointed for all living, is the reward of human guilt. Mortality is our portion, death is our inheritance; there is no discharge in that war, no delivery from that trial, no method of escape from the stroke of the last enemy: we are sentenced to death for the commission of an evil; and behold, brethren, the solemnity,—judgment and eternity succeed the king of terrors! The sentence pronounced upon us for sin is severe, and it condemns us to shame, and everlasting contempt. It assigns us our lot in "Tophet, which was prepared of old: it is made deep and large; the pile thereof is fire and much wood; the breath of the Lord, like a stream of brimstone, doth kindle it." This is the sentence declared against the evil work, and it is—

3. Strictly just. Would it be at all consistent with the attributes and perfections of the Deity, if he were to be regardless of the contempt that is cast upon his authority; the disaffection men express to his government; or the temerity with which they violate his commands? Would he, then, be a God jealous of his honor? But we know, that to him it belongeth justly to punish sin. Shall sin, which intruded itself into our world, which otherwise would have been a blissful paradise of pleasure; shall sin, which has usurped his dominion, be unnoticed or unpunished by him? To vindicate his own character, to display the glory of his own perfections, especially to manifest to all his unspotted holiness and purity, to show that he will not wink at sin, he has pronounced sentence on all who practise it. You have just viewed the evil of sin, yea, seen that it has occasioned incalculable and irreparable mischief: I leave it with yourselves to judge, whether the sentence pronounced against it be not just. Yes, brethren, in the con-

fidence of this fact, the justice of God in sentencing sin, "every mouth shall be stopped, and all the world become guilty before God."

This is a sentence, too, that is—

4. Certain of its accomplishment. For hath the Lord spoken, and shall it not be done? Hath he commanded, and shall it not stand fast? Be it known to you, brethren, that though the sons of Belial take the timbrel and harp, and rejoice at the sound of the organ, and spend their days in wealth, yet in a moment they shall go down to the grave, and the candle of the wicked shall be put out. The sentence that God passes against the workers of iniquity, must be, in all its rigor and severity, put in force, that the terror of the Almighty's frown may be manifested, and the malignity of sin displayed. The fulfillment of the severe determination, respecting the doom of sinners, rests on the justice of God; nor is there one threat that goes out of his mouth, which he will not awfully put in force, and that to all eternity, upon the devoted head of the impenitent miserable offender. This is the sentence then which is declared against this evil work. But now I am to remark,—

III. That the execution of this sentence is frequently deferred.

It "is not" (in the language of my text) "executed speedily." This cannot be from any want of power in the Almighty to put it in immediate force, because it requires no peculiar exertion from him, to dash a world to atoms, or send a soul to hell. He could take you away with a stroke; could call you, sinner, from the midst of this congregation into eternity; yet he delays, and "sentence against an evil work is not executed speedily." He might, indeed, summon more than he does to appear before his bar, from the scene of pleasure and from the couch of sensual indulgence; but often, whilst they are doing these things, God keeps silence. Yet shall he, hereafter, come as the Lion of the tribe of Judah, to tear his enemies in pieces. But this circumstance of God refusing to execute the sentence speedily, arises—

1. From the forbearance of God. There is not a greater truth stated within this holy book, than that the Lord is long-suffering; that he bears with our manners in this wilderness: hence he does not now deal with mankind as he did of old, when he said, he would destroy man, whom he had created, from the face of the earth; but now he, in his long-suffering, waits: he is, as his word acknowledges him to be, "slow to anger, gracious, and full of compassion;" hence it is that the sons of Jacob are not consumed: since there is this disposition in the Almighty, his sentence is not executed speedily; "his mercies fail not." Here, then, we have human preservation, in the midst of dangers and snares, traced to its proper source, and we see why it is that his wrath delays. Again, Is sentence against an evil work, in many instances, yet unexecuted?

2. This represents our life as a state of trial. It shows us that the Lord is leading us in the wilderness, to humble and to prove us, to know what is in our heart, whether we would serve the Lord our God or not: it proves to us that this is a probationary state: it sets this matter beyond the possibility of a doubt, that whilst we are sojourners and pilgrims here, as all our fathers were, the eye of God is upon us, that he inspects our conduct, and spies out all our ways; he gives us space and opportunity for repentance. O that we may, whilst sentence against an evil work is not

executed speedily, properly fill up our days, and, by fleeing to Jesus, avert the threatened danger. For, if the sentence is yet unfulfilled, I remark—

3. This lays a foundation for hope

The messenger, Death, has not yet visited you; you may perhaps have yet no peculiar cause to imagine that you are going the way whence you shall not return; then, whilst the lamp of life burns, the trumpet of the gospel sounds; whilst the sentence is unexecuted, the blood of Christ has all-powerful efficacy. This thought, sinner, that as yet you are out of hell, should constrain you to look all around for help; should operate on your mind to lead you to the door of mercy, where, even now, if you knock, it shall be opened unto you. But, oh, I am obliged, from the sentiment and spirit of my text, to observe,—

IV. That this circumstance, through the depravity of man, often produces the worst effects. On account of it, my text assures us, that "the heart of the sons of men is fully set in them to do evil." Here is mercy abused, long-suffering despised, compassion slighted. What ought to be the effect of the patience of God with sinners? It should lead them to repentance. If he comes so often, and so long, seeking fruit, ought he not to find it? But God says, "Moab has been at ease from his youth, and he has settled on his lees, and hath not been emptied from vessel to vessel, neither hath he gone into captivity, therefore his taste remaineth in him, and his scent is not changed." Your hearts are hardened, sinners, by the forbearance of God; you become more and more resolved on iniquity, and determined in sin; your hearts are fully set in you to do evil. Here observe that, because sentence against sin is not yet executed,—

1. Mankind imagine that it will not be so dreadful as scripture represents it. Men act as if they thought that every day they spent in sin, diminished, instead of added, to their future sufferings; and "though favor is shown to the wicked, yet will he not learn righteousness; even in the land of uprightness he will deal unjustly, and will not behold the majesty of the Lord. He is wearied in the greatness of his way; yet, says he not, There is no hope:" he is not sufficiently grieved He determines to do evil, because, as the sentence is not yet executed, he foolishly wishes and persuades himself, that what is so long delayed, may probably be tolerable to bear. But further, because the former part of my text is true,—

2. Sinners presume that judgment never will come. Since it is delayed, they look not forward to the period when it will be awfully felt; they suppose the Almighty to be altogether such a one as themselves, and therefore "their hearts are set in them to do evil." Thus, when Pharaoh saw that there was respite, he hardened his heart and hearkened not, as the Lord had said; neither would he let the people go. Because the sentence against sinners is not speedily executed, they say, in their hearts, "We shall not be moved, for we shall never be in adversity:" they tantalize those who are looking forward to the day of God's wrath, and say, "Where is the promise of his coming, for, since the fathers fell asleep, all things continue as they were from the beginning?" They do not see, "that one day is with the Lord as a thousand years, and a thousand years as one day;" but they determine to do evil, because they would persuade themselves that justice sleeps, and

vengeance will never fall on them. There is one step more in this stage of impiety, and that is, that many of them are, from this circumstance, resolved to do evil, because,—

3. They boldly and impiously challenge the divine wrath. "They draw iniquity with cords of vanity, and sin as it were with a cart-rope;" they say, "Let him make speed and hasten his work, that we may see it; and let the counsel of the Holy One of Israel draw nigh, and come, that we may know it:" and because the Lord delayeth his coming, this "evil servant begins to smite his fellow-servants, and to eat and drink with the drunken:" their hearts are set in them to do evil; they encourage this propensity; they indulge this evil bias; by drinking deeper and deeper of the fountain of pleasure, they endeavor to fortify their minds against the fear of ruin: with hell in all its terrors before their eyes, they go on to sin.

But, oh, how awful is the state of obstinate sinners! God often lets them take their course, nor stops them in the road to hell. But, sinner, stay, "We are sure that the judgment of God is according to truth against them which commit such things. And thinkest thou this, O man, that judgest them which do such things, and doest the same, that thou shalt escape the judgment of God? Or despisest thou the riches of his goodness, and forbearance, and long-suffering; not knowing that the goodness of God leadeth thee to repentance? But, after thy hardness and impenitent heart, treasurest up unto thyself wrath against the day of wrath and revelation of the righteous judgment of God; who will render to every man according to his deeds." Rom. ii. 2–6. The promises of God are no less true than his threatenings. He has pardoned believers;

he will not revoke it: but will encourage to holiness: how consolatory, &c.* Let uspray for sinners—

Swift may thy mercy, Lord, arise,
  Ere justice stops their breath;
And lighten those deluded eyes,
  That sleep the sleep of death.

* No doubt, Mr. Spencer enlarged here in the delivery of this Discourse, as was his custom in the improvement of his subjects.

SERMON XVI.

GOD'S ABILITY TO BESTOW INCONCEIVABLE BLESSINGS.

"Now unto him that is able to do exceeding abundantly above all that we ask or think, according to the power that worketh in us; unto him be glory in the church by Christ Jesus, throughout all ages, world without end. Amen."—EPHESIANS iii. 20, 21.

THERE certainly cannot be a more astonishing subject for human or angelic contemplation, than the love of Christ. It is, indeed, immense and unsearchable,—vast in extent, —without any commencement,—enduring to eternity—unfathomable in its depths, and superlative in its heights: it challenges the most enlarged powers fully to comprehend it. All the ideas that may be entertained of it by men or angels are infinitely surpassed, since no stretch of thought can embrace its nature, or the grand manifestations that have been given of it. And yet, mysterious as this subject is, God has thought fit to enlighten the minds of a favored few, in every age of the world, so that they are enabled to understand, at least somewhat of that divine theme, the full excellence of which cannot be told.

Hence the great apostle of the Gentiles is emboldened to ask for the believing Ephesians no small boon; but to beg the Father of our Lord Jesus Christ to make them able to comprehend, as far as a human mind can, the love of Christ; that they might feel its virtue, power, and sweetness, and be favored with a delightful view of its boundless riches. And when he had asked this great, and apparently to many, hard thing, lest they should suppose for a moment, that they ought not to dare to expect such a favor, or that it was too much for God to grant, he intimates that even this, and more than this, can be accomplished for us by the God of all grace; and therefore, to raise their expectations and confirm their faith, he says, "Now unto him who (I can tell you, if you think this a great request) is able to do exceeding abundantly above all that we ask or think, according to the power that worketh in us; unto him be glory in the church by Christ Jesus, throughout all ages, world without end. Amen."

In proposing this text for your contemplation, I remark, that it gives us an insight into Jehovah's ability to bestow the greatest blessings on his saints,—the proof that he has already given of it,—and the honor that should be ascribed to him on account of it. Hoping that our reflections will be made useful to strike us with admiration of the exceeding riches of grace, we will, in the first place, indulge a few thoughts on,—

I. Jehovah's ability to bestow the greatest blessings on his saints.

"He is able," says my text, "to do exceeding abundantly above all that we ask or think." And who (may some say) can doubt it? Do we not all know that he is God all-mighty? Have we not often heard, that nothing is too hard for the Lord? Do you think that any of us doubt that with God all things are possible? But, O believers, have you always faith in this? Does your experience and your conduct show, that you always believingly rest your soul upon the divine omnipotence? Rather do you not, by your needless fears, frequently give us reason to suppose that you do not believe in the power of the arm of God? This being the case, let your minds be stirred up by way of remembrance, that you may be encouraged to trust in the Lord Jehovah, by beholding, that "in the Lord Jehovah is everlasting strength." We are not now called to dwell upon Jehovah's creating power, or to see how easily he can dash a world to pieces. It is not the power of his anger, which solicits your attention now. It is not what he can do to beautify and bless angels, or to torment with eternal anguish the lost spirits in hell; but it is what he can do in your behalf; what he can accomplish for you, who are, without his assistance, helpless as the new-born infant, or weaker than the feeble worm. And let us observe, that he is able to fulfill and to exceed the most enlarged prayer of faith,—or the most vast desire of the heart. Our text shows us that he can exceed,—

1. The most enlarged prayer of faith. "He is able," says my text, "to do exceeding abundantly above all that we ask." In our petitions at the throne of the heavenly Majesty, we never need be afraid to ask too much. "Open thy mouth wide," says the Lord of all, "and I will fill it;" be not scanty in your desires. Ask what I shall give thee, and for the sake of Jesus it shall be all bestowed. Is any grievous trial before you? O, display the same faith in the power of God, that Shadrach, Meshach, and Abednego did, when they said, "Our God, whom we serve, is able to deliver us from the burning fiery furnace, and he will deliver us out of thine hand, O king." Are you fearing that the Redeemer's interest will not succeed in the

world, when you plead the cause of Zion? Recollect that he is able, of these stones, to raise up children unto Abraham. Are you afraid that you shall one day fall into the hand of your enemy, or backslide from the Lord that bought you, when you pray for persevering grace? Remember, that "he is able to make you stand." Are the stores of the divine bounty exhausted? Is there not a perfect fullness of grace in the Saviour? Cannot our God supply all our need "according to his riches in glory by Christ Jesus?"

Ask then for spiritual blessings in heavenly places in Christ, and you shall receive them; for God is able to bestow them. Not only will he fulfill the desire of them that fear him, but he will far exceed it; for "he is able to do exceeding abundantly above all that we ask." This is illustrated in a memorable part of the experience of Solomon: he asked wisdom of the Lord; he gave it him, but said to him, "And I have also given thee that which thou hast not asked, both riches and honor; so that there shall not be any among the kings like unto thee, all thy days."

Abraham, the father of the faithful, seemed to be, in the midst of trial, firmly persuaded of the truth stated in my text, that God was able to do exceeding abundantly above all that he could ask or think; hence, says the apostle, "he offered up Isaac, of whom it was said, that, in Isaac shall thy seed be called; accounting that God was able to raise him up, even from the dead; from whence also he received him in a figure." So let us all believe and act upon the truth, that he is able to save to the very uttermost, all that come unto him by the Son of his love. And when a Christian has been constantly praying for years, and has asked for all the blessings, the need of which his mind suggested, he may still say, He is able to do exceeding abundantly above all that I ask. He is able also to exceed,—

2. The most secret desires of the heart. He can do exceeding abundantly above all that we ask or think. There are some periods in our experience, when certain blessings can only be thought on by us, and we have not faith to plead for them with our heavenly Father; we seem to look at them with a wishful eye, but scarcely dare say, Lord, make them mine! But the ability of our covenant God, however, extends to this. Let us not limit the Holy One of Israel, but see that he can exceed all that we can even think. When a child of God has received any particular blessing from Heaven, for which he is, as he ought to be, especially thankful, we may say to him, as the man of God said to Amaziah, "The Lord is able to give thee much more than this." For it has not entered into the heart of man to conceive, what God has prepared for them that love him; and therefore he must do more than we can think. We sometimes see the cup of blessing in the dear Redeemer's hand, and secretly long to taste. Well, at that time he shall say, "Drink, yea, drink abundantly, O beloved." Our highest thoughts shall be surpassed by the stores of his grace, and that grace shall be exceeding abundant towards us with faith and love, which are in Christ Jesus. Yea, though at times we dare not think of possessing hereafter a station among God's redeemed ones in glory: yet "an entrance shall be administered to us abundantly, into the everlasting kingdom of our Lord and Saviour Jesus Christ." O, then, let us not stagger at the promises, but "be strong in faith, giving glory to God." Let us rejoice, that what he has promised he is able to perform; and if he

is so abundant in goodness and truth, as to exceed our strongest and largest desires, surely his loving-kindness is excellent; "therefore the children of men put their trust under the shadow of his wings." Yea, "we shall be abundantly satisfied with the fatness of his house, and he shall make us drink of the river of his pleasures, for with him is the fountain of life, and in his light shall we see light."

Think over as many temporal and spiritual blessings as you can; anticipate as many favors from the hand of God as possible; enumerate covenant blessings till you can proceed no further; and yet say, "He is able to do exceeding abundantly above all that we think." Surely he gives like a God, and withholds no good thing from them that walk uprightly. This is what God will do. Let us view,—

II. The proof that he has already given of it.

Even in the power that worketh in us; for says my text, "He is able to do exceeding abundantly above all that we ask or think, according to the power that worketh in us." Thus intimating, that the energy of divine grace, as operative on the heart, is the best evidence that God could give us of his ability to exceed our desires and wishes.

This power, you know, was exerted in snatching you as a brand from the burning, in calling you from darkness to light. It made you willing to submit to the righteousness of God; it worked effectually in you; hence you threw down your weapons of hostility against the Saviour, and took up, yea, put on, the whole armour of God, that you might go forth to fight the battles of the Lord. You would have had no grace in your heart, had it not been communicated with power from on high; and so even now this mighty power worketh in you, whereby he is able to subdue your evil passions and propensities to himself, and shall ever be exerted in your behalf.

The apostle's argument then seems to stand thus: there is a divine power continually exerted in your behalf, constantly maintaining the life of faith in your soul: now, since God has exerted, and continues to exert, his potent arm in your behalf, you may learn from it, that he will even exceed your largest desires, and give you all necessary good. And we might indeed dwell with peculiar pleasure on this part of our subject, in endeavoring to show how it is that the power of divine grace, as exerted within us, affords us an evidence of the truth of Jehovah's ability to exceed all that we ask or think; but we will briefly remark, that this power displays itself—in subduing our corruptions,—in confirming our faith,—in preserving us near to himself,—and in enabling us to glorify his name; and that all this is but an earnest of better things.

1. This power is put forth in subduing our corruptions. What but the arm of Omnipotence could crucify the old man? What but the effectual working of the Redeemer's power could mortify the flesh with its affections and lusts? And this power does prevent sin from having dominion over us; it restrains our appetites and passions; it keeps the body of death in subjection. Inbred corruption would indeed prevail against us, were it not for the power that worketh in us; but there is a secret, silent operation of God upon the soul, which subdues the power of sin; and it shall soon appear, to our joy and satisfaction for ever, that the grace of God is much stronger than our sins, and more powerful than corruption itself. Surely, then, we have every encouragement to believe, that if the arm of the Lord

has been lifted up to slay our corruptions, he will not refuse even to do for us "exceeding abundantly above all that we ask or think."

2. See this power exerted in confirming our faith. To believe in the Son of God, without the assistance of the Lord himself, is utterly impossible; as well might you attempt to create a new world. Did not he first teach you to believe? And must not the same spirit of faith be given to you now, to teach you always to believe that he is faithful who has promised? It is only by being assisted with power from on high, that you can cast anchor upon the Rock of Ages, or do the will of God by believing in him whom he has sent into the world. But a constant act of faith is preserved in the soul by this mighty power. Moral suasion could not work faith in your heart; the Lord must give it and increase it. Those who are ordained unto eternal life, and believe the gospel, are the men on whose minds the Spirit of God works in a most gracious and effectual way; and this he does to give them to know that he will do yet more, and to make them persuaded that he is able to do exceeding abundantly above all that we ask or think.

3. You may learn this, too, from considering that the power of God appears, in preserving us near to himself. Does it not require divine agency to keep you near to Christ, from whom, alas, you would be always wandering, did he not engage to put his fear in your heart, that so you might not depart from him? The blessings of communion and fellowship with the Saviour, would, alas, be all strange things to us, did not God, by his powerful hand, raise us to that state of dignity in which we may enjoy them. God answers the prayers of the Saviour, by keeping us through his own name, and so influencing our conduct, that we are led on to

follow the Lamb whithersoever he goeth. When our sinful inclinations would lead us from him, he gently, delightfully, restrains us, by saying to our souls, "I am your salvation," and causes us to esteem the light of his countenance more than any other enjoyment. If he does this for us, never let us fear but he will convince us of his ability to do exceeding abundantly above all that we ask or think.

4. What gracious power does he evince, in enabling us to glorify his name! Without divine strength, should we ever adorn the doctrine of God our Saviour in all things, or, with well-doing, put to silence the ignorance of foolish men? Left to ourselves, should we not rather bring a reproach upon that worthy name by which we are called? This divine energy assisted the apostle Paul in his labors; hence he said, "Whereunto I also labor, striving according to his working, which worketh in me mightily;" and again, "I labored more abundantly than they all; yet not I, but the grace of God which was with me." This power working in us, too, shall influence our conduct; shall make us fill up our days to the divine glory; and serve our generation according to the divine will. But, oh, never let us forget that the same power which makes a man a Christian in this untoward generation, will also exceed all that he asks or thinks. This is the mighty power of God, which will accomplish so much for our good

III. Consider the honor that should be ascribed to him on account of it.

"To him," says the apostle, "be glory." And is it not equitable that we should give unto the Lord, the glory due unto his name; and that, since we can view the attribute of divine power engaged on our behalf, we should give him the praise he so justly demands; for his is the kingdom, the power and the glory. But observe three things in the honor we must give to God; for, being able to exceed our desires,—it must be ascribed to him in all the churches;—it must be presented to him through the mediation of Christ;—and it must be rendered to him to the latest period of time, and throughout eternity. The text shows us—

1. That honor must be ascribed to Christ in all the church. Unto him be glory, says my text, in the church. For this power, you know, can be exerted on the behalf of every individual member of his church, however mean or contemptible in the eyes of the world; therefore the joy, occasioned by the contemplation of it, shall pervade all the members of the mystical body of Christ. Every Christian who has experienced proofs of this ability, has a right to call upon those members of the church of Christ with whom he is connected, to rejoice with him; and the gladness should be like the precious oil that ran down from the beard, even Aaron's beard, and went down to the skirts of his garment. For this power God is alike praised by men below and saints above, whether we regard the church militant or triumphant; they praise him for the glory of his mighty acts, and they say, "Thine, O Lord, is the greatness, and the power, and the glory, and the victory, and the majesty; for all that is in the heaven, and in the earth, is thine. Thine is the kingdom, O Lord, and thou art exalted as head above all: both riches and honor come of thee, and thou reignest over all; and in thine hand is power and might, and in thine hand it is to make great, and to give strength unto all."

2. This glory must be presented to him through the

mediation of Christ. To him be glory in the church by Christ Jesus. We should never have dared to offer the sacrifice of praise to God, had it not been for this glorious Redeemer; since he has by his cross glorified the divine perfections, we can contemplate them with holy pleasure and delight, and adore him for them all. But he would spurn at our attempts at adoration, if we had no reference to the atonement of his Son. Our praises will never be acceptable in his sight, unless they are offered through faith in Christ Jesus. Besides, he must present them to God, even the Father; hence we rejoice that "we have a High Priest passed into the heavens, Jesus the Son of God," who bears our praises to the eternal throne. Yes, he stands at the altar, "having a golden censer, and there is given unto him much incense, that he should offer it with the prayers of all the saints upon the golden altar which is before the throne." How pleasing is the thought, that our imperfect praises are conveyed to God the Judge of all, by the Angel of the covenant. What need have we of saints to be our advocates, when we have Christ Jesus? Who else can render our acknowledgments worthy of the acceptance of the eternal Father, but Jesus only? hence,

Jesus alone shall bear my cries
Up to his Father's throne;
He, dearest Lord, perfumes my sighs,
And sweetens every groan.

And so shall it be with our songs of praise, even till we are admitted into his presence. Oh, to him be glory by Jesus Christ.

3. The honor must be rendered to him to the latest

period of time, and throughout eternity. "To him be glory in the church by Christ Jesus, throughout all ages, world without end. Amen." So long as Jehovah possesses this divine power, so long must he be honored on account of it. And I leave with yourselves to judge, whether this will not be forever and ever. It must be throughout all ages; when the present generation shall have passed away, and another shall have come; when our heads shall be all laid beneath the clods of the valley, and the worms feed sweetly on our bodies; even then there will be a generation to call Jehovah blessed, and a seed to serve him. For then this power shall be exerted, and the people that shall be created shall praise the Lord. Yea, till all his saints are gathered in, must the Head of the church be glorified, and world without end. When all the redeemed shall be united in Christ, this glory shall be rendered to Jehovah; since the sweet work of praise shall be our employment in heaven, forever and ever.

Now, to all this, you are called upon to add the solemn word—Amen. My text is a prayer for the glory of God. Oh, offer it up from the bottom of your hearts!

And what think you, sinner, of the power of God? it will be exerted in destroying you. Oh, dread his anger, and take refuge in Jesus, the Sanctuary.*

* We have before noticed, that Mr. Spencer was accustomed to enlarge on his written notes, in the improvements of his Sermons: we annex the following specimen, which was taken down in short-hand.—

"Now, to all this, my dear hearers, you are required to pronounce the solemn word—Amen! Because God possesses this power, you ought to rejoice in it; because he can do exceeding abundant above all that you can ask or think, you ought to entreat him, from the bottom of your hearts, that he would do it for you.

"My text is a prayer, a prayer for the glory of God, to which all our exertions ought to be directed. Is this, then, the object to which your exertions are directed? Are you saying, by your lives and conversations, 'Worthy is the Lamb?' Are you glorifying Jesus by your lives? Remember, that you have now an opportunity of showing that you desire to glorify him; and I trust that Jesus will receive a revenue of praise, within the walls of this place, at this opportunity.

"Sinners! what aspect does the mighty power of God wear toward you? It wears the most terrific aspect. You may think of defying the power of God; but once hath God spoken, yea, twice have I heard this, that power belongeth unto God; and power to destroy as well as to save. I have told you that there was a power that worked in the hearts of them that believe; but oh! you have not submitted to it; your lusts are your guide; and God may say of you, He is joined to his idols, let him alone! He is able to inflict exceeding abundantly more pain upon you than you can think; he has so much ability, that he can terrify you by his anger, frown you into hell, and make you the eternal subject of the gnawing of the worm that never dies. Whither will you flee from his anger? Jesus shall be a sanctuary; but if you refuse him, whither will you flee from the divine anger? A man shall be a covert from the tempest, and a shelter from the wind, and you can only take shelter in that way. But so soon as you have embraced him, he will present you to God as one who has received his good Spirit. The moment you lay hold on the hope set before you, that moment the omnipotence of God shall be engaged on your behalf, and the prayer of Christ shall be answered, 'Keep through thine own name, thosewhom thou hast given me.''

'Now to the God whose power can do
More than our thoughts or wishes know,
Be everlasting honors done,
Through all the church, by Christ his Son.'
Amen."

SERMON XVII.

INFLUENCE OF THE GOSPEL ON THOSE WHO BELIEVE IT.

"For the grace of God that bringeth salvation, hath appeared to all men, teaching us that denying ungodliness and worldly lusts, we should live soberly, righteously, and godly, in this present world."—Titus ii. 11, 12.

If any thing is calculated to excite the tears of commiseration from a generous mind, surely the wretched state of the lost sons of Adam must produce such an effect. Placed upon the stage of life as they are, with a propensity to evil, and pursuing, as they do with eagerness, the desires of the flesh and of the mind; surely when we recollect that state of primeval dignity and eminence in holiness from which they have so awfully, so deeply fallen, we must say, "How is the gold become dim, how is the most fine gold changed!" The children of men, from their natural depravity, and the influence of habits acquired by continuance in sin, are all unholy and impure; the image of God, which was once impressed in such lively and pleasing characters upon the heart of their first parent, their head and representative, is now entirely lost, the glory is departed. Sin, that abominable thing which God's righteous soul hateth, which breaks his law, opposes his government, and insults his Spirit, is the delight, the unhallowed source of pleasure to the creatures he has made. He looks down from his high throne in glory, he sees men walking in a vain show, and he says, concerning us, considered in the condition in which we were born, "There is none that doeth good, no, not one." Well may we then look around us for help; it surely becomes us to enquire what shall raise us from this abject state of sin, and deliver us from those iniquities which prevail against us. How shall our tempers, which are by nature evil, become excellent and divine? How shall our conduct, which is that of the children of disobedience, be so changed as to become that which men shall love, angels admire, and God himself approve?

Shall we sit at the feet of heathen sages? They will, indeed, give us excellent precepts, but they cannot touch the springs of action; they cannot reach the heart. Their advice may be excellent, but the reformation which it can accomplish is, after all, but partial; it arises from no noble principle: it is imperfect, it is unacceptable in the sight of God. Shall the law of Moses produce in us that holiness, without which no man shall see the Lord? Its commands are, indeed, represented by the pen of inspiration, as holy, just, and good: it is a transcript of the divine mind; it is an exact rule for the conduct of men; but instead of possessing power to render us Israelites indeed, in whom there is no guile, its office is, by its own spirituality, to show us our exceeding sinfulness, to condemn us, and to declare to us that we are accursed, because we have not continued in all things written in the book of the law to do them. Whither then shall he who hungers and thirsts after righteousness direct his attention? Where shall those of us, who, sensible of the plague of our hearts, and the sins of our lives, long for purity, and grasp after holiness, find that which we so eagerly desire? It devolves on me to show you that it may be found in the gospel of Jesus. Descending from the skies, it points out to us the path of piety and peace; it shows us the mount of holiness, bids us climb it, and gives us strength to reach its summit. This holy guide, then, shall direct our enquiries, yea, it shall do more, it shall influence our hearts. It is not enough that we hear a voice, saying, "This is the way, walk ye in it;" but we wretched and depraved as we are by nature, must, by the potent, the blessed influence of the glorious gospel of the blessed God, become holy in all manner of conversation and godliness. Then shall we display to the world, the triumphs of grace, the genuine effects of religion, and the vast superiority of the gospel, to all the schemes that men devise.

Permit me, then, with as much brevity as possible, to establish the fact, that the gospel does produce the most salutary effects on the mind and deportment;—and to trace it in the mode of its operations.

I. We will establish the fact, that the gospel does produce the most salutary effects on the mind and deportment.

We mean to say, that the gospel, by its holy power, produces a radical, a total change; that it forms us new creatures in Christ Jesus; and makes us partakers of a divine nature: the members of the body, and the faculties of the soul, are alike affected by its blessed influence; that tongue, which was once an unruly member, full of deadly poison, now tells the wonders of redeeming grace; those eyes, that were once evil and full of adultery, are now turned to heaven with pious adoration, or gushing with tears of penitence for sin; those ears which before could listen to nothing but what was sinful and depraved, are now opened to attend to the things of the kingdom; the hands are lifted up to God in prayer; the lips praise the name of Jesus. That heart, which was once a cage full of unclean birds, is now a temple for God to dwell in, through the eternal Spirit. When the power of the gospel is experienced in the heart, the obstinate become mild; the self-willed, submissive; the careless, thoughtful; and the dissolute, holy. It is not enough that the gospel enlightens the judgment, and elevates the affections, but it must do more; it must transform both soul and body into the image of Christ, and thus affect the temper and the conduct; and that it does this, may be proved—from the design of God,—and the testimony of example. Learn that the gospel produces a holy effect upon the disposition and deportment of mankind,—

1. From the design of God.

Jehovah determined to accomplish, by the inspiration and diffusion of the gospel, what the law could not do, in that it was weak; he chose it to be the grand means of turning men from darkness to light, and from the power of sin and Satan to God. He ordained it to be the sword of his Spirit, that should slay our corruptions; the rod of his strength that should rule in our hearts; and the noblest display of the power of God, in raising us to a high elevation of mental and moral excellence. He resolved in his eternal mind, that his word should heal the nations of the deadly plague of sin, and clothe the people in the garments of purity. Then, surely, the purpose of the Lord must stand, and he will do all his pleasure, because he wisely determined that it should be so; therefore his gospel powerfully influences the temper and conduct. This may be also seen—

2. By the testimony of example.

Let those who have received the gospel in the love of it, be viewed by us as a long cloud of witnesses to its truth and divine effects; for into what heart has it darted its influence that has not, from being obdurate and hard, become tender and susceptible? Who is there that firmly believes the gospel testimony, that does not adopt a different line of conduct from that which is pursued by the children of disobedience? Through the power of the gospel, those who were cruel and profane, as Manasseh, like him begin to seek the Lord their God, and repent with full purpose of heart. Those who were as extortionate as Zaccheus, when the salvation of the gospel comes to their ears and their hearts, like him feel a spirit of pure benevolence to the world, and love to Him, who caused his grace to abound much more than sin. Those who persecuted the saints, like Saul of Tarsus, when the light of the gospel shines into their souls, throw down their weapons of hostility to Christ and his chosen, and determine to war a good warfare under the protection of the Captain of salvation. When all other attempts at reforming the character have failed, the gospel has gloriously succeeded. It has taught the liar to become sincere; the intemperate to become sober; the proud to become humble; the wanton to become chaste; and the self-righteous to submit to the obedience of faith. Yea, am I not addressing some who glory in the thought that they are trophies of its power, and who stand in the church of Christ as monuments of its grace: though ye were sometimes foolish and disobedient, the time past of your life has sufficed you, wherein to have wrought the will of the Gentiles; and you now desire to serve God in all holiness and righteousness. What, though I might, after I had mentioned some of the slaves of sin, say, "And such were some of you:" yet I rejoice that I am able to add, "but ye are washed, but ye are justified, but ye are sanctified, in the name of the Lord Jesus, and by the Spirit of our God;" and therefore you display the influence of the gospel, in your temper and conduct. But I shall detain you no longer in attempting to prove what must, to those who know the purity of the gospel, appear a self-evident proposition; but shall now,—

II. Trace the gospel in the mode of its operation, or show how it is that it produces so happy an effect; and admire the wise adaptation of the means to the accomplishment of the end.

The gospel, then, influences the conduct,—as it strikes a death-blow at our evil propensities,—as it implants new principles in the soul,—as it presents us with a perfect pattern of all that is excellent,—as it proposes the noblest motives to purity of heart and life,—and, as by the enjoyment of its consolations, it gives us strength to obey its precepts.

1. The gospel is every way calculated to influence the conduct, because it strikes a death-blow at our evil propensities. When we believe the record that God hath given us of his Son, our corruptions begin to weaken; and the man of sin dies daily. The gospel nails our abominable rebellion to the cross of Jesus, and takes away the enmity of the heart; this being done, that which before opposed the will of God is removed, and we desire to run

in the way of his commandments, since he has enlarged our hearts. Well has the immortal Cowper said—

> "Let this hint suffice;
> The cross once seen, is death to every vice;
> Else He that hung there, suffer'd all his pain,
> Bled, groan'd, and agoniz'd, and died in vain."

The gospel controls the power and dominion of sin within us; it subdues the enmity of the heart; and therefore bends us to obey the laws of Heaven.

2. When we receive the gospel in the love of it, new principles are implanted in the soul. For it imparts to us a taste for holiness; a perception of its beauty; an ardent desire to cultivate Christian purity in the thoughts we indulge, the words we speak, and the actions we perform. As soon as the gospel has come to us, as it is indeed and in truth the word of God and not of man, we begin to love the divine law; we discover a tendency to holiness; an increase in grace; yea, an earnest aspiration after being perfect, even as our Father in heaven is perfect. By the gospel, the seeds of divine grace are sown in the naturally barren soil of the human heart, which, under the blessing of Heaven, spring up, and present us with those fruits of righteousness, which are by Jesus Christ, to the praise and glory of God.

3. The gospel influences the conduct too, as it proposes the noblest motives to purity of heart and life. It gives us to feel that the love of Christ constrains us. This is indeed a spring of action, an incentive to obedience, with the force of which the unregenerate are totally unacquainted, yet the power of which is mighty beyond conception; for whenever the soul of an individual is touched with the love of Christ, he readily yields him implicit and constant

obedience. The gospel secures a pleasing change in our spirit and temper immediately, as it makes us glow with affection to its glorious subject, its adorable Author. This justifies us in saying—

> Talk they of morals? O thou bleeding Love!
> Thou Teacher of true morals to mankind!
> The grand morality is love of Thee!

The gospel teaches us to aim to please God, as well as to show to the world that we are travelers to a heavenly city, within whose gates nothing that defileth, or is defiled, can ever enter.

4. The gospel presents us with a perfect pattern of all that is excellent. It sets before us Jesus the Son of God, whose immaculate purity heaven and earth can attest. In him, indeed, all the rays of moral excellence meet as in one point; and we not only view in him the brightness of the Father's glory and the express image of his person, but we behold human nature adorned and dignified, by a lively combination of all the virtues of which it is capable. And after the gospel has exhibited to us the holy Jesus, it says to us, "Let the same mind be in you which was also in him." Yea, by its heavenly power, it assimilates us to his image; it changes us into his likeness; it forms us upon a divine model; for we all with open face beholding, in the glass of the gospel, the glory of the Lord, are changed into the same image, from glory to glory, even as by the Spirit of the Lord. Oh, blessed influence of the glorious gospel!

5. The enjoyment of its consolations gives strength to obey its precepts. If you ask here, Does the gospel influence the temper and conduct? we can tell you that it takes you to Christ's banqueting house, where his banner over you is love; it places you at his table, where you

hear him say, "Eat, O friends, drink, yea, drink abundantly, O beloved!" and where you are abundantly satisfied with his presence, and drink of the wine of the kingdom. Sentiments of gratitude are then excited in your mind to the Founder of the feast; you feel thankful to him, and you rise from your seat animated by his favor, and sensible of his love. You evidence that you are not only refreshed by his bounty, but determined to execute his commands; and when you have enjoyed the most, you say, "Lord, what wilt thou have me to do?" So much life and vigor are imparted to our minds by a firm belief of the glad tidings of the gospel, that no duty appears too hard for us to discharge, no trial too heavy to bear; but our triumphant exclamation is, "I can do all things through Christ which strengtheneth me!" Hence follows a cheerful acquiescence in the duties we owe to one another, to God, and to the world.

Our tempers, by those frequent and solemn interviews with which we are indulged, become spiritual, heavenly, and divine; admiring spectators see that we have been with Jesus: like Enoch, we walk with God, and, like him, shall be wafted away to the world of purity and peace.

And are these the triumphs of the gospel? Does it indeed produce so divine a change in the moral world? Then surely it is worthy of its Author; of him "for whom are all things, and by whom are all things." Is it any disgrace to the wisdom that devised it, or the love that gave it to the nations? No: for in the gospel God has declared the glory of all his perfections, and particularly does his holiness shine in it with radiant lustre.

Is it the tendency of the gospel to refine and exalt the character; to make the temper and conduct such as God requires? Then who would not long for its general diffusion? Who would not exclaim with ardor, "Fly abroad, thou mighty gospel?" Who would not love those noble institutions which have in view its wider circulation, and which God has honored for the conveyance of its blessings to the children of men?

But oh! are there not many who profess to love the gospel, and to feel its power, who are filled with envy, malice, and all uncharitableness! Yes, there are! But O thou blessed Jesus, are these thy disciples! Most glorious gospel! are these the men in whose hearts thy truths have made a deep impression? The Saviour and the gospel alike disown them; and, "Depart from me, I never knew you," will hereafter be uttered to them by God the Judge of all.

I dare not persuade myself to leave this pulpit without asking my hearers, What has the gospel done for you? In the presence of God and all his holy angels, I would put this question to you, and leave you with all solemnity to consult God and your own consciences on the subject. But O, do remember that you may hear the gospel; you may avow your attachment to it; you may liberally support its interests, and yet die after all without experiencing its blessings, and have a neglected gospel rise up in judgment against you to aggravate your condemnation.

Here, however, allow me to turn from man to God; suffer me to express my wishes for all who compose this congregation; and, looking around you, permit me to say to the God of purity and the God of the gospel, "Sanctify them all through thy truth—thy word is truth."*

* This Sermon was preached at the Anniversary of Hoxton College.

SERMON XVIII.

CHRIST AT EMMAUS.

"And they said one to another, did not our hearts burn within us, while he talked with us by the way, and while he opened to us the Scriptures?"—LUKE xxiv. 32.

THE connection of this text shows us, that after the death and resurrection of the great Messiah, two of the disconsolate disciples, who knew not that he was raised from the dead, went to a village called Emmaus; that on their way thither they conversed, as was likely they would do, upon the wonderful events that had lately transpired in Jerusalem, and spake of him they loved. His person—his actions—his sermons—his prophecies—and, above all, his most extraordinary exit occupied their solemn attention, and afforded a subject for the most interesting discourse. Whilst they were thus engaged in conversing about him, with whom they had before been familiar, and from whom they had learned most excellent lessons, a third came up and joined them; this indeed was Jesus of Nazareth, who had been raised from the dead by the glory of the Father. But he chose, for wise ends, to conceal himself from them, and to cause that their eyes should be holden, that they should not know him, appearing to them as a stranger desirous of knowing the subject of their conversation, and the cause of their grief, and to sympathize with them under their sorrow—weeping with them that wept. They intimated to him their wonder that *he*, even supposing that he were but a stranger in Jerusalem, should be unacquainted with the things which were come to pass there in those days; then proceeding to tell him how Jesus, a prophet, mighty in deed and word before God and the people, was condemned to death and crucified; giving him to understand at the same time, that the hopes they had entertained of him were most sanguine, for they trusted that it had been he which should have redeemed Israel; and, finally, they informed him of some peculiar phenomena that had been witnessed by certain women of their acquaintance at his sepulchre, where his body could not be seen, though they saw a vision of angels, who said that he was alive. The courteous and mild fellow traveler then began to speak and detain them with delightful converse; for he showed them "that Christ ought to suffer these things, and then to enter into his glory." He spread before them the mysteries of the inspired page, and showed how they were illustrated in the life and death of their best friend. Sooner than they thought they arrived at their journey's end, where he made as though he would have gone further; but they prevailed on him, by their great importunity, to go in and tarry with them—with them he took bread, blessed it, break it, and gave unto them—then first their eyes were opened to behold him as the same Jesus who was crucified, and to discover in him the lovely features of their Lord who had done all things well—when, lo! he vanished out of their sight, and was seen no more. After which, we may reasonably suppose to have taken place—a solemn silence;

and then they used to each other the admirable expression we have selected as a text—"Did not our hearts burn within us, while he talked with us by the way, and while he opened to us the Scriptures?" Having, then, taken a slight glance at the whole account of this wonderful circumstance, in confining our attention more particularly to the words of the text, we shall view them as leading us to reflect on—the conversation of our Lord with his disciples—and the effects it produced upon their minds—"their hearts burned within them, while he talked with them by the way." Behold

I. The conversation of our Lord with his disciples.

And here the passage presents us with the kind familiarity which he displayed, and the lustre that he cast on the divine word—the first remarkable thing in our Lord's conversation with the travelers to Emmaus, is—

1. The kind familiarity which he displayed—their own expression is, "He talked with us by the way." It is condescension in the Son of God, to notice the concerns and accept the worship of his holy angels; how much more must it be so to sojourn with mankind—to go where they go—and freely to tell them the secrets of his heart. The Saviour was now, you remember, even on earth, a most dignified character—he was now no longer to suffer and be cruelly entreated—he had now finished the work his Father had given him to do—and had shortly after to ascend to claim his high seat in glory. He now showed himself to be the Christ, the Son of God, and confirmed the reality of his appointment and mission, by his bursting the bars of the tomb. He would not now be viewed by any as a common character, but as the most wonderful being that had ever appeared in the world—as such even his enemies

must consider him. Yet all this did not make him forget his friends, or cause him to lose any thing of that social and condescending disposition he had ever before manifested: but almost as soon as he was risen, he goes to meet some of the members of his little family, and confirm them further in himself. "He talked with them by the way." Oh! what a heaven does Christ here by his example stamp upon Christian intercourse and sacred friendship. Behold he talks with his disciples, proving to them that "as ointment and perfume rejoice the heart, so doth the sweetness of a man's friend, by hearty counsel." And to this day we are permitted to converse with our God—"he talks with us by the way"—tells us our true character, and reveals his own excellence—he appears as our wonderful counsellor! and to whatever place we journey, we should be concerned to have him talking with us by the way. The next remarkable circumstance in this conversation of our Lord, mentioned in the text, is—

2. The lustre that he cast upon the divine word—"He talked with us by the way, and opened to us the Scriptures." And well he might, for he told us before that "the Lord had given him the tongue of the learned; that he should know how to speak a word in season, to him that is weary." "He began," says the evangelist, "at Moses and all the prophets, and expounded to them in all the Scriptures, the things concerning himself"—blessed interpreter—divine teacher. We have no reason to suppose that he forgot the first promise that was made of him; even in the garden of Eden, that he should bruise the head of the serpent: no doubt but the intended sacrifice of Isaac, the patriarch's son—the erection of the brazen serpent on the pole—and the various sacrifices under the law,

were all delightfully commented on by Jesus the Saviour. He did justice to all the passages—he showed their full import—he gave them an insight into the meaning of all the prophecies respecting his death and glory—he took up every part of Scripture in its bearing upon himself, he showed [that he] was "all in all"—even in the Old Testament; and thus by his teachings they discovered far more of the beauty, harmony, and fulfillment of the word of God, than they ever did before, or ever would have done without his instruction. And does he not now give his people to understand the doctrines of his word—does he not now daily open to us the Scriptures—has he not given to us his Holy Spirit in order to make us more wise in the mysteries of his kingdom—and are we not directed to seek for him in the field of divine truth as for hid treasure? Oh! how much is there respecting Christ in this holy book, and who is so able to make us know it as himself—"he opens our understanding that we may understand the Scriptures"—he ever teaches his ministers to open and allege "that Christ must needs have suffered and risen again from the dead, and that this Jesus whom we preach unto you is Christ,"—as he taught his apostles to "testify the kingdom of God, persuading men concerning Jesus, both out of the law of Moses, and out of the prophets, from morning till evening." Having then admired the conversation of our Lord with his disciples on the way to Emmaus, we notice—

II. The effects it produced in their minds.

It was not at all probable that this discourse should be without effect, or fail deeply to interest their minds, since it was the very theme on which they chose to dwell; and it was conducted in so wise and endearing a manner—it was such that, according to their own confession, it made their hearts to burn within them while he talked with them by the way—and surely I need not say this was not the glow of *shame*, lest they should be found in his company.—No, brethren, they would not have cared who of all the great men of the land had met them in company with this most intelligent stranger—they felt themselves highly honored by his company, even before they knew his name. Nor was this the heat of *anger*, or of any bad passion excited by any thing that he delivered; his communications were sweet and soothing. Had they been so disposed, they could find nothing in them that was improper, untrue, or provoking;—he talked with them as a man talks with his friend; the communion was sweet, and the intercourse highly gratifying; hence, though their hearts burned within them, it was neither with shame, nor anger. But this, brethren, permit me to say, was the glow of fixed surprise; of grateful feeling, of humble love, and of holy animation of soul. Observe it was the glow

(1) of fixed surprise.

They wondered much that he who appeared a stranger, not only to them, but also to the place where they were, should know so much about them, Jerusalem and Jesus; they were astonished at his wisdom, at his eloquence. I almost fancy that they exclaimed, "Never man spake like this man." With emotions of amazement, they perceived that his "word was quick and powerful, and sharper than any two edged sword, piercing even to the dividing asunder of soul and spirit, and of the joints and marrow; and that it is a discoverer of the thoughts and intents of the heart." With what prying eyes must they have looked upon him;

and yet not so as to behold him who he was, because himself had prevented it; yet their hearts burned within them; sentiments of unutterable admiration were hid in their breasts whilst he opened to them the Scriptures. Again it was the glow

(2) of grateful feeling.

They must have discovered that they were greatly indebted to this benevolent stranger, who had so effectually enlightened their judgments, and alleviated their sorrows. Their hearts burned within them with the sensation of thankfulness; they saw that he was a praiseworthy character, and, methinks, were devising some acknowledgments for his attention to them, little thinking that is was the Lord. Did your hearts ever glow in this way with a sense of utter incapability of making any suitable returns to him that loved you, and revealed to you his will? For your fellowship with him, have you ever said, what shall I render to the Lord? Did you ever feel the high honor of being with Jesus; admitted into his presence, and being made partakers of his grace? All your hearts, Christians, should glow with gratitude, and burn with love. Hence, we remark again, their hearts burned within them with the sensation

(3) of humble love.

Finding as they did, that his words "were found of them, and they did eat them," and they were to them the joy and the rejoicing of their hearts, they manifested a strong attachment to him whom they supposed to be a new friend. He engaged their affections, hence they desired more of his company, and said, when their fears were excited lest he should depart from them: "Abide with us, for it is toward evening." So do the hearts of the people of God burn within them to the present day, with like sensations under similar enjoyments; the flame of divine love is kindled in their souls; the words of his mouth appear to them sweeter than the honey of the honeycomb; his doctrine drops like the rain, and distils like the dew, and sensible that none teacheth like him, they admire and love him before all others. Oh! how excellent a thing it is thus to love the Saviour. Let it be our happiness to sit at his feet; and with meekness receive the ingrafted word of truth, which is able to save the soul, so shall its admirable Author rise daily more and more in our estimation. Finally it was the glow

(4) of holy animation of soul.

Divine light broke in upon their minds, and dispersed their remaining unbelief; they were elevated above the world to the contemplation of their adorable Redeemer. He touched their finest feelings; he filled their souls with the sublime joys of his salvation; he inspired them with pure devotion, and fixedness of heart, and while he led them to the consideration of Him who endured such contradiction of sinners against himself, he prevented them from being weary and fainting in their minds. And oh! Christians, what sweet moments; rich in blessing, have you enjoyed, when in converse with Immanuel. "Whether in the body, or out of the body," you have hardly been able to tell; drops of heaven have been bestowed upon you here below, the light of the Divine countenance has caused you to take your harp from the willows, and make every string speak to the praise of love divine. Did not your hearts burn within you? Were you not like Peter on the mount, who, in an ecstasy of joy said, "Lord, it is good to be here?" You anticipated the joys of the blessed, you drank of the brook by the way, and seemed ready to depart and to be with Christ, to drink wine new with him, in the kingdom of his Father. This holy delight in God is real, and not enthusiastic; it is bestowed only on the new born heirs of grace, and it is given them as a pledge of joys to come; their hearts burn within them while he talks with them by the way.

In reflecting on this subject we are struck with the idea that we often have to blame ourselves for not sufficiently estimating our mercies during the time of their continuance.

These disciples, notwithstanding the pleasure they had found in his society, did not, till just as he left them, discover him to be their Lord; to the present day Joseph often knows his brethren, whilst they know him not. And then afterwards they say, did not our hearts burn within us? True, they did. But why did not we value the blessing while we enjoyed it? Why did we not say, as the word of wisdom dropped from his mouth, it is the Lord?

Again, a review of past favors greatly supports the mind under present bereavements.

When we seem forsaken; when our affections towards Christ appear but cold, oh! what a privilege it is to be enabled to revert to a period when our hearts did burn within us, while he talked with us by the way. This thought cheers the drooping spirits, and raises the fainting head; it excites our hope, too, that he will be with us again, and hold converse with us, even till the hour of death; yea, it makes us argue, that if the Lord had intended to destroy us, he would not have made our hearts burn within us by his divine communications.

It is the duty and interest of us all earnestly to pray for the society and conversation of Christ.

The blessing itself is so desirable, for it is to have the honor of dwelling and walking with Christ, and the sensations which he, by his discourse excites in the mind, are so pleasing and delightful, that we ought earnestly to beseech him to tarry with us; if he is an instructor and companion, how short will the distance to heaven appear, and how light and momentary the trials of tho way.—Lastly,

If those who travel with the Saviour, are thus blessed, how miserable are they who are altogether alienated from him.

Sinner, you never yet enjoyed the society of Christ, nor do you wish it. You are loading him with reproaches, and will have none of his counsel, and he will never say of you, "they shall walk with me in white, for they are worthy;" the fever of lust, and the torment of envy shall be your curse, while you live in the pains of hell, your portion after death, when you will burn in the "fire that never can be quenched, and the smoke of your torments shall ascend up for ever and ever." Oh! may we, instead of this awful doom, be honored and glorfied with his constant presence in a better world; so shall the chosen of Nazareth be praised and adored by us for ever and ever.

SERMON XIX.

DEATH BY ADAM—ETERNAL LIFE BY CHRIST.

" As we have borne the image of the earthy, we shall also bear the image of the heavenly."—1 CORINTHIANS xv. 49.

" THE proper study of mankind is man;" and the best science to which any of us can attain is, to know ourselves; for " all wisdom centres there." Human nature is a fit subject of investigation, and will well repay the mind's attention to it; it has frequently been represented in unjust and improper points of view; men have formed very mistaken ideas of themselves and of their condition, and have too often represented their case to be rather what they wished it, than what it really is. The testimony of the Bible, however, viewed in connection with facts which we are every day called to witness, will appear to be the best teacher of what we are in our true character, our real condition, and our bounden duty. Here we learn what man originally was, what he now is, and to what standard of excellence he ought to attain. From the Bible alone, that fruit of heavenly wisdom, can we derive proper ideas of human nature. Here its past excellence, its present degradation, and the only means by which it can possibly be restored, are detailed with unquestionable veracity, and told by the Spirit of God. Here we learn that, as in Adam all whom he represented, the whole human race, fell and died; so in Christ Jesus all to whom he is a covenant head shall live forevermore: and that as these characters, before conversion, gave awful evidence of fatal union to their head, so by the grace of God shall they now be made to resemble Jesus, who is given as a covenant of the people, who is the Head of the body, the church. "As we have borne the image of the earthy, we shall also bear the image of the heavenly." Here, then, you perceive the depth of misery to which you fell, and the height of happiness to which you are raised. My text shows you the man, by whose disobedience you lost your peace, your happiness, your God. My text presents you also with that glorious Redeemer, who has restored that which he took not away, and given you more blessings than your father lost. In discoursing upon this text, we must—

I. Confirm the lamentable fact, that, by nature, we all bear the image of the earthy.

II. Rejoice in the glorious truth, that, as believers, we shall bear the image of the Lord from heaven.

It is necessary that I—

I. Show that we all bear the image of the earthy Adam. So says my text; so says experience, the melancholy experience of all ages and nations; so witness the shrieks, the groans of dying infants; so testify our own eyes, beholding the miseries that are abroad in the world; so witness our own feelings in the endurance of those ills to which mortality is subject. Here, too, let it be remembered, that the mischief we lament is universal; that the evils we deplore are experienced all over the world; that all mankind suffer from their connection with their first parent; that every individual on the globe bears the image of the earthy Adam. Oh, show us, if you can, the spot of earth to which the effects of the curse have not yet reached; and tell us, if among all the tribes of men in Europe, Asia, Africa, or America, there are any to be found who do not discover a depraved nature, who do not bear the image of the earthy. So extensive are the calamities introduced into the world by sin; so general the dire effect of our first parent's disobedience to the will of Heaven.

In order that we may enter into the import of the expression, "bearing the image of the earthy," permit us to observe, that we bear this image in our bodies—and that we bear it in our souls. Behold it—

1. In our bodies, which are earthy, frail, and tending to dissolution.

Observe this image is evident in our bodies, as they are earthy; for the Lord God formed man of the dust of the ground: so poor in our origin that we have no pretension at all to nobility of descent, but must look upon the earth as our common parent, and say, Oh, how poor a creature is man, that is a worm, and the son of man, that is a worm! Oh, what a lecture does the constitution of our frame read us upon the folly of human pride, upon the ridiculous absurdity of towering ambition! Never let us suppose ourselves to be some great ones, since it is evident that we are vile as the dust; and the ground we tread on contains the materials of our formation, and the means of our support. Verily, our bodies are but clods of clay, and soon must they return to the earth out of which they were taken. Now the condition of our frame points out the resemblance between Adam and all his race, between the father and his children. It is the image of the earthy Adam.

Our bodies are also frail, and thus bear the image described in the text. To what a long train of diseases and disorders are they liable! To what a list of accidents and ills are they exposed! What is your life? It is even a vapor that appeareth for a little while, and then vanisheth away. Our bodies are easily borne down by weariness and fatigue, are soon brought low by affliction. How little can they sustain or endure! With what numerous proofs of their weakness are they daily presenting us! How shortly may the strongest among us, the man who boasts most of the soundness of his health and the vigor of his constitution, be confined to the chamber of sickness! Ah! God may weaken your strength in the way; he may shorten your days. We that are in this tabernacle do groan, being burdened. And is the body a tabernacle?

> Weak cottage where our souls reside,
> Flesh but a tottering wall;
> With frightful breaches gaping wide,
> The building bends to fall.
>
> All round it storms of trouble blow,
> And waves of sorrow roll;
> Cold waves, and wintry storms beat through,
> And pain the tenant soul.

O Adam! what hast thou done!

Again, Our bodies tend to destruction. They give us repeated proofs that this is not their final abode; they show that they are hasting to the grave, and that in its gloomy repository they must all shortly lie. Death reigns, and all men are his subjects: before the king of terrors we all must shortly bow; he will change our countenances and send us away. Now, in the whole of our passage to the house appointed for all living, in every step we take to the solemn dwelling of the dead, we are bearing the image of the earthy. You lose a friend; a dear relative leaves you and life, and enters the world to come, whereof we speak; his immortal spirit has ascended to God who gave it; but here, with you, he has left his body, to be placed in the ground till the morning of the resurrection. Before you inter it in the gloomy cavern, its destined abode, you gaze on it with the most gloomy and inexpressible feelings. Oh, who can tell your sensations, as you behold that cabinet now without its jewel; that tabernacle of the soul now without its tenant: as long as you can, you retain it near you; you are unwilling to part with the remains of your companion, and your friend; you appear to grudge the earth its due, and the worm its prey; till at length you are obliged to say, Bury my dead out of my sight! The ghastly, the loathsome ruins of your well-beloved friend offend you. But, as you draw near, to take the last, last look of all that was mortal in your friend, let me ask, What is that you behold, and at which you shudder? What is that in the cold corpse which shocks the feelings of humanity, and harrows up the soul? What is it? It is the image of the earthy Adam! And ere long you shall bear it too. It is seen in the countenance of the dead.

2. We all bear this image in our souls. You have seen the impression of it upon our mortal part; now let us behold it upon that within us, which can never die, the soul, the immortal principle which was at first endowed with the

noblest faculties, pervaded with the finest feelings, and rendered capable of glorifying its great Creator; the soul, that once appeared the resemblance of the Deity, the genuine copy of the mind of God, now bears this inscription, Ichabod, the glory is departed. It now bears the image of the earthy Adam, for observe,—It is defiled with sin,—and it is exposed to divine wrath.

1. Our souls are defiled with sin.

Oh, how impure, how unholy is the mind of man! It has received such a taint, such a stain, as you cannot remove. The moment we come into the world we bring with us the most hateful, the most perverse dispositions; a tendency, a bias to evil; and we bear the imputation of the guilt of Adam's sin. Now who can bring a clean thing out of an unclean? What but renovating grace can purify the polluted soul of man? Our guilt, how deep it stains! How loathsome! how offensive! how guilty are our souls before God! This is bearing the image of the earthy Adam.

2. Our souls are exposed to divine wrath, and thus bear the image of the earthy.

While we remain in the condition in which we were born, God is angry with us every day. Our souls are by nature fit subjects of the divine vengeance; and well will it be for us if the vials of divine wrath are not poured upon our devoted heads for ever and ever. The soul that sinneth, it shall die. It is the decree of Heaven,—the judgment of the skies,—the doom of man. I have, says the great Eternal, kindled a fire in mine anger, which shall burn to the lowest hell; and our exposure to all this wrath, our fearful looking-for of judgment and fiery indignation which shall devour the adversaries, shows us the image of the earthy Adam. Here you behold an awful representation of the dire effect of human crimes, and see to what miseries and consequences sin has exposed us. Well may we mourn over the lost image of God! Surely, if we have feelings, they must be excited here. Shall no anxiety be roused on account of the dreadful the universal depravity of human nature? Shall no concern be discovered at the miseries of the world? God forbid! O that our head were waters, and our eyes, as it were, fountains of tears, that we might weep over the melancholy condition of our own souls, the souls of our brethren, of our countrymen, and of all mankind; for all these bear the image of the earthly Adam.

But the more pleasing part of our subject now courts our attention. Let us therefore,—

II. Rejoice in the glorious truth, that, as believers, we shall also bear the image of the Lord from heaven. "As we have borne the image of the earthy, we shall also bear the image of the heavenly."

The second Adam shall restore
The ruins of the first,
Hosanna to that sovereign power
That new creates our dust.

And here I cannot but pause for a moment to observe, what an illustrious character is here introduced to our attention, the Second Adam! This is He who has been declared to be the Son of God with power. It is Jesus, the first-born among many brethren! And behold the excellences that meet in his character; see his superiority to the first Adam! The first Adam was of the earth, earthy; the second Adam is the Lord from heaven: the first Adam transgressed the divine command, and suffered for his fault;

the second Adam magnified the law, and made it honorable: the first Adam ruined himself, and all his posterity; the second Adam gives us abundance of grace, imputes to us his own righteousness, and causes us to bear his image in the world. This divine image, however, is not borne by all the human race, but by those alone to whom Christ is a covenant head; for, as in Adam all those, whose representative he stood, fell and died; so in Christ Jesus all, in whose stead he suffered and bare the curse, shall be made alive to God, and to the enjoyment of happiness. These characters evince, that they were chosen in him from before the foundation of the world, by their belief of the gospel while they live; and all these characters shall, according to the promise, and through the grace of their heavenly Father, bear the image, and reflect the glory of Christ, their great Redeemer. Concerning this blessed image, I make three remarks—It is first impressed upon us at the time of our regeneration,—It shall visibly discover itself through the whole course of our Christian life,—It shall be rendered more conspicuous and glorious in the morning of the resurrection.

1. It is first impressed upon us at the time of our regeneration. For that is the time when it pleases God, who separated us from our mother's womb, to call us by his grace, and to reveal his Son in us; then it is that we are enabled "to put off the old man with his deeds, and to put on the new man, which, after God, is created in righteousness and true holiness." Effectual grace then gives a new bias to the mind, and the Father of the spirits of all flesh then makes us new creatures in Christ Jesus. O most memorable day, when we were sealed to the day of redemption! O day, well worthy to be remembered with grateful

feelings, when the image of Christ was first impressed upon our minds! With what new powers, what new feelings, what new desires, were we then enriched! The Saviour imparted to us the principle of grace; he made us, who before lived only for folly and sin, to pant after holiness, as our noblest pursuit; to grasp after purity, as our noblest attainment. Oh, what a difference did this make in our character! We were, indeed, formed anew; we were made partakers of Christ, and of a divine nature; we then first began to bear the image of the heavenly: there is a people, a host of worshippers, whom Jehovah has formed for himself, and they shall shew forth his praise; every one of them has had a divine impression made upon his mind by the Eternal Spirit, which altogether rendered him a new creature, and made him to bear the image of the heavenly. Never let us forget, that nothing but the regenerating grace of the Holy Spirit can make us bear this sacred image; for without his gracious work upon the heart, the children of men remain still the slaves of Satan, the heirs of destruction, and God is not in all their thoughts; his word has not taken root in their minds; his image has not yet been impressed upon their hearts. But ye who believe have an unction from the Holy One; ye know all things; you bear the image of the heavenly.

2. This image shall visibly discover itself through the whole course of the Christian's life.

It shall be seen in the walk and deportment of a good man, that he bears the image of the heavenly. This lovely image shall produce a happy effect upon his temper, his passions, his pursuits; it shall make him to speak, to look, to live, like the children of God. To the world, to angels, and to men, it shall appear that he bears the image of the heavenly Adam; but if ever this holy image is made particularly visible, it is at the time when we walk closely with God, and live in the delightful enjoyment of intercourse with Heaven. Oh, what a lustre of piety does this shed over all that we do and say! O God! Blessed are the men that habitually draw nigh unto thee! The men who are most with God have imparted to them by their familiarity with their Maker, and the holy discoveries they enjoy, a general, a holy dignity in them; we behold the grace of God, the power of God, the image of God.

I will endeavor to illustrate what I mean, by an example or two contained in the inspired records. When Moses had been with God on the mount of communion, he wist not that the skin of his face shone, but Aaron his brother, and all the children of Israel saw it, and the lustre was so great that he was obliged to put a veil upon his face, because they were dazzled with the sight; and I would enquire, What was this that rendered his appearance so glorious? What was that effulgence of glory and splendor, at which they were so astonished and almost afraid? What was it? It was the image of the Lord from heaven. Stephen, you know, was once summoned before the Jewish council, to give an account of the doctrines he preached, of the holy doctrines which ever inspired his mind with the liveliest joy, and the persuasion of the importance of which ever quickened his zeal, and enabled him to suffer and die for Jesus; and while these divine realities occupied his thoughts, and were the subject of his communication with those before whose tribunal he appeared, it is said, All that sat in the council saw his face as it had been the face of an angel. It was the image of the heavenly Adam. By nothing else could such an effect have been produced; and we may be certain, that in one way or other, the same image will, more or less, discover the reality of its existence in all them that believe.

3. This image shall be rendered more striking and glorious on the resurrection morning.

Beloved, now are we the sons of God, and it doth not yet appear what we shall be; but we know that when He shall appear, we shall be like him, for we shall see him as he is." Such are the rational, the well-founded, the solid and certain hopes of the favorites of the second Adam. With eager anticipation and joyful hope, they look forward to the day when the trumpet shall sound, and the dead shall be raised; for then they are persuaded, that the image of the heavenly Adam will be far more conspicuous and glorious than it had been before, whether we regard their bodies or their souls. It will appear in our bodies; for "He shall change our vile bodies, and fashion them like unto his own glorious body, according to the working whereby he is able to subdue all things unto himself." These now frail and dying bodies shall then be formed upon the model of the glorified body of the Redeemer: and in holiness and purity our souls shall resemble our Lord's, since they shall sin no more, but be entirely and for ever freed from every corruption, purified from every moral stain, and constituted holy and unblamable before him in love. The image of the heavenly Adam will then gloriously appear in all the saints; to his likeness they shall all be conformed; his glory they shall all reflect; they will then for ever beautify and adorn the palace of our God. "Then shall the righteous shine forth as the sun in the kingdom of their Father," while their enemies will be obliged to say, We fools counted their lives to be madness, and their end to be without honor; but now how are they numbered with the just, and their portion is with the righteous. Now it is as certain that believers shall thus bear the image of the heavenly Adam, as it is that all mankind bear the image of the earthy; and this is the force of the apostle's reasoning: "As we have borne the image of the earthy, we shall also bear the image of the heavenly." And to show that this is no foolish conjecture, or absurd speculation, consider that this is the end of predestination,—of the inspiration of the Scriptures,—and of the afflictions with which believers are exercised, that they should bear this lovely image.

It is the end of their predestination. "For whom he did foreknow, he also did predestinate to be conformed to the image of his Son; that he might be the first born among many brethren." Jehovah elected them for this express purpose, that they might resemble the Saviour; he chose them in Christ, that they might be like unto Christ; and by the sovereign purpose of his will he secured their real, evident, beautiful, and everlasting conformity to Christ, their living head. These his all-wise designs, his excellent counsels, would not be fulfilled, if his servants did not bear the image of the heavenly.

So, also, this is the design of the inspiration of the Scriptures. The Bible was written and circulated that we all, "with open face beholding, as in a glass, the glory of the Lord, might be changed into the same image, from glory to glory, even as by the Spirit of the Lord." Our hearts are purified by the love of the truth, and the written word ever directs us to the incarnate Word. The holy oracles of God are the means of sanctifying the souls of his servants, for his word directs them, and when applied by his spirit, enables them to bear the image of the heavenly Adam.

Finally, This is the object to be promoted by all their afflictions. The apostle represents himself, and his fellow-laborers, as enduring a great fight of afflictions; as tried, distressed, perplexed, and persecuted; but, he adds, "always bearing about in our body the dying of the Lord Jesus, that the life also of Jesus might be made manifest in our body;" and God is daily teaching his saints to glorify him in the fires. Often are the trying exercises of his servants the happy means of furthering their resemblance to Christ, and of promoting within them the life of faith upon him. When our imperfections and sins would render the possession of this blessed image doubtful to ourselves or to others, those afflictions are sent again to discover it, and to impart to it fresh lustre and excellence. When our afflictions have answered their designed end, we leave the chamber of sickness, or the scene of our sorrows, wherever it be, to evidence more strikingly our possession of the image of the heavenly Adam.

Permit me now,—having finished the discussion of my subject,—permit me to ask you, my hearers, Whose image and superscription do you bear? I shall not ask you whether you bear the image of the earthy Adam, because I know it well; for here "every mouth must be stopped, and all the world become guilty before God." But we wish you to be concerned to ascertain whether a new and divine impression has been made upon your souls? Are you, then, daily departing from all iniquity? hourly aspiring after conformity to Christ? Some men carry the mark of the beast, and bear the image of the devil; not only do they show us their connection with Adam, but their alliance with the powers of darkness. We speak this to their shame. O that they may be confounded before God, and led to pray that, instead of their being the very vassals of Satan, they may be numbered among the friends of Immanuel!

What thanks are due to the Redeemer, for the restoration which he hath made of peace and happiness to man!

My text shows us how the great Saviour has triumphed over human depravity and satanic force; and how, by his own grace, he hath restored the image of God in the soul, and directed our hopes to a better world, where this image shall be perfect, this resemblance inimitably correct. And has he indeed done all this; then—

> Praise! flow for ever, (if astonishment
> Will give thee leave,) my praise for ever flow;
> Praise ardent, cordial, constant, to high Heaven
> More fragrant than Arabia sacrific'd,
> And all her spicy mountains in a flame.

O Saviour! stamp thine holy image upon our souls; there let it appear; there let it shine, in life, in death, and for ever! Amen.

SERMON XX.

RELIGIOUS HEROISM.

FAREWELL SERMON AT HOXTON.

"But none of these things move me, neither count I my life dear unto myself, so that I might finish my course with joy, and the ministry which I have received of the Lord Jesus, to testify the gospel of the grace of God."—Acts 20 : 24.

This is not the language of stoical apathy; the man who uttered these words, my hearers, was a man possessed of the keenest sensibility; a man of real, honest, and exquisite feeling; in his heart, cold indifference and unfeeling stubbornness had no place: nor do the words express philosophical heroism; a foolish bravado; for our apostle derives his support from sources far different from these; he was animated by principles; he was delighted with prospects which the natural man never possesses; the power of which principles, and the view of which prospects, produce an effect which is mighty beyond all conception. The passage I have read you introduces to our view Paul the preacher, at the time of his departure from his friends, when his mind was led to expect, and prepared to meet bonds and afflictions in every place; and the words of the text do most strikingly show us the way in which the principles of the gospel discover themselves, and prove their power to strengthen and support. Viewing this passage as not unsuitable to the present opportunity, I shall exhibit it to your view, as showing us that the principles of the gospel of Christ display their power and virtue.

I. In rendering us insensible to the power of affliction; "none of these things move me."

II. In raising us superior to the love of life; "neither count I my life dear unto me, so that I may finish my course with joy, and the ministry which I have received of the Lord Jesus." Let us behold here the glorious gospel of the blessed God. How the religion of Christ displays its potent influence; its mighty efficacy.

I. In rendering us insensible to the power of affliction. Its supports enabled the holy, zealous apostle to say of painful separation—of the labors of the ministry, and of the large measure of persecution which in that age of the church every where attended the preachers of the gospel, "none of these things move me." Paul had, however, without doubt, the feelings of humanity; and, as I have already intimated, these things would affect his soul as a *man*, and occasionally overwhelm his spirits; but when he felt the happy influence of the gospel in all its power, he triumphed over these difficulties; he heroically conquered himself, subdued his own feelings, and appeared a ready, a joyful martyr for Christ. Thus did Paul, yet did not he, but the grace of God which was in him. These trials, then, these difficulties, which to many would be insurmountable, did not "move" him: that is, the anticipation of them, the endurance of them, did not so move him as to damp his *ardor;* as to discourage his soul, or as to make him wish to exchange with the world. Observe, they did not so move him—

As to damp his ardor. These trials and apparent obstacles to the success of his work, and to his own happiness in it, did not make him less anxiously desirous of doing good in the world, did not at all diminish the fervent wishes of his soul to be the means of conducting many sons unto glory. Notwithstanding these difficulties, he was still "steadfast, unmovable, always abounding in the work of the Lord, forasmuch as he knew that his labor was not in vain in the Lord." And as he had this ministry, as he had received mercy, so he fainted not; hence he could say to others—no man should be moved by these afflictions, for yourselves know that we were appointed thereunto. He remembered the long cloud of witnesses who, through much tribulation, had entered the kingdom, and he determined to imitate their example; he did more; he considered Jesus, who endured such contradiction of sinners against himself; and this prevented him from being weary, or from fainting in his mind: he looked unto Jesus, the author and finisher of his faith, and by that means obtained encouragement to proceed, and grace sufficient for him. Oh! never let the servants of the most high God relax in their endeavors to do good, or grow cold in their desires after the immortal welfare of mankind because some difficulties await them: of these difficulties they ought to say "none of these things move me." Nor did these trials so affect the apostle—

As to discourage his soul; that is, to make him shrink at the thought of enduring them; to make him afraid to meet them: no, for supported by the consolations of the gospel, he could welcome reproaches, pain and death; yea, rejoice and be exceeding glad that he was counted worthy to suffer for the sake of the Lord Jesus. "What mean ye," says he elsewhere, "what mean ye to weep and to break my heart, for I am ready not to be bound only, but also to die at Jerusalem for the name of the Lord Jesus." Divine grace so supported him that, though he was troubled on every side, he was not distressed; though perplexed, he was not in despair; though persecuted, he was not forsaken; though cast down, he was not destroyed. I suffer, says he, these things, nevertheless I am not ashamed; "for I know in whom I have believed, and am persuaded that he is able to keep that which I have committed unto him, until that day." Thus he could endure, and the Saviour enabled him to suffer as well as to preach for him, and none of these things moved him.

Finally, they did not so move him as to make him wish to exchange with the world.

Because he thus reckoned that the sufferings of this present life are not worthy to be compared with the glory that should be revealed in us. He saw that "our light affliction, which is but for a moment, worketh out for us a far more exceeding and eternal weight of glory." He looked not at the things which are seen, which are temporal, but at the things which are not seen, which are eternal. There was a pleasure even connected with the sufferings which far excelled the joy of worldlings: hence he says, "I am filled with comfort, I am exceeding joyful in all our tribulations." For the Lord stood by him and strengthened him; yea, the Lord delivered him from every evil work, and preserved him to his heavenly kingdom. The apostle, taught by the Spirit of God, loved even the difficulties of his Master's service far better than the ease and the pleasures of the world. Oh! that, like him, we may wisely count the reproach of Christ greater riches than all the treasures of this world; prefer even the worst, the most painful circumstances in the cause of the Saviour, to the most fascinating pleasures of the world; to the enjoyments which the men who know not God reckon most valuable and most dear; thus shall we show that we are willing to be any thing that the Saviour chooses, so that he may be glorified; thus shall we show that we speak the feelings of our hearts when we say of the difficulties of our work, "none of these things move me." Thus was the apostle enabled to enjoy strong consolations in the midst of trials. Thus did Immanuel's grace quicken him to diligence and fortify his mind against the numerous ills that flesh is heir to. Oh! that the Spirit of glory and of God would rest on us also; that all our duties may be so discharged, and all our trials to endured, as that the power of the gospel may be evinced, and the supporting grace of the great Head of the Church abundantly magnified. And what can so teach us to endure trials as the religion of Christ? What supports have infidels, mere moralists, and speculative philosophers, like those which may be derived from the fullness of our Lord Jesus Christ? Theirs are refuges of lies, ours a never-failing foundation. "Their rock is not as our rock, even our enemies themselves being judges." The gospel of Christ presents the only sovereign balm for human woe; it supplies us with real, and with sure support; it emboldens us to say, in the face of difficulties, dangers, and death, "None of these things move me." The gospel, however, does not merely display its power in rendering us insensible to the power of affliction, but—

II. In raising us superior to the love of life.

For, adds the apostle, "neither count I my life dear

unto myself, so that I may finish my course with joy." "Skin for skin, yea, all that a man hath, will he give for his life." The preservation of life is the first law of nature. That man is unworthy the character of a rational being, who intentionally shortens, or daringly terminates his own life. And yet here a man comes forward and says, "neither count I my life dear unto myself"—and he is taught to form this estimation of life, too, by the gospel of Jesus! How is this? The apostle did not choose strangling rather than life; but the case may be stated thus. The gospel taught him the right use of life, and made him earnestly to desire to fulfill it; the gospel taught him as a minister, that life was only valuable to him so far as he accomplished its purposes—the joyful completion of his Christian race, the honorable close of his ministerial exertions. Further than this, life was not dear to him, or highly prized by him, for he was willing to be "absent from the body, and to be present with the Lord." His earnest expectation and his hope was, that in nothing he should be ashamed, but that with all boldness, as always, so now, Christ should be magnified in his body, whether it were by life or by death. "Yea," says he, "and if I be offered upon the sacrifice and service of your faith, I joy and rejoice with you all." Oh! what a noble principle is this that renders a man willing to suffer and to die for Christ, "for herein perceive we the love of God, because he laid down his life for us; and we ought also to lay down our lives for the brethren." And now it is said of the apostle, and all who like him triumphed over Satan, "they were faithful unto death." They overcome him by the blood of the Lamb, for they loved not their lives unto death. But I digress from the subject. Observe, then, that the gospel raised the mind of Paul superior to the love of life, as it showed him that it was only useful for two purposes.

1. That he might joyfully complete his Christian race. So he says, "that I may finish my course with joy." The course to which he alludes is the Christian race, which he had some time before undertaken in divine strength. God had called him so to run that he might obtain, and hence he "laid aside every weight, and the sin which so easily beset him, and ran with patience the race set before him, looking unto Jesus." He set out with a full determination never to grow weary, or to decline his eager pursuit after glory, honor and immortality. Hitherto he had pursued it with alacrity; he did not count himself to have apprehended; but this one thing he did, forgetting those things which were behind, and reaching forth unto those things which were before, he pressed toward the mark for the prize of the high calling of God in Christ Jesus. Personal religion had flourished in his soul, and he had not left the path marked out for him, by the great forerunner, to be led aside either to the right hand or to the left, and now he wished to finish it with joy: and that man finishes his course with joy when he expresses gratitude for any ardor he has discovered in it, and when he has a full view of the crown of glory, and prospect of eternal rest. To finish our course with joy, we must express our gratitude for the assistance grace has offered us in it. [When a Christian can say, through the good hand of my God upon me, the care of his love, and the animation of his grace, "I have finished my course."] Oh! what pleasure it must afford a believer who completes his race on earth, to look back upon the path he has trod, and to remember even the trials he endured, and to

bless God that he was enabled to persevere to the end. The Christian race cannot be joyfully completed without a bright prospect of eternal glory and a splendid crown. The man finished this race with joy, who could say, "henceforth there is laid up for me a crown of righteousness, which the Lord, the righteous judge will give me in that day." Let others run to obtain a corruptible crown, we do it for an incorruptible. And oh! that when we finish our course it may be with this firm persuasion, that we shall enter into the joy of our Lord, where toil and fatigue will be known no more. For this purpose life is of use, as it conducts us to the end of the Christian race. But the apostle views himself not only as a Christian, but as a minister of the New Testament, and therefore he views life as desirable.

2. That he might honorably close his ministerial exertions. That I may finish, says he, my course with joy, and ministry which I have received of the Lord Jesus. Here you behold the author of the gifts and the graces of ministers, "the Lord Jesus." The Lord had said of Paul, "he is a chosen vessel unto me, to bear my name unto the Gentiles. And he had received his ministry of the Lord Jesus. The subjects of his ministry came from him, or he taught him to preach human depravity the atonement of Christ, and the influence of the Spirit, and to be witness unto all, for Jesus, of what he had seen and heard. His call to the ministry was from the Lord Jesus. He told him to publish the gospel, and immediately he conferred not with flesh and blood. He was an apostle not of man, nor by man, but by Jesus Christ and God the Father. His qualifications for the ministry came from the Lord Jesus—he gave him a freedom of speech—he

made him apt to teach—he furnished him with wisdom and knowledge—he made him a minister that needed not to be ashamed, rightly dividing the word of truth. His success in the ministry was from the Lord Jesus—he made him fruitful and he made him useful—he opened the hearts of his hearers—he attended his message with the power of his Spirit—he gave testimony to the word of his grace. Thus he assisted him in his work—owned him as an honored servant, nor suffered him to labor in vain, or spend his strength for naught. Now, he wishes to close this ministry with joy. He does not want to leave it, to quit it for worldly ease; but to go on in it to the end of his life. He does not wish to grow weary in well doing; but to persevere to the last; and thus finishing his work, he would do it with joy, as he would review instances of usefulness, and behold the grace of the Lord of the harvest, in raising up more laborers to enter into his vineyard. A minister closes his work with joy when he reviews instances of usefulness, when he knows that there are many whom he may view as his joy and crown of rejoicing—that he shall have to say of a goodly number, here am I, Father, and the children which thou hast given me. Thus our Lord rejoiced at the close of his labors, saying, "I have given them thy word; I have finished the work which thou gavest me to do." So also does the good minister finish his course with joy, when he beholds other laborers crowned with success in the vineyard; when he dies with the full confidence that Zion's glory increases, and that the work of the Lord is promoted. He rejoices that others shall enter into his labors, and that by their exertions the Saviour will be honored when he is cold in dust. Thus he rejoices, that instead of the fathers he raises up the children, and that the Saviour's name shall be known to all generations. Happy man! Like Simeon, thou shalt depart in peace; like him, thou shalt have the Saviour enclosed in thine arms, and eternal glory full in thy view.

Let those of us who are aged in the ministry imitate the apostle's example.

Students, be diligent; honor Christ and the Holy Spirit; aim sincerely to do good; be not afraid of difficulties; let us go on, &c., &c.

In so doing, we shall both save ourselves and those that hear us. Amen.

SERMON XXI.

GOD'S GRACIOUS REGARD FOR THE PENITEFT.

"He looketh upon men, and if any say I have sinned, and perverted that which was right, and it profitted me not; he will deliver his soul from going into the pit, and his life shall see the light."—JOB xxxiii. 27, 28.

How desirable a thing is genuine penitence; it appears eminently so from the attention God pays to it; from the salutary and holy feelings it calls into exercise; from the blessed effects which arise from it to the penitent individual, for "They that sow in tears shall reap in joy;" from the pleasure it occasions in heaven, for "There is joy in the presence of the angels of God over one sinner that repenteth." All this you may see in the testimony of God, and in the experience of every true penitent. O that you may see it in your own!

We will endeavor now to gain instruction upon this sub ject, from the passage I have read to you, a passage replete with consolation, and fraught with the richest truths. O that while we meditate upon it, its goodness and suitableness to our case, its kind report of the mercy of the Lord Jehovah, may dissolve our hearts in thankfulness, and melt our eyes to tears! "He looketh upon men, and if any say I have sinned, and perverted that which was right, and it profited me not, he will deliver his soul from going into the pit, and his life shall see the light." Observe here, how this text—

I. Presents to us the extent of the divine inspection, "He looketh upon men."

II. Unfolds the language of genuine repentance, "I have sinned, and perverted that which was right, and it profited me not."

III. Discovers the triumphs of reigning grace, "He shall deliver his soul from going into the pit, and his life shall see the light."

And all these things are closely connected together; for the truth of my text is, that God, in surveying the different ranks of men, beholds a penitent individual, hears his earnest cry, and forgives him the iniquity of his sin. We say, then, that our text,—

I. Presents to us the extent of the divine inspection.

"Jehovah looketh upon men." God's omniscience ought to make us adore and tremble; for He confines not his observation to the heavens, in which he more particularly dwells, but he also looketh upon men. Though He surveys the bright armies of saints and angels, who are ever before him, hearkening to the voice of his word, yet he also looketh upon men. Mortals are beheld by him. The inhabitants of the earth are looked on as grasshoppers, yet not one escapes his notice. He watches over their actions, and there is no darkness, or shadow of death, where the workers of iniquity may hide themselves from his eye. The text teaches us that he looketh upon men universally, and at once. I say, he surveys men universally. He looks upon all the tribes and conditions of men, from the helpless babe to the hoary sage; he sees them all. Every one of the human race must exclaim, "Thou God seest me!" For "the eyes of the Lord run to and fro throughout the whole earth, to show himself strong in behalf of them whose heart is perfect before him." "The Lord is in his holy temple; the Lord's throne is in heaven; his eyes behold, his eyelids try the children of men." "O Lord, thou hast searched me and known me: thou knowest my down-sitting and mine up-rising, thou understandest my thoughts afar off; thou compassest my path and my lying down, and art acquainted with all my ways; for there is not a word in my tongue, but lo, O Lord, thou knowest it altogether: thou hast beset me behind and before, and laid thine hand upon me." Thus he does from his throne behold all the dwellers upon earth; and here the wise and the illiterate, the righteous and the wicked, the just and the unjust, meet together; the Lord is the observer of them all! So he surveys them at once. He looketh upon men, he sees them all at one glance, in one view; his eyes behold all that is done upon the face of the earth, and the darkness and the light are both alike to him. At once the Lord looketh from heaven upon the children of men, for "the ways of man are always before the eyes of the Lord, and he pondereth all his goings." The eyes of the Lord are at one moment in every place, beholding the evil and the good. "Can any hide himself in secret places, that I should not see him, saith the Lord? Do not I fill heaven and the earth, saith the Lord?" "All things, then, are naked and open before the eyes of Him with whom we have to do." Yet are there, amongst the numerous objects which engage his notice, some particular ones that attract his special and marked attention; while he sees all, some he observes with peculiar pleasure, as well as with the nicest inspection; for "Though the Lord be high, yet hath he respect unto the lowly;" his name is holy and he dwells on high, yet to that man he looks, and with him he also dwells, that is poor and of a contrite spirit, and trembleth at his word. For among all the tribes of men that pass before him, it is not the rich man, it is not the mighty man, it is not the self-righteous man, that attracts his notice; but he that confesses his sins with "a humble, lowly, penitent, and obedient heart." He sees and he loves to see, he hears and he loves to hear, the man who says, "I have sinned and perverted that which was right, and it profited me not." Having attempted to illustrate the text, on the divine inspection, let us now behold how it—

II. Unfolds the language of unfeigned repentance.

For here God fixes his eyes upon one who says, "I have sinned, and perverted that which was right, and it profited me not." The man who makes a confession like this, is far better in the sight of God, than he who says he has no sin, and thus deceives himself. The humbled publican shall go down to his house justified, rather than the vaunting pharisee. This is a confession which deserves attention; it is one that will suit us all. It is a confession, an acknowledgment, 1st, of having committed enormous crimes, "I have sinned;" 2d, of having abused the best of blessings, "I have perverted that which was right;" 3d, of having experienced disappointment from sinful pursuits, "and it profited me not." This is, I say,—

1. A confession of having by sin offended against God.

He says, "I have sinned." Like Job, a penitent appears to say, "Behold I am vile." "I have sinned, what shall I do unto thee, O thou Preserver of men?" Like David to Nathan, he says, "I have sinned against the Lord." Like the prodigal, he cries, saying, "Father, I have sinned against Heaven, and in thy sight, and am no more worthy to be called thy son." I am "verily guilty concerning this thing." Wherever the Spirit of God has begun to work upon the soul, there will be this sense of unworthiness; this conviction of sin; this inward consciousness that all has not been right between God and the soul. "God be merciful to me a sinner," is a cry which the great God knows well would suit us all. "I have sinned." Born in sin and shapen in iniquity, as I grew up to manhood I gave awful proofs of the depravity of my nature. I neglected God and prayer; I secretly loved and cherished sin; I walked in the broad road that leadeth to destruction. There must be a measure of shame and confusion of face upon every one of us, when we approach a holy God; and the true penitent, feeling that it is of no use to attempt to conceal sin, because God looketh upon men, and knows it all; I say, being conscious of this, he confesses and forsakes his sin. He sees his guilt and shame, and casts himself upon the pure, free mercy of God in Christ.

2. This is a confession of having abused the best of blessings. "I have perverted that which was right." That is, thy holy providence gave me many peculiar and rich favors, which I employed to a bad purpose, or entirely neglected: a true penitent confesses that the goodness of God had not, till lately, led him to repentance. There are various right things, excellent blessings, which, in the state of nature, we have perverted. Divine forbearance is a great

good; for, "It is of the Lord's mercies that we are not consumed;" and yet, perhaps I am addressing some, who, because sentence against an evil work has not been executed speedily, have their hearts fully set in them to do evil.

This was perverting that which was right. The time of youth is a season of peculiar importance, and gives special advantages; but how many a penitent has had to regret that he perverted it, wasted its precious hours, and his own strength, in the ways of folly and sin; did not remember his Creator in the days of his youth, but passed them in carelessness, or perhaps in open depravity! Health is a great blessing, but how little have we estimated it, how much have we perverted and abused it! forgetting to be thankful for the favors we have received, we have not glorified the God "in whose hand our breath is, and whose are all our ways." Time is a great blessing, but how have we squandered it, idled it away in unnecessary visits, perhaps in unlawful amusements, or tried to kill time, while, in fact, time has been gradually killing us! Providential supplies are great blessings; but we have perverted them by luxury, by profaneness. The tables of the luxurious man cry out against him; you may fancy that they groan under the weight of the abused creatures of God. The glutton, the wine-bibber, the man that is prodigal in any thing, perverts that which is in itself right. Money, property, possessions, are all right in themselves, but foolish man perverts them all. But oh, a true penitent most of all regrets that he has abused the Bible, and the publication of the gospel. "The law of the Lord is right, the commandment of the Lord is perfect and pure;" yet, oh, may a penitent say, How I abused it, how I neglected its calls, its invitations, its promises! How I refused to behold Christ crucified, to look unto the Saviour of sinners! I perverted that which was right; despising the book, the day, the people of God: so have I abused the best of blessings.

3. This is a confession of having experienced disappointment in the ways of sin. I have done all this, "and it profited me not." Some men foolishly and wickedly say, It profiteth a man nothing that he should delight himself in God; but every penitent can truly testify, that the way of transgressors is hard, and that it ensures disappointment and dissatisfaction,—"it profiteth me not." Now can I testify that it is all vanity and vexation of spirit. We may try the pursuit of gold, of fame, or of lawless pleasure; but, "What shall it profit a man, if he gain the whole world, and lose his own soul?" "For when ye were the servants of sin, what fruit had ye then in those things whereof ye are now ashamed?" The sincere penitent confesses, that he was quite mistaken in the hope of happiness from the world; that as yet he has not obtained it; that all has been delusion and deceit; that he has grasped at shadows, and thus proved his own folly and misery. "It profiteth me not." Oh, sinner, if you never made this confession before, I am sure you will make it on a dying bed; you will then see that the things which now please and amuse you, profit you not. O that you would now go and tell this to God before that solemn hour arrives. Humbled for sin, confess the cheat the world has played on you; it has profited you nothing.

III. My text discovers the triumph of reigning grace. "For if we confess our sins, God is faithful and just to forgive us our sins, and to cleanse us from all unrighteousness." "I have, surely," says God, "heard Ephraim bemoaning himself thus: Thou hast chastised me, and I was chastised, as a bullock unaccustomed to the yoke; turn thou me, and I shall be turned, for thou art the Lord my God. Surely, after that I was turned, I repented; and after that I was instructed, I smote upon my thigh: I was ashamed, yea, even confounded, because I did bear the reproach of my youth. Is Ephraim my dear son? Is he a pleasant child? for since I spake against him, I do earnestly remember him still: therefore my bowels are troubled for him; I will surely have mercy upon him, saith the Lord." "Whoso confesseth and forsaketh his sins shall find mercy." This humble penitent, who sincerely makes the confession I have mentioned, and looks to the Redeemer, obtains grace in his sight; for the Lord—

1st, prevents his soul from enduring eternal perdition.

2d, raises him to the everlasting enjoyment of divine illumination.

1. The Lord prevents his soul from enduring eternal perdition. "He will deliver his soul from going into the pit:" evidently implying, that to a pit of misery he was rapidly tending, and of falling into it was afraid; perhaps he was saying, "Let not the water-floods overflow me, neither let the deep swallow me up, and let not the pit shut her mouth upon me." Then God says, "Deliver him from going down to the pit, for I have found a ransom." Jesus is a sufficient Saviour, I will accept him for his righteousness' sake. It may be, that there is here a reference to the grave, in allusion to which, it is said in Scripture, "They shall go down to the bars of the pit, where our rest together is in the dust." But does it not rather

refer to that awful pit of destruction, mentioned in the 20th chapter of the Revelation, where Satan is bound, where sinners are lost?

"Behold," says a penitent, "for peace I had great bitterness, but thou hast in love to my soul delivered it from the pit of corruption; for thou hast cast all my sins behind thy back." Jesus, the Redeemer, then, delivers us from the wrath to come, saves from the power of death and hell; he prevents our souls from going into the pit, from whence there is no redemption. On us the second death hath no power.

2. The Almighty raises him to the perpetual enjoyment of divine illumination. "And his life shall see the light." This implies the dispersion of his melancholy, the introduction of happiness and peace to his soul: for, through the grace of the great ransom, Jesus, "the people that walked in darkness have seen a great light; they that dwell in the land of the shadow of death, upon them hath the light shined." But further, this expression carries our thoughts to the period when we shall behold the light of heaven: for God intends to bring every believing penitent to that city of which it is written, that God and the Lamb are the light thereof. We, "who truly repent and unfeignedly believe his holy gospel," shall possess the inheritance of the saints in light, shall be for ever illuminated and encircled by the rays of the Sun of righteousness, and so shall we be ever with the Lord. The Lord shall be our light, our God shall be our glory, and the days of our mourning shall be ended.

Learn from the subject,—

The richness of God's pardoning mercy, extending even to sins of perverseness.

The madness of impenitent sinners : they must be banishod to the pit, never to see the light.

The importance of imploring daily a penitential spirit : we sin daily, therefore beg always for mercy. Believe in the testimony of God, " I, even I, am he that blotteth out thy transgressions for mine own sake, and will not remember thy sins."

SERMON XXII.

THE SEARCHER OF HEARTS.

"All things are naked and opened to the eyes of him with whom we have to do."—HEBREWS iv. 13.

WHERE should a creature look, but to his Creator? and what being should engage so much of our attention, as the God that made us? O my soul, forget, forget thy trifling cares; relinquish thy foolish chase after the world and sin, thy eagerness for the things of time and sense, and look upward to the Being who ever looks on thee.

Think on his perfections, adore him for his greatness, and tell of the glorious majesty of his kingdom. He, my hearers, who is God over all, blessed for ever, requires us frequently to meditate on his ways; to consider in what relation we stand to him; to remember our own accountableness; and to think how holy and reverend is his name.

We will therefore now contemplate that divine and holy Being, who made us, preserves us, and before whose bar we shall all shortly stand; we will remember, that to him all hearts are open, all desires known; and that his power no creature is able to control; "neither is there any creature that is not manifest in his sight;" but, says the passage I have read for my text, " All things are naked and opened to the eyes of Him with whom we have to do." Let us then,—

I. Take that interesting view of Jehovah, with which the text presents us: He is the God with whom we have to do.

II. Glance at his penetrating omniscience as connected with such a view of him, " All things are naked and open in his sight."

III. Deduce from the subject some suitable reflections.

1. Let us take that interesting view of Jehovah, which the text presents to us: as the God with whom we have to do. Here you perceive the great God described, not so much by what he is in himself, as by what he is to us: here you are allowed to indulge no idle speculation upon the nature of the Godhead, for you cannot by searching find him out, nor trace the Almighty to perfection; but you have the awful relation in which you stand to him, strikingly set before you. We might speak of God, indeed, as happy in himself, as independent and self-existent, but we wish to excite you to prayer; we want to urge you to adore and tremble; and therefore, instead of answering your fancies, pleasing your ears, or entertaining your imaginations by discussing those perfections of the Deity, or those parts of his works, with which we are not so immediately concerned; we shall rather lead you to view him as the God, " with whom we all have to do." Yes, with this God, " glorious in holiness, fearful in praises, doing wonders," we shall have some solemn transactions, transactions that will never be forgotten. Here I may address every one of my hearers, whether a lost sinner, or an heir of God

through Christ, and say, It is He with whom thou hast to do. O solemn thought! Ye careless sinners, ye artful hypocrites, ye deluded votaries of sensuality and uncleanness, ye unholy and profane, ye all have to do with God; there is to be a commerce between your souls and the great Eternal. And ye blest saints that love him too, have communications to carry on with heaven, he is the God with whom you have to do, in the way of solemn dedication, habitual dependence, and lively hope that you shall be found accepted of him. He is indeed and in truth, the God with whom we all have to do, especially on these memorable occasions;—in the seasons of religious exercises,—at the day of death,—and at the last judgment. In each of these times Jehovah is the God with whom we have to do. Let us look at our vast concerns with him—

1. In religious exercises. And thus we shall be able to ascertain the importance, and discover the solemnity of our engagements at the throne of grace, and in the house of God. Be it known unto you, men and brethren, then, that when we pray and sing, and attend public ordinances, we are carrying on commerce with heaven; we have to do with God. How ought the thought of creatures to be altogether banished from our minds, when we profess to worship! for the place where we stand is holy ground. The worship in which we engage has Jehovah for its object, as well as its minute observer; it is intercourse with Heaven. It is having to do with "the high and the lofty One that inhabiteth eternity." It is bringing our powers and our services into his august and awful presence: it is dust and ashes speaking to the great Lord of the universe, and begging him not to be angry with us. Remember, ever remember, in all your acts of worship, the God with whom you

have to do. Careless worshippers do not, will not recollect that they are dealing with God! but oh, will they not be destroyed by his anger, and consumed by his fury, since they are offering the Lord strange fire, which he commanded them not?

O that the great God we worship would himself convince us, and impress us with the truth, that we are, in every act of prayer and praise, dealing with "the King eternal, immortal, and invisible!"

2. We have to do with God in the hour of death. To that solemn hour, every pulse we tell brings us nearer. The youngest may say, Soon this hand will cease to move, this throbbing heart be still. And oh, as soon as we have drawn our last gasp, and uttered our last sigh, we shall have to do with God, in a way we never had before! "Prepare to meet thy God, O Israel:" thy God must be met and terrible indeed will he appear to thee in that dread moment, unless thou hadst before had dealings with him through Christ, as the God of salvation, the hearer and answerer of prayer! Yes, we shall have to do with him; for he is coming to stop the warm current of existence and call us to himself; we shall have to do with him; for yet a little while, and he will call our spirits to his bar, and take them kindly to himself, or assign them their lot with the wretched beings on whom his wrath is poured out for ever, without the least mixture of mercy. In the hour of death, let every soul solemnly recollect, he shall have to do with God; may it be to say, "Into thine hands I commit my spirit." "I have waited for thy salvation, O Lord." May the exchange be this: for me to give him a spirit redeemed by the blood of the Lamb, and renewed by the Spirit of God; and for him to give me heaven and himself

for my everlasting portion. Then I shall not regret, that in death he will appear the God with whom I have to do. Once more, we shall particularly have to do with God,—

3. At the last judgment. "For God shall bring every work into judgment, with every secret thing, whether it be good, or whether it be evil." We shall then have to do with him: for he is coming in his glory, and all the holy angels with him, sitting upon the throne of his glory; before him shall be gathered all nations: "for the hour is coming, in the which all that are in their graves shall hear his voice, and shall come forth; they that have done good unto the resurrection of life, and they that have done evil, unto the resurrection of damnation." Is there not a "day appointed in which the God with whom we have to do, will judge the world in righteousness, by that man whom he has ordained?" Yes, he will in that day "judge the secrets of men by Jesus Christ, according to my gospel." "Why then dost thou judge thy brother? or why dost thou set at naught thy brother? for we shall all stand before the judgment seat of Christ." "For it is written, As I live, saith the Lord, every knee shall bow to me, and every tongue shall confess to God. So then every one of us shall give account of himself to God." The dead, small and great, shall stand before God, the books shall be opened, and the dead shall be judged out of those things which are written in the books. We shall all have to do with God as our King, our Lawgiver, and our Judge: we shall all stand before him either pale, trembling and in despair, or in all the ecstacy of holy joy. Each of us shall hear the voice, Well done; or the sound, Depart. Thus shall we have to do with God at the last day.

Having endeavored to illustrate the view of Jehovah, with which the text presents us; we will now—

II. Glance at his penetrating omniscience, as connected with such a view of him. For "all things are naked and opened to the eyes of Him with whom we have to do."

All things are naked and open to his view. He beholds the whole universe, and every thing done in it. He knows all that passes in heaven, for there he displays his glory, and sees his servants ever before him, standing to hear his wisdom, or occupied in singing his praise. The dark abodes of despair, too, are inspected by him. Hell is naked before him, and destruction is without a covering. But his minute attention to individuals, is what I wish to enforce upon you now, that you may see how every mortal is immediately concerned in the omnipresence and omniscience of Jehovah; for "all things are naked and opened to the eyes of him with whom we have to do."

They are exposed to his view, they are marked by him. All the things we did in our infancy, in our youth, and all we are doing now. This shows us, I remark, by way of distinction and impression, that he is acquainted—with our state,—our feelings,—and our characters.

I. He knows well our state. It is naked and open before him. The God with whom we have to do, perceives accurately the circumstances of our condition. At once he knows, whether we are "in the gall of bitterness, and in the bond of iniquity," or whether we have been "translated into the glorious liberty of the children of God." "Be not deceived; God is not mocked; for whatsoever a man soweth, that shall he also reap." A hypocrite's heart alway lies naked and open to the eyes of Him with whom we have to do. Christ's members and ministers may be deceived, in the estimation they form of a man's personal religion, but God cannot be deceived. As he looks now upon this assembly, he knows, to the nicest certainty, who fears him, and who fears him not: he recognizes the men that have been in their closets in prayer to-day; he sees the sincere worshipper, and distinguishes him from the cold formalist, and the pharisaical professor. The state of every one of us, as a child of God, or an heir of hell, is "naked and opened to the eyes of him with whom we have to do."

2. So also he knows and is privy to all our feelings. Those not accepted, which we foolishly think are locked up in our hearts, and hidden from perception; he knows them altogether. The secret desires any of you may entertain after sinful gratifications, and unhallowed pleasures, are all witnessed by him, and recorded in his book. Your desires to check conviction, to flee from remorse, to kill time, to obtain worldly honors; all these "are naked and open to the eyes of Him with whom we have to do." All your hopes, whether well founded, or resting on false foundations, are all known to God. All your attempts at self-deception, or to deceive others. Ah! he knows them all. All your fears of dying, your dread of hell, these things are ever before him. The sensations of your mind, the feelings of your heart, which prompt you to the performance of the actions you accomplish, he detects, he sees even afar off. No wonder, then, that—

3. All our characters "are naked and opened to the eyes of Him with whom we have to do." What we are at home, and what we are abroad; what we are in the closet, what we are in the family, what we are in the church, and what we are in the world. The proportion of what is

called virtue, and what is styled vice, that forms our character, is "all known by Him with whom we have to do;" and hence "There is no darkness, nor shadow of death, where the workers of iniquity may hide themselves from his view."

Almighty God, thy piercing eye
  Strikes through the shades of night,
And our most secret actions lie
  All open to thy sight.

'There's not a sin that we commit,
  Nor wicked word we say,
But in thy dreadful book 'tis writ,
  Against the judgment-day.

"All things are naked and opened to the eyes of Him with whom we have to do." Let us,—

III. Deduce from the subject some suitable reflections. And oh! how this voice of God may be heard to urge us,—

1. To evince holy reverence. A being, like Jehovah, privy to every thought, acquainted with all our ways, understanding even the secrets of our minds, should be looked up to and addressed with holy awe. His name is so holy and reverend, that when we approach him, we ought even to rejoice with trembling. O, let us never dare trifle before him: let us entertain for him the highest sentiments of veneration: let us not even mention his name, but with the most solemn feelings of holy reverence; for we are not worthy even to take his name upon our polluted lips. He is in heaven, and we are upon earth; all the things we do, and say, and think, are naked and open before him. Let us think on him, then, with all reverence and awe.

2. Learn hence to practice devout circumspection.

Watch over your hearts, and guard against every sin, for God's eye is ever upon you. Were an intelligent, upright, and dignified fellow-creature always to inspect your actions, ever to attend you, to witness all your conduct by night and by day, would you not, oh! would you not, be, in every respect, a different character from what you are? And shall all this alteration of conduct be occasioned by a fellow-creature's presence; and shall not the scrutiny of omniscience alarm you? shall not the inspection of God lead you to consider your ways? O, set a watch upon every thought and deed, for "all things are naked and opened to the eyes of Him with whom we have to do." Let us learn—

3. To seek after internal sincerity. For oh, what a disgusting spectacle must the heart of the hypocrite present to the God who "searcheth the hearts and trieth the reins of the children of men!" Oh, if every thing is witnessed, known, and recorded by him, how essentially desirable is it, that we should be upright characters; wearing no mask, assuming no characters which do not belong to us! How necessary that we should be Israelites indeed, in whom there is no guile.

As God inspects us, O let him see that we wish to appear in our true light; that we have renounced the hidden things of dishonesty; and now conduct ourselves with the carriage which simplicity and godly sincerity warrant and enjoin. O that we were but always sincere before God!

4. Learn to make perpetual approaches to the Lord Jesus Christ. For in him alone have you a shelter from the wrath of God, and a covert from the storm. "Hide me, O my Saviour, hide." The Lord Jesus Christ renders even the omniscience of God, a friend to sinners; for God

beholds us in him, and accepts us for his sake. Nor need any one who believes in his name, and loves and serves him, at all fear, or be alarmed from the consideration, that "all things are naked and opened to the eyes of Him with whom we have to do;" for he knows the desires of them that fear him; he knows every act of worship, and approves them all. Interested in Christ, we can deal with a holy God, with satisfaction, profit, and joy. Escape for thy life then, sinner, flee to him; nor need you fear, though "all things are naked and opened unto the eyes of Him with whom you have to do."

ADDRESS

AT LAYING THE FOUNDATION-STONE OF THE NEW CHAPEL.

"*And this stone, which I have set for a pillar, shall be God's house.*" So said the patriarch Jacob on a memorable occasion, and so may we say, assembled as we are to lay the foundation-stone of an edifice to God. We have found out a place for the Lord—an habitation for the mighty God of Jacob: beholding this spot of ground on this interesting morning, a thousand delightful sensations pervade our souls, and we are ready to anticipate the presence of the Great Eternal in this place, or "is not this the hill which God hath chosen to dwell in it for ever?" Let us please ourselves with believing, that here holy incense shall ascend to God—that from this place the voice of prayer and praise shall rise tuneful to the court of heaven—that here pious men shall enjoy the sublime happiness of devotion—that here the ungodly and the sinner shall be induced to begin their lives anew. How often may many have to say, on the very ground we tread, "How dreadful is this place! this is none other than the house of God, and the gate of heaven." The Master of worshipping assemblies, Jehovah, by whose call congregations assemble, and by whose blessing their souls are benefited, may here afford his watchful care, his animating smiles: we have every reason to believe he will do it, entreated by the earnest and fervent supplications of the men he loves;

himself inclined to bless the gates of Zion, his eyes and his heart shall be here perpetually; with pleasure will he behold the favored spot; and in the liberality of his heart afford to his assembled saints an earnest, a foretaste, a lively representation of what those happy spirits know and feel who are ever with the Lord.

We flatter ourselves, that the erection of an edifice like this is the effect of benevolent feeling to mankind, and an ardent love to the Great Lord of all. We unite in endeavoring to maintain the honor of the Saviour's name, and to support the glory of his cross. We feel, and deeply too, the necessity of possessing somewhat more than this earth can afford: we regard men as immortals, and we know that there are blessings, without the enjoyment of which, those souls will experience continued disappointment here, and will languish forever in another world. These necessary and holy blessings, the Eternal has chosen to communicate by the instrumentality of a preached gospel. We know that Jehovah, in making up the number of his elect, works by means; therefore it is that we endeavor to bring that gospel, the report of which is indeed a joyful sound, to the ears of mankind, praying that the blessed Spirit would send it to their hearts. The erection of this place is a direct attack against—against whom? say my hearers, alarmed at the idea of hostility—against the Church of England? No! God forbid; the very reverse of all this. We cheerfully take the present opportunity of informing this numerous auditory, that the doctrines which will be proclaimed on this ground will exactly correspond, will be just the same, with those contained in the doctrinal articles of the Church of England, which are the bulwarks of its faith, and may be read in most of the

Books of Common Prayer. Is it, then, you ask again, an attack against any other congregation, or body of professing Christians? My soul revolts and spurns at the idea; for in the cause of Immanuel we wish cordially and constantly to unite with all those who believe in the Lord Jesus, both theirs and ours. But in one word, this is an attack directed against the kingdom of Satan, and the prince of darkness. Its object is the translation of our fellow creatures from his hateful power and dominion, and their transition into the family of the blessed household of their Redeemer. With the sword of the Spirit we wish to combat the old serpent the devil. In this large and populous town he has maintained his seat, he has reigned and triumphed: we long to see him fall, like lightning from heaven; and hence we preach that glorious gospel, which opposes his works, which rescues from his power, which gives us to expect a final triumph over him and his followers.

Here we expect that the preaching of the cross will be heard—that self-righteousness will in no shape meet with encouragement—that man will be represented as nothing, and Christ as all in all. We erect no altar to an unknown God, but are boldly confessing, that we wish every day to approach the Father of Spirits, through the mediation of God our Saviour, and all this by the gracious aid of the Holy Spirit. And are any of us so hardened, through the deceitfulness of sin, as not to wish that here many souls may be born to God—may be trained up for heaven; or shall we not, at the last great day, rejoice to see a goodly company of men, who on this spot shall have met with the Saviour Jesus, and commenced an honorable path to heaven. We rejoice in the thought, that the cause is God's, and must prevail, and with pleasure we celebrate the growing empire of our King. His church must flourish, because it is purchased with his blood, and preserved by his grace. The names of the several denominations among which it is scattered may be lost and forgotten, but its numbers shall increase, and its honors spread to the end of time.

The Episcopalian church may totter to the ground; the Presbyterian church may be known no more; the Independent church may no longer exist as a separate body; but the *true* church, made up of many of all these, and confined to no one of them, shall increase yet more and more, and ever be acknowledged the Zion of the Lord, the city of the Holy One of Israel.

This morning have we cause for gratitude, that amidst the spread of infidelity, and a vain philosophy, the work of God is not forgotten: that still his churches rise and flourish; that still souls are born to God, and the saints shout aloud for joy. In the sanctuaries where we worship, we have the solace of our cares, a kind refreshment afforded us in our journey to heaven, and new light and joy bestowed. May all this be known amongst us—be known by posterity when we are cold in death.

I cannot lose sight of the opportunity which this morning affords me, of assuring this large and mixed assembly, that real religion is a personal thing; that the gospel we preach must be believed, and its consolations enjoyed, or there remains for us no hope of pardon or of peace. My fellow immortals, you have all sinned, and come short of the glory of God; but we exhibit to you a blessed and perfect Redeemer! Believe in him, and you shall not be confounded world without end. And when I meet you in an assembly far larger and more solemn than this, I mean at the judgment day, you shall be accepted of him; yea, believing in him, you shall then enter a temple, not made with hands eternal in the heavens; and for ever adore the hand that formed it, the grace that conducted us to it, and the Saviour who fills it with his glory. Amen.

www.ingramcontent.com/pod-product-compliance
Lightning Source LLC
LaVergne TN
LVHW020914110826
845150LV00004B/674

* 9 7 8 1 4 2 5 5 5 6 0 8 2 *